Writing Analytically

Third Edition

David Rosenwasser

Jill Stephen

Muhlenberg College

THOMSON
™
HEINLE

Australia   Canada   Mexico   Singapore   Spain   United Kingdom   United States

Writing Analytically, Third Edition
David Rosenwasser and Jill Stephen

Publisher, English: Michael Rosenberg
Acquisitions Editor: Dickson Musslewhite
Sr. Developmental Editor: Michell Phifer
Sr. Production Editor: Maryellen E. Killeen
Director of Marketing, Higher Education:
    Lisa Kimball
Marketing Manager: Ken Kasee

Sr. Manufacturing Coordinator: Mary Beth
    Hennebury
Text Design, Composition, Project Management,
    Photo Research: Thompson Steele, Inc.
Cover Designer: Gina Petti, Rotunda Design
Printer: Phoenix Color

For permission to use material from this
text or product contact us:
Tel   1-800-730-2214
Fax   1-800-730-2215
Web   www.thomsonrights.com

ISBN: 0-15-505874-6

Rosenwasser, David.
   Writing analytically / David Rosenwasser,
Jill Stepen.--3rd ed.
     p. cm.
   Includes bibliographical references and index.
   ISBN 0-15-505874-6 (alk. paper)
    1. English language--Rhetoric. 2. Inter-
disciplinary approach in education. 3. Critical
thinking. 4. Academic writing. I. Stephen, Jill
II. Title.
PE1408 .R69 2002
808'.042--dc21   2002024270

Contents in Brief

Contents

PART III Matters of Form   189

CHAPTER 10 Introductions and Conclusions   191

Preface

This is not a book that tries to be all things to all teachers and students. Instead, it concentrates on one kind of writing—analysis—which we define as the search for meaningful pattern. This book argues that analysis, rather than dissecting information, fosters an exploratory attitude toward experience. By searching out questions before rushing to answers, analysis aims at a complex understanding of what something means.

Writing Analytically was born of frustration about the gap between, on the one hand, the lively quality of students' thinking in class discussion and informal writing, and, on the other hand, the inert, evasive, and simplistic finished products they submitted to us. This book seeks to bridge that gap.

We focus on analysis because it is the skill most often called for in higher education and beyond. Analysis offers alternatives to oversimplified thinking of both the like/dislike, agree/disagree variety and the cut-and-paste compilation of sheer information. Implicit throughout the book is an argument for the value of reflection in an age that seems increasingly unaware of it as an option. Toward this end, *Writing Analytically* teaches students to distinguish between an idea and mere opinion and to respect the complexity of subjects that have no single right answer. *Writing Analytically* is about how to have and develop *ideas* in an academic setting.

There are, of course, many causes of mediocre writing, but the primary culprit this book attacks is an overly rigid notion of thesis proffered in many writing textbooks and school settings—that the thesis is an unchanging claim that a paper sets out to prove. In practice, this conception of thesis leads writers to spend most of their time trying to organize superficial ideas rather than testing and evolving them. It leads them to judge prematurely, usually settling for obvious generalizations, rather than use their writing to explore the evidence, finding the questions that intrigue them. And it is at odds with the way that most good writing actually operates. The solution, we believe, is to reorient students from judging to understanding.

How does the book attempt to accomplish these ends? Here is a radically compressed version of the book's project, its essential advice to students.

- Dwell longer than customary with the evidence. Notice more before reducing scope and making the interpretive leap to a thesis.

- Make the thesis evolve in response to evidence. The confrontation with evidence should not only confirm but refine the thesis.

- Converse with sources rather than agreeing/disagreeing or parroting.

- Share your thought process with readers, not just your conclusions but how you arrived at them.

The book does not, by the way, denigrate thesis-driven writing, nor does it slight the importance of producing clear, well-organized finished products. But the book does argue that students should not be pressed to formulate and argue thesis statements without first being taught how to examine evidence in depth, in an open-ended, exploratory way that constant position-taking discourages.

Writing Analytically also has more to say about what students shouldn't do than is usually the case in writing texts. While we are sensitive to the dangers of negativism, we have found that students have a hard time developing new skills until they've come to understand what is counterproductive about features of their current practice. We believe in the value of talking overtly with students about where their writing typically goes wrong. So, for example, we discuss at some length the shortcomings of the slot-filler organizational scheme known as *five-paragraph form,* and we offer a chapter on kinds of weak thesis statements, with explanations of why they are weak and practical advice on how to fix them.

WHAT'S NEW IN THIS EDITION

The book has been significantly rewritten and reorganized for this edition. It is now arranged into a three-part sequence that takes students from specific short exercises in observation, interpretation, and reading (Part I), to methods of arriving at thesis-driven and researched papers (Part II), to matters of form—organization, style, and basic writing errors (Part III). Chapters from the second edition have generally been shortened or divided in two to make them more teachable, except for the "Topics" chapter, which has been dispersed into other chapters.

Part I, "Making Meaning: Essential Skills," consists of four new chapters, written out of our conviction that the primary reason students get frustrated, can't write, and don't have ideas is because they lack a storehouse of *methods* for looking at evidence that would help them to notice something to write about in the first place. More than the first two editions of *Writing Analytically*, this edition attends to the skills that allow students to find patterns in the evidence and to make plausible interpretive leaps.

The first of the new chapters, "Habits of Mind: Getting Ready to Have Ideas," leads with the idea that much of what passes for thinking is merely reacting: right/wrong, good/bad, loved it/hated it, couldn't relate to it, boring. The first step toward writing analytically, it argues, is to start recognizing and blocking the kinds of mental reflexes—such as judging, either/or thinking, and over-personalizing—that clog perception and substitute prefabricated generic "answers" for thinking.

As the title of the second chapter—"Noticing: Learning to Observe"—suggests, we have come to recognize that it is not enough to ask writers to collect data; they need to be taught a series of procedures and prompts for noticing and then for organizing what they notice. The following chapter, "Interpreting: Asking 'So What?'"

offers additional prompts and procedures for moving writers from observation to implication. It also counters some of the more common and debilitating misconceptions that people have about the interpretive process, such as the Fortune Cookie School (X has one, hidden meaning) and its opposite but near cousin, the Anything Goes School of Interpretation (we can make of X whatever we want).

The last of the new chapters, "Reading: How to Do It and What to Do with It," premises the inseparability of effective writing and careful reading. The chapter targets the common assumption among students that they should read for a general or global impression, thereby not attending closely enough to the language of the reading to see questions and unearth implications—which is what reading in the best sense is all about. The chapter also shows students how to use readings in ways that get beyond the matching exercise, plugging primary subject A into theory grid B without any real exploration of either.

This edition has reconceived its approach to writing assignments. Brief exercises under the heading *Try this* replace the longer "Applications" of the previous edition. Designed for in-class writings or homework, the "Try this" exercises offer a quick way to apply the book's lessons. We have also included at the ends of most chapters a paper topic keyed to the chapter's focus.

Writing Analytically is designed to be used in first-year writing courses or seminars, as well as more advanced writing-intensive courses in a wide variety of subject areas. An assumption of the book is that most teachers will want to supply their own subject matter for students to read and write about. Both the brief writing exercises and the paper topics can be adapted to a wide range of course contents.

The book does acknowledge that various academic disciplines differ in their expectations of student writing. Interspersed throughout the text are boxes labeled *Voices from Across the Curriculum*. These were written for the book by professors in various disciplines who offer their disciplinary perspective on such matters as reasoning back to premises and determining what counts as evidence. These *Voices* are especially prominent in Chapter 11, "Forms and Formats," which explains the rationale for disciplinary formats and offers advice on how to use these to arrive at ideas rather than just to arrange the final product.

Writing Analytically is prescriptive, but it does not impose a system that students and professors must follow in every particular. It scrupulously attempts to avoid patronizing students, instead addressing them as thinking adults. Our hope is to provide a basis for conversation—between faculty and students, between students and students, and especially, between writers and their own writing.

ABOUT THE AUTHORS

David Rosenwasser and Jill Stephen are Professors of English at Muhlenberg College in Allentown, Pennsylvania, where they have co-directed a Writing Across the Curriculum (WAC) program since 1987. They began teaching writing to college students in the early 1970s—David at the University of Virginia and then at the College of William and Mary, and Jill at New York University and then at Hunter College (CUNY). *Writing Analytically* has grown out of their undergraduate teaching and the seminars on writing and writing instruction that they have offered to faculty at Muhlenberg and at other colleges and universities across the country.

ACKNOWLEDGEMENTS

We have had the good fortune to garner many friends for this book, people who have believed in it and generously given us advice about how to improve it. The rethinking that has gone into the third edition is especially indebted to Georgina Hill, Christine Farris, John Schilb, and Paul Heilker. Thanks too to those who have invited us to their campuses recently to try out our ideas: Christine and John, as well as Lin Spence, Bernadette Glaze, and all the workshops' attendees for their useful advice (especially Mathew Johnson and Ted Leahy). We are also grateful for the friendship and advice of Dean Ward, Mary Ann Cain, George Kalamaras, Anna Adams, Hank Noordam, and Rich Bullock, and for the wisdom and camaraderie of the WPA.

We continue to appreciate the contributions from the faculty of Muhlenberg College, without whom this textbook would never have been conceived. The insights they shared with us in the summer seminars on writing across the curriculum and the questions they raised forever changed the way we think about writing. More specifically, we are grateful to the Muhlenberg colleagues who contributed to the *Voices from Across the Curriculum* sections: Karen Dearborn, Jack Gambino, James Marshall, Robert Milligan, Richard Niesenbaum, Frederick Norling, Ellen Poteet, Laura Snodgrass, Alan Tjeltveit, and Bruce Wightman. And we are especially indebted to reference librarian Kelly Cannon for his lengthy contribution to Chapter 9. Nor could we have written the book without the many students who have generously contributed samples of their work—in particular, Jenn Axe, Dennis Slade, Theresa Leinker, Sarah Kersh, and Dana Ferrelli.

Further thanks are due to Thomas Cartelli, a prince among department heads; to Carol Proctor, who was always there when we needed her; to the many colleagues at Muhlenberg who have given us feedback after using the book, most notably Barri Gold, Jim Bloom, and Grant Scott; and to Dean Curtis Dretsch for continually supporting our attendance at conferences.

We would also like to thank the many colleagues who reviewed the book; we are grateful for their insight: Bonita Dattner-Garza, St. Mary's University; Christine Farris, Indiana University; Georgina Hill, Western Michigan University; Joe Law, Wright State University; and Gardner Rogers, University of Illinois at Urbana–Champaign.

The book continues to be indebted to Karl Yambert, who taught us how to write textbooks, and to John Meyers, who gave the book its start.

Sincere appreciation goes to everyone who contributed to the book at Heinle: Michell Phifer, senior developmental editor; Dickson Musslewhite, acquisitions editor; Michael Rosenberg, publisher; and Maryellen Eschmann-Killeen, production editor.

Finally, special thanks to our families—Mark, Lesley, and Sarah; Deborah and Elizabeth—for their continued support.

PART I

Making Meaning:
Essential Skills

1

Habits of Mind:
Getting Ready to Have Ideas

This is a book about one kind of writing: writing analytically. The definition of that term will grow as the book unfolds, but for now let's say that writing analytically is the practice of using words (writing) to figure out what things mean. To analyze something is to ask how something does what it does or why it is as it is. Learning to write analytically is primarily a matter of becoming more aware of the act of thinking. Thinking is a process, an activity. Ideas don't just happen; they're made. We have chosen to write about analysis because analysis, more than any other form of thought, is what college and postcollege writing calls for. Of all the skills you acquire as a writer and thinker, analysis is likely to have the greatest impact on the way you learn. This is so because the more you write analytically, the more actively and patiently you will think.

Analyzing often gets a bad rap. It is sometimes thought of as destructive—*breaking things down* into their component parts or, to paraphrase a famous poet, murdering to dissect. Other detractors attack it as the rarefied province of intellectuals and scholars, beyond the reach of normal people. In fact, we all analyze all of the time, and we do so not simply to break things down but to *construct* our understandings of the world we inhabit.

If, for example, you find yourself being followed by a large dog, your first response, other than breaking into a cold sweat, will be to analyze the situation. What does being followed by a large dog mean for me, here, now? Does it mean the dog is vicious and about to attack? Does it mean the dog is curious and wants to play? Similarly, if you are losing a game of tennis or if you've just left a job interview or if you are looking at a painting of a woman with three noses, you will begin to analyze. How can I play differently to increase my chances of winning? Am I likely to get the job, and why (or why not)? Why did the artist give the woman three noses?

If we break things down as we analyze, we do so in order to search for meaningful patterns or to uncover what we had not seen at first glance—or just to understand more closely how and why the separate parts work as they do. Why do this in writing?

Because writing provides a method for expanding our ability to notice things, to have ideas about what we notice, and to arrive ultimately at some plausible interpretation.

In short, writing analytically can make you smarter. It can get you beyond thinking that what things mean is simply a matter of opinion. It can help you understand and synthesize other people's ideas en route to ideas of your own.

And it can be learned. As this book will try to show, analyzing is surprisingly formulaic. It consists of a fairly limited set of basic moves. Before we get to these, though, we first want to isolate some counterproductive habits of mind that are amazingly hardy and pervasive (like weeds).

A lot of what passes for thinking is merely reacting: right/wrong, good/bad, loved it/hated it, couldn't relate to it, boring. Responses like these are habits, reflexes of the mind. And they are surprisingly tough habits to break. Experiment. Ask someone for a description of a place, a movie, or a new CD, and see what you get. Too often it will be a diatribe. Offer a counterargument and be told, huffily, "I'm entitled to my opinion."

The first step toward writing analytically is to start recognizing and blocking the kinds of mental reflexes that clog perception and substitute prefabricated generic "answers" for thinking.

Why is this so?

We live in a culture of inattention and cliché. It is a world in which we are perpetually assaulted with mind-numbing claims (Arby's offers "a baked potato so good you'll never want anyone else's"), flip opinions ("Bush [or Clinton] is an idiot"), and easy answers ("Be yourself" or "Provide job training for the unemployed, and we can do away with welfare"). We're awash in such stuff.

That's one reason for the prominence of the currently popular buzz phrase "thinking outside the box"—which appears to mean getting beyond outworn ways of thinking about things. But more than that, the phrase assumes that most of the time most of us are trapped inside the box—inside a set of prefabricated answers (clichés) and like/dislike responses. This is not a new phenomenon, of course. Two hundred fifty years ago the philosopher David Hume, writing about perception, asserted that our lives are spent in "dogmatic slumbers," so ensnared in conventional notions of just about everything that we don't really see; we just rehearse what we've been told is there.

Growing up, we all become increasingly desensitized to the world around us; we tend to forget the specific things that get us to feel and think in particular ways. Instead we respond to our experience with a limited range of generalizations, and more often than not, these are shared generalizations—that is, clichés.

The way out of this trap is an attitude of skepticism, which is the very lifeblood of analysis. Like analysis, skepticism tends to get a bad rap. It is not the enemy of optimism, as people sometimes unquestioningly assume; it's the enemy of blind optimism and of blindness in general. Skeptics believe in asking questions, in not automatically accepting the same old narrow set of answers as accurate and right. A skeptic values doubt, in the words of one scholar, "because everywhere one looks there are those selling their version of the truth as the only version of the truth" (Owens xiii).

Just as analyzing a subject is not a negative move to "rip things apart," adopting a skeptical attitude toward life is not a move to wallow in negativity, assuming the futility of everything. The skeptic wants not to deny life but to affirm a version of life that is more accurate—to arrive at a better explanation of what things mean, to locate and solve problems that others don't see. In this sense, skepticism is careful and intelligent optimism.

In sum, a skeptical attitude goes hand in hand with writing analytically. Together they aim not to close things down but to open things up, *habitually seeking out live questions over inert answers.* By asking questions you'll discover that the world is filled with interesting things to analyze.

Here's a survey of habits of mind—some of them potentially blinding—and alternatives to them.

A. BANKING

The theorist Paolo Freire is now widely known for his attack on educational practices that he called "banking." In the banking model of education, the student is given information that he or she later gives back in more or less the same form. There is, in other words, a deposit and later a withdrawal. Like the number-bearing account through which money passes, the learner is a passive conduit taking things in and spitting them back out.

As only one part of the learning process, banking isn't really such a bad habit. We all need information to think with; the worst kind of opinion-mongering is starved of information. Opinion-mongerers think what they think because they think it, because they heard it somewhere, although they often have forgotten where. How can we arrive fairly at ideas and judgments with no information of the world, nothing to go on beyond our own limited experience?

But an education consisting entirely of banking—information in/information out—does not teach thinking. Being able to recite the ideas other people have had does not automatically render a person capable of thinking about these ideas or producing them. Of course, repetition, imitation, and memorization can develop our minds and help us retain information, but it is possible to repeat what we don't understand, to merely accept where we should be asking questions, and never learn how to think about all that has been taken in. *Passivity is a primary retardant of learning.* As we show in a later chapter on reading critically, it is possible to acquire and respect other people's ideas but also to get beyond just cutting and pasting them into mental scrapbooks, agreeing and disagreeing with them in reflex fashion.

There are several things you can try in order to get beyond banking. One of these is an activity whose usefulness is too often underestimated: paraphrasing. Paraphrasing something is not the same as summarizing it or generalizing about it. Summarizing and generalizing are further removed from the language of the reading than paraphrasing. A paraphrase takes the language of the reading and restates it in other words.

Why is paraphrasing useful? Why isn't it just a mechanical and labor-intensive form of banking? The answer has to do with words—what they are and what we do with them. When we read, it is easy to skip quickly over the words, assuming we know what they mean. Yet when people start talking about what they mean by particular words—the difference, for example, between "assertive" and "aggressive" or the meaning of ordinary words like "polite" or "realistic" or "gentlemanly"—they usually find less agreement than they expected. Most words mean more than one thing and mean different things to different people. Words matter. They are our primary means of negotiating the space between ourselves and others and of figuring out our relation to the world. It pays to take the time to notice them and find ways of thinking more carefully about what they mean. Try, for example, to come up with as many words as you can think of that name different kinds of anger. What does this reveal?

Paraphrasing, in short, is a prime alternative to just banking, and it certainly involves more than mechanically reproducing the reading. When you recast a sentence or two, finding the best synonyms you can think of for the original language, translating it into a parallel statement, you are thinking actively about what the words mean.

❧ *Try this:* Select a short paragraph or even a key sentence from something you are currently reading. Recast the substantive language in the passage into other words that mean as close to the same thing as possible. Try not to make the language more general, and don't condense it into a summarizing statement. Then reflect and take some notes on what you notice about the passage that you may not have noticed when you read it the first time. □

The next few chapters offer more tactics for reading actively, but here is another one to start using now. Read with an eye to problems. Virtually all writing can be seen as trying to address some problem or problems. Generally speaking, writers write because they have determined that something needs to be done to correct some idea or situation, whether in their own lives or in the world. You can read more actively by trying to figure out from the language of the reading what its author is worried about and what he or she is trying to "fix." Once you figure out what the reading is reacting against, what it wants to better understand or change, you will have a far clearer understanding of how the reading operates, why it does what it does. This is true even of textbooks: informational reading still has a point of view. Whenever you can, find the position the reading is trying to resist, revise, or replace.

B. GENERALIZING

What it all boils down to is . . . What this adds up to is . . . The gist of her speech was . . .

Like banking, generalizing is not always a bad habit. Reducing complex events or theories or books or speeches to a reasonably accurate summarizing statement requires practice and skill. We generalize from our experience because this is one way of arriving at ideas. The problem with generalizing as a habit of mind is that it removes the mind—usually much too quickly—from the data that produced the generalization in the first place.

People tend to remember their reactions and impressions. The dinner was dull. The house was beautiful. The music was exciting. But they forget the specific, concrete causes of these impressions (if they ever fully noticed them). As a result, people deprive themselves of material to think with—the data that might allow them to reconsider their initial impressions or share them with others.

So, one common denominator of an analytical habit of mind is that it pays attention to detail. We analyze because our global responses—to a social problem, for example, or to a film or a speech—are too general to be of much use. To understand a subject we need to get past our first broad (and usually evaluative) response in order to discover the particulars that best explain the character of the whole.

Consider for a moment what you are actually asking others to do when you offer them a generalization such as "His stories are very depressing." Unless the recipient of this observation asks a question—such as "Why do you think so?"—he or she is being required to take your word for it: the stories are depressing because you say so. What happens instead if you offer a few details that caused you to think as you do? Clearly, you are on riskier ground. Your listener might think that the details you cite are actually not depressing or that this is not the most interesting or useful way to think about the stories. He or she might offer a different generalization, a different reading of the data, but at least conversation has become possible. There is something available to think with: the actual stuff of experience from which further generalizations can be made.

In a reply to a young writer who had solicited his advice, Ernest Hemingway recommended what he referred to as his five-finger exercise. The exercise, like playing scales on a piano, is a kind of mental scale playing. In it you train yourself to habitually trace your own responses back to their causes in the concrete stuff of experience. The same five-finger exercise will make you a better reader and learner. Vagueness and generality are major blocks to learning because, as habits of mind, they allow you to dismiss virtually everything you've read and heard except the general idea you've arrived at. Often the generalizations that come to mind are so broad that they tell us nothing. To say, for example, that a poem is about love or death or rebirth, or that the economy of a particular emerging nation is inefficient, accomplishes very little, since the generalizations could fit almost any poem or economy. In other words, your generalizations are often sites where you stopped thinking prematurely, not the "answers" you've thought they were.

The simplest antidote to the problem of generalizing is to train yourself to be more self-conscious about where your generalizations come from. We say more about this kind of mental training in the next chapter, but for now, *press yourself to trace your general impressions back to the particulars that caused them.* What three details about the classroom or meeting room (or some public space you regularly spend time in), for example, seem most responsible for the attitude you tend to have toward that place and the way it makes you feel? Why? This tracing of attitudes back to their concrete causes is the most basic—and most necessary—move in the analytical habit of mind. It will help you go through the world in less of a haze. Deciding to be more conscious of our own responses to the world and their causes is also an antidote to the inevitable numbing, the desensitizing, that takes place as habit takes control of our daily lives. Choose to notice more and to keep noticing.

Here's another strategy for bringing your thinking down from high levels of generality. Think of the words you use in terms of an *abstraction ladder*. The more general and vague the word, the higher its position on the abstraction ladder. "Mammal," for example, is higher on the abstraction ladder than "cow." Saying that a poem is about loss is more general—higher on the abstraction ladder—than saying that the poem records the struggle of a grown child to understand the departure of a parent very different in temperament from herself.

You might try using "Level 3 Generality" as a convenient tag phrase reminding you to steer clear of the higher reaches of abstract generalization, some so high up the ladder from the concrete stuff that produced them that there is barely enough air to sustain the thought. Why "Level 3" instead of "Level 2"? There aren't just two categories, abstract and concrete: the categories are the ends of a continuum, a sliding scale. And too often when writers try to concretize their generalizations, the results are still too general: they change "animal" to "mammal," but they need "cow" or, better, "black angus."

Try this: Locate a word above (more abstract than) and a word below (more concrete than) each of the following words: society, food, train, taxes, school, government, cooking oil, organism, story, and magazine. □

If you experiment with the abstraction ladder, you will find that it takes some practice to learn to distinguish between abstract words and concrete ones. A concrete word is one that appeals to the senses. Abstract words are not available to our senses of touch, sight, hearing, taste, and smell. "Submarine" is a concrete word. It conjures up a mental image, something we can physically experience. "Peace-keeping force" is an abstract phrase. It conjures up a concept, but in an abstract and general way. We know what people are talking about when they say there is a plan to send submarines to a troubled area. We can't be so sure what is up when people start talking about a peace-keeping force. Start experimenting with the rather tricky divide between concrete and abstract words.

Try this: Make a list of the first ten words that come to mind and then arrange them from most concrete to most abstract. Then repeat the exercise by choosing key words from a page of something you have written recently. □

C. JUDGING

It would be impossible to overstate the mind-numbing effect that the judgment reflex has on thinking. Why? Consider what we do when we judge something and what we ask others to do when we offer them our judgments. "Ugly," "realistic," "pretty," "boring," "wonderful," "unfair," "crazy." Notice that the problem with such words is a version of the problem with all generalizations—lack of information. What have you actually told someone else if you say that X is ugly or boring or realistic?

In its most primitive form—most automatic and least thoughtful—judging is like an on/off switch. When the switch gets thrown in one direction or the other— good/bad, right/wrong, positive/negative—the resulting judgment predetermines and overdirects any subsequent thinking we might do. Rather than thinking about what X is or how X operates, we lock ourselves prematurely into proving that we were right to think that X should be banned or supported.

The psychologist Carl Rogers has written at length on the problem of the judgment reflex. He claims that our habitual tendency as humans—virtually a programmed response—is to evaluate everything and to do so very quickly. Walking out of a movie, for example, most people will immediately voice their approval or disapproval, usually in either/or terms: I liked it *or* didn't like it; it was right/wrong, good/bad, interesting/boring. The other people in the conversation will then offer their own evaluations plus their judgments of the others' judgments: I think that it was a good movie and that you are wrong to think it was bad. And so on.

There are several problems with this kind of reflex move to evaluation. Like the knee jerk in response to the tap from the physician's silver hammer, reflex judgments are made without conscious thought (the source of the pejorative term "knee-jerk thinking"). They close off thinking with likes and dislikes and instant categories. The fact that you liked or didn't like a movie probably says more about you—your tastes, interests, biases, and experiences—than it does about the movie. What makes a movie boring? That it doesn't have enough car chases? That its plot resembles half the plots on cable channels? That the leading man is miscast or the dialogue too long-winded? At the least, in such cases, you'd need to share with readers your *criteria* for judgment— your reasons and your standards of evaluation. Without such careful explanation, judgments will always appear to be reflex, and others will assume that you are motivated more by your desire to defend your position than by your desire to understand what the film was trying to accomplish.

When people leap to judgment, they usually land in the mental pathways they've grown accustomed to traveling, guided by family or friends or popular opinion. If you can break the evaluation reflex and press yourself to analyze before judging a subject, you will often be surprised at how much your initial responses change. As a general rule, you should seek to understand the subject you are analyzing before moving to a judgment about it. Try to *figure out what your subject means before deciding how you feel about it.*

This is not to say that all judging should be avoided. Obviously, our thinking on many occasions must be applied to decision making—deciding whether we should or shouldn't vote for a particular candidate, should or shouldn't eat french fries, or should or shouldn't support a ban on cigarette advertising.

A writer needs to take into account how the judgment has been affected by the particular situation (context) and to acknowledge how thinking about these details has led to restricting (qualifying) the range of the judgment: X is *sometimes* true in these particular circumstances; Z is *probably* the right thing to do *but only when* A and B occur. Ultimately, in other words, analytical thinking does need to arrive at a point of view—which is a form of judgment—but analytical conclusions are usually not phrased in terms of like/dislike or good/bad. They disclose what a person has come to understand about X rather than how he or she imperiously rules on the worth of X.

In some ways, the rest of this book consists of a set of methods for blocking the ever-present judgment reflex in favor of more thoughtful responses. For now, here are two things to try in order to short-circuit the judgment reflex and begin replacing it with a more thoughtful, more patient, and more open-mindedly curious habit of mind. First, try the cure that Carl Rogers recommended to negotiators in industry and government. Do not assert an agreement or disagreement with another person's position until you can repeat that position in a way the other person would accept as fair and accurate. This is surprisingly hard to do because we are usually so busy calling up judgments of our own that we barely hear what the other person is saying.

Second, try eliminating the word "should" from your vocabulary for a while, since judgments so often take the form of recommendations. The analytical habit of mind is characterized by the words "why," "how," and "what." Analysis asks the following: What is the aim of the new law? Why do laws of this sort tend to get passed in some parts of the country rather than in others? How does this law compare with its predecessor? Judgments take the form of "should statements." We should pass the law. We should not consider putting such foolish restrictions into law.

You might also try eliminating evaluative adjectives—those that offer judgments with no data. "Green" is a descriptive, concrete adjective. It offers something we can experience. "Beautiful" is an evaluative adjective. It offers only judgment.

Try this: The dividing line between judgmental and nonjudgmental words is often more difficult to discern in practice than you might assume. Categorize each of the terms in the following list as judgmental or nonjudgmental, and be prepared to explain your reasoning: monstrous, delicate, authoritative, strong, muscular, automatic, vibrant, tedious, pungent, unrealistic, flexible, tart, pleasing, clever, and slow. □

Try this: One way of keeping tabs on your own habits of mind is to evaluate the kinds of adjectives and adverbs that you use. Some are evaluatively neutral, offering information without telling you what to think about it. Others are not neutral; they name evaluative responses, usually offering little or no concrete information. Consider the following sentence: "The gypsy was walking heel to toe, insultingly, like a ballroom dancer." The words in this sentence do each of the four different things that go on when we describe: they offer details, make comparisons, name, and overtly judge. Locate an example of each of these different descriptive activities in the sentence. Then, write a paragraph of description—on anything that comes to mind—without using any evaluative adjectives or adverbs. Alternatively, analyze and categorize the word choice in a piece of your own recent writing. □

D. DEBATE-STYLE ARGUMENT

People are customarily introduced to writing arguments through the debate model. They are taught to argue pro *or* con on a given position or issue, with the aim of defeating an imagined opponent and convincing an audience of the rightness of one side of the argument. To its credit, the debate model teaches writers to consider more than a single viewpoint, their opponent's as well as their own. But unfortunately, it can also train them, even if inadvertently, to see the other side only as the opposition and to concentrate their energy only on winning the day. The problem with this approach is that it overemphasizes the bottom line—aggressively advancing a claim for *or* against some view—without *first* engaging in the exploratory interpretation of evidence that is so necessary to arriving at thoughtful arguments.

Thus, debate-style argument produces a frame of mind in which defending positions matters more than taking the necessary time to develop ideas worth defending. And, very possibly, it nourishes the mudslinging and opinionated mind-set—attack first—that proliferates in editorials and television talk shows, not to mention the conversations you overhear in going about your life. We are not saying that people should forget about making value and policy decisions and avoid the task of persuading others. We are saying that too many of the arguments we all read, hear, and participate in every day are based on insufficient analysis.

In sum, adhering to the more restrictive, debate-style definition of argument can create a number of problems for careful analytical writers:

1. By requiring writers to be oppositional, it inclines them to discount or dismiss problems with the side or in the position they have chosen; they cling to the same static position rather than testing it as a way of allowing it to evolve.
2. It inclines writers toward either/or thinking rather than encouraging them to formulate more qualified positions (carefully limited, acknowledging exceptions, and so forth) that integrate apparently opposing viewpoints.
3. It overvalues convincing someone else at the expense of developing understanding.

The remedy, we suggest, is the temporary suspension of the pro/con, debate-style habit of mind. Argument and analysis are profoundly connected, but their stances toward subject matter and audience differ so much that most people need to learn them separately before being able to put them back together. And because the argumentative habit of mind is so aggressively visible in our culture, most people never get around to experimenting with the more reflective and less combative approach that analysis embraces. Thus, this book asks you to turn off the argument switch, not forever, but for as long as it takes for you to cultivate other habits of mind that argument might otherwise overshadow.

Although analysis and argument proceed in essentially the same way, they differ in the kinds of questions they try to answer. Argument, at its most dispassionate, asks "What can be said with truth about X or Y?" In common practice, though, the kinds of questions that argument more often answers are more committed, directive, and should-centered, such as "Which is better, X or Y?," "How can we best achieve X or Y?," and "Why should we stop doing X or Y?"

Analysis, by contrast, asks "What does X or Y mean?" In analysis the evidence (your data) is something you wish to understand, and the claims are assertions about what that evidence means. The claim that an argument makes—for example, readers should or shouldn't vote for bans on smoking in public buildings, or they should or shouldn't believe that gays can function effectively in the military—is often an answer to a "should" question. The writer of an analysis is more concerned with discovering how each of these complex subjects might be defined and explained than with convincing readers to approve or disapprove of them.

The factor that most clearly separates argument and analysis is the closer association of argument with the desire to persuade. A writer concerned with persuading others may feel the need to go into the writing process with considerable certainty about the position he or she advocates. The writer of an analysis, on the other hand, usually begins and remains for an extended period in a position of uncertainty. Analysis is thus more exploratory, more tentative, and more dispassionate than argument (especially debate-style argument).

Analytical writers are frequently more concerned with persuading themselves, with discovering what they believe about a subject, than they are with persuading others. The writer of an analysis is thus more likely to begin with the details of a subject he or she wishes to better understand than with a position he or she wishes to defend. Analysis, in sum, is concerned with having better ideas about how things operate rather than with whether or not we should approve or disapprove of them.

It's important to remember that, in practice, analysis and argument are inevitably linked. Even the most tentative and cautiously evolving analysis shares with argument the aim of having readers accept a particular interpretation of a set of data. Similarly, even the most passionately committed argument engages in analysis, arranging details into patterns and explaining what they mean. But as should now be clear, the aims of analysis and argument can sometimes be in conflict.

E. EITHER/OR THINKING (BINARIES)

Analytical thought is unthinkable without categories. Categorical thinking is an unavoidable and distinctive feature of how all human beings make sense of the world: in order to generalize from particular experiences, we try to put those experiences into meaningful categories. When we contract an illness, for example, doctors diagnose it by type. When we study personality theory, different behaviors are grouped by personality type. Subject areas in school are categorized into divisions: the natural sciences, the social sciences, and the humanities.

But categorical thinking can also be dangerous. It can lead us into oversimplification. This is especially the case with one of the most common forms of categorical thinking, the use of *binaries*.

In human thinking as in a computer, a binary is a pair of elements, usually in opposition to each other, as in off/on, yes/no, right/wrong, agree/disagree, approve/disapprove, real/unreal, accurate/inaccurate, believable/unbelievable, and so on. As the philosopher Herbert Marcuse says, "We understand that which is in terms of that which is not": light is that which is not dark; masculine is that which is not feminine; and civilized is that which is not primitive. We can't help but think in binary terms; creating opposing categories is fundamental to defining things.

Binaries become a problem when they are used uncritically, leading to what is called *reductive thinking*. Reductive thinking oversimplifies a subject, eliminating alternatives between two extremes—for example, that women are *either* virgins *or* whores, or teachers *either* instill a love of learning in students *or* alienate them from their feelings.

Because binaries are part of how humans think, we can't avoid the problem of reductive thinking by just avoiding binaries altogether. In fact, noticing and naming binaries is an excellent way to improve your reading skills and to generate ideas. The issue is how to make productive rather than reductive use of binaries. You can start by keeping the following points in mind.

1. Most subjects cannot be adequately considered in terms of only two options—either this or that, with nothing in between.
2. The arrangement of two terms into opposing categories usually implies a value hierarchy even when the valuing of one side of the binary over the other is not intended. The binaries black/white or primitive/civilized may in the writer's mind be value neutral, but the fact that the terms appear in opposed pairs suggests that one side is right, the other wrong, one side desirable, the other less so.

In sum, *it is useful and necessary to construct binaries, but it is dangerous to ignore the gray areas in between and the value judgments that binaries tend to conceal.*

Often the trouble starts with the ways that binaries are phrased. Two of the most common and potentially counterproductive ways of phrasing binaries are *either/or* and *agree/disagree*. In the vast majority of cases, there are more than two alternatives, but the either/or or agree/disagree phrasing prevents you from looking for them. And it does not acknowledge that both alternatives may have some truth to them. A new environmental policy may be both visionary and blind, or some combination of the two. And there may be more accurate categories than visionary and blind for considering the merits and demerits of the policy.

Framing an issue in either/or terms can be useful for stimulating a chain of thought, but it is usually not a good way to end one. Consider the either/or binary "Was the Civil War fought over slavery or economics?" You could begin this way, but if you're not careful—conscious of the all-or-nothing force of binary formulations—you could easily get trapped in an overly dichotomized position; in this case, that economics caused the war and that slavery had nothing to do with it, or vice versa.

You can't analyze without binaries, but you need to be wary of putting everything into big, undifferentiated categories, labeled all black or all white, with nothing in between.

F. PERSONALIZING (LOCATING THE "I")

In one sense all writing is personal: you are the one putting words on the page, and inevitably you see things from your point of view. Even if you were to summarize what someone else had written, aiming for maximum impersonality, *you* would be making the decisions about what to include and exclude. Most effective analytical prose has a strong personal element—the writer's stake in the subject matter. As readers, we want the sense that a writer is engaged with the material, cares about what he or she says about it, is sharing what he or she finds interesting about it.

But in another sense, no writing is strictly personal. As contemporary cultural theorists are fond of pointing out, the "I" is not a wholly autonomous free agent who writes from a unique point of view. Rather, the "I" is always affected by forces outside the self—social, cultural, educational, historical, and so forth—that shape the self. The extreme version of this position allots little space for what we like to think of as individuality at all: the self is a site through which dominant cultural ways of understanding the world (ideologies) circulate. That's a pretty disarming notion, but one worth pondering. From this perspective we are like actors who don't know that we're actors, reciting various cultural scripts that we don't realize are scripts.

This is, of course, an extreme position. A person who believes that civil rights for all is an essential human right is not necessarily a victim of cultural brainwashing. The grounds of his or her belief, shaped by participation in a larger community of belief (ethnic, religious, family tradition, and so forth) are, however, not merely personal.

To return to a claim that began this chapter, overpersonalizing substitutes merely reacting for thinking. Rather than open-mindedly exploring what a subject might mean, the overpersonalizing writer tends to use a limited range of culturally conditioned likes and dislikes to close the subject down. Is a reader who dislikes a character in a novel or television show—Madame Bovary or Elaine Bennis—doing any useful analytical thinking? If Elaine reminds him of his own whiny sister and so he dislikes her, (bluntly) who cares? What if a viewer hates a film because she suffered from her parents' divorce and the film's star divorced his wife and left his children? These are responses that, however valid in themselves, are merely personal.

Along similar lines, it's a mistake for a person to assume that because he or she experiences X, everyone else does too. It is surprisingly difficult to break the habit of treating our points of view as self-evidently true—not just for us but for everyone. What is common sense for one person and, so, not even in need of explaining can be quite uncommon and not so obviously sensible to someone else. More often than not, "common sense" really means "what seems obvious to me and therefore should be obvious to you."

❋ *Try this:* Paraphrase the phrase "common sense." Your aim is to extend our discussion of what people are doing when they fall back on the idea of common sense. You also may wish to think of recent situations in which someone you know has appealed to common sense or remarked on its absence. ☐

One tell-tale sign of an overpersonalizing writer is his or her tendency to let personal narratives substitute for careful consideration of a subject. When you substitute personal narrative for analysis, your own experiences and prejudices tend to become an unquestioned standard of value. Your own disastrous experience with a health maintenance organization (HMO) may predispose you to dismiss a plan for nationalized health care, but your writing needs to examine in detail the holes in the plan, not simply evoke the three hours you lingered in some doctor's waiting room. Paying too much attention to how a subject makes you feel or fits your previous experience can seduce you away from paying attention to how the subject itself operates.

This is not to say that there is no learning or thinking value in telling our experiences. Storytelling has the virtue of offering concrete experience—not just the conclusions the experience may have led to. Personal narratives can take us back to the source of our convictions. The problem comes when "relating" to someone's story becomes an habitual substitute for thinking through the ideas and attitudes that the story suggests. What do people mean when they say, "I can relate to that"? By and large, "relating" to someone else's experience is an overly generalized response, one in which you do not stop to isolate either the precise grounds of the emotional identification or the various assumptions that the story rests on but does not make overt.

If our experience is not necessarily applicable to others, if our feelings about X are not self-evident truths about it, what then is the role of the personal in thinking and writing analytically? The problem with "the personal" really has to do with how that term is commonly (mis)understood. It is usually located as one-half of a particularly vicious binary that might be schematized thus:

subjective		objective
personal expression		impersonal analysis
passionately engaged	Versus	detached, impassively neutral
genuinely felt		heartless

Like most vicious binaries, this one overstates the case and obscures the considerable overlap of the two sides. Analysis is not separate from feeling and engagement; these are attitudes necessary to energize it. *Analysis is always personal but not overly personal;* it is somewhat detached but not cold and heartless.

The antidote to the overpersonalizing habit of mind is, as with most habits you want to break, to become more self-conscious about it. If you keep in mind that the "I" you tend to lead with is not simply a free agent but also a product of cultural influences, you will be more likely to notice your first responses and become curious about them. Is this what you really believe? Asking that question is a healthy habit to cultivate and one that can often help you see the logic of other possible responses to the position you've initially taken. And of course, some intuitive responses provide valuable beginnings for constructive thinking; so, get in the habit of *tracing your own responses back to their causes.* If you find an aspect of your subject irritating or funny or disappointing, locate the exact details that evoked your emotional response, and begin to analyze those details.

G. OPINIONS (VERSUS IDEAS)

Perhaps no single word causes more problems in the relations between students and teachers, and for people in general, than the word "opinion." In the opening to this chapter, we cited that most common but nonetheless strange claim, "I'm entitled to my opinion." This phrase is worth exploring. What is an opinion? How is it (or is it) different from a belief or an idea? If I say that I am entitled to my opinion, what am I asking you to do or not do?

Many of the opinions people fight about are actually clichés, pieces of much-repeated conventional wisdom. For example, "People are entitled to say what they want. That's just my opinion." But, of course, this assertion isn't a private and personal revelation. It is an exaggerated and overstated version of one of the rights in the U.S. Bill of Rights, guaranteeing freedom of speech. Much public thinking has gone on about this private conviction, and it has thus been carefully qualified. A person can't, for example, say publicly whatever he or she pleases about other people if what he or she says is false and damages the reputation of another person.

Our opinions are learned. They are products of our culture and our upbringing—not personal possessions. It is okay to have opinions. Everyone does. It is not okay, however, to give too many of our views, our opinions, protected-species status, walling them off into a reserve, not to be touched by reasoning or evidence.

Some things, of course, we do have to take on faith. Religious convictions, for example, are more than opinions, though they operate in a similar way: we believe where we can't always prove. But even our most sacred convictions are not really harmed by thinking. The world's religions are constantly engaged in interpreting and reinterpreting what religious texts mean, what various traditional practices mean, and how they may or may not be adapted to the attitudes and practices of the world as it is today.

For purposes of writing analytically, you need to think about the difference between an idea and an opinion. The discovery and careful wording of ideas is one of

---

Voices from Across the Curriculum

Ideas Versus Opinions

Writers need to be aware of the distinction between an argument that seeks support from evidence and mere opinions and assertions. Many students taking political science courses often come with the assumption that in politics one opinion is as good as another. (Tocqueville thought this to be a peculiarly democratic disease.) From this perspective any position a political science professor may take on controversial issues is simply his or her opinion to be accepted or rejected by students according to their own beliefs/prejudices. The key task, therefore, is not so much substituting knowledge for opinions, but rather substituting well-constructed arguments for unexamined opinions.

What is an argument, and how might it be distinguished from opinions? Several things need to be stressed: (1) The thesis should be linked to evidence drawn from relevant sources: polling data, interviews, historical material, and so forth. (2) The thesis should make as explicit as possible its own ideological assumptions. (3) A thesis, in contrast to mere statement of opinion, is committed to making an argument, which means that it presupposes a willingness to engage with others. To the extent that writers operate on the assumption that everything is an opinion, they have no reason to construct arguments; they are locked into an opinion.

—Jack Gambino, Professor of Political Science

the primary aims of analysis. To get to ideas, we have to learn to *see the questions* that are suggested by whatever it is we are studying. Opinions, particularly for people who have a lot of them, get in the way of having ideas because opinions are so often habitual responses—mental reflexes.

H. WHAT IT MEANS TO HAVE AN IDEA

This is a book about how to have ideas. It's one thing to acquire knowledge, but you also need to learn how to produce knowledge, to think for yourself. The problem is that people get daunted when asked to arrive at ideas. They dream up ingenious ways to avoid the task. Or they get paralyzed with anxiety.

What is an idea? Must an idea be something that is entirely "original"? Must it revamp the way you understand yourself or your stance toward the world?

Such expectations are unreasonably grand. Clearly, a writer in the early stages of learning about a subject can't be expected to arrive at an idea so original that, like one in a Ph.D. thesis, it revises complex concepts in a discipline. Nor should you count as ideas only those that lead to some kind of life-altering discovery.

What, then, does it mean to have an idea? We can probably best understand what ideas are by considering what ideas do and where they can be found. Here is a partial list:

- An idea may be the discovery of a question where there seemed not to be one.
- An idea usually starts with an observation that is puzzling, with something that you want to figure out rather than with something that you think you already understand.
- An idea may make explicit and explore the meaning of something implicit—an unstated assumption upon which an argument rests or a logical consequence of a given position.
- An idea may connect elements of a subject and explain the significance of that connection.
- An idea often accounts for some *dissonance*—that is, something that seems not to fit together.
- An idea answers a question; it explains something that needs to be explained.

Most strong analytical ideas launch you in a process of resolving problems and bringing competing positions into some kind of alignment. They locate you where there is something to negotiate, where you are required not just to list answers but also to ask questions, make choices, and engage in reasoning about the significance of your evidence.

When we wrote this book our aim was to serve the needs of writers not just in English courses but across the curriculum and beyond school altogether. Some would argue that ideas are in fact discipline-specific, which is to say that what counts as an idea in psychology is quite different from what counts as an idea in history or philosophy or business. And surely the context does affect the way that ideas are shaped and expressed. As you go through your education, you will find it interesting to think about how different disciplines seem to define what an idea is, what it does, and how you recognize one.

This book operates on the premise, however, that ideas across the curriculum share common elements. All of the items in the list above, for example, seem to us to be common to ideas and to idea-making in virtually any context. As you read the book, we hope that you will try to add to our list, to develop your own sense of what it means to have an idea.

I.   ANALYSIS AND CREATIVITY

We conclude this chapter on habits of mind with our short answer to a long-standing vicious dichotomy—that between creativity and analysis. This version of the head/heart false dichotomy, which has been making trouble since before the Enlightenment (circa 1750), is absolutely disabling to people on both sides of the supposed analytical/creative divide.

It has been one project of this chapter to show that analysis and creativity go hand in hand. A person who possesses an analytical cast of mind

- aims to notice more.
- is more inclined to see the questions rather than to settle for clichéd answers or to leave his or her own assumptions unacknowledged.
- is suspicious of rigid dichotomies (heart/head, creative/analytical, feeling/thinking).
- is slow to leap to generalizations and judgments, instead choosing to dwell longer with detail in an open, exploratory way.
- knows that formulating an idea, searching out what something means, *is* creative.
- recognizes that creative writing isn't just about feelings but is also a way of thinking about feelings.

In future chapters we explore—and we hope, explode—the myths that artificially separate analytical from creative writing. All good writing, we believe, is *both*.

ASSIGNMENTS

1. Among the habits of mind that this chapter recommends, one of the most useful (and potentially entertaining) is to trace impressions, reactions, sudden thoughts, moods, and so forth, back to their probable causes. Practice this skill for a week, recording at least one impression a day in some detail (that is, recording what you both thought and felt). Then determine at least three concrete causes of your responses. That is, go after specific sensory details. For class purposes, pick one or two of your journal writings, and revise them to a form that can be shared with other members of the class.

   Interesting subjects for such writing might include your response to your first-year student orientation, some other feature of the beginning of the school year, or your response to selected places on campus. What impact do certain places have on you? Why?

2. Visit a professor in a discipline you find interesting and interview him or her about what constitutes an idea in that discipline. Ask for one or two single-sentence statements of ideas that the professor may have seen lately in a journal in his or her field or may be working on in his or her research. You might also ask the professor to share with you a couple of good ideas that past students have arrived at in his or her courses. Write an account of your interview, including examples of what your interviewee considered to be good ideas and why.

2

Noticing: Learning to Observe

Learning to think means learning how to look at and analyze information. Before we can train ourselves to look at things—to notice more—we have to unlearn habits of mind (like overgeneralizing, the judgment reflex, and either/or thinking) that make us blind. As we argue in Chapter 1, these are culturally ingrained moves; you had to learn them, and fortunately, you can unlearn them. But what do you put in their place?

In a word, *observation*.

The meaning of observation is not self-evident. If you had five friends over and asked them to write down one observation about the room you were all sitting in, it's a sure bet that many of the responses would be generalized judgments—"It's comfortable" or "It's a pigsty." And why? Because the habits of mind that come to most of us most readily and that are further encouraged by the culture tend to shut down the observation stage so that we literally notice and remember less. We go for the quick impression and dismiss the rest.

Of course, we all have methods of observation, but most of us are very little aware of these. And so, if we are to become better observers, we need to become more aware of what observation involves. This is the purpose of this chapter, which first explains what gets in the way of observation and then offers several systematic ways of improving your observational skills.

The fundamental principle we want to communicate in this chapter—the key to becoming a better observer and thus a better thinker—is that you need to *slow down,* to stop trying to draw conclusions before you've spent time openly attending to the data, letting yourself notice more. Better ideas grow out of a richer acquaintance with whatever it is you are looking at. The trick—and it requires both willpower and practice—is to give yourself permission to dwell longer and more closely with the data. The poet Emily Dickinson once wrote that "Perception of an object/ Costs precise the object's loss." When we leap prematurely to our perceptions about a thing, we place a filter between ourselves and the "object," shrinking the amount and kinds of information that can get through to our minds and our senses.

Often, it is not just carelessness or a judgmental cast of mind that closes down the information-gathering stage. People sometimes have unreasonable expectations of themselves when it comes to having ideas. They think that they should get to ideas right away, that arriving at a "thesis," some governing idea about a subject, is a necessary starting point for analysis. We call this kind of idea–first–look–later anxiety *the dogfish problem*. In the dogfish problem, a writer trying to start with a thesis before looking more openly at the data is in the same predicament as a scientist being expected to propose a theory about the dogfish after having had only a cursory look at one.

What would a scientist studying a particular species of fish actually do in order to formulate a theory? He or she would start with observation. She'd look at its habitat. She'd watch its habits—how it eats, swims, and reproduces. She'd undoubtedly dissect it. Or how about those studies by Jane Goodall and others of apes in the wild? These scientists spend years observing creatures in their habitats, collecting data, before they're ready to start publishing their ideas.

You, on the other hand, don't have years to get your writing done. But you have more time to spend at the data–gathering end than you are probably accustomed to spending. Slow down; it's worth it. Don't fall victim to the dogfish problem. If you give yourself more time to look at your subject matter and see what you notice, ideas will come.

You will also need to cultivate a more positive attitude toward not knowing. Uncertainty—even its more extreme version, confusion—is a productive state of mind, a precondition to allowing yourself to have ideas. Rather than court confusion, most of us seek the comfort of feeling that we understand. But when people decide too quickly that they understand something, they actually cause themselves to see less. Once they've made a mental note of their general impression and the details that created it, they usually stop looking (and forget the details). A more productive approach is to *deliberately assume that you don't understand,* that you may not yet fully see what is going on in whatever it is you are looking at. By training yourself to be more comfortable with not knowing, you give yourself license to start working with your material, the data, *before* you try to decide what you think.

In short, the major shift this chapter asks you to make is to locate more of your time and attention in the observation stage that necessarily precedes the thesis-formulating phase. Train yourself to stay open longer to what you can notice in your subject matter. Do this by starting not with "What do I think?" or, worse, with "What do I like/dislike?" but with "What do I *notice?*"

Here are a few more thoughts about noticing and what gets in its way. Some people, perhaps especially the very young, are good at noticing things. They see things that the rest of us don't see or have ceased to notice. But why is this? Is it just that people become duller as they get older? The poet William Wordsworth, among others, argued that we aren't the victims of declining intelligence but of habit. That is, as we organize our lives so that we can function more efficiently, we condition ourselves to see in more predictable ways and to screen out things that are not immediately relevant to our daily needs.

You can test this theory by considering what you did and did not notice this morning on the way to work or class or wherever you regularly go. Getting where we need to go, following a routine for moving through the day, can be done with minimal engagement of either the brain or the senses. Our minds are often, as we say, "somewhere else." As we walk along, our eyes wander a few feet in front of our shoes or stare blankly in the direction of our destination. Moving along the roadway in cars, we periodically realize that miles have gone by while we were driving on automatic pilot, attending barely at all to the road or the car or the landscape. Arguably, even when we try to focus on something that we want to consider, the habit of not really attending to things stays with us. We glide over the top. We go for rapidly acquired impressions and then relax our attention.

The deadening effect of habit on seeing and thinking has long been a preoccupation of artists as well philosophers and psychologists. Some people have even defined the aim of art as "defamiliarization." "The essential purpose of art," writes the novelist David Lodge, "is to overcome the deadening effects of habit by representing familiar things in unfamiliar ways." The man who coined the term "defamiliarization," Victor Shklovsky, wrote "Habitualization devours works, clothes, furniture, one's wife, and the fear of war. . . . And art exists that one may recover the sensation of life" (Lodge 53).

In this context we come back around to the perhaps peculiar-sounding suggestion made earlier about not knowing, about accepting uncertainty and even confusion as beneficial states of mind on the way to the discovery of ideas. Curiosity may in fact kill cats, but it has the opposite effect on the human brain.

The problem with convincing ourselves that we have the answers is that we are thus prevented from *seeing the questions,* which are usually much more interesting than the temporary stopping points we have elected as answers. In the last chapter, which ends with a definition of what it means to have an idea, we offer one definition of idea as the answer to a good question. An idea, we propose, often consists of seeing a question where one seemed not to exist or of finding a connection between things that seem not to be connected. Having ideas is dependent on allowing yourself to notice things in your subject that you want to better understand rather than glossing over things with a quick and too easy understanding.

In light of this brief rationale, we now offer two formulas for developing the ability to dwell longer and more insightfully with data, with the stuff of experience, rather than pushing on prematurely to conclusions. The first of these, *Notice and Focus,* is very basic but nevertheless represents a significant shift for most people. The second procedure, a somewhat more elaborate but still basic set of steps, we call *The Method,* because it is widely applicable to a range of thinking, reading, and writing tasks.

A. NOTICE AND FOCUS (RANKING)

This exercise is governed by repeated return to the question "What do you notice?" Most people's tendency is to generalize and thus to rapidly move away from whatever it is they are looking at. The question "What do you notice?" redirects attention to the subject matter itself and delays the pressure to come up with answers, with a closing off of the experience.

So, the first step is for you to repeatedly answer the question "What do you notice?" Be sure to cite actual details of the thing being observed rather than move to more general observations about it. (Note that this is more difficult than it sounds.) This phase of the exercise should produce an extended and unordered list of details—features of the thing being observed—that call attention to themselves for one reason or another.

The second step is the focusing part in which you *rank* (create an order of importance) for the various features of your subject you have noticed. (Note that sometimes it is useful to start right away with this second step in in-class writing exercises and discussion.) Answer the question "What three details (specific features of the subject matter) are most interesting (or significant or revealing or strange)?" The purpose of relying on "interesting" or one of the other suggested words is that these will help to deactivate the like/dislike switch, which is so much a reflex in all of us, and replace it with a more analytical perspective.

The third step in this process is to say why the three things you selected struck you as the most interesting. We are postponing discussion of this move—the interpretive leap from observation to conclusion—until the next chapter. For now, we only ask you to start looking at things—at everything—using Notice and Focus.

Remember to start by noticing as much as you can about what you are looking at. Dwell with the data. Record what you see. Don't move to generalization or, worse, to judgment. What this procedure will begin to demonstrate is how useful description is as a tool for arriving at ideas. Stay at the description stage longer (in that attitude of uncertainty we recommend), and have better ideas. Training yourself to notice is fun. It will improve your memory, your ability to think, and probably also your conversation.

✻*Try this:* Do Notice and Focus with the room you're in. List a number of details about it, and then rank the three most important ones. Use in your focusing question any of the four words suggested above—"interesting," "significant," "revealing," or "strange." Or come up with your own focus for the ranking, such as three aspects of the room that seem most to affect the way you feel and behave in the space. Then, try this exercise with other possibilities—a picture, a cartoon, an editorial, eavesdropping around campus, looking at people's shoes, and so forth. □

B. THE METHOD

Although in subsequent chapters of the book we offer other formulas for seeing, for dwelling with the data, and for arriving at ideas, The Method underlies them all. The Method, once you've learned how to use it, can become, as it is in our classes, a universal assignment, something you always do with whatever it is you are working on: making sense of something you are reading, contemplating revision of a piece of your own or a friend's writing, or gathering firsthand information on something you plan to write about.

We've been talking about trying to write about what you see, starting with details rather than generalizations. It takes most people a while to grasp this idea because they don't readily distinguish between generalizing about, for example, a picture and writing about what is actually in the picture.

We've also tried to suggest that arriving at ideas is not a mystical process, that, in fact, most people already have formulas—mental procedures—that they use whenever they're called upon to do analysis. The problem is that people are insufficiently aware of these, and, so, it is difficult to learn to use them more consciously and efficiently.

Finally, we've been saying that people don't spend enough time in the information-gathering stage, nor do they think enough about the discrete activities that information gathering brings into play. This is to say that people need to learn how to notice things. Especially, they need to learn how to go about selecting some things as potentially more important or more interesting than others.

The Method is not about arranging an argument and getting quickly to the bottom line; it's about really looking at things—reducing anxiety by getting rid of the bottom-line mentality and giving yourself something quasimechanical to do that will let your mind play freely with the material. Listing is a great form of brainstorming; The Method makes the listing activity more coherent and systematic.

The Steps of The Method: Making Observation Systematic and Habitual

Hold yourself initially to doing the steps one at a time and in order. Start with step 1 and do it as thoroughly as you can before moving on. As you get good at using The Method, you will be able to record your answers under each of the three steps simultaneously. Use The Method to guide you in circling, underlining, and drawing connecting arrows among things you notice in whatever you are reading or observing. Then make lists following the directions below.

Step 1. Locate *exact repetitions*—identical or nearly identical words or details—and note the number of times each repeats.

> For example, if the word "seems" repeats three times, write "seems × 3." Consider different forms of the same word—"seemed," "seem"—as exact repetitions. Similarly, if you are working with images rather than words, the repeated appearance of high foreheads or of bare midriffs would constitute exact repetitions.

Step 2. Locate repetition of the same kind of detail or word. We call this a *strand*—a grouping of same or similar kind of words or details. (For example, "polite, courteous, mannerly" or "accuse, defense, justice, witness" are strands.)

> Be able to explain the strand's connecting logic, how the words are linked. Some people find it useful to think of strands as clusters or word–detail families that repeat throughout a verbal or visual subject.

Step 3. Locate details or words that form or suggest binary oppositions. We call these *binaries* or *organizing contrasts*. Here are some examples: open/closed, naïve/self-conscious, and gray/brown (note the opposition doesn't have to be as stark as black/white or light/dark).

> Start with what's on the page. Gradually move to implied binaries but keep these close to the data. Images of rocks and water, for example, might suggest the implied binary permanent/impermanent or the binary unchanging/changing.

Step 4. Choose what you take to be the key repetitions, strands, and binaries—which may involve renaming or labeling them—and *rank* them in some order of importance.

Notice that choosing which binaries, strands, and repetitions are key is already an interpretive activity.

> At this point in the process (and not before) you can give yourself more space to start making the leap from data to claims (that is, from observations to conclusions). If, for example, you had been analyzing a picture, your leap might answer the question "What does this picture 'say'?" There will always be more than one plausible answer to this question. We say more on this final step in Chapter 3, "Interpreting: Asking 'So What?'" For now, you should concentrate on practicing the first four steps—the data-gathering phase—and recognize that your choices of what goes with what, what is key, and so forth, already constitute moves toward interpretation.

Step 5. Write up the three lists that you have been composing and then write one healthy paragraph in which you explain your choice of one repetition *or* one strand *or* one binary as especially significant. (We refer to step 5 as the *Universal Assignment*.)

Rationale for The Method: Looking for Pattern

We have been defining analysis as the search for meaningful pattern, an understanding of parts in relation to each other and to a whole. But how do you know which parts to attend to? What makes some details in the material you are studying more worthy of your attention than others? Here are some principles for selecting significant parts of the whole:

Looking for exact repetition and resemblance, that is, strands (*steps 1 and 2*)   In virtually all subjects, repetition is a sign of emphasis. In a symphony, for example, certain patterns of notes repeat throughout, announcing themselves as major themes. In a legal document, such as a warranty, a reader will quickly become aware of words that are part of a particular idea or pattern of thinking, for instance, disclaimers of accountability.

The repetition may not be exact; in Shakespeare's play *King Lear,* for example, references to seeing and eyes call attention to themselves through repetition. So, a reader of the play would do well to look for various occurrences of words and other details that might be part of this pattern. Let's say you notice that references to seeing and eyes almost always occur with another strand—a pattern of similar kinds of language—having to do with the concept of proof. How might noticing this pattern lead to an idea? You might make a start toward an idea by inferring from the pattern that the play is very concerned with ways of knowing (proving) things—with seeing as opposed to other ways of knowing, such as faith or intuition.

Looking for organizing contrasts (*step 3*)   Sometimes patterns of repetition that you begin to notice in a particular subject matter will be significant because they are part of a contrast—a basic opposition—around which the subject matter is structured. Some examples of organizing contrasts are nature/civilization, city/country, public/private, organic/inorganic, and voluntary/involuntary. One advantage of detecting repetition is that it will lead you to discover organizing contrasts, which are key in helping you to locate central issues and concerns in the material you are studying.

As we note in the discussion of either/or thinking in Chapter 1, binaries are deeply engrained in the ways that we think. Thinking is not possible without them. But discovering binaries is not the end goal.

Why is it useful to find binaries? They are sites of uncertainty, of more than one point of view. As such, they are the breeding ground of ideas. If you can locate and begin to think about—to complicate—the binaries in anything, you will usually be able to detect what is at stake in the subject that you are studying.

Let's think further about what binaries are and what they reveal. When you run into a binary opposition in your own thinking, it is like a fork in the road, a place where two paths going in different directions present themselves and you pause to choose the direction you will take. Binaries thus announce a point of tension, a place where something is being opened to decision. When you find a binary opposition in an essay, a film, or a political campaign, you locate the argument, the struggle that the film, essay, or political campaign is having with itself, the place where something is at issue.

As a general rule, *favor live questions*—where something remains to be resolved— *over inert answers,* places where things are already pretty much nailed down and don't leave much space for further thinking. Finding binaries will help you to find the questions that whatever you are studying is organized around. That's why we call them "*organizing* contrasts."

❧*Try this:* Use The Method on the following student poem. Write up the three lists plus one healthy paragraph in which you explain your choice of one repetition, strand, or binary as most significant. (Note that this is the Universal Assignment in step 5 of The Method.)

Brooklyn Heights, 4:00 A.M.
Dana Ferrelli

sipping a warm forty oz.
Coors Light on a stoop in
Brooklyn Heights. I look
across the street, in the open window;
Blonde bobbing heads, the
smack of a jump rope, laughter

of my friends breaking
beer bottles. Putting out their
burning filters on the #5 of
a Hopscotch court.
We reminisce of days when we were
Fat, pimple faced—
look how far we've come. But tomorrow

a little blonde girl will
pick up a Marlboro light filter, just to play.
And I'll buy another forty, because
that's how I play now.

Reminiscing about how far I've come □

❧*Try this:* Do the same assignment as in the "Try this" on page 27, using the following pen and ink drawing.

The Dancers by Sarah Kersh. Pen and ink drawing, 6"x 13.75". □

Anomaly

After you have produced your three ranked lists and the paragraph called for by The Method, you are ready to add an additional step to the process of looking for patterns. *Look for anomalies—things that seem unusual, seem not to fit.* An anomaly (*a*, meaning "not," and *nom* meaning "name") is literally something that cannot be named, what the dictionary defines as deviation from the normal order. Along with looking for patterns, it is also fruitful to attend to anomalous details—those that seem not to fit the pattern. Anomalies help us to revise our stereotypical assumptions. A recent television commercial, for example, chose to advertise the Philadelphia Phillies baseball team by featuring its star, Scott Rolen, reading a novel by Dostoyevsky in the dugout during a game. In this case, the anomaly, a baseball player who reads serious literature, is being used to subvert (question, unsettle) the stereotypical assumption that sports and intellectualism don't belong together.

Like searching out binary oppositions, searching out anomalies often takes you to those places in your subject matter where something is going on—where some kind of breaking out of an old pattern or some attempt at "re-seeing" is beginning. Why add anomalies as a separate activity? Anomalies become evident only after you have begun to discern a pattern, so it is best to locate repetitions, strands, and organizing contrasts—things that fit together in some way—before looking for things that seem not to fit. Once you see an anomaly, you will often find that it is part of a strand that you had not detected, a strand that may be the other side of a previously unseen binary. In this respect, looking for anomalies is great for shaking you out of your settled convictions and getting you to consider other possible interpretations.

Just as people tend to leap to evaluative judgments, they also tend to avoid information that challenges (by not conforming to) opinions they already hold. In the desire to make things fit and keep explanations simple, people often screen out anything that would ruffle the pattern they've begun to see. The result is that they ignore the evidence that might lead them to a better theory. (For more on this process of using anomalous evidence to evolve an essay's main idea, see Chapter 6, "The Evolving Thesis.") Anomalies are important because noticing them often leads to new and better ideas. Most advances in scientific thought, for example, have arisen when scientists observed phenomena that do not fit with prevailing theories.

Using The Method: An Example

Examine the following excerpt from a draft of a paper about Ovid's *Metamorphoses*, a collection of short mythological tales dating from ancient Rome. We have included annotations in blue to suggest how the writer's ideas evolve as she looks for patterns (repetition, strands, and binaries) and anomalies, constantly remaining open to reformulation.

The draft actually begins with two loosely connected observations—one that males dominate females and another that many characters in the stories lose the ability to speak and thus become submissive and dominated. In the excerpt, the writer begins to connect these two observations and speculate about what this connection means.

> There are many other examples in Ovid's *Metamorphoses* that show the dominance of man over woman through speech control. In the Daphne and Apollo story, Daphne becomes a tree to escape Apollo, but her ability to speak is destroyed. Likewise, in the Syrinx and Pan story, Syrinx becomes a marsh reed, also a life form that cannot talk, although Pan can make it talk by playing it. [The writer establishes a pattern of similar detail.] Pygmalion and Galatea is a story in which the male creates his rendition of the perfect female. The female does not speak once; she is completely silent. Also, Galatea is referred to as "she" and never given a real name. This lack of a name renders her identity more silent. [Here the writer begins to link the contrasts of speech/silence with the absence/presence of identity.]

> Ocyrhoe is a female character who could tell the future but who was transformed into a mare so that she could not speak. One may explain this transformation by saying it was an attempt by the gods to keep the future unknown. [Notice how the writer's thinking expands as she sustains her investigation of the overall pattern of men silencing women: here she tests her theory by adding another variable—prophecy.] However, there is a male character, Tiresias, who is also a seer of the future and is allowed to speak of his foreknowledge, thereby becoming a famous figure. (Interestingly, Tiresias during his lifetime has experienced being both a male and a female.) [Notice how the Ocyrhoe example has spawned a contrast based on gender in the Tiresias example. The pairing of the two examples demonstrates that the ability to tell the future is not the sole cause of silencing, because male characters who can do it are not silenced—though the writer pauses to note that Tiresias is not entirely male.] Finally, in the story of Mercury and Herse, Herse's sister, Aglauros, tries to prevent Mercury from marrying Herse. Mercury turns her into a statue; the male directly silences the female's speech.

The woman silences the man in only two stories studied. [Here the writer searches out an anomaly—women silencing men—that grows in the rest of the paragraph into an organizing contrast.] In the first, "The Death of Orpheus," the women make use of "clamorous shouting, Phrygian flutes with curving horns, tambourines, the beating of breasts, and Bacchic howlings" (246) to drown out the male's songs, dominating his speech in terms of volume. In this way, the quality of power within speech is demonstrated: "for the first time, his words had no effect, and he failed to move them [the women] in any way by his voice" (247). Next the women kill him, thereby rendering him silent. However, the male soon regains his temporarily destroyed power of expression: "the lyre uttered a plaintive melody and the lifeless tongue made a piteous murmur" (247). Even after death Orpheus is able to communicate. The women were not able to destroy his power completely, yet they were able to severely reduce his power of speech and expression. [The writer learns, among other things, that men are harder to silence; Orpheus's lyre continues to sing after his death.]

The second story in which a woman silences a man is the story of Actaeon, in which the male sees Diana naked, and she transforms him into a stag so that he cannot speak of it: "he tried to say 'Alas!' but no words came" (79). This loss of speech leads to Actaeon's inability to inform his own hunting team of his true identity; his loss of speech leads ultimately to his death. [This example reinforces the pattern that the writer began to notice in the Orpheus example.]

In some ways these paragraphs of draft exemplify a writer in the process of discovering a workable idea. They begin with a list of similar examples, briefly noted. As the examples accumulate, the writer begins to make connections and formulate trial explanations. We do not include enough of this draft to get to the tentative thesis the draft is working toward, although that thesis is already beginning to emerge. What we want to emphasize here is the writer's willingness to accumulate data and to locate it in various patterns of similarity and contrast.

C. THINKING RECURSIVELY: REFOCUSING BINARIES

Thinking is not simply linear and progressive, from point A to point B to point C, like stops on a train. Careful thinkers are always retracing their steps, questioning their first—and second—impressions, assuming that they've missed something. All good thinking is *recursive*—that is, it repeatedly goes over the same ground. In a thinking technique called looping, for example, a writer might repeatedly go over the same material but from different starting points, seeing what would happen if he or she reformulates, begins with different details, and moves in a slightly different direction. Imagine writing an autobiographical sketch of your life as a student that begins with getting singled out for winning a spelling bee. Then, imagine beginning instead with getting beaten up on the playground in fourth grade.

For the purposes of using The Method, recursive thinking is essential. You need to view and review the material to find repetition. Working with strands is an inherently recursive activity because you'll tend to first think that one set of words or details fits together as a strand and then you'll find yourself regrouping—reformulating your strands as new patterns begin to strike you. And as you have no doubt already experienced, as you begin to notice repetitions, these tend to suggest strands, and strands tend to beget organizing contrasts.

Nowhere is it more important to reformulate than in working with organizing contrasts. This is because, as you have seen, the habit of mind called binary thinking can retard thought through oversimplification—through a tendency toward rigidly dichotomized (either/or) points of view. But finding binary oppositions as a means of locating what is at issue and then using the binaries to *start* rather than end your thinking process is not reductive. Notice how in the Ovid example the writer keeps reforming her ways of categorizing her data.

Here are some other examples of what working productively with binaries looks like. Let's consider a brief example in which a writer starts with the binary "Was the poet Emily Dickinson psychotic, or was she a poetic genius?" This is a useful if overstated starting point for prompting thinking. Going over the same ground, the writer might next decide that the terms "insanity" and "poetic genius" don't accurately name the issue. He or she might decide, as the poet Adrienne Rich did, that poetic genius is often perceived as insanity by the culture at large and, thus, it's not a viable either/or formulation. This move, by the way, is known as *collapsing the binary:* coming to see that what had appeared to be an opposition is really two parts of one complex phenomenon. Perhaps the insanity/poetic genius binary would be better reformulated in terms of conventionality/unconventionality—a binary that might lead the writer to start reappraising the ways in which Dickinson is not as eccentric as she first appeared.

There seem to be four mental operations that people go through when they think recursively with binaries. Here they are with another example.

Step 1. Locate a number of different binaries suggested by your subject.

Consider, for example, the binaries contained in the following question: Does the model of management known as Total Quality Management (TQM) that is widely used in Japan work in the American automotive industry? The most obvious binary in this question is work/not work. But there are also other binaries in the question—Japanese/American, for example, and TQM/more traditional or more traditionally American models of management. These binaries imply further binaries. Insofar as TQM is acknowledged to be a team-oriented, collaborative management model, the question requires a writer to consider the accuracy and relative suitability of particular traits commonly ascribed to Japanese versus American workers, such as being communal and cooperative versus being individualistic and competitive.

Step 2. Analyze and define the opposing terms.

What, for example, does it mean to ask whether TQM "works" in the American automotive industry? Does "work" mean make a substantial profit? Produce more cars more quickly? Improve employee morale? Too often people start arguing either/or before they have figured out what the key terms mean.

Step 3. Question the accuracy of the binary.

Having begun to analyze and define your terms, you would next need to determine how accurately they define the issues raised by your subject. You might consider, for example, whether American management styles actually differ from the Japanese version of TQM. In the process of trying to determine if there are significant differences, you could start to locate particular traits in these management styles and in Japanese versus American culture that might help you to formulate your binary more precisely. *Think of the binary as a starting point—a kind of deliberate overgeneralization—that allows you to set up positions you can then test in order to refine.*

Step 4. Substitute "To what extent?" for "either/or."

The best strategy in using binaries productively is usually to locate arguments on both sides of the either/or choice that the binary poses and then choose a position somewhere in between the two extremes. Once you have arrived at what you consider the most accurate phrasing of the binary, you can rephrase the original either/or question in the more qualified terms that asking "To what extent?" allows. Making this move would not release you from the responsibility of taking a stand and arguing for it. But by analyzing the terms of the binary, you would come to question it and ultimately to arrive at a more complex and qualified position to write about.

Admittedly, in reorienting your thinking from the obvious and clear-cut choices that either/or formulations provide to the murkier waters of asking "To what extent?" your decision process will be made more difficult. The gain, however, is that the to-what-extent mind-set, by predisposing you to assess multiple and potentially conflicting points of view, will enable you to address more fairly and accurately the issues raised by your subject.

Applying these steps will usually cause you to do one or more of the following:

a. Discover that you have not adequately named the binary and that another opposition would be more accurate.
b. Weight one side of your binary more heavily than the other, rather than seeing the issue as all or nothing.
c. Discover that the two terms of your binary are not really so separate and opposed after all but are actually part of one complex phenomenon or issue (collapsing the binary).

Try this: Locate some organizing contrasts in anything—something you are studying, something you've just written, something you saw on television last night, something on the front page of the newspaper, something going on at your campus or workplace, and so forth. As we've said, binaries are pervasive in the way we think; therefore, you can expect to find them everywhere. Consider, for example, the binaries suggested by current trends in contemporary music or by the representation of women in birthday cards. Having selected the binaries you want to work with, pick one and try out the four steps we suggest for working with binaries. □

Try this: Or, if you wish, write a couple of pages in which you work with the binaries suggested by the following familiar expression: "School gets in the way of one's education." Keep the focus on working through the binaries implicit in the quotation.

What other terms would you substitute for "school" and "education"? Coming up with a range of synonyms for each term will clarify what is at stake in the binary. Remember to consider the accuracy of the claim. To what extent, and in what ways, is the expression both true and false? ☐

D. PREREQUISITES TO GETTING SMARTER

If you persist in working with the observational skills offered in this chapter, you will surprise yourself with all the things you find yourself noticing and with your increasing confidence in your own ability to have ideas. There are, however, certain prerequisites—attitudes and expectations—that you will need to bring to the task of thinking and writing more analytically. Here they are.

1. Look for questions.

What all of our suggestions have in common is the single requirement that you train yourself to look for questions rather than leaping too quickly to answers. It is this orientation that will move you beyond merely reporting information and lead you to think with and about it.

The best way to become a better thinker is to actively search out an area of your subject where there are no clear and obvious answers—to look for something that needs explaining rather than to reiterate the obvious.

Although disciplines vary in the kinds of questions they characteristically ask, every discipline is concerned with asking questions, exploring areas of uncertainty, and attempting to solve or at least clarify problems. Rather than leading you to a single or obvious answer, an analytical attitude aims to find a space in which you can have ideas about (explore the questions in) what you've been learning. In short, you are usually better off to begin with something that you don't understand very well and want to understand better. Begin by asking what kinds of questions the material poses.

2. Suspect your first responses.

If you settle for your first response, the result is likely to be superficial, obvious, and overly general. A better strategy is to examine your first response for ways in which it is inaccurate and then develop the implications of the overstatement (or error) into a new formulation. In many cases, writers go through this process of proposing and rejecting ideas ten times or more before they arrive at an angle or approach that will sustain an essay.

A first response is okay for a start, as long as you don't stop there. For example, many people might agree, *at first glance,* that no one should be denied health care, that a given film or novel that concludes with a marriage is a happy ending, or that the U.S. government should not pass trade laws that might cause Americans to lose their jobs. On closer inspection, however, each of these responses begins to reveal its limitations. Given that there is a limited amount of money available, should everyone, regardless of age or physical condition, be accorded every medical treatment that might prolong life? And might not a novel or film that concludes in marriage signal that the society offers too few options or, more cynically, that the author is feeding the audience an implausible fantasy to blanket over problems raised earlier in the work? And couldn't trade laws resulting in short-term loss of jobs ultimately produce more jobs and a healthier economy?

As these examples suggest, first responses—usually pieces of conventional wisdom—can blind you to rival explanations. (See the section entitled "Weak Thesis Type 3: The Thesis Restates Conventional Wisdom" in Chapter 7.)

3. Expect to become interested.

Writing gives you the opportunity to cultivate your curiosity by thinking exploratively. Rather than approaching subjects in a mechanical way or putting off writing to the last possible moment and doing the work grudgingly, try giving yourself and the subject matter the benefit of the doubt. If you can suspend judgment and start writing, you will often find yourself uncovering interests where you had not seen them before. In other words, accept the idea that *interest is a product of writing—not a prerequisite.*

If you repeatedly reject things because they don't interest you, you will deprive yourself of the opportunity to discover interests. Banish the word "boring," if you can, from your vocabulary for awhile. Expect interest to come, and it will. People who are easily bored and not shy about saying so reveal more about themselves than about the subject matter in which they find no interest. Or as an acerbic colleague of ours marvels, "My students think that when they find Shakespeare boring, they are saying something about Shakespeare."

4. Write all of the time about what you are studying.

Because interest is so often a product and not a prerequisite of writing, it follows that writing informally about what you are studying while you are studying it is probably the single best preparation for developing interesting ideas. By writing spontaneously about what you read, you will accustom yourself to being a less passive consumer of ideas and information, and you will have more ideas and information available to think actively with and about. In any case, you should not wait to start writing until you think you have an idea you can organize a paper around. Instead, use writing to get you *to* the idea. We say more on this score in the next chapter.

ASSIGNMENTS

1. Find a subject to analyze using Notice and Focus and then The Method. Your aim here initially is not to write a formal paper but to do data-gathering on the page. After you have recorded your responses to the Universal Assignment (step 5 of The Method) and perhaps discussed these with another writer or in a small group setting, revise your work into more coherent form. Don't worry too much at this point about form (having an introductory paragraph, for example) or your thesis. Just write at greater length about what you noticed and what you selected as most revealing or interesting or strange or significant and why.

   You might use as a model the student essay on stories from Ovid's *Metamorphoses,* but you would choose your own subject in which to look for significant patterns of repetition and organizing contrasts. It could be a story, essay, or poem by a writer you like. It could be a painting or an artistic photograph. It could be the cover of a magazine. (Covers from the *New Yorker* magazine are prime examples.) The Method could yield interesting results when applied to the architecture on your campus, the student newspaper, campus clothing styles, or the latest news about the economy.

2. Revisit the first "Try this" at the end of the section entitled "Thinking Recursively: Refocusing Binaries" (page 32). As noted there, binaries are pervasive in the way we think, and, thus, you can expect to find them everywhere. Pick a subject and then apply the four steps for refocusing binaries. Experiment! Try renaming the terms more accurately. Weigh one side more heavily than the other; then weigh the other side more heavily. Try collapsing the binary—that is, demonstrating how the two sides of your opposition are not really so separate after all.

   You might consider, for example, some of the either/or categories that students tend to put each other, or their teachers, in. You might consider current events in the world or in some more local arena and find the binaries that seem to divide people or groups. You might look for the binaries in the work of some artist or performer that you like. What binaries do you find in the book of Genesis? What binaries fuel a current sports controversy?

3

Interpreting: Asking "So What?"

So, let's assume that you have begun to practice the skills laid out in the book so far. You've begun to catch yourself when leaping to judgments, using Level 3 Generalities and clichés, and adopting rigidly dichotomized points of view. You've been trying to avoid words like "should" and "shouldn't" that prompt a move to judgment rather than to analysis and interpretation. You've been practicing dwelling with the data using various tools: Notice and Focus, The Method (repetitions, strands, and binaries), looking for anomalies, and reformulating binaries. Inevitably, these observational strategies will have led you to begin experimenting with ways of generating ideas. In this chapter we want to get more specific about this phase of the thinking process—the phase in which you make an interpretive leap from your data to ideas, to theories about the meaning of your data.

An interpretation is a theory, a hypothetical (still open to question and to testing) explanation of what something means. An interpretation offers a reading of what is at stake, what is driving or motivating the character of something that you have been observing. Since interpretations are always shaped by context, it is difficult to generalize about the interpretive process. But we can start by saying simply that interpretation is what happens when you make certain kinds of moves with your data. Later on in this chapter— in a section called "Where Do Meanings Come From?"—we'll tackle interpretation anew in more complexity. But for now, let's talk about why certain moves are useful in getting to interpretation.

A. PROMPTS: "INTERESTING" AND "STRANGE"

Consider, for example, the verbal prompts that we proposed in Chapter 2: "interesting," "strange," "revealing," and "significant." What do these do? First of all, they offer alternatives to the judgment reflex (like/dislike, right/wrong, and should/shouldn't). The prompts shift attention from pro/con argument to thinking aimed at understanding, at theorizing about the nature of things. The same words also press you to notice and to stay more aware of the connections between your responses (moods, attitudes, beginnings of ideas) and the particulars that gave rise to them.

What does it mean to find something "interesting"? Often we are interested by things that have captured our attention without our clearly knowing why. Interest and curiosity are near cousins. Interest is also related to confidence. When you can allow yourself to feel that you don't have to have all the answers immediately, you can trust yourself to dwell with questions, a primary characteristic of good thinking.

The word "strange" is a useful prompt because it gives us permission to notice oddities, the things we called anomalies in the preceding chapter. "Strange" invites us to *defamiliarize,* rather than to normalize, things within our range of notice. "Strange," in this context, is not a judgmental term but one denoting features of a subject or situation that aren't readily explainable. Where you locate something strange, you will have something to interpret—to figure out what makes it strange and why.

Along similar lines, the words "revealing" and "significant" work by requiring you to make choices that can lead to interpretive leaps. If something strikes you as revealing, even if you're not yet sure why, you will eventually have to produce some theories on what it reveals. If something strikes you as significant, you will motivate yourself to come up with some things that it might signify or "say." Words matter: your choice of some words as verbal starting points can direct you onto more productive pathways.

❧ *Try this:* Try using one or more of the four prompts with something immediately available to you, such as a recent event or a trend in music, fashion, television advertising, or fast food. Select one to talk about with a small group, perhaps following focused freewriting, and see what the verbal prompts can do by way of stimulating and focusing interpretation. □

B. PUSHING OBSERVATIONS TO CONCLUSIONS: ASKING "SO WHAT?"

A prompt we now want to add to your repertoire is what we call the "So what?" question. Asking "So what?" forces the issue, so to speak. It presses you to make some kind of claim about something you've noticed in your data.

Asking "So what?" is a calling to account, which is why, in conversation, its force is potentially rude. That is, the question intervenes rather peremptorily with a "Why does *this* matter?" It is thus a challenge to make meaning through a creative leap—to move beyond the patterns and emphases you've been observing in the data to what tentative conclusions these observations suggest.

Asking yourself "So what?" is thus a central way to spur yourself to leap, to hazard an interpretation. It can and should be posed all of the time as you think and write, not just at the end of your thinking process. At the least, consider asking and answering "So what?" at the ends of paragraphs. And then, if you ask "So what?" again of the first answer you've offered, you'll often tell yourself where your thinking needs to go next.

For example, let's say you make a number of observations about the nature of e-mail communication—it's cheap, informal, often grammatically incorrect, full of abbreviations ("IMHO"), and ephemeral (impermanent). You rank these and decide that its ephemerality is most interesting. So what? Well, that's why so many people use it, you speculate, because it doesn't last. So what that its popularity follows from its ephemerality? Well, apparently we like being released from the hard-and-fast rules of formal communication; e-mail frees us. So what? Well, . . .

The peremptoriness of the "So what?" question can, we think, be liberating. Okay, take the plunge, it says. Start laying out possible interpretations. And, when you are tempted to stop thinking too soon, asking "So what?" will press you onward. In Part II, "Writing the Thesis-Driven Paper," we have more to say about what to do when your answer to "So what?" calls to mind conflicting data or an opposing idea, and thus interferes with the forward flow of your thinking. For now, start experimenting with asking, "So what?"

Moving from Description to Interpretation: An Example

Where does interpretation begin? When does analysis become interpretation? What we have suggested thus far is that the process of noticing, of recording selected details and patterns of detail, is already the beginning of interpretation. *Analysis and interpretation are, by and large, inseparable. Analysis implies a search for meaning.*

Let's work through a more extended example, using as our subject matter the well-known painting, *Arrangement in Black and Grey: The Artist's Mother*, popularly known as *Whistler's Mother*, shown in Figure 3.1. We chose a painting for our example

FIGURE 3.1
Arrangement in Black and Grey: The Artist's Mother by James Abbott McNeill Whistler, 1871.

because it is a relatively compact subject, one that can fit on a single page. The ways of thinking about the painting are, we believe, applicable to most kinds of subject matter. First, spend some time at the observation phase.

✸ *Try this:*   Apply The Method to the painting. What details repeat in the picture? What patterns of similar detail (strands) can you find? What details and patterns of detail seem to fall into organizing contrasts? Compile your three lists in writing; then rank the top three in each category, and write a paragraph on why you would choose one of these as most important. □

A primary aim of the observation practice we call The Method, as you will recall, is to shift your attention from premature generalizing about a subject—in this case the painting—to recording detail that actually appears in it. Description is the best antidote to what we call in Chapter 2 the "dogfish problem"—trying to start with an idea about your subject without first really looking at it. What do you notice about the picture? Not what do you think, but what do you notice?

Using The Method will produce a *description* of the painting. We offer our own description in Figure 3.2, but we urge you to do yours first. That way you will more easily discover a cardinal rule of interpretation: there is always a range of plausible interpretations, depending, in part, on the differing descriptions that underlie them.

As you can see, the observations in the interpretive-leaps column in Figure 3.2 go beyond describing what the painting contains, moving on to ideas about what its details imply, what the painting invites us to make of it and by what means. Notice how intertwined the descriptive analysis is with the interpretations. Laying out the data is key to any kind of analysis not simply because it keeps the analysis accurate but also because, crucially, it is *in the act of carefully describing a subject that analytical writers often have their best ideas.*

Here is a sample interpretive analysis of the painting, based on the details we chose to emphasize and the leaps we initially made in response to the "So what?" prompt:

> The painter's choice to portray his subject in profile contributes to our sense of her separateness from us and of her nonconfrontational passivity. We look at her, but she does not look back at us. Her black dress and the fitted lace cap that obscures her hair are not only emblems of her self-effacement, shrouds disguising her identity like her expressionless face, but also the tools of her self-containment and thus of her power to remain aloof from prying eyes. What is the attraction of this painting (this being one of the questions that an analysis might ask)? What might draw a viewer to the sight of this austere, drably attired woman, sitting alone in the center of a mostly blank space? Perhaps it is the very starkness of the painting, and the mystery of self-sufficiency at its center, that attracts us.

You may not agree with this reading of the painting, neither the details we have emphasized nor the conclusions ("the mystery of self-sufficiency") we have drawn

FIGURE 3.2

Summary and Analysis of *Whistler's Mother*

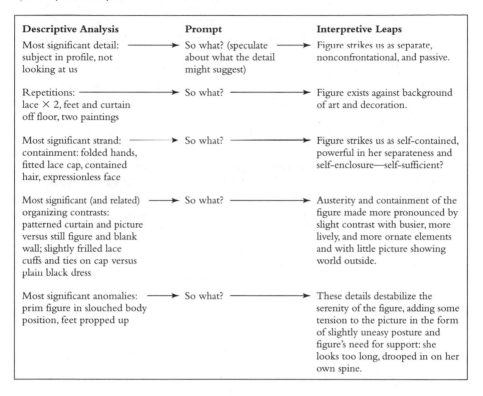

Descriptive Analysis	Prompt	Interpretive Leaps
Most significant detail: subject in profile, not looking at us	So what? (speculate about what the detail might suggest)	Figure strikes us as separate, nonconfrontational, and passive.
Repetitions: lace × 2, feet and curtain off floor, two paintings	So what?	Figure exists against background of art and decoration.
Most significant strand: containment: folded hands, fitted lace cap, contained hair, expressionless face	So what?	Figure strikes us as self-contained, powerful in her separateness and self-enclosure—self-sufficient?
Most significant (and related) organizing contrasts: patterned curtain and picture versus still figure and blank wall; slightly frilled lace cuffs and ties on cap versus plain black dress	So what?	Austerity and containment of the figure made more pronounced by slight contrast with busier, more lively, and more ornate elements and with little picture showing world outside.
Most significant anomalies: prim figure in slouched body position, feet propped up	So what?	These details destabilize the serenity of the figure, adding some tension to the picture in the form of slightly uneasy posture and figure's need for support: she looks too long, drooped in on her own spine.

about them. Nor is it necessary that you agree, because there is no single right answer to what the painting means. The absence of a single right answer does not, however, mean that anything goes, that any reading is as good as any other. Some readings are better—better evidenced, better reasoned—than others.

A reader's willingness to accept an analytical conclusion is powerfully connected to his or her ability to see its *plausibility*—that is, how it follows from both the supporting details that the writer has selected and the language used in characterizing those details. The writer who can offer a plausible description of a subject's key features is likely to arrive at conclusions about possible meanings that others would share. This is often the best you can hope for: not that others will say, "Yes, that is obviously right," but rather, "Yes, I can see where it might be possible and reasonable to think as you do."

Try this: Return to your own lists of key details, and word the interpretive leaps that they might plausibly prompt. Then, generate in a paragraph or two your own interpretation of *Whistler's Mother.* □

C. WHERE DO MEANINGS COME FROM?

Our last example, the interpretation of *Whistler's Mother,* raises some theoretical questions about interpretation, about where meanings come from. The discussion may also have raised in you some of the reservations that the interpretive process tends to evoke. And so, we will now pause to consider a few issues about the making of meaning.

Although analysis is an activity we call on constantly in our everyday lives, many people are deeply suspicious of it. "Why can't you just enjoy the movie rather than picking it apart?" they'll say. Or, "Oh, you're just making that up!" You may even be accused of being an unfeeling person if you adopt an analytical stance, because it is typical of the anti-intellectual position to insist that feeling and thinking are separate and essentially incompatible activities.

Though he was among the most astutely analytical of thinkers, the nineteenth-century English Romantic poet, William Wordsworth, made the famous remark that we mention in Chapter 1, "we murder to dissect," giving voice to the still common anxiety that analysis takes the life out of things. This anxiety—so common in Romanticism as to be virtually a defining characteristic of that intellectual and artistic movement—arose in reaction against an equally extreme position from the eighteenth century (the so-called Age of Reason or Enlightenment), known for its indictment of emotion as the enemy of rationality. In response to the eighteenth century's elevation of reason over all other human faculties, the nineteenth century sought to correct the imbalance by elevating the faculties of feeling and imagination. Few thinkers of either century really adhered to these positions in such extreme forms, but suffice it to say that analysts of human beings seem always to have been perplexed about how our various capacities fit together into a functional whole. One aim of this book is to demonstrate that taking refuge in either side of the opposition between thinking and feeling is not only counterproductive but also unnecessary.

The Limits on Interpretation

Where do meanings come from? The first thing to understand about meanings is that they are *made,* not ready-made in the subject matter. They are the product of a transaction between a mind and the world, between a reader and a text or texts. That is, the making of meaning is a process to which the observer and the thing observed both contribute. It is not a product of either alone.

If meanings aren't ready-made, there to be found in the subject matter, what's to prevent people from making things mean whatever they want them to—say, for example, that *Whistler's Mother* is a painting about death, with the black-clad mother mourning the death of a loved one, perhaps a person who lived in the house represented in the painting on the wall? There are in fact limits on the meaning-making process.

- Meanings must be reasoned from sufficient evidence if they are to be judged plausible. Meanings can always be refuted by people who find fault with your reasoning or who can cite conflicting evidence. In the case of the mourning the-

ory, for example, black need not signify only mourning, and this interpretation is
based on little else.
* Meanings, to have value outside one's own private realm of experience, have to
make sense to other people. The assertion that Whistler's mother is an alien astro-
naut, her long black dress concealing a third leg, is unlikely to be deemed acceptable by enough people to give it currency. This is to say that the relative value of
interpretive meanings is socially (culturally) determined. Although people are free
to say that things mean whatever they want them to mean, simply saying doesn't
make it so.

Cultural context is primarily responsible for the mourning theory being more
plausible than the alien-astronaut theory. Black clothes often indicate mourning. This is
culturally accepted, a recognized sign. But with only the black dress and perhaps the
sad facial expression (if it is sad) to go on, the mourning theory gets sidetracked from
interpreting what is there into storytelling. It is less made up than the alien-astronaut
theory, but it still relies too heavily on what is not there, on a narrative for which there
is not sufficient evidence in the painting itself.

Multiple Meanings and Interpretive Contexts

In the last section we demonstrated that there are certain limits on interpretation,
chiefly that interpretation has to follow the rules of evidence. It is useful and reassuring
to know that a person can't just make up meanings and say they are true simply
because he or she says so. As you've already seen, however, meanings are multiple.
Evidence usually will support more than one plausible interpretation.

Consider, for example, a reading of *Whistler's Mother* that a person might produce
if he or she began with noticing the actual title, *Arrangement in Black and Grey: the
Artist's Mother.* From this starting point, a person might focus observation on the dispo-
sition of color exclusively and arrive at an interpretation that *Arrangement* is a painting
about painting (which is why there is also a painting on the wall). The figure of the
mother then would only mean insofar as it contained those two colors, and its human
content would be ignored. This is a promising and plausible idea for an interpretation.
It makes use of different details from previous interpretations we've suggested—the
title, the painting—but it would also address some of the details already targeted (the
dress, the curtain) from an entirely different context, focusing on the use and arrangement of color.

To generalize: two equally plausible interpretations can be made of the same thing.
It is not the case that our first reading, focusing on the profile view of the mother and
suggesting the painting's concern with mysterious separateness, is right, while the aesthetic view, building from the clue in the title, is wrong. They operate within different
contexts. As these examples illustrate, very often the starting point for an interpretation
(the profile, the title) in effect determines its context. However the context is arrived
at, an important part of getting an interpretation accepted as plausible is to *argue for the
appropriateness of the interpretive context you use,* not just the interpretation it takes you to.

Intentionality As an Interpretive Context

Let's turn now to an interpretive context that frequently creates problems: authorial intention. People relying on authorial intention as their interpretive context typically assert that the author—not the work itself—is the ultimate and correct source of interpretations. The work means what its author says it means, and even without his or her explicit interpretation, we are expected to guess at it.

Let's say that an enterprising person discovered that after Whistler did the painting, he wrote a letter to a friend in which he commented upon his intention—say, because his mother had been needling him that painters never amount to anything, he had deliberately painted her unflatteringly in somber puritanical tones as an act of revenge. As an interpretation of the painting, the revenge against puritanism is not more correct than the separateness or aesthetic readings. Whatever an author thinks he or she is doing is often a significant part of the meaning of what he or she creates, but it does not outrank or exclude other interpretations. It is simply another context for understanding, that of authorial intention.

Why is this so? In our earlier discussion of personalizing, we suggested that people are not entirely free agents, immune to the effects of the culture they inhabit. It follows that when people produce things, they are inevitably affected by that culture in ways of which they both are and are not aware. The culture, in other words, speaks through them. In the early 1960s, for example, a popular domestic sitcom entitled *Leave It to Beaver* portrayed the mother, June Cleaver, usually impeccably dressed in heels, dress, and pearls, doing little other than dusting the mantlepiece and making tuna fish sandwiches for her sons. Is the show then intentionally oppressing June by implying that the proper role for women is that of domestic helper? Well, that meaning is in the show, if we choose to view it in this gendered context. But to conclude that *Beaver* promoted a particular stereotype about women does not mean that the writers got together every week and asked, "How should we oppress June this week?" It is cultural norms asserting themselves here, not authorial intent.

It is interesting and useful to try to determine from something you are analyzing what its makers might have intended. But, by and large, you are best off concentrating on what the thing itself communicates as opposed to what someone might have wanted it to communicate. As a rule, *intention does not finally control the implications that an event, a text, or anything else possesses.*

Look at the drawing entitled *The Dancers* on page 28. What follows is the artist's statement about how the drawing came about and what it came to mean to her.

> This piece was created completely unintentionally. I poured some ink onto paper and blew on it through a straw. The ink took the form of what looked like little people in movement. I recopied the figures I liked, touched up the rough edges, and ended with this gathering of fairy-like creatures. I love how in art something abstract can so suddenly become recognizable.

In this case, interestingly, the author initially had no intentions beyond experimenting with materials. As the work evolved, she began to arrive at her own interpretation of what the drawing might suggest. Most viewers would probably find the artist's interpretation plausible, but this is not to say that the artist must have the last word and that it is somehow an infraction for others to produce alternative interpretations. But suppose the artist had stopped with her first two sentences. Even this explicit statement of the artist's lack of intention would not prohibit people from interpreting the drawing in some of the ways that the artist later goes on to suggest. The artist's initial absence of a plan doesn't require viewers to interpret *The Dancers* as only ink on paper.

Where do meanings come from? In the maker? In the thing itself? While the maker's personal intentions don't control meaning, it is interesting and useful to infer from the material itself what a creator might have been trying to accomplish.

What about analyzing things that were not intended to mean anything, like entertainment films and everyday things like blue jeans and shopping malls? Writers sometimes resist analysis on the grounds that some things were not intended to mean outside of a limited context, such as entertainment, and so should not be analyzed from any other point of view. Barbie dolls are toys intended for young girls. Should the fact that the makers of Barbie intended to make money by entertaining children rather than trying to create a cultural artifact rule out analysis of Barbie's characteristics (built-in earrings and high-heeled feet), marketing, and appeal as cultural phenomena?

What the makers of a particular product or idea intend is only a part of what that product or idea communicates. The urge to cordon off certain subjects from analysis on the grounds that they weren't meant to be analyzed unnecessarily excludes a wealth of information—and meaning—from your range of vision. It is right to be careful about the interpretive contexts we bring to our experience. It is less right—less useful—to confine our choice of context in a too-literal-minded way to a single category. To some people, baseball is only a game, and clothing is only there to protect us from the elements.

Notice how in the following analysis the student writer's interpretation relies on his choice of a particular interpretive context, post–World War II Japan. Had he selected another context, he might have arrived at some different conclusions about the same details. Notice also how the writer perceives a pattern in the details and queries his own observations (asking "So what?") to arrive at an interpretation.

The series entitled "Kamaitachi" is a journal of [Japanese photographer Eikoh] Hosoe's desolate childhood and wartime evacuation in the Tokyo countryside. He returns years later to the areas where he grew up, a stranger to his native land, perhaps likening himself to the legendary Kamaitachi, an invisible sickle-toothed weasel, intertwined with the soil and its unrealized fertility. "Kamaitachi #8" (1956), a platinum palladium print, stands alone to best capture Hosoe's alienation from and troubled expectation of the future of Japan. [Here the writer chooses a biographical approach as his interpretive context.]

The image is that of a tall fence of stark horizontal and vertical rough wood lashed together, looming above the barren rice fields. Straddling the fence, half-crouched and half-clinging, is a solitary male figure, gazing in profile to the horizon. Oblivious to the sky above of dark and churning thunderclouds, the figure instead focuses his attentions and concentrations elsewhere. [The writer selects and describes significant detail.]

It is exactly this *elsewhere* that makes the image successful, for in studying the man we are to turn our attention toward him and away from the print. He hangs curiously between heaven and earth, suspended on a makeshift man-made structure, in a purgatorial limbo awaiting the future. He waits with anticipation—perhaps dread?—for a time that has not yet come; he is directed away from the present, and it is this sensitivity to time which sets this print apart from the others in the series. One could argue that in effect this man, clothed in common garb, has become Japan itself, indicative of the post-war uncertainty of a country once-dominant and now destroyed. What will the future (dark storm clouds) hold for this newly-humbled nation? [Here the writer notices a pattern of "in-between-ness" and locates it in an historical context in order to make his interpretive leap.]

Remember that regardless of the subject you select for your analysis, you should directly address not just "What does this say?" but also, as this writer has done, "What are we invited to make of it, and in what context?"

"Hidden" Meanings: What "Reading Between the Lines" Really Means

"You're reading between the lines." That's a claim we've all heard. Depending on the context, it can be an accusation or a compliment, though it's usually the former. When it's uttered as an accusation, it implies that the accused is not actually reading the words on the page but the white space between the sentences. So, presumably, the charge means that the person producing the analysis is basing it on nothing—on white space. In other words, it's all in his or her imagination, not really "there."

The kind of thinker prone to attack analysis as reading between the lines would probably find all of our interpretations of *Whistler's Mother* equally made up, imposed upon the painting. He or she would maintain that the painting is only what the subtitle declares, a portrait of the artist's mother, and that any further interpretation is "reading into" the painting things that are not there. But what does "not there" really mean? It really means that the *meanings are not overt, not tangible, not extractable ready-made (like fortune cookie fortunes) from the thing being analyzed*. As we've seen, that's accurate: interpretation is the product of a leap.

The naïveté of people who make the reading-between-the-lines attack lies in their unstated assumption that all communication is or *should be* a matter of direct statement. In effect, they are committing themselves to the position that everything in life means what it says and says what it means, that meanings are always obvious and understood the same by everyone and thus don't require interpretation.

This view—that all communication is a matter of direct statement—is easily opened to question. You need think only of what people's body positions "say" in addition to (sometimes in opposition to) the words they speak in order to see the error in assuming that all things can be communicated directly.

It is in fact an inherent property of language, linguists tell us, that it always means more than and thus other than it says. How often have you heard a person respond to a challenging personal question with, "I don't know," when what he or she really means is, "I don't want to talk about it"? And doesn't the "How you doin'?" that we toss at others as we pass them in the hallway really mean "I acknowledge that you and I are acquaintances"—because in most cases we have neither the time nor the inclination to find out how they are really doing? If you don't believe this, the next time someone asks you how you're doing, give him or her a line of Hemingway's—"Sometimes I see me dead in the rain"—and see what kind of response you get.

As these examples demonstrate, people are remarkably adept at sending and receiving complex and subtle—that is, indirect—signals. Though we may not pause to take notice, we are continually processing what goes on around us for the indirect or suggested meanings it contains. If you observe yourself for a day, you'll find yourself interpreting even the most direct-seeming statements. There's an old cartoon about the anxiety bred by the continual demands of interpretation: a person who says, "Good morning," causes the one addressed to respond, "What did she mean by that?"

The truth to which this cartoon points is that a statement can have various meanings, depending on various circumstances and how it is said. *The relationship between words and meaning is always complex.* Marshall McLuhan, one of the fathers of modern communication theory, noted that communication always involves determining not just what is being said but also "what kind of message a message is." Depending on tone and context, "Good morning" can mean a number of things.

Why does so much communication take place indirectly? When we want to understand a complex subject like love or death, we sometimes need to arrive at that understanding indirectly—by comparison with more tangible and accessible subjects like the weather, the seasons, or baseball, or chess. This is because sometimes it is possible to communicate complex ideas or feelings or situations only through comparison with something that is more immediate and more concrete. It is also the case that human beings seem inclined to think by *association* and by *analogy* (likeness). At the root of indirect communication lies *metaphor*—a mode of expression in which one thing stands for (represents) something else that remains unnamed.

Metaphor is not confined to the arts; it is a pervasive feature of communication. Many linguists argue that all language is metaphor, that we are always talking about things in terms of other things. This is the case not only when we say, "My love is like a red, red rose," but also when we say, "That movie was a piece of trash" or "I could kill you for that." The leap to language is itself metaphorical: the word spelled *c-a-t* is not the same thing as the four-legged feline that purrs.

You can easily test some of these assertions yourself as you go through an ordinary day. What, for example, does your choice of wearing a baseball cap to a staff meeting or a class—rather than no hat or a straw hat or a beret—"say"? Note, by the way, that a communicative gesture such as the wearing of a cap need not be premeditated and entirely conscious in order to communicate something to those who see it. The cap is still "there" and available to be "read" by others as a sign of certain attitudes and a culturally defined sense of identity, with or without your intention. Things communicate meaning to others whether we wish them to or not, which is to say that the meanings of most things are always to some extent socially rather than privately and individually determined.

As we have repeatedly argued, it helps to remember that *interpretive leaps*—conclusions arrived at through analysis about what some gesture or word choice or clothing combination or scene in a film *means*—follow certain established rules of evidence. One such rule is that the conclusions of a good analysis do not rest on details taken out of context; you should instead test and support claims about the details' significance by locating them in a pattern of similar detail (see "The Method" in Chapter 2). In other words, analytical thinkers are not really free to say whatever they think, as those who are made uneasy by analysis sometimes fear.

We should acknowledge, with respect to the reading-between-the-lines charge, that analysis sometimes does draw out the implications of things that are not there, because they have been deliberately omitted. Usually we recognize such omissions because we have been led to expect something that we are not given, making its absence conspicuous. An analysis of the Nancy Drew mysteries, for example, might attach significance to the absence of a mother in the books, particularly in light of the fact that biological mothers, as opposed to wicked stepmothers, are pretty rare in many kinds of stories involving female protagonists, such as fairy tales ("Hansel and Gretel," "Cinderella," and "Snow White"). Taking note of mothers as a potentially significant omission could lead to a series of analytical questions, such as the following: How might this common denominator of certain kinds of children's stories be explained? What features of the stories' social, psychological, historical, economic, and other possible contexts might offer an explanation? As this example suggests, things are often left out for a reason, and a good analysis should therefore be alert to potentially meaningful omissions.

But what about meanings that are neither intentionally omitted nor directly and overtly present, such as the baseball cap worn backwards—are they hidden or not?

The Fortune Cookie School of Interpretation
Versus the Anything Goes School

The Fortune Cookie School of Interpretation believes that things have a single, hidden, "right" meaning, and if a person can only "crack" the thing, it will yield an extractable and self-contained "message." There are several problems with this conception of meaning. First of all, the assumption that things have single hidden meanings interferes with open-minded and dispassionate observation. The thinker looks solely for clues pointing to *the* hidden message and, having found these clues, discards the rest. But worse, the fortune-cookie approach forecloses on the possibility of multiple plausible meanings, each within its own context. When you assume that there is only one right answer, you are also assuming that there is only one proper context for understanding and, by extension, that anybody who happens to select a different starting point or context and who thus arrives at a different answer is necessarily wrong.

Most of the time practitioners of the fortune-cookie approach aren't even aware that they are assuming the correctness of a single context, because they don't realize a fundamental truth about interpretations: they are always limited by contexts. In other words, we are suggesting that claims to universal truths are always problematic, if not downright dubious. Things don't just mean in some simple and clear way for all people in all situations; they always mean within a network of beliefs, from a particular point of view. The person who claims to have access to some universal truth, beyond context and point of view, is either naïve (unaware) or, worse, a bully—insisting that his or her view of the world is obviously correct and must be accepted by everyone.

At the opposite extreme from the single-right-answer-obsessed Fortune Cookie School lies the completely relativistic Anything Goes School. The problem with the anything-goes approach is that it tends to assume that *all* interpretations are equally viable, that meanings are simply a matter of individual choice, irrespective of evidence or plausibility. Put another way, it overextends the creative aspect of interpretation to absurdity, arriving at the position that you can see in a subject whatever you want to see.

As we suggest throughout this book, it is simply not the case that meaning is up to the individual. Some readings are clearly better than others: the aesthetic or separateness readings of *Whistler's Mother* are better than the mourning or, especially, alien-astronaut interpretations. The better interpretations have more evidence and rational explanation of how the evidence means what they claim—qualities that make these meanings more public and negotiable because they are more plausible. Plausible interpretations are multiple but not infinite: anything doesn't go.

It is probably worth noting here that in the field of logic there is a principle known as *parsimony,* which holds that "no more forces or causes should be assumed than are necessary to account for the facts" (*Oxford English Dictionary*). In other words, the explanation that both explains the largest amount of evidence (accounts for facts) and is the simplest (no more than necessary) is the best. There are limits to this rule as well: sometimes focusing on what appears to be an insignificant detail as a starting point can provide a revelatory perspective on a subject. But as rules go, parsimony is a useful one to keep in mind as you start sifting through your various interpretive leaps about a subject.

Implication and Inference: Hidden or Not?

Sometimes, as earlier noted, the ability to read between the lines is commended as a talent. In this context, the assumption is not that the reader is inventing meanings that are not there but rather *making explicit (overtly stated) what is implicit (suggested but not overtly stated).* This is a definition of analytical writing to which this book will return repeatedly. The process of converting suggestions into direct statements is essential to analysis. It's one of the activities that makes analysis valuable.

Let's look at a hypothetical example of this process of drawing out implications but pause first to offer a couple of definitions. The process of drawing out implications is also known as *making inferences.* "Inference" and "implication" are related but not synonymous terms, and the difference is a useful one to know. The term "implication" is used to describe something suggested by the material itself. The term "inference" is used to describe your thinking process. In short, *you infer what the subject implies.*

Now, let's move on to the example, which will suggest not only how the process of making the implicit explicit works but also how often we do it in our everyday lives. Imagine that you are driving down the highway and find yourself analyzing a billboard advertisement for a brand of beer. Such an analysis might begin with your noticing what the billboard photo contains, its various "parts"—six young, athletic, and scantily clad men and women drinking beer while pushing kayaks into a fast-running river. At this point, you have produced not an analysis but a summary—a description of what the photo contains. If, however, you go on to consider what the particulars of the photo *imply,* your summary would become analytical.

You might infer, for example, that the photo implies that beer is the beverage of fashionable, healthy, active people, not just of older men with large stomachs dozing in armchairs in front of the television. Thus, the advertisement's meaning goes beyond its explicit contents; your analysis would lead you to *convert to direct statement meanings that are suggested but not overtly stated,* such as the advertisement's goal of attacking a common, negative stereotype about its product (that only lazy, overweight men drink beer). The naming and renaming of parts that you undertake when analyzing should carry you from the actual details to the meanings they imply. By making the implicit explicit (inferring what the ad implies), you can better understand the nature of your subject.

❦ *Try this:* Locate any magazine ad that you find interesting. Ask yourself, "*What are we invited to make of this and by what means?*" Use our hypothetical beer ad as a model for making the implicit explicit. Don't settle for just one or even three answers. *Keep answering the question in different ways,* letting your answers grow in length as they identify and begin to interpret the significance of telling details. Attend to your choice of language, because your word choice as you summarize details will begin to suggest to you the ad's range of implication. Remember to *write about what you see,* the details of the ad, rather than generalizing too soon about it. ☐

Seems to Be About X but . . .

This chapter and the one before it have focused your attention on three prerequisites to becoming a more perceptive analytical thinker:

- Training yourself to observe more fully and more systematically—dwelling longer with the data before leaping to generalizations, using Notice and Focus (ranking), The Method, looking for anomalies, and reformulating binaries.
- Pushing yourself to make interpretive leaps by describing carefully and then querying your own observations by repeatedly asking "So what?"
- Getting beyond common misconceptions about where meanings come from— that meanings are hidden, that they are "read into" something but are really "not there" (reading between the lines), that there are single right answers or that anything goes, that meanings are multiple and not controlled by a maker's intentions, that some things should not be analyzed because they weren't meant to be, and so forth.

A useful verbal prompt founded on these prerequisites is *"seems to be about X but is really (or could also be) about Y."*

This formula can open up your thinking about all manner of thinking and writing situations: analysis of reading, problems, complex situations, behavior, art, popular culture, current events, and so forth. Here's why the formula works. Frequently, the nominal (in name only) subject matter—what a book or speech or X appears to be about, what it says it is about—is not what the book or speech or X is most interested in. The nominal subject, in other words, is a means to some other end; it creates an opportunity for some less overtly designated matter to be put forward. This is so regardless of intention. Consider the following example.

A recent highly successful television ad campaign for Nike Freestyle shoes contains sixty seconds of famous basketball players dribbling and passing and otherwise handling the ball in dextrous ways to the accompaniment of court noises and hiphop music. The ad seems to be about X (basketball or shoes) but is *really* (*also*) about Y. At Y, either a rapid-fire list might follow or a filling in of the blanks (Y) might prompt a more sustained exploration of a single point.

Here is one version of a rapid-fire list, any item of which might be expanded.

Seems to be about basketball but is really about dance
Seems to be about selling shoes but is really about artistry
Seems to be about artistry but is really about selling shoes
Seems to be about basketball but is really about race
Seems to be about basketball but is really about the greater acceptance of black culture in American media
Seems to be about the greater acceptance of black culture in American media but is really about targeting black basketball players as performing seals or freaks
Seems to be about individual expertise but is really about working as a group

Here is one version of a more sustained exploration of a single seems-to-be-about-X statement.

The Nike Freestyle commercial seems to be about basketball but is really about the greater acceptance of black culture in American media. Of course it is a shoe commercial and so aims to sell a product, but the same could be said about any commercial. What makes the Nike commercial distinctive is its loving embrace of African-American culture. The hip hop soundtrack, for example, which coincides with the rhythmic dribbling of the basketball, places music and sport on a par, and the dexterity with which the players (actual NBA stars) move with the ball—moonwalking, doing 360s on it, balancing it on their fingers, heads, and backs—is nothing short of dance. The intrinsic cool of the commercial suggests that Nike is targeting an audience of basketball lovers, not just African-Americans. If I am right, then it is selling blackness to white as well as black audiences. Of course, the idea that blacks are cooler than whites goes back at least as far as the early days of jazz and might be seen as its own strange form of prejudice. . . . In that case, maybe there is something a little disturbing in the commercial, in the way that it relegates the athletes to the status of trained seals. I'll have to think more about this.

Note: Don't be misled by our use of "really" in the prompt into thinking that there should be some single hidden right answer. Rather, "really" aims to prompt you to think recursively, to come up with a range of less obvious landing sites for your interpretive leap. The word "really" is in the prompt in order to get you past a recitation of the obvious—for example, that the ad appears to be about basketball but is really about selling shoes. Both basketball and shoe sales are the ad's nominal subjects, what it is overtly about. But as we demonstrate, nominal subjects allow for the expression of other less immediately obvious ideas and attitudes. To look for these ideas and attitudes is not to condition yourself to see sinister and manipulative plots everywhere. It is instead to recognize that communication is not simple but, rather, that most things we want to understand are complexly embedded in particular cultural contexts. It is this embedding and the complexity of the verbal and visual gestures that permeate our world that analysis equips us to better understand and enjoy.

As we say in our discussion of where meanings come from, meanings are not simply "there" to be found, ready-made and directly stated in what you are studying. They are the product of a transaction between a mind and materials. "Seems to be about X . . ." can give you practice at making the implicit explicit and at accepting the existence of more than one plausible meaning for the same thing, depending on interpretive context or starting point. "Seems to be about X . . ." gives you license to try on all kinds of inter-pretive possibilities, but the one you pick will most likely not say that the ad appears to be about basketball but is really about alien astronauts in professional sport today.

❦ *Try this:* "The reading seems to be about X, but it's really about Y" is a useful for-mula for quickly getting past your first responses. An alternative version of this formula is "Initially I thought X about the reading, but now I think Y." Take any reading assign-ment you have been given for class, and prior to the class meeting, write either formula at the top of a page, fill in the blanks, and then explain the statement for a few para-graphs. You might also try these formulas when you find yourself getting stuck while drafting a paper. □

ASSIGNMENT

Write an essay in which you make observations about some cultural phenomenon, some place and its social significance, or an event (in terms of its significance in some context of your choice) and then push these observations to tentative conclusions by repeatedly asking "So what?" Be sure to query your initial answers to the "So what?" question with further "So what?" questions, trying to push further into your own thinking and into the meaning of whatever it is you have chosen to analyze. Trends of some sort are good to work with. Marketing trend? So what? Trends in movies about unmarried women or married men or . . . So what? And so forth.

Since the chapter offers sample analyses of paintings and advertisements, you might choose one of these. Cartoons are interesting subjects. Here you would really have to think a lot about your choice of interpretive context. Gender? Politics? Humor? Family life? American stereotypes?

What are we invited to make of this and by what means and in what context? That is the primary question this chapter addresses. Answer it with something of your choice.

CHAPTER

4

Reading: How to Do It and What to Do with It

A. HOW TO READ: WORDS MATTER

In a sense, the world is a text. As any child psychology textbook will tell you, as we acquire language, we acquire knowledge of the world. We can ask for things, say what's on our mind. But it's language, arguably, that fills our minds and gives us something to say in the first place. A well-known twentieth century philosopher, Ludwig Wittgenstein, noted, in a famous phrase, that we cannot make a proposition about the world; we can only make a proposition about another proposition about the world. Think about that remark for a minute. Try paraphrasing it.

The statement implies that we live in a world of language. This is not to say that everything is words, that words are the only reality. But to an enormous extent, we understand the world and our relation to it by working through language, "reading." Words matter: they are how we process the world.

As you have probably noticed, this book has been using the word "reading" to mean "interpreting." This usage hearkens back to the idea of the world as a text. The idea wasn't new with Wittgenstein, by the way. The Puritans also envisioned the world as a text in which God read their lives, and so, predictably, they started reading their lives too, reflecting on events that befell them, querying whether what was happening in their lives were signs of salvation or damnation. (The stakes for being a good reader couldn't have been higher!) In short, reading for them meant gathering evidence and analyzing it to arrive at ideas or conclusions.

That more generalized notion of reading remains with us today. In interpreting the world, we are reading it as a text that is largely made knowable to us through words. And, obviously, for most of us a significant amount of that interpretation actually consists of the more literal act of reading—that is, moving our eyes along a line of printed words and processing what the words signify ("reading comprehension," as the standardized tests call it). And so reading suggests two related activities: (1) reading in the literal sense of tackling words on the page, written materials and (2) reading in the metaphorical sense of gathering data that can be analyzed as primary evidence to produce ideas.

Considering how central both kinds of reading are in our lives, it's amazing how little we think about words themselves. We use words all the time, but often unthinkingly. We don't plan out our sentences before we utter them, for example, and the same goes for most of the ones that we write. In the last chapter we put forth the notion that things mean multiply. So do words; check any dictionary, and you will find more than one definition for virtually every word.

Most of us live, however, as if there were a consensus about what words mean. Often—much more than you suspect—there isn't a consensus. We tend to assume that things mean simply or singly. Don't believe it. Words are promiscuous; they won't stay put, won't stick to a single meaning. This is often a source of the comic. A recent posting on the Internet of the year's best headlines included "Teacher Strikes Idle Kids," "Panda Mating Fails: Veterinarian Takes Over," "New Vaccines May Contain Rabies," "Local High School Drop-outs Cut in Half," and "Include Your Children When Baking Cookies" (or if you prefer, "Kids Make Nutritious Snacks"). Another posting included sentences such as "The bandage was wound around the wound" and "After a number of injections my jaw got number." It's often a nutty language, and we need to remember this fact whenever we start getting too complacent about the meanings of words being singular and obvious.

If you want to better understand something that you're reading—or revising in your own writing—ask yourself what certain key words mean, even if you think you know what they mean. As was mentioned in our discussion of banking in Chapter 1, paraphrasing, the act of recasting words, is one of the best ways to make the move to analysis. Whether you are in a school setting or not, paraphrase is a great way to figure out how to respond to questions. Consider, for example, the question "Is feminism good for Judaism?" You would first want to figure out what "good" means and in what interpretive context. (For another example, look back at the treatment of the word "work" in the section called "Thinking Recursively: Refocusing Binaries" in Chapter 2.) So, if you want to read more effectively, two guidelines are to *expect complexity* and to *ask yourself what the words mean and paraphrase them* (which will reveal the complexity you may not have initially noticed).

Becoming Conversant Versus Reading for the Gist

Many readers operate under the dubious impression that they are to "read for the gist"—for the main point that is to be gleaned through a glancing speed-reading. Quite simply, you cannot expect to demonstrate your control of the information without getting closer to it than generalizations allow. One of the most crippling and frustrating things for many students is to expect that, if they read through something once and then look away, they should be able either to accurately and productively restate it or to have an idea about it. The vast majority of writing tasks that you will encounter require as a prerequisite your *conversancy* with material that you have read, not inert generalizations about it.

It is a reasonable expectation both in academic courses and in the workplace that you should become *conversant* with the material. To become conversant means that

1. after a significant amount of work with the material, you should be able to talk about it conversationally with other people and answer questions about it without having to look everything up.
2. you should be able to converse with the material—to be in some kind of dialogue with it, to see the questions the material asks, and to pose your own questions about it.

Few people are able to really understand things they read or see without making the language of that material in some way their own. We can only learn, in other words, by finding ways to actively engage material rather than moving passively through it. This is why skills such as note-taking, paraphrasing, and outlining—all forms of summary—are not just empty mechanical tasks. They are the mind's means of acquiring material, both the ideas and the language, that make it possible to work with these ideas. Let's pause to examine a few of these key tools; if you want to improve your reading, they will work.

Paraphrase × 3

The exercise we call *Paraphrase × 3* offers the quickest means of seeing how a little writing about what you're reading can lead to having ideas about it. (Paraphrasing is an activity we introduce in our discussion of banking in Chapter 1.) Paraphrase is commonly misunderstood as summary—a way of shrinking an idea you've read about—or perhaps as simply a way to avoid plagiarism by "putting it in your own words." Rather, *the goal of paraphrase is to open up the possible meanings of the words*; it's a mode of inquiry.

If you force yourself to paraphrase a key passage from a reading several times (or, arbitrarily, pick three times), you will discover that it gets you actually working with the language. But you have to work slavishly at it. Don't go for the gist; aim to replace all of the key words. The new words you will be forced to come up with represent first stabs at interpretation, at having (small) ideas about what you are reading by unearthing a range of possible meanings embedded in the passage. Then, you will have *something to do* with your writing about the reading beyond simply recording it or agreeing/disagreeing with it.

✻Try this: Do Paraphrase × 3 with the following sentence: "I am entitled to my opinion." Next write a paragraph about what you've discovered this common remark actually means. Then, select something more challenging—say, a passage you find central or difficult in any of your assigned reading—and repeat the exercise. Resist the temptation to talk about the words on the page. Instead, use synonyms to make the words speak. ☐

Summary

Summary is the standard way that reading—not just facts and figures but also other people's theories and observations—enters your writing. The aim of summary is to recount (in effect, to reproduce) someone else's ideas, to achieve sufficient understanding of them to productively converse with what you have been reading.

Summary and analysis go hand in hand. Neither aims to approve or disapprove of its subject; the goal for both is to understand rather than evaluate. Summary is a necessary early step in analysis because it provides *perspective* on the subject as a whole by explaining the meaning and function of each of that subject's parts. Within larger analyses—papers or reports—summary performs the essential function of *contextualizing* your subject accurately. It creates a fair picture of what's there. If you don't take the time to get your whole subject in perspective, you will be more prone to misrepresenting it in your analysis.

But summarizing isn't simply the unanalytical reporting of information; it's more than just shrinking someone else's words. To write an accurate summary, you have to ask analytical questions, such as

- Which of the ideas in the reading are most significant? Why?
- How do these ideas fit together?
- What do the key passages in the reading mean?

Summarizing is, then, like paraphrasing, a tool of understanding and not just a mechanical task. But a summary stops short of in-depth analysis because summary typically makes much smaller interpretive leaps. A summary of a picture, for example, would tell readers what the picture includes, which details are the most prominent, and even what its overall effect seems to be. A summary of the painting *Whistler's Mother* (discussed in the interpretation chapter) might say that it possesses a certain serenity and that it is somewhat spare, almost austere. This kind of language still falls into the category of *focused description*, which is what a summary is.

Strategies for Making Summaries More Analytical

What information should be included and what excluded? That's the perennial question that summarizing raises. When summaries go wrong, they are just lists. A list is a simple "this and then this and then this" sequence. Sometimes lists are random, as in a shopping list compiled from the first thing you thought of to the last. Sometimes they are organized: fruit and vegetables here, dried goods there. At best, they do very little logical connecting among the parts beyond "next."

Summaries that are just lists tend to dollop out the information monotonously. They omit the *thinking* that the piece is doing—the ways it is connecting the information, the contexts it establishes, and the implicit slant or point of view. Be aware that the thinking the piece is doing is not necessarily the same as the ideas it may contain. Two articles on European attitudes towards the Bush presidency, for example, may contain essentially the same information but vary widely in how they assemble it, how they connect the dots. Writing analytical summaries can teach you how to read for the connections, the lines that connect the dots. And when you're operating at that level, you are much more likely to have ideas about what you are summarizing.

Here are five strategies for seeing and connecting the dots in what you are reading and, by extension, for deciding what to include and exclude in your summaries.

1. Look for the underlying structure.

Use The Method. Even if you just apply The Method (see Chapter 2) to a few selected paragraphs, it will provide you with the terms that get repeated, and these will almost always suggest strands, which in turn make up the organizing contrasts. The Method, in other words, works to categorize and then further organize information and, in so doing, to bring out the underlying structure of the reading that you are summarizing.

2. Select the information that you wish to discuss on some principle other than general coverage (usually "and-then" lists) of the material.

Use Notice and Focus to *rank* these items in some order of importance (see Chapter 2). Let's say that you are writing a paper on major changes in the tax law or on recent developments in U.S. policy toward Eastern Europe. Rather than simply collecting the information, try to arrange it into hierarchies. What are the least or most significant changes or developments, and why? Which are most overlooked or most overrated or most controversial or most practical, and why? All of these terms—"significant," "overlooked," and so forth—have the effect of *focusing* the summary. In other words, they will guide your decisions about what to include and exclude. As you rank, however, it is important to distinguish between the rankings that are implicit within the piece (for a strict summary) and your own rankings of the material (for beginning to use the summary in a context of your own).

3. Reduce the scope of what you choose to summarize, and say more about less.

Both The Method and Notice and Focus inevitably involve some loss of breadth; you won't be able to cover everything. But this is usually a trade-off worth making. Your ability to rank parts of your subject or choose a particularly revealing feature or pattern to focus on will give you surer control of the material than if you just reproduced what was in the text. You can still begin with a brief survey of major points to provide context, before narrowing the focus.

Reducing scope is an especially efficient and productive strategy when you are trying to understand a reading you find difficult or perplexing. It will move you beyond just banking and towards having ideas about the reading. If, for example, you are reading Chaucer's *Canterbury Tales* and start cataloguing what makes it funny, you are likely to end up with unanalyzed plot summary—a list that arranges its elements in no particular order. But narrowing the question to "How does Chaucer's use of religious commentary contribute to the humor of 'The Wife of Bath's Tale'?" reduces the scope to a single tale and the humor to a single aspect of humor. Describe those as accurately as you can, and you will begin to notice things.

4. Get some detachment: shift your focus from *what* to *how* and *why?*

Most readers tend to get too single-minded about absorbing the information. That is, they attend only to the *what:* what the reading is saying or about. They take it all in passively. But through an act of will, as a tool in your repertoire, you can deliberately shift your focus to *how* it says what it says, and *why.* If, for example, you were asked to discuss the major discoveries that Darwin made on *The Beagle,* you could avoid simply listing his conclusions by redirecting your attention to *how* he proceeds. You could choose to focus, for example, on Darwin's use of the scientific method, examining how he builds and, in some cases, discards hypotheses. Or you might select several passages that illustrate how Darwin proceeded from evidence to conclusion and then *rank* them in order of importance to the overall theory. Notice that in shifting the emphasis to Darwin's thinking—the *how* and *why*—you would not be excluding the *what* (the information component) from your discussion.

Let's take one more example. If you were studying the reasons that the American colonies rebelled against England, so broad a subject would tend to produce passive summary—a list of standard generalizations about the American revolution. But what if you narrowed the focus to the Boston Tea Party and considered *how* American and British history textbooks differ in their treatment of this crucial event? Note that this question would still enable you to address, though in much more focused form, the broader question of why the colonies rebelled.

5. Attend to the pitch, the complaint, and the moment.

Consider that whatever you are reading, and this is even true in such apparently neutral material as textbooks, is at least three things other than just an assemblage of information.

A reading is an argument, a presentation of information that makes a case of some sort, even if the argument is not explicitly stated. When you write a summary, look for language that reveals the position or positions the piece seems interested in having you adopt. As we say in Chapter 1, it is not only debate-style argument that makes a case for things. Analysis, for example, argues for understanding a subject in a particular way.

A reading is a reaction to some situation, some set of circumstances, that the piece has set out to address. An indispensable means of understanding and summarizing someone else's writing is to figure out what seems to have caused the person to write the piece in the first place. Writers write, presumably, because they think something needs to be addressed. What? Look for language in the piece that reveals the writer's starting point. If you can find the position or situation he or she is trying to correct, you will find it much easier to locate the argument, the position the piece asks you to accept.

A reading is a response to the world conditioned by the writer's particular moment in time. In your attempt to figure out not only what a piece says but where it is coming from (the causes of its having been written in the first place and the positions it works to establish), history is significant. When was the piece written? Where? What else was going on at the time that might have shaped the writer's ideas and attitudes? You don't necessarily have to run to a history book for every summary you write, but neither do you want to ignore the extent to which writers are conditioned by their times.

Passage-Based Focused Freewriting

Passage-based focused freewriting is one of the best analytical exercises you can do in order to get ideas about what you are reading. It works on the assumption that you'll be ready to have a smarter appreciation of how the whole works when you've seen how a piece works.

In general, freewriting is a method of arriving at ideas by writing continuously about a subject for a specified period of time (usually ten to twenty minutes) without pausing to edit or correct or bite your pen or stare into space. The rationale behind this activity can be understood through a well-known remark by the novelist E. M. Forster (in regard to the "tyranny" of prearranging everything): "How do I know what I think until I see what I say?" Freewriting gives you the chance to see what you'll say.

In passage-based focused freewriting, you narrow the scope to a single passage, a brief piece of the reading (at least a sentence, at most a paragraph) to anchor your analysis. You might choose the passage in answer to the question, "What is the one passage in the reading that needs to be discussed, that poses a question or a problem, or that seems (in some way perhaps difficult to pin down) anomalous or even just unclear?" You can vary this question by selecting the passage that you find most puzzling or most important or most dissonant or whatever.

One advantage of focused freewriting is that it forces you to articulate what you notice as you notice it, not delaying—or, as is more common, simply avoiding—thinking in a persistent and relatively disciplined way about what you are reading. There is no set procedure for such writing, but it usually involves the following:

- It selects out key phrases or terms in the passage and paraphrases them, trying to tease out the possible meanings of these words.
- It relentlessly asks "So what?" about the details: so what that the passage uses this language, moves in this way, arrives at these points? and so forth.
- It addresses how the passage is representative of broader issues in the reading; perhaps it will refer to another, similar passage.
- It attends briefly to the context surrounding the passage, summarizing the larger section of which the passage is a part.

As you can see, passage-based focused freewriting thus makes use of the other skills that we have been discussing in this chapter as well: paraphrasing, summarizing, and narrowing the focus. It is an effective way of preparing for class discussion and of testing possible target areas of concentration for a paper.

☞ *Try this:* Select a passage from any of the material that you are reading and copy it at the top of the page. Then do a twenty-minute focused freewrite on it, using the bulleted items on page 59 as guidelines. Strive by the end of the time allotted to make some kind of interpretive leap, some consolidation of what you have learned about the reading by doing the exercise. ☐

B. WHAT TO DO WITH THE READING: AVOIDING THE MATCHING EXERCISE

What does it mean "to do something with the reading"? Well, obviously, you can paraphrase, summarize, or do a focused freewrite with it; but these exercises aim primarily to establish an accurate understanding of what the reading is doing and saying. That's why they are included under the heading "How to Read: Words Matter." When, by contrast, you *do* something with the reading, you use it for purposes that are different from the aims of the reading itself. This distinction holds for all kinds of reading, not just the academic or literary varieties. In a guide to bike repair, you might paraphrase the directions for replacing the brakes to make sure your understanding of this complex procedure was sufficiently clear. But if you used the knowledge you'd gained to fix the brakes on some other machine, adapting what you'd learned, you'd be doing something with the reading.

Since analysis relies so heavily on reading, we address in much of the rest of this book, either directly or implicitly, ways of negotiating what you read. In a later chapter, for example, we concentrate on how to use secondary research. For now, we will discuss three basic approaches to doing things with the reading:

* Applying a reading as a lens for examining something else
* Comparing one reading with another
* Uncovering the assumptions in a reading—where the piece is "coming from"

We'll introduce and do basic troubleshooting on the first two approaches, foregrounding the major problems and how to solve them. But we'll concentrate on the third, with which you are probably least familiar.

Applying a Reading as a Lens

> **Problem:** A matching exercise, a mere demonstration of applicability.
> **Solution:** Emphasize the shift in context, and then actively seek out areas of dissonance to analyze.

We apply what we read about all the time. It's a standard academic assignment. You read an article on gender and blue jeans and then connect its ideas to something else—how, for example, magazine ads represent jeans-wearing with respect to gender. Or you study Freud's *The Interpretation of Dreams* and then analyze a dream of your own or a friend's as you project what Freud would have done. Or you apply his theory of repression to the behavior of a character in a novel or to some newfound realization about your mother's occasional bouts of frenzied housecleaning or your father's zealous weeding when he's upset. Freud thus becomes a *lens* for seeing the subject.

But what about taking an article on liberation theology as practiced by certain Catholic priests in Latin America and applying it to the rise of Islamic fundamentalism in the Middle East? Or for that matter, what about applying the directions for fixing the brakes on a bicycle to the analogous task on a car? Obviously, the original texts may be somewhat useful, but there are also significant differences between the two religious movements and between the two kinds of brakes.

So what should you do? When using a reading as a lens for better seeing what is going on in something you are studying, assume that the match between the lens and your subject will never be exact. It is often in the area where things don't match up exactly that you will find your best opportunity for having ideas. Here are two guidelines for applying lens A to some subject matter B.

1. Think about how lens A both fits *and* does not fit subject B: avoid the matching-exercise mentality.

The big problem with the way most people apply a reading is that they do so too indiscriminately, too generally. They essentially construct a *matching exercise* in which each of a set of ideas drawn from text A is made to equate with a corresponding element (an idea or a fact) from subject B, often in virtual list-like fashion. Matching exercises are more useful in some contexts than in others (great for fixing your bike's brakes, less so for analyzing your parents). At their worst, matching exercises are static, mindlessly mechanical, and, worst of all, inaccurate. This is because they concentrate on similarities and forget the rest. As a result, the lens screens out what it cannot bring into focus, and the writer applying it distorts what he or she sees. Like an optometrist figuring out the new prescription for your glasses, you need to constantly adjust the lens whenever you bring it to new material. Don't just apply A as a blanket: really think about how A both fits *and* doesn't fit B.

Remember that whenever you apply lens A to a new subject B, you are taking A from its original context and using its ideas in at least somewhat different circumstances for at least somewhat different purposes. Don't just nod to the shift in context; really think about how this shift changes things and, thus, how it may require you to refocus the lens. Freud's theory of repression wasn't actually talking about your father, after all. And there are probably other explanations for his weeding frenzies to be explored. Again, the goal is not to dismiss Freud but to adjust his thinking to the particular case. You don't want to use the reading that you are applying as a club to bludgeon your subject into submission.

2. Actively seek out the differences between lens A and subject B; use these differences to probe both A and B ("Yes, but . . .").

If you undertake applications assuming that A does not fit B completely and accurately, you are bound to find areas of mismatch—ideas in the reading that don't apply and information and ideas in your subject that don't fit. This is not a problem. It's an opportunity, giving you something to *do* with the reading. On the basis of the differences you detect, you can probe both A and B.

Say, for example, you are applying an article on the racist implications of the recent vogue for black/white buddy films to a film you've seen recently that was not discussed in the article. "Yes, but . . . ," you find yourself responding: there are places where the film does appear to fit within the pattern that the article claims, but there are also exceptions to the pattern. What do you do? What *not* to do is either choose a different film that "fits better" or decide that the article is wrong-headed.

Instead, start with the "yes"; talk about how the film accords with the general pattern. Then, focus on the "but"; talk about the claims in the reading (the lens) that seem not to fit or material in your subject not adequately accounted for by the lens. Although you're not out to attack the reading you have been applying, neither should you believe that applying a reading as a lens is a process of merely nodding repeatedly about how neatly everything fits. In fact, a careful application of a reading will usually lead you to refine one or more of its ideas (to adjust the lens) and bring you to new, small additions to or changes in the thinking offered by the reading. We have more to say about this subject—the reciprocal relationship between claims and evidence—in later chapters.

❧ *Try this:* Apply the two preceding guidelines and the following generalization about talk shows to a talk show of your choice: "These shows obviously offer a distorted vision of America, thrive on feeling rather than thought, and worship the sound-byte rather than the art of conversation" (Stark 243). Alternatively, take any general claim you find in your reading and apply it to some other text or subject. Either way, strive to produce several paragraphs in which you avoid the matching exercise and instead probe both lens A and subject B. □

Comparing and Contrasting One Reading with Another

Problem: Stopping too soon, with only a list of similarities and differences.
Solution: Look for difference within similarity or for similarity despite difference.

Comparing and contrasting is another traditional assignment done with readings that falls flat when it turns into a mechanical matching exercise. Comparing readings resembles applying a reading as a lens. These activities are not intended as ends in themselves; they almost always contribute to some larger process of understanding.

The rationale for working comparatively is that you can usually discover ideas about a reading much more easily when you are not viewing it in isolation. You can observe it from a different perspective, in relation to something else. When used in this way, the comparison is usually not a 50–50 split; you've moved to a comparison of A with B because you want to better understand A.

In short, *a good comparison should open up a reading, not close it down.* It does more than demonstrate that you've "done the reading." We're all completely familiar with the formulaic conclusions to the comparisons produced by the matching-exercise mentality: "Thus, we see there are many similarities and differences between A and B." Perfunctory, pointless, and inert lists: that's what you get if you stop the process of comparing and contrasting too soon, before you've focused and explored something interesting that you notice.

How do you avoid the ubiquitous matching-exercise habit? Here are three guidelines for productively comparing A with B:

1. Focus the comparison to give it a point.

A comparison won't have a point inherently—you need to consciously give it one. It's often useful to assume that what you have originally taken for a point has not yet gone far enough, is still too close to summary. Rather than sticking with a range of broad comparisons, try to focus on a key comparison, one that you find interesting or revealing. (The Method, Notice and Focus, and other tools can help you here to select your focus.) Although narrowing the focus in this way might seem to eliminate other important areas of consideration, in fact it usually allows you to incorporate at least some of these other areas in a more tightly connected, less list-like fashion.

If, to return to an earlier example, you were to compare the representations of the Boston Tea Party in British and American history texts, you would *begin but not stop* with identifying similarities and differences. The goal of your reading would be to focus on some particular matches that seem especially revealing—for example, that British and American texts trace the economic background of the incident in different ways. Then, in response to the "So what?" question, you could attempt to develop some explanation of what these differences reveal and why they are significant. You might, for example, decide that the British texts view the matter from a more global economic perspective, while American texts emphasize nationalism.

2. Look for significant difference between A and B, given their similarity.

One of the best ways to arrive at a meaningful and interesting focus is to follow a principle that we call *looking for difference within similarity*. The procedure is simple but virtually guaranteed to produce a focused idea.

   a. First, deal with the similarity. Identify what you take to be the essential similarity and then ask and answer, "So what?" Why is this similarity significant?

   b. Then, in this context, identify the differences that you notice.

   c. Choose one difference you find particularly revealing or interesting, and again ask, "So what?" What is the significance of this difference?

You can repeat this procedure with a range of key similarities and differences. If you do so, look for ways that the various differences are connected.

The phrase "difference within similarity" is to remind you that once you have started your thinking by locating apparent similarities, you can usually refine that thinking by pursuing significant, though often less obvious, distinctions among the similar things. In Irish studies, for example, scholars characteristically acknowledge the extent to which contemporary Irish culture is the product of colonization. To this extent, Irish culture shares certain traits with other former colonies in Africa, Asia, Latin America, and elsewhere. But instead of simply demonstrating how Irish culture fits the general pattern of colonialism, these scholars also isolate the ways that Ireland *does not fit* the model. They focus, for example, on how its close geographical proximity and racial similarity to England, its colonizer, have distinguished the kinds of problems it encounters today from those characteristic of the more generalized model of colonialism. In effect, looking for difference within similarity has led them to locate and analyze the anomalies.

3. Look for unexpected similarity between A and B, given their difference.

A corollary of the preceding principle is that you should focus on *unexpected similarity rather than obvious difference.* The fact that in the Bush presidency Republicans differ from Democrats on environmental policy is probably a less promising focal point than their surprising agreement on violating the so-called lockbox policy against tapping Social Security funds to finance government programs. Most readers would expect the political parties to differ on the environment, and a comparison of their positions would likely involve mostly summarizing. But a surprising similarity, like an unexpected difference, necessarily raises questions for you to pursue: do the parties' shared positions against the lockbox policy, for example, share the same motives?

❦ *Try this:* Choose any item from the list below, and practice reading comparatively. After you've done the research necessary to locate material to read and analyze, list as many similarities and differences as you can: go for coverage. Then, review your list, and select the two or three most revealing similarities and the two or three most revealing differences. At this point, you are ready to write a few paragraphs in which you argue for the significance of a key difference or similarity. In so doing, you may find it interesting to focus on an *unexpected* similarity or difference—one that others might not initially notice. (We recommend trying the "unexpected" gambit.)

1. accounts of the same event from two different newspapers or magazines or text-books
2. two CDs (or even songs) by the same artist or group
3. two ads for the same kind of product
4. graffiti in men's bathrooms versus graffiti in women's bathrooms
5. the political campaigns of two opponents running for the same or similar office ☐

Uncovering the Assumptions in a Reading

Everything you read has basic assumptions that underlie it. What are assumptions in this context? They are the basic ground of beliefs from which a position springs, its starting points or "givens," its basic operating premises. The *Oxford English Dictionary* defines a "premise"—from a Latin word meaning "to put before"—as "a previous statement or proposition from which another statement is inferred or follows as a conclusion." All arguments or articulations of point of view have premises—that is, they are based in a given set of assumptions, which are built upon to arrive at conclusions.

A lot of the time, though, the assumptions are not visible; they're implicit (which is why they need to be inferred). They're usually not actively concealed by writers—writers hiding from readers the subterranean bases of their outlooks—which might be considered unethical. Rather, many writers (especially inexperienced ones) remain unaware of the premises that underlie their points of view—probably because they were never taught to be aware of them. Similarly, most readers don't know that they should search out the starting points of what they read and, so, of course, they also don't know how.

Especially if it's in a book, most readers tend to credit what they read as true, or at least relatively neutral. In other words, most people aren't aware that everything they read (and write) comes from given sets of assumptions. It follows that the ability to uncover assumptions is a powerful analytical procedure to learn—it gives you insight into the roots, the basic givens that a piece of writing (or a speaker) has assumed are true. When you locate assumptions in a text, you understand the text better—where it's coming from, what else it believes that is more fundamental than what it is overtly declaring. You also find things to write about; uncovering assumptions offers one of the best ways of developing and revising your own work. Uncovering assumptions can help you to understand why you believe X, or it may reveal to you that two of your givens are in conflict with each other.

To uncover assumptions, you need to read "backwards"—to ask *what a reading must also already believe*, given that it believes what it overtly claims. In other words, you need *to imagine or reinvent the process of thinking by which a writer has arrived at a position.* You can do this by employing some of the skills already discussed in this chapter, in particular, identifying the underlying structure of a reading, asking what particular words mean, and shifting your focus from *what* to *how* and *why*.

Say you read a piece that praises a television show for being realistic but faults it for setting a bad example to the kids who watch it. What assumptions might we infer from such a piece? Here are some:

- Television should attempt to depict life accurately (realistically).
- Television should produce shows that set good examples.
- Kids imitate or at least have their attitudes shaped by what they watch on television.
- Good and bad examples are clear and easily recognizable by everyone.

Note that none of these assumptions is self-evidently true—each would need to be argued for. And some of the assumptions conflict with others—for example, that shows should be both morally uplifting and realistic, given that in "real life" those who do wrong often go unpunished. These are subjects an analytical response to the piece (or a revision of it) could bring out.

Procedure for Uncovering Assumptions

How do you actually go about uncovering assumptions? Here's a fairly flexible procedure, which we will apply step-by-step to the claim "Tax laws benefit the wealthy."

1. Paraphrase the explicit claim.

This activity will get you started interpreting the claim, and it may begin to suggest the claim's underlying assumptions. We might paraphrase the claim as "The rules for paying income tax give rich people monetary advantages" or "The rules for paying income tax help the rich get richer."

2. List the implicit ideas that the claim seems to assume to be true.

Here are two: "Tax laws shouldn't benefit anybody" and "Tax laws should benefit those who need the benefit, those with the least money."

3. Determine the various ways that the key terms of the claim might be defined, as well as how the writer of the claim has defined them.

This process of definition will help you to see the key concepts upon which the claim depends. How does the writer intend "benefit"? And does he or she mean that tax laws benefit only the wealthy and presumably harm those who are not wealthy? And where does the line between wealthy and not wealthy get drawn?

4. Try on an oppositional stance to the claim to see if this unearths more underlying assumptions.

Regardless of your view on the subject, suppose for the sake of argument that the writer is wrong. This step allows you to think comparatively, helping you to see the claim more clearly, to see what it apparently *excludes* from its fundamental beliefs. Knowing what the underlying assumption leaves out helps us to see the narrowness upon which the claim may rest; we understand better its limits. Two positions that the claim appears to exclude are "Tax laws benefit the poor" and "Tax laws do not benefit the wealthy."

Whether you encounter a claim such as "Tax laws benefit the wealthy" in your reading or start writing a paper from that position, you will get into trouble as you develop your claim (move it forward) if you don't move backwards as well, for the claim conceals a set of more fundamental assumptions about the *purpose* of tax laws. To find these assumptions, you need to query the claim before going on to make some kind of argument about it. Is the purpose of tax laws to redress economic inequities, as the claim seems to imply? Is the purpose of tax laws to spur the economy by rewarding those who generate capital, in which case tax laws don't benefit only the wealthy? You might go to the U.S. Constitution and/or to legal precedents to resolve such questions, but our point here is that regardless of the position your paper adopts—attacking tax laws, defending them, showing how they actually benefit everyone, or whatever—you risk proceeding blindly if you have failed to question the purpose of tax laws in the first place.

❦ *Try this:* Apply the four-step procedure for uncovering assumptions to the following brief excerpt from a student paper: paraphrase, list implicit assumptions, define key terms, and try on an oppositional stance. The result of this process should be a list of the premises upon which the writer's argument operates that the paragraph has not made sufficiently clear. At this point, if you wish, you might write a page about the paragraph, providing the results of your analytical reading.

> In all levels of trade, including individual, local, domestic, and international, both buyers and sellers are essentially concerned with their own welfare. This self-interest, however, actually contributes to the health and growth of the economy as a whole. Each country benefits by exporting those goods in which it has an advantage and importing goods in which it does not. Importing and exporting allow countries to focus on producing those goods that they can generate most

efficiently. As a result of specializing in certain products and then trading them, self-interest leads to efficient trade, which leads to consumer satisfaction. □

❧ *Try this:* Here's another statement for uncovering assumptions. In the reference application sent to professors for students who are seeking to enter a student-teaching program, the professor is asked to rank the student from one to four (unacceptable to acceptable) on the following criterion: "The student uses his/her sense of humor appropriately." Use the procedure for uncovering assumptions to compile a list of the assumptions embedded in the quotation. □

A Sample Essay: Having Ideas by Uncovering Assumptions

As an analytical activity, uncovering assumptions is not limited to reading. Like other tools we discuss, it can also lead you to have ideas and formulate a point of view about the reading—in effect, to become a writer. We'll now examine a newspaper editorial (from the *New York Times*) that demonstrates this process. The editorial illustrates how a writer reasons forward to his own conclusions by reasoning backward to the premises assumed in the positions of others. As you will see, the piece also shows how the strategy of refocusing binaries (discussed in Chapter 2) operates in tandem with uncovering assumptions.

As you read this editorial on the controversial rules established at Antioch College to govern sexual conduct among its students, try to focus not only on the content of the argument but also on its form—that is, how the writer moves from one phase of his thinking to the next. Toward this end, we have added our own summaries of what each paragraph of the editorial accomplishes. At the end of the editorial we sum up the writer's primary developmental strategies as guidelines that you can apply to your own reading and writing.

"Playing by the Antioch Rules"
by Eric Fassin

[1] A good consensus is hard to find, especially on sexual politics. But the infamous rules instituted last year by Antioch College, which require students to obtain explicit verbal consent before so much as a kiss is exchanged, have created just that. They have provoked indignation (this is a serious threat to individual freedom!) as well as ridicule (can this be serious?). Sexual correctness thus proves a worthy successor to political correctness as a target of public debate. [The writer names the issue: the complaint that Antioch's rules threaten individual freedom.]

[2] Yet this consensus against the rules reveals shared assumptions among liberals, conservatives and even radicals about the nature of sex in our culture. [The writer identifies members of an unlikely consensus and focuses on a surprising similarity despite difference.]

[3] The new definition of consent at Antioch is based on a "liberal" premise: it assumes that sexual partners are free agents and that they mean what they say—yes means yes, and no means no. But the initiator must now obtain prior consent, step by step, which in practice shifts the burden of clarification from the woman to the man.

The question is no longer "Did she say no?" but "Did she say yes?" Silence does not indicate consent, and it becomes his responsibility to dispel any ambiguity. [The writer identifies assumption of freedom underlying the rules.]

[4] The novelty of the rules, however, is not as great as it seems. Antioch will not exert more control over its students; there are no sexual police. In practice, you still do what you want—as long as your partner does not complain . . . the morning after. If this is censorship, it intervenes *ex post facto*, not *a priori*. [The writer questions the premise that rules will actually control individual freedom more than present norms do.]

[5] In fact, the "threat" to individual freedom for most critics is not the invasion of privacy through the imposition of sexual codes, but the very existence of rules. Hence the success of polemicists like Katie Roiphe or Camille Paglia, who argue that feminism in recent years has betrayed its origins by embracing old-style regulations, paradoxically choosing the rigid 1950s over the liberating 1960s. Their advice is simply to let women manage on their own, and individuals devise their own rules. This individualist critique of feminism finds resonance with liberals, but also, strangely, with conservatives, who belatedly discover the perils of regulating sexuality. [The writer locates an antiregulatory (laissez-faire) premise beneath the freedom premise.]

[6] But sexual laissez-faire, with its own implicit set of rules, does not seem to have worked very well recently. Since the collapse of established social codes, people play the same game with different rules. If more women are complaining of sexual violence, while more men are worrying that their words and actions might be misconstrued, who benefits from the absence of regulation? [The writer attacks the laissez-faire premise for ineffectiveness.]

[7] A laissez-faire philosophy toward relationships assumes that sexuality is a game that can (and must) be played without rules, or rather that the invention of rules should be left to individual spontaneity and creativity, despite rising evidence that the rule of one's own often leads to misunderstandings. When acted out, individual fantasy always plays within preordained social rules. These rules conflict with the assumption in this culture that sex is subject to the reign of nature, not artifice, that it is the province of the individual, not of society. [The writer uncovers an assumption beneath the laissez-faire premise: sex is natural and thus outside social rules.]

[8] Those who believe that society's constraints should have nothing to do with sex also agree that sex should not be bound by the social conventions of language. Indeed, this rebellion against the idea of social constraints probably accounts for the controversy over explicit verbal consent—from George Will, deriding "sex amidst semicolons," to Camille Paglia railing, "As if sex occurs in the verbal realm." As if sexuality were incompatible with words. As if the only language of sex were silence. For *The New Yorker*, "the [Antioch] rules don't get rid of the problem of unwanted sex at all; they just shift the advantage from the muscle-bound frat boy to the honey-tongued French major." [The writer develops the linguistic implications of the natural premise and questions the assumption that sex is incompatible with language.]

[9] This is not very different from the radical feminist position, which holds that verbal persuasion is no better than physical coercion. In this view, sexuality cannot be entrusted to rhetoric. The seduction of words is inherently violent, and seduction itself is an object of suspicion. (If this is true, Marvell's invitation "To His Coy Mistress" is indeed a form of sexual harassment, as some campus feminists have claimed.) [The writer develops a further implication: that the attack on rules masks a fear of language's power to seduce—and questions the equation of seduction with harassment.]

[10] What the consensus against the Antioch rules betrays is a common vision of sexuality which crosses the lines dividing conservatives, liberals and radicals. So many of the arguments start from a conventional situation, perceived and presented as natural: a heterosexual encounter with the man as the initiator, and the woman as gatekeeper—hence the focus on consent. [The writer redefines consensus as sharing the unacknowledged premise that conventional sex roles are natural.]

[11] The outcry largely results from the fact that the rules undermine this traditional erotic model. Not so much by proscribing (legally), but by prescribing (socially). The new model, in which language becomes a normal form of erotic communication, underlines the conventional nature of the old one. [The writer reformulates the claim about the antirules consensus: rules undermine attempts to pass off traditional sex roles as natural.]

[12] By encouraging women out of their "natural" reserve, these rules point to a new definition of sexual roles. "Yes" could be more than a way to make explicit the absence of "no"; "yes" can also be a cry of desire. Women may express demands, and not only grant favors. If the legal "yes" opened the ground for an erotic "yes," if the contract gave way to desire and if consent led to demand, we would indeed enter a brave new erotic world. [The writer extends the implication of the claim: rules could make sex more erotic rather than less free.]

[13] New rules are like new shoes: they hurt a little at first, but they may fit tomorrow. The only question about the Antioch rules is not really whether we like them, but whether they improve the situation between men and women. All rules are artificial, but, in the absence of generally agreed-upon social conventions, any new prescription must feel artificial. And isn't regulation needed precisely when there is an absence of cultural consensus? [The writer questions the standard by which we evaluate rules; the writer proposes reformulating the binary from artificial versus natural to whether or not rules will improve gender relations.]

[14] Whether we support or oppose the Antioch rules, at least they force us to acknowledge that the choice is not between regulation and freedom, but between different sets of rules, implicit or explicit. They help dispel the illusion that sexuality is a state of nature individuals must experience outside the social contract, and that eroticism cannot exist within the conventions of language. As Antioch reminds us, there is more in eroticism and sexuality than is dreamt of in this culture. [The writer culminates with his own idea: rules are good because they force us to acknowledge as a harmful illusion the idea that sex operates outside social conventions.]

The strategies that direct the thinking in this editorial offer a model for reading to uncover assumptions in the service of arriving at ideas. If you examine what the writer has done—not just what he has said—you might arrive at the following primary moves, which can be phrased as general guidelines for reading analytically:

1. Paraphrase the explicit claims; search out the meanings of key terms.

The writer does not begin by offering his own conclusion on whether the views he has thus far described are right or wrong. Instead, he slows down the forward momentum toward judgment and begins to analyze what the consensus against the Antioch rules might mean—the "shared assumptions" it reveals "among liberals, conservatives and even radicals about the nature of sex in our culture." In fact, the author spends the first three-quarters of the essay trying on various answers to this question of meaning.

2. Uncover assumptions to decide what is really at issue.

Rather than proceeding directly to a judgment on whether or not the rules threaten individual freedom, the writer carefully searches out the assumptions—the premises and the givens—underlying the attacks on the rules. He proposes, for example, that underneath the attack by the consensus on the rules and its defense of individual freedom lies a basic assumption about sex and society, that sexuality should not be governed by rules because it is natural rather than cultural: "These rules conflict with the assumption in this culture that sex is subject to the reign of nature, not artifice, that it is the province of the individual, not of society" (paragraph 7).

3. Attend to organizing contrasts; but be alert to the possibility that they may be false dichotomies, and reformulate them as necessary.

A false dichotomy (sometimes called a false binary) inaccurately divides possible views on a subject into two opposing camps, forcing a choice between black and white when some shade of gray might be fairer and more accurate. As we discuss under "Either/Or Thinking (Binaries)" in Chapter 1, it is always a good strategy to question any either/or dichotomy. Consider whether its opposing terms define the issue fairly and accurately before accepting an argument in favor of one side or the other.

Consider, too, how you might reject *both* choices offered by an either/or opposition in order to construct an alternative approach that is truer to the issues at hand. (See "Thinking Recursively: Refocusing Binaries" in Chapter 2.) This is what the author of the editorial does. He outlines and then rejects as a false dichotomy the assumption he has uncovered that is held by the consensus view—that sexual behavior is either a province of individual freedom or is regulated by society:

False Dichotomies

freedom versus regulation

natural versus artificial

no rules versus rules

It is here, evidently, that reasoning back to premises and reformulating binaries has led the writer to his primary idea. He argues that much of what we perceive to be natural, such as the notion of men as sexual initiators and women as nay-sayers and gate-keepers, is in fact governed by social rules and conventions. He proposes that what is really at stake—the root assumption shared by the antirules consensus—is a different dichotomy, a choice between two sets of rules, one implicit and one explicit. If you use The Method on the editorial, new organizing contrasts emerge:

Reformulated Dichotomies
rules versus rules
implicit versus explicit
not working versus might work
based on "no" versus based on "yes"

The editorial concludes that we need to decide questions of sexual behavior—at Antioch and in the culture at large—by recognizing and evaluating the relative merits of the two sets of rules rather than by creating a false dichotomy between rules and no rules, between regulation and freedom: "The choice is not between regulation and freedom, but between different sets of rules" (paragraph 14).

4. When you write your analysis of the reading, rehearse for your readers the thinking process by which you have uncovered the assumptions—not just the conclusions to which the process has led you.
Notice that virtually the entire editorial has consisted of uncovering assumptions as a way of arriving at new ways of thinking. This matter of sharing your thinking with readers as you develop and fine-tune your ideas is the primary subject of Part II of this book.

ASSIGNMENTS

1. Write a summary of a piece of writing using one or more of the following methods:
   a. Paraphrase × 3
   b. Ranking and reducing scope
   c. Finding the underlying structure
   d. Attending to the pitch, the complaint, and the moment
   e. Passage-based focused freewriting

2. Use a reading as a lens for examining a subject. For example, look at a piece of music or a film through the lens of a review that does not discuss the particular piece or film you are writing about. Or you might read about a particular theory of humor and use that as a lens for examining a comic play, film, story, television show, or stand-up routine.

3. Compare and contrast two readings on the same or similar subjects by looking for significant difference, given their similarities, or unexpected similarity, given their differences.

4. Using the editorial on the Antioch rules as your model, write an essay in which you develop a position by uncovering the assumptions in a reading or set of

related readings. You might try this with an editorial or a batch of editorials on the same subject. Reviews are often a good target for this assignment, because they tend to offer judgments. You could also uncover the assumptions of a policy decision at your school or place of work. This will work best if you have not just the policy but some kind of written manifesto on it. (Policies relating to student life are often quite revealing of what the institution actually thinks of its students.)

5. Write a personal essay that develops a thesis by reasoning back to premises. Once you have had some practice in unpacking concealed assumptions, you might wish to use this strategy to examine some idea or attitude of your own, preferably one that has undergone some kind of change in recent years (for example, your attitude toward the world of work, toward marriage, toward family life, toward community, toward religion, and so forth).

PART II

Writing the
Thesis-Driven Paper

5

Linking Evidence and Claims:
10 on 1 Versus 1 on 10

Thus far, we have been concerned with developing the primary skills and habits of mind that go into thinking and writing analytically. Now, in Part II of this book, we turn to ways of using those skills to write a thesis-driven paper.

Perhaps no aspect of writing causes more problems and attracts more unsound advice than the question of how to construct an effective thesis. In Part I we deliberately skirt this subject for a good reason: a primary problem in thesis construction is that people think about it too early in the analytical process, leaping to a thesis too soon. And so we haven't even used the word "thesis," instead opting for a synonym, "claim."

By way of definition, a *claim* is an assertion that you make about your evidence— an idea that you believe the evidence supports. The primary claim in a paper is the *thesis*. In analytical writing, the thesis is a theory that explains what some feature or features of a subject mean. The subject itself, the pool of primary material (data) being analyzed, is known as *evidence*.

Of course, we have, using different terms, been talking about approaches to evidence and thesis all along. The chapter on observation (Chapter 2), for instance, is about ways of looking at evidence; the chapter on interpretation (Chapter 3) is about making claims; and the chapter on reading (Chapter 4) is vitally concerned with the connection between evidence and claims. *If we were to summarize the whole point of the book so far, it would be that you should avoid settling for premature leaps to generalities and then looking at evidence only to find things that fit the claim.* Instead, the approach we suggest is to look at evidence more openly. When you find yourself arriving at generalizations, don't stop with these. Go back to the details, look for patterns, find the organizing contrasts, and come up with a range of synonyms to describe what is there. These tactics will give rise to better ideas.

At some point, however, you are going to need to move from exploratory evidence-gathering and preliminary interpretation to producing a more finished paper, one with a thesis and an introduction, a conclusion, and an orderly review of your evidence. This is not to say that The Method, Notice and Focus, and asking "So what?" won't get you to a paper—they will, if you will stick with them.

But when the time comes to compose a formal paper with a thesis, it is very common for writers who have been thinking well while doing these preliminary activities to abandon both the thinking they have been doing and the skills that have produced it. Faced with the challenge of constructing a *thesis,* they panic and revert to old habits: "Now I better have my one idea and be able to prove to everybody that I'm right." So, out goes careful attention to detail. Out goes any evidence that doesn't fit. Instead of analysis, they substitute the kind of paper we call a *demonstration*.

Demonstrations are the result of two primary mistaken assumptions about what an analytical paper is, one having to do with thesis, the other with evidence.

- The misconception about a thesis is that a thesis should be static and unchanging.
- The misconception about evidence is that the sole function of evidence is to corroborate (confirm) the thesis—in other words, that evidence is limited to "the stuff that proves I'm right."

If these are misconceptions, then what are the better, more accurate understandings to acquire about the thesis and the use of evidence? Here's the short answer, after which we take up these matters in more detail:

- A strong thesis *evolves:* it changes as a paper progresses. The changes in the thesis are galvanized by its repeated encounters with evidence. A strong thesis is not static.
- Evidence has a second function beyond corroborating claims: to test and develop and evolve the thesis, making the thesis more precise. Evidence is not to be treated as static, as just a means of confirming and reasserting unchanging ideas.

Now let's slow down and explore these two misconceptions, starting with what's wrong with the idea of a static thesis.

A. DEVELOPING A THESIS IS MORE THAN REPEATING AN IDEA ("1 ON 10")

Perhaps the most common misunderstanding about the thesis is that it must appear throughout the paper in essentially the same form. In fact, this absence of change is the primary trait of a weak thesis. Like an *inert* (unreactive) material, a weak thesis neither affects nor is affected by the evidence that surrounds it.

A paper produced by repeating a single idea generally follows the form we call *1 on 10:* the writer makes a single and usually very general claim ("History repeats itself," "Exercise is good for you," and so forth) and then proceeds to affix it to ten examples. (See Figure 5.1.) The problem with 1 on 10 is that it tries to cover too much ground and often ends by noticing little more than some general similarity that might be the starting point but should not be the final outcome of a paper. The number ten, we should add, is arbitrarily chosen. You could cite four, five, or seven examples. Whatever the number, the evidence would remain insufficiently analyzed, the thesis

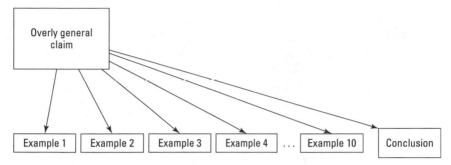

FIGURE 5.1
Doing 1 on 10. The horizontal pattern of 1 on 10 (in which "10" stands arbitrarily for any number of examples) repeatedly makes the same point about every example and in the conclusion. Its analysis of evidence is superficial.

would remain inert, and the paper would amount to little more than a list if all you did was reassert the same idea about each example. By contrast, in nearly all good writing the thesis evolves by *gaining in complexity* and, thus, in accuracy as the paper progresses.

Even in cases where, for disciplinary reasons, the thesis itself cannot change, there is still movement between the beginning of the paper and the end. In the report format of the natural and social sciences, for example, the hypothesis as initially worded must be either confirmed or denied, but it still undergoes much conceptual development. Rather than *simply* being confirmed or rejected, its adequacy is considered from various angles; and alternatives, along with alternative methodologies for testing the original hypothesis again, are often proposed. (We discuss later in a section of Chapter 6 entitled "Locating the Evolving Thesis in the Final Draft" the differences and especially the similarities in the ways various disciplines locate and use thesis statements.)

Weak thesis statements (poorly formulated and inadequately developed) are most easily detected not only by their repetitiveness but also by their predictability. The writer says the same thing again and again, drawing the same overgeneralized conclusion from each piece of evidence ("And so, once again we see that . . ."). A thesis that functions as an inert formula closes down a writer's thinking rather than guiding and stimulating it.

Inert thesis statements are, at least in part, products of a writer's adhering to an overly rigid and mechanical organizational scheme. Such schemes have the advantage of guaranteeing order, which they achieve by arranging everything under some single unifying point. Any data that do not conform, however, remain unnoticed or are studiously ignored. Thus, a thesis such as "Government welfare programs stifle initiative" will exclude welfare success stories, and a thesis such as "Marlowe's *Doctor Faustus* is a play about greed" will screen out the main character's moments of generosity.

Where do writers get the idea in the first place that a thesis should be static? In most cases they learned it early in their writing careers as part of a stubbornly inflexible organizational scheme known as five-paragraph form.

What's Wrong with Five-Paragraph Form?

Perhaps the best introduction to what's wrong with five-paragraph form can be found in Greek mythology. On his way to Athens, the hero Theseus encounters a particularly surly host, Procrustes, who offers wayfarers a bed for the night but with a catch. If they do not fit his bed exactly, he either stretches them or lops off their extremities until they do. This story has given us the word "procrustean," which the dictionary defines as "tending to produce conformity by violent or arbitrary means."

Five-paragraph form is a procrustean formula that most students learn in high school. While it has the advantage of providing a mechanical format that will give virtually any subject the appearance of order, it usually lops off a writer's ideas before they have the chance to form or stretches a single idea to the breaking point. In other words, this simplistic scheme blocks writers' abilities to think deeply or logically, restricting rather than encouraging the development of complex ideas.

A complex idea is one that has many sides. To treat such ideas intelligently, writers need a form that will not require them to cut off all of those sides except the one that most easily fits the bed. Most of you will find the basic five-paragraph form familiar:

1. An introduction that announces the writer's main idea, about which he or she will make three points
2. Three paragraphs, each on one of the three points
3. A conclusion beginning "Thus, we see" or "In conclusion" that essentially repeats the introduction

Here is an example in outline form:

Introduction: The food in the school cafeteria is bad. It lacks variety, it's unhealthy, and it is always overcooked. In this essay I will discuss these three characteristics.

Paragraph 2: The first reason cafeteria food is bad is that there is no variety. (Plus one or two examples—no salad bar, mostly fried food, and so forth)

Paragraph 3: Another reason cafeteria food is bad is that it is not healthy. (Plus a few reasons—high cholesterol, too many hot dogs, too much sugar, and so forth)

Paragraph 4: In addition, the food is always overcooked. (Plus some examples— the vegetables are mushy, the "mystery" meat is tough to recognize, and so forth)

Conclusion: Thus, we see . . . (Plus a restatement of the introductory paragraph)

Most high school students write dozens of themes using this basic formula. They are taught to use five-paragraph form because it seems to provide the greatest good—a certain minimal clarity—for the greatest number of students. But the form does not promote logically tight and intellectually aggressive writing. It is a meat grinder that can turn any content into sausage. The two major problems it typically creates are easy to see.

1. The introduction reduces the remainder of the essay to *redundancy*. The first paragraph tells readers, in an overly general and listlike way, what they're going to hear; the succeeding three paragraphs tell the readers the same thing again in more detail and carry the overly general main idea along inertly; and the conclusion repeats what the readers have just been told (twice). The first cause of all this redundancy lies with the thesis. As in the example above, the thesis (cafeteria food is bad) is too broad—an unqualified and obvious generalization—and substitutes a simple list of predictable points for a complex statement of idea.

2. The form arbitrarily divides content: why are there three points (or examples or reasons) instead of five or one? A quick look at the three categories in our example reveals how arbitrarily the form has divided the subject. Isn't overcooked food unhealthy? Isn't a lack of variety also conceivably unhealthy? The format invites writers to list rather than analyze, to plug supporting examples into categories without examining the examples or how they are related. Five-paragraph form, as is evident in our sample's transitions ("first," "another reason," and "in addition"), counts things off but doesn't make logical connections. At its worst, the form prompts the writer to simply append evidence to generalizations without saying anything about it.

The subject, on the other hand, is not as unpromising as the format makes it appear. It could easily be redirected along a more productive pathway. (If the food is bad, what are the underlying causes of the problem? Are students getting what they ask for? Is the problem one of cost? Is the faculty cafeteria better? Why or why not?)

Now, let's look briefly at the introductory paragraph from a student's essay on a more academic subject. Here we can see a remarkable feature of five-paragraph form—its capacity to produce the same kind of say-nothing prose on almost any subject.

> Throughout the film *The Tempest*, a version of Shakespeare's play *The Tempest*, there were a total of nine characters. These characters were Calibano, Alonso, Antonio, Aretha, Freddy, the doctor, and Dolores. Each character in the film represented a person in Shakespeare's play, but there were four people who were greatly similar to those in Shakespeare, and who played a role in symbolizing aspects of forgiveness, love, and power.

The final sentence of the paragraph reveals the writer's addiction to five-paragraph form. It signals that the writer will proceed in a purely mechanical and superficial way, producing a paragraph on forgiveness, a paragraph on love, a paragraph on power, and a conclusion stating again that the film's characters resemble Shakespeare's in these three aspects. The writer is so busy *demonstrating* that the characters are concerned with forgiveness, love, and power that she misses the opportunity to analyze the significance of her own observations. Instead, readers are drawn wearily to a conclusion; they get no place except back where they began. Further, the demonstration mode prevents her from analyzing connections among the categories. The writer might consider, for example, how the play and the film differ in resolving the conflict between power and forgiveness (focusing on difference within similarity) and to what extent the film and the play agree about which is the most important of the three aspects (focusing on similarity despite difference).

These more analytical approaches lie concealed in the writer's introduction, but they never get discovered because the five-paragraph form militates against sustained analytical thinking. Its division of the subject into parts, which is only one part of analysis, has become an end unto itself. The procrustean formula insists upon a tripartite list in which each of the three parts is separate, equal, and, above all, *inert*.

Here are two *quick checks* for whether a paper of yours has closed down your thinking through a scheme such as five-paragraph form:

1. *Look at the paragraph openings.* If these read like a list, each beginning with an additive transition like "another" followed by a more or less exact repetition of your central point ("Another example is . . . " or "Yet another example is . . ."), you should suspect that you are not adequately developing your ideas.
2. *Compare the wording in the last statement of the paper's thesis (in the conclusion) with the first statement of it in the introduction.* If the wording at these two locations is virtually the same, you will know that your thesis has not responded adequately to your evidence.

An Alternative to Five-Paragraph Form: The All-Purpose Organizational Scheme

Five-paragraph form sacrifices thinking for organization—a losing bargain—but organization does matter. The various analytical techniques and prompts that we offer in its place, from "interesting" and "strange" to looking for difference within similarity, will encourage thinking, but how do you go about organizing that thinking? We address many aspects of organization in Part III of the book, "Matters of Form"; but for now, let's leap ahead to a template that you can adapt to many kinds of analytical writing. It is constructed upon several premises that we have already mentioned in Part I:

- An analytical writer approaches evidence to refine and sharpen his or her thesis, not just to support it,
- A productive thesis changes (evolves) as it encounters evidence, and
- The paper itself should reenact in more polished form for the reader the chains of thought that led the writer to his or her conclusions (the editorial, "Playing by the Antioch Rules" on page 67 in Chapter 4 being a case in point).

Some of the steps below will become clearer by the end of the chapter, and there will be further discussion of organization in succeeding chapters. In any case, here is the template:

1. Write an introduction.

Begin analytical papers by defining some issue, question, problem, or phenomenon that the paper will address. An introduction is not a conclusion. It lays out something you have noticed that you think needs to be better understood. Use the introduction to get your readers to see why they should be more curious about the thing you have noticed. Aim for half a page.

2. State a working thesis.

Early in the paper, often at the end of the first paragraph or the beginning of the second (depending on the conventions of the discipline you are writing in), make a tentative claim about whatever it is you have laid out as being in need of exploration. The initial version of your thesis, known as *the working thesis,* should offer a tentative explanation, answer, or solution that the body of your paper will go on to apply and develop (clarify, extend, substantiate, qualify, and so on).

3. Begin querying your thesis.

Start developing your working thesis and other opening observations with the question "So what?" This question is shorthand for questions like "What does this observation mean?" and "Where does this thesis get me in my attempts to explain my subject?"

4. Muster supporting evidence for your working thesis.

Test its adequacy by seeing how much of the available evidence it can honestly account for. That is, try to prove that your thesis is correct, but also expect to come across evidence that does not fit your initial formulation of the thesis.

5. Seek complicating evidence.

Find evidence that does not readily support your thesis. Then explore—and explain—how and why it doesn't fit.

6. Reformulate your thesis.

Use the complicating evidence to produce new wording in your working thesis (additions, qualification, and so forth). This is how a thesis evolves, by assimilating obstacles and refining terms.

7. Repeat steps 3 to 6.

Query, support, complicate, and reformulate your thesis until you are satisfied with its accuracy.

8. State a conclusion.

Reflect on and reformulate your paper's opening position in light of the thinking your analysis of evidence has caused you to do. Culminate rather than merely restate your paper's main idea in the concluding paragraph. Do this by getting your conclusion to again answer the question "So what?" In the conclusion, this question is shorthand for "Where does it get us to view the subject in this way?" or "What are the possible implications or consequences of the position the paper has arrived at?" Usually the reformulated (evolved) thesis comes near the beginning of the concluding paragraph. The remainder of the paragraph gradually moves the reader out of your piece, preferably feeling good about what you have accomplished for him or her.

As should be apparent, following the template will require you to shift your approach not only to a thesis (abandoning the notion of a fixed and static one) but also to evidence. Let's turn now to consider more carefully the nature and function of evidence.

B. LINKING EVIDENCE AND CLAIMS

Evidence matters because it always involves authority: the power of evidence is, well, *evident* in the laboratory, the courtroom, the classroom, and just about everywhere else. Your SAT scores are evidence, and they may have worked for or against you. If they worked against you—if you believe yourself smarter than the numbers on this standardized test indicate—then you probably offered alternative evidence, such as class rank or extracurricular achievements when you applied to college. As this example illustrates, there are many kinds of evidence; and whether or not something qualifies as acceptable evidence, as well as what it may show or prove, is often debatable. Are high school grades a more reliable predictor of success in college than a score of six hundred on the verbal portion of the SAT? What exactly is an SAT score evidence of?

The types and amounts of evidence necessary for persuading readers and building authority also vary from one discipline to another, as does the manner in which the evidence is presented. While some disciplines—the natural sciences, for example—will require you to present your evidence first and then interpret it, others (the humanities and some social sciences) will expect you to interpret your evidence as it is presented. But in all disciplines—and virtually any writing situation—it is important to support claims with evidence, to make your evidence lead to claims, and especially to be explicit about *how you've arrived at the connection between your evidence and your claims* (see Figure 5.2).

The first step in learning to explain the connection between your evidence and your claims is to remember that *evidence rarely, if ever, can be left to speak for itself.* When you leave evidence to speak for itself, you are assuming that it can be interpreted in only one way and that others will necessarily think as you do.

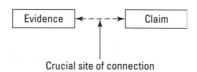

Crucial site of connection

FIGURE 5.2
Linking Evidence and Claims

Writers who think that evidence speaks for itself generally do very little with it. Sometimes they will present it without making any overt claims, stating, for example, "There was no alcohol at the party" and expecting the reader to understand this statement as a sign of approval or disapproval. Alternatively, they may simply place the evidence next to a claim. Such writers will say, for example, "The party was terrible: there was no alcohol" or "The party was great: there was no alcohol." Merely juxtaposing the evidence to the claim (just putting them next to each other) leaves out the *thinking* that connects them and thereby implies that the logic of the connection is obvious. But even for readers prone to agree with you, just pointing to the evidence, assuming it will speak for itself, is not enough.

Of course, before you can attend to the relationship between evidence and claims, you first have to make sure to include both of them. The two most fundamental problems that writers must surmount, then, are unsubstantiated claims and pointless evidence. Let's pause to take a look at how to remedy these problems.

Unsubstantiated Claims

Problem: Making claims that lack supporting evidence.
Solution: Learn to recognize and support unsubstantiated assertions.

Unsubstantiated claims occur when you concentrate only on conclusions, omitting the evidence that led to them. At the opposite extreme, pointless evidence results when you offer a mass of detail attached to an overly general claim. To solve both of these problems, remember two rules. Whenever you make a claim, make sure that you (1) offer your readers the evidence that led you to it and (2) explain how the evidence led you to that conclusion. The word "unsubstantiated" means "without substance." An unsubstantiated claim is not necessarily false; it just offers none of the concrete "stuff" upon which the claim is based. When you make an unsubstantiated claim you assume that readers will believe you just because you say this or that.

Perhaps more important, unsubstantiated claims deprive you of details. Without details, you're left with nothing concrete to think about. If you lack some actual "stuff" to analyze, you can easily get stuck in a set of abstractions, which tend to overstate your position, inhibit your thinking, and leave your readers wondering exactly what you mean. The further away your language gets from the concrete, from references to physical detail—things that you can see, hear, count, taste, smell, and touch—the more abstract it becomes. An aircraft carrier anchored outside a foreign harbor is concrete; the phrase "intervening in the name of democracy" is abstract.

You can see the problem of unsubstantiated assertions not only in papers but also in everyday conversation. It occurs when people get in the habit of leaping to conclusions—forming impressions so quickly and automatically that they have difficulty even recalling what it was that triggered a particular response. Ask such people why they thought a party was boring or a new acquaintance pretentious, and they will rephrase the generalization rather than offer the evidence that led to it: the party was boring because nobody did anything; the person is pretentious because he puts on airs.

Rephrasing your generalizations rather than offering evidence tends to starve your thinking; it also has the effect of shutting out readers. If, for example, you defend your judgment that a person is pretentious by saying that he puts on airs, you have ruled on the matter and dismissed it. (You have also committed a logical flaw known as a *circular argument,* because "pretentious" and "putting on airs" mean virtually the same thing and using one in support of the other is arguing in a circle.) If, by contrast, you include the *grounds* upon which your judgment is based—the fact that he uses big words or that he always wears a bow tie—you have given readers a glimpse of your criteria. Readers are far more likely to accept your views if you give them the chance to think *with* you about the evidence. The alternative—offering groundless assertions—is to expect them to take your word for it.

There is, of course, an element of risk in providing the details that have informed your judgment. You leave yourself open to attack if, for example, your readers wear bow ties or speak in polysyllables. But this is an essential risk to take, for, otherwise, you leave your readers wondering why you think as you do or, worse, unlikely to credit your point of view. Moreover, in laying out your evidence, you will be more likely to anticipate your readers' possible disagreements. This will make you more inclined to think openly and carefully about your judgments.

In order to check your drafts for unsubstantiated assertions, you first have to know how to recognize them. One of the most fundamental skills for a writer to possess is the ability to *distinguish* evidence from claims. It is sometimes difficult to separate facts from judgments, data from interpretations of the data. Writers who aren't practiced in this skill can believe that they are offering evidence when they are really offering only unsubstantiated claims. In your own reading and writing, pause once in a while to label the sentences of a paragraph as either evidence (E) or claims (C). What happens if we try to categorize the sentences of the following paragraph in this way?

> The owners are ruining baseball in America. Although they claim that they are los-
> ing money, they are really just being greedy. A few years ago, they even fired the
> commissioner, Fay Vincent, because he took the players' side. Baseball is a sport, not
> a business, and it is a sad fact that it is being threatened by greedy businessmen.

The first and last sentences of the paragraph are claims. They draw conclusions about as yet unstated evidence that the writer will need to provide. The middle two sentences are harder to classify. If particular owners have stated publicly that they are losing money, the existence of the owners' statements is a fact. But the writer moves from evidence to claims when he suggests that the owners are lying about their financial situation and are doing so because of their greed. Both of these assertions are unsubstantiated claims. Unless the writer proceeds to ground them in evidence—relevant facts—they amount to little more than name-calling. Similarly, it is a fact that commissioner Fay Vincent was fired, but the assertion that he was fired "because he took the players' side" is another unsubstantiated claim. The writer needs to offer evidence in support of this claim, along with his reasons for believing that the evidence means what he says it does.

Without evidence and the reasoning you've done about it, your writing asks readers to accept your opinions as though they were facts. The central claim of the baseball paragraph—that greedy businessmen are ruining baseball—is an example of an opinion treated as though it were factual information. While many readers might be inclined to accept some version of the claim as true, they should not be asked to accept the writer's opinion as a self-evident truth.

The word "evident" comes from a Latin verb meaning "to see." To say that the truth of a statement is "self-evident" means that it does not need proving because its truth should be plainly seen by all. The problem is that very few ideas—no matter how much you may believe in them—readily attest to their own truth. And precisely because what people have taken to be common knowledge ("Women can't do math," for example, or "Men don't talk about their feelings") so often turns out to be wrong, you should take care to avoid unsubstantiated claims.

You need to be stingy, therefore, about treating your claims and evidence as factual. The more concrete information you gather, the less likely you will be to accept your opinions, partial information, or misinformation as fact. The writer of the baseball paragraph, for example, offers as fact that the owners claim they are losing money. If he were to search harder, however, he would find that his statement of the owners' claim is not entirely accurate. The owners have not unanimously claimed that they are losing money; they have acknowledged that the problem has to do with poorer "small-market" teams competing against richer "large-market" teams. This more complicated version of the facts might at first be discouraging to the writer, since it reveals his original thesis ("greed") to be oversimplified. But then, as we have been saying, the function of evidence is not just to corroborate your claims; it should also help you to *test* and *refine* your ideas and to *define* your key terms more precisely.

✻*Try this:* Take an excerpt from your own writing, at least two paragraphs in length—perhaps from a paper you have already written or a draft you are working on—and at the end of every sentence, label the sentence as either evidence (E) or claim (C). For sentences that appear to offer both, determine which parts of the sentence are evidence and which are claim, and then decide which one, E or C, predominates. What is the ratio of evidence to claim, especially in particularly effective or weak paragraphs? ☐

Pointless Evidence

Problem: Presenting a mass of evidence without explaining how it relates to the claims.

Solution: Make details speak. Explain how evidence confirms and qualifies the claim.

Your thinking emerges in the way that you follow through on the implications of the evidence you have selected. You need to interpret it for your readers. It is not enough to insert evidence after your claim, expecting readers to draw the same conclusion about its meaning that you have. You cannot assume that the facts can speak for themselves. You have to make the details speak, conveying to your readers why they mean what you claim they mean.

The following example illustrates what happens when a writer leaves the evidence to speak for itself.

> Baseball is a sport, not a business, and it is a sad fact that it is being threatened by greedy businessmen. For example, Eli Jacobs, the previous owner of the Baltimore Orioles, recently sold the team to Peter Angelos for one hundred million dollars more than he had spent ten years earlier when he purchased it. Also, a new generation of baseball stadiums have been built in the last decade—for the Orioles in Baltimore, for the White Sox in Chicago, for the Rangers in Arlington, for the Indians in Cleveland, and most recently, for the Giants in San Francisco, the Brewers in Milwaukee, and the Astros in Houston. These parks are enormously expensive and include elaborate scoreboards and luxury boxes. The average baseball players, meanwhile, now earn over a million dollars a year, and they all have agents to represent them. Alex Rodriguez, the shortstop for the Texas Rangers, is paid over twenty million dollars a season. Sure, he set a record for most homers in a season by a shortstop, but is any ballplayer worth that much money?

Unlike the previous example, which was virtually all claims, this paragraph, except for the opening claim and the closing question, is all evidence. The paragraph presents what we might call an "evidence sandwich": it encloses a series of facts between two claims. (The opening statement blames "greedy businessmen," presumably owners, and the closing statement appears to indict greedy, or at least overpaid, players.) Readers are left with two problems. First, the mismatch between the opening and concluding claims leaves it not altogether clear what the writer is saying that the evidence suggests. And second, he has not told readers why they should believe that the evidence means what he says it does. Instead, he leaves it to speak for itself.

If you look again at the example, you'll see that each sentence after the opening claim offers facts but does not overtly interpret those facts by connecting them to the claims. The closest connection between claims and evidence is between the fact that Alex Rodriguez earns twenty million dollars per year and the writer's implicit claim (phrased as a question) that no player is worth that much. Otherwise, the items of evidence do not bear directly on the claims made.

If readers are to accept the writer's implicit claims—that the spending is too much and that it is ruining baseball—he will have to show *how* and *why* the evidence supports these conclusions. The rule that applies here is that *evidence can almost always be interpreted in more than one way.*

You might, for instance, formulate at least three conclusions from the evidence offered in the baseball paragraph. You might decide that the writer believes baseball will be ruined by going broke or that he is saying its spirit will be ruined by becoming too commercial. Worst of all, you might disagree with his claim and conclude that baseball is not really being ruined, since the evidence could be read as signs of health rather than decay. The profitable resale of the Orioles, the expensive new ballparks (which, the writer neglects to mention, have drawn record crowds), and the skyrocketing salaries all could testify to the growing popularity rather than the decline of the sport.

How can you ensure that your readers will at least understand your interpretation of the data? Begin by constantly reminding yourself that the thought connections that have occurred to you will not automatically occur to others. This doesn't mean that you should assume your readers are stupid, but you shouldn't expect them to read your mind and to do for themselves the thinking that you should be doing for them.

You can make the details speak if you take the time to stop and look at them, asking questions about what they imply. The two steps to follow are (1) to say explicitly what you take the details to mean and (2) to state exactly how the evidence supports or qualifies your claims.

The writer of the baseball paragraph leaves some of his claims and virtually all of his reasoning about the evidence implicit. What, for example, bothers him about the special luxury seating areas? What does this piece of information imply? Attempting to uncover his assumptions, we might speculate that he intends it to demonstrate how economic interests are taking baseball away from its traditional fans because seats in the new seating areas cost far more than the average person can afford to pay. This interpretation of the evidence could be used to support the writer's governing claim, but he would need to spell out the connection, to reason back to his own premises. He might say, for example, that baseball's time-honored role as the all-American sport—democratic and grass roots—is being displaced by the tendency of baseball as a business to orient its efforts around attracting higher box office receipts and wealthier fans.

The writer could then make more explicit what his whole paragraph implies, that baseball's image as a popular pastime in which all Americans can participate is being tarnished by players and owners alike, whose primary concerns appear to be making money. In making his evidence speak, the writer would also refine his claim by being clear about which aspect of baseball he thinks is being ruined. He could clarify in his revision, for instance, that the "greedy businessmen" to whom he refers include both owners and players.

There is a final lesson to glean from this example. Notice that when you focus on tightening the links between evidence and claim, the result is almost always a "smaller" claim than the one you set out to prove. This is what evidence characteristically does to a claim: it shrinks and restricts its scope. This process, also known as *qualifying a claim* or generalization, is the means by which a thesis evolves.

Sometimes it is hard to give up on the large, general assertions that were your first response to your subject. But your sacrifices in scope are exchanged for greater accuracy and validity. The sweeping claims you lose ("Greedy businessmen are ruining baseball") give way to less resounding but also more informed, more incisive, and less judgmental ideas ("Market pressures may not bring the end of baseball, but they are certainly changing the image and nature of the game").

C. ANALYZING EVIDENCE IN DEPTH: "10 ON 1"

How do you move from making details speak and explaining how evidence confirms and qualifies the claim to actually composing a paper? One way is through the practice we call *10 on 1:* a focused analysis of a representative example. (See Figure 5.3.) Doing 10 on 1 is the opposite of doing 1 on 10—the phrase we introduced at the beginning of this chapter to describe the static demonstration paper that repeats the same point as its "answer" for ten similar examples or issues.

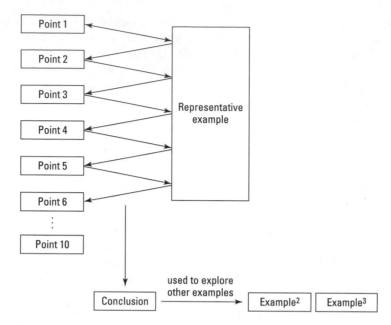

FIGURE 5.3

Doing 10 on 1. The pattern of 10 on 1 (in which "10" stands arbitrarily for any number of points) successively develops a series of points about a single representative example. Its analysis of evidence is in–depth.

Phrased as a general rule, 10 on 1 holds that *it is better to make ten observations or points about a single representative issue or example than to make the same basic point about ten related issues or examples (as in 1 on 10).* The number "10," let us hasten to add, is arbitrarily chosen. You could make four or five or seven observations and points.

We bring together in 10 on 1 the various skills that the book has been discussing thus far. It offers an efficient and productive way to look at evidence, to formulate claims about it, and, ultimately, to organize your analysis into a paper. We get to the organizational element shortly; for now the important idea we intend 10 on 1 to communicate is that you should *draw out as much meaning as possible from your best examples.* Doing 10 on 1 depends, in other words, upon *narrowing your focus and then analyzing in depth.*

Once most writers decide that all the evidence points to the same conclusion, they tend to stop really looking at the evidence. If you were to use all of your examples to repeatedly corroborate the same point, the repetition would deter you from exploring the evidence in more depth. Writing would then become not a matter of finding things out or developing an idea but simply of dropping each example into place next to an unchanging conclusion. Here is a brief example: say that you were writing an essay on the role of disease in *The X-Files.* You locate a number of examples that all point to the same conclusion: now that the Cold War is over, the threat to America's security lies within. *Rather than catalogue* all of the instances of festering innards in *The X-Files,* you would do better to *scrutinize the most revealing instance and then locate it in a pattern of other like instances.* By drawing out its implications, you would more likely discover the questions and understand the cultural issues that surround disease in *The X-Files* or exist in any subject.

In sum, you can use 10 on 1 to accomplish various ends: (1) to locate the range of possible meanings your evidence suggests, (2) to make you less inclined to cling to your first claim inflexibly and open the way for you to discover a way of representing more fully the complexity of your subject, and (3) to slow down the rush to generalization and thus help to ensure that when you arrive at a working thesis, it will be more specific and better able to account for your evidence.

But what exactly are the "1" and the "10," and how do you go about finding them? The "1" is a representative example, what you have narrowed your focus to. How do you select the "1"? One of the best ways is to use The Method to identify a strand or pattern and then to choose the example of it you find most interesting, strange, revealing, and so forth. Here, in effect, you do 1 on 10 as a preliminary step—locating ten examples that share a trait—and then focus on one of these for in-depth analysis. Proceeding in this way would guarantee that your example was representative. It is essential that your example be representative because in doing 10 on 1 you will take one part of the whole, put it under a microscope, and then generalize about the whole on the basis of your analysis. In the preceding section we used the baseball example in this way, doing 10 on 1 with the student's paragraph as a way of anchoring our generalizations about giving evidence a point. We address the issue of representativeness in more detail shortly.

As for the "10," they are comprised of both observations and interpretive leaps that you make about the "1," both what you notice about the evidence and what you make of what you notice. To get the "10"—to analyze in depth—use the various tools, prompts, and procedures that have been introduced in this book thus far:

- Look at the example and ask yourself what you notice.
- Use The Method to identify patterns of repetition and contrast.
- Locate anomalies and query them.
- Locate, name, and reformulate binaries.
- Try saying something "seems to be about X but is *also* about Y."
- Employ Paraphrase × 3 on key sentences or phrases if your evidence has a verbal component.
- Actively seek to uncover the assumptions in your example.
- As you try on different interpretations, repeatedly ask, "So what?" to develop the implications of your thinking.
- As a major claim begins to emerge (and it will), seek out conflicting evidence to enable you to qualify the claim still further.

Pan, Track, and Zoom: The Film Analogy

To understand how 10 on 1 can generate the form of a paper, let's turn to an analogy. The language of filmmaking offers a useful way for understanding the different ways that a writer can focus evidence. The writer, like the director of a film, controls the focus through different kinds of shots.

The pan—The camera pivots around a stable axis, giving the viewer the big picture. Using a pan, we see everything from a distance. Pans provide a context, some larger pattern, the "forest" within which the writer can also examine particular "trees." Pans establish the representativeness of the example the writer later examines in more detail, showing that it is not an isolated instance.

The track—The camera no longer stays in one place but follows some sequence of action. For example, whereas a pan might survey a room full of guests at a cocktail party, a track would pick up a particular guest and follow along as she walks across the room, picks up a photograph, proceeds through the door, and throws the photo in a trash can. Analogously, a writer tracks by moving in on selected pieces of the larger picture and following them in order to make telling connections among them.

The zoom—The camera moves in even closer on a selected piece of the scene, allowing us to notice more of its details. For example, a zoom might focus in on the woman's hand as she crumples the photograph she's about to throw away or on her face as she slams the lid on the trash can. A writer zooms by giving us more detail on a particular part of his or her evidence and by making the details say more. The zoom is the shot that enables you to do 10 on 1.

In a short paper (three to five pages), you might devote as much as ninety percent of your writing to illustrating what one example (the "1"—your zoom) reveals about the larger subject. Even in a paper that uses several examples, however, as much as fifty percent might still be devoted to analysis of and generalization from a single case. The remaining portion of the paper would *make connections with other examples, testing and applying the ideas you arrived at from your single case.* In-depth analysis of your best example thus creates a center from which you can move in two directions: (1) toward generalizations about the larger subject and (2) toward other examples, using your primary example as a tool of exploration.

Faced, for example, with writing a paper about the role slavery played in causing the Civil War, an inexperienced writer might offer a broad survey with a few paragraphs on abolitionism, a few paragraphs on various congressional attempts to legislate the slavery issue, and a few paragraphs on economic rivalries between the industrial North and the agrarian South. You could cover the same body of information in far more depth, however, by focusing almost entirely on the Missouri Compromise as a representative instance. Your analysis of this legislative battle would necessarily include discussion of the abolitionists' role and the economic interests of both parties, but it would do so within a tightly focused framework. Your assumption would be that if readers can see the collision of interests that led to this compromise and its failure, they will obtain a deeper understanding of the slavery issue than a survey could provide.

This same model, applicable across a wide variety of writing situations, can be reduced to a series of steps:

1. Find (using The Method) a revealing pattern or tendency in your evidence.
2. Select a representative example.
3. Provide in-depth analysis (doing 10 on 1) of your example.
4. Test your results in similar cases.

An analysis of the representation of females on television, for example, would fare better if you focused on one show—say, *Buffy, the Vampire Slayer*—narrowed the focus to teenage girls, and tested your results against other shows with teenage girl characters, such as *Felicity, The Gilmore Girls,* and *Seventh Heaven*. Similarly, a study of the national debt might focus on Social Security, analyzing it in order to arrive at generalizations to be tested and refined in the context of, say, health care or military spending. A close look at virtually anything will reveal its complexity, and you can bring that complex understanding to other examples for further testing and refining.

It is, of course, important to let your readers know that you are using the one primary example in this generalizable way. Note how the writer of the following discussion of the people's revolt in China in 1989 sets up his analysis. He first explains how his chosen example—a single photograph (shown in Figure 5.4) from the media coverage of the event—illuminates his larger subject. The image is of a Chinese man in a white shirt who temporarily halted a line of tanks on their way to quell a demonstration in Tiananmen Square in Beijing.

FIGURE 5.4
Tiananmen Square, Beijing, 1989.

The tank image provided a miniature, simplified version of a larger, more complex revolution. The conflict between man and tank embodied the same tension found in the conflict between student demonstrators and the Peoples' Army. The man in the white shirt, like the students, displayed courage, defiance, and rebellious individuality in the face of power. Initially, the peaceful revolution succeeded: the state allowed the students to protest; likewise, the tank spared the man's life. Empowered, the students' demands for democracy grew louder. Likewise, the man boldly jumped onto the tank and addressed the soldiers. The state's formerly unshakable dominance appeared weak next to the strength of the individual. However, the state asserted its power: the Peoples' Army marched into the square, and the tanks roared past the man into Beijing.

The image appeals to American ideology. The man in the white shirt personifies the strength of the American individual. His rugged courage draws on contemporary heroes such as Rambo. His defiant gestures resemble the demonstrations of Martin Luther King Jr. and his followers. American history predisposes us to identify strongly with the Chinese demonstrators: we have rebelled against the establishment, we have fought for freedom and democracy, and we have defended the rights of the individual. For example, the *New York Times* reported that President George Bush watched the tank incident on television and said, "I'm convinced that the forces of democracy are going to overcome these unfortunate events in Tiananmen Square." Bush represents the popular American perspective of the Chinese rebellion; we support the student demonstrators.

This analysis is a striking example of doing 10 on 1. In the first paragraph, the writer constructs a detailed analogy between the particular image and the larger subject of which it was a part. The analogy allows the writer not just to describe but also to interpret the event. In the second paragraph, he develops his focus on the image as an image, a photographic representation tailor-made to appeal to American viewing audiences. Rather than generalizing about why Americans might find the image appealing, he establishes a number of explicit connections (does 10 on 1) between the details of the image and typical American heroes. By drawing out the implications of particular details, he manages to say more about the significance of the American response to the demonstrations in China than a broader survey of those events would have allowed.

The rule of thumb here is to say more about less, rather than less about more, to allow a carefully analyzed part of your subject to provide perspective on the whole.

Demonstrating the Representativeness of Your Example

Problem: Generalizing on the basis of too little and unrepresentative evidence.
Solution: Survey the available evidence and argue overtly for the representativeness of the examples on which you focus.

One significant advantage of concentrating on your single best example is its economy: you can cut quickly to the heart of a subject. But with this advantage comes a danger: that the example you select will not in fact be representative. Thus, it's not enough just to select an example you think is representative. You also need to overtly demonstrate its representativeness. In other words, you must *show that your example is part of a larger pattern of similar evidence and not just an isolated instance.*

In terms of logic, the problem of generalizing from too little and unrepresentative evidence is known as an *unwarranted inductive leap.* That is, the writer leaps from one or two instances to a broad claim about an entire class or category. For example, just because you see an economics professor and a biology professor wear corduroy jackets, you should not leap to the conclusion that all professors wear corduroy jackets.

The surest way you can guard against the problem of unwarranted inductive leaps is by reviewing the range of possible examples to make certain that the ones you choose to focus on are representative. If you were writing about faith as it is portrayed in the book of Exodus, for example, you might suggest the general trend by briefly panning across instances in which the Israelites have difficulty believing in an unseen God. Then, you could concentrate (zoom in) on the best example.

Not all illogical leaps are easy to spot. Here is a brief example from a writer who makes an unwarranted inductive leap.

> Some people feel that rock music videos are purely sexist propaganda and that they stereotype women as sex objects. I feel this is a generalization and far from the truth. Many types of videos exist, a lot of which show no women in them at all. Others do contain women and could be considered sexist only if you choose to look at them from that point of view.

The writer of this paragraph next offers three examples in support of her generalization that rock videos do not stereotype women as sex objects. One video consists entirely of concert footage. In another, the lead singer hugs and kisses his mother. The third shows a female passenger in a Jaguar trying to get the attention of the male singer, who is driving—a scenario that leads the writer to assert, "If anyone is being presented as the sex object, it is he."

Clearly, this writer is trying to correct the overgeneralization that all rock videos are sexist in their depiction of women, but her argument falls prey to the same kind of overgeneralization. Her *sample is too small.* Three examples of videos that do not depict women as sex objects constitute too small a sample to dismiss the charge of sexism. Also, her *sample is too selective.* It does not confront examples that would challenge her point of view, examples that an opponent might use to prove that videos do stereotype women as sex objects. In other words, she avoids the difficult evidence, deliberately picking videos that may well be exceptions to the rule and then arguing that they are the rule.

Most of the time, unwarranted leaps result from making too large a claim and avoiding examples that might contradict it. As a rule, you should *deliberately seek out the single piece of evidence that might most effectively oppose your point of view and address it.* Doing so will prompt you to test the representativeness of your evidence and, in many cases, to qualify the claims you have made for it. The writer of the rock video example, for instance, can argue on the basis of three videos for a *more limited* version of her claim—that the representation of men and their relationship to women in rock videos is more varied and complex than the charge of sexism has allowed. In sum, if you select more complicated examples or actively search out complication in evidence that at first seems simple and obvious, then you will be less likely to use unrepresentative examples to arrive at a claim that does not respond to the full range of relevant evidence.

❋ Try this: Take a piece of evidence—a representative example—from something you are studying and do 10 on 1. The key to doing 10 on 1 successfully is to slow down the rush to conclusions so that you can allow yourself to notice more about the evidence and make the details speak. The more observations you assemble about your data *before* settling on your main idea, the better that idea is likely to be. Remember that a single paragraph from something you are reading can be enough to practice on, especially since you are working on learning to say more about less rather than less about more. Pictures and poems or the front page of a newspaper, because they present a lot of detail in a relatively small space, are good to work with if you have nothing else at hand. Or you can try doing 10 on 1 with the room you are sitting in: make ten observations about elements of the space that you have not paid much attention to before, and then see what ideas these observations suggest to you. □

10 on 1 and Disciplinary Conventions

In some cases, the conventions of a discipline would appear to discourage doing 10 on 1. The social sciences in particular tend to require a larger set of analogous examples to prove a hypothesis (tentative claim). Especially in certain kinds of research, the focus of inquiry rests on discerning broad statistical trends over a wide range of evidence. The inexperienced writer is likely to obey this disciplinary convention by providing a list of unanalyzed examples. But some trends deserve more attention than others, and some statistics similarly merit more interpretation than others. The best writers learn to choose examples carefully—each one for a reason—and to concentrate on developing the most revealing ones in depth; the interpretive and statistical models for analyzing evidence are not necessarily opposed to one another.

For instance, proving that tax laws are prejudiced in particularly subtle ways against unmarried people might require a number of analogous cases along with a statistical summary of the evidence. But even with a subject such as this, you could still concentrate on some examples more than others. Rather than moving through each example as a separate case, you could use your analyses of these primary examples as *lenses* for investigating other evidence.

A Template for Using 10 on 1

Here is a variant on the template offered earlier as an alternative to five-paragraph form. It is adapted for use with 10 on 1. Think of it not as a rigid outline but as a way of moving from one phase of your paper to the next.

1. In your introduction, start by noting (panning on) an interesting pattern or tendency you have found in your evidence. Explain what attracted you to it—why you find it potentially significant and worth looking at. This paragraph would end with a tentative theory (working thesis) about what this pattern or tendency might reveal or accomplish.

2. Zoom in on your representative example, some smaller part of the larger pattern. Argue for the example's representativeness and usefulness in coming to a better understanding of your subject.

3. Do 10 on 1—analyze your representative example—sharing with your readers your observations (what you notice) and your tentative conclusions (answers to the "So what?" question).

4. In a short paper you might at this point move to your conclusion, with its qualified, refined (evolved) version of your thesis and brief commentary on what you've accomplished—that is, the ways in which your analysis has illuminated the larger subject.

5. In a longer paper you would move from your initial zoom to another zoom on a similar case, to see the extent to which the thesis you evolved with your representative example is in need of further adjusting to better reflect the nature of your subject as a whole. This last move is the primary topic of our next chapter.

ASSIGNMENT

The technique we call 10 on 1 is the primary thinking strategy we offer in this chapter. Write a paper in which you do 10 on 1 with a single, representative example of something you are trying to think more carefully about. This could be a representative passage from a story or a representative story from a volume of stories by a single author. It could be a representative poem from a short volume of poetry or a representative passage from a nonfiction book or article. It could be a passage from a favorite columnist or a single representative song from a CD. It could be a single scene or moment or character from a film or play or other performance. It could be one picture or work of art that is representative of a larger exhibit.

Brainstorm your "1" on the page, making observations and asking "So what?" Draw out as much meaning as possible from your representative example. Go for depth. And then use this example as a lens for viewing similar examples. See the template in the previous section.

CHAPTER

6

The Evolving Thesis

You now know what a thesis is—a claim about the meaning of some feature or features of your subject—but what does a thesis *do?* What is its function? Its function is to focus inquiry, providing a principle of selection that makes some evidence more relevant than other evidence. It also works to guide development of your ideas, leading you to greater precision and accuracy about what things mean. The static thesis, as we demonstrate in the previous chapter, provides organization but sacrifices thinking. By contrast, the evolving thesis both prompts and organizes your thinking.

The first step in composing a productive working thesis is to recognize that one will not appear to you, ready-made, in the material you are analyzing. In other words, a restatement of some idea that is already clearly stated in your subject is not itself a thesis (though summarizing analytically may help you to find a thesis). The process of finding a thesis—an idea about the facts and ideas in your subject—begins only when you start to ask questions about the material, deliberately looking for places where there is something to be curious about—something, in short, that seems to you to require analysis.

The second step in composing a productive working thesis is to recognize that a working thesis will only be relatively adequate. It won't explain all of the relevant evidence equally well. More often than not, when inexperienced writers face a situation in which evidence seems to be unclear or contradictory, they tend to make one of two unproductive moves: they either ignore the conflicting evidence, or they abandon the problem altogether and look for something more clear-cut to write about.

In fact, you should *expect* to find evidence that will complicate your thesis. *Complicating evidence is something for which your thesis does not account.* When you don't seek to complicate—to find exceptions to and questions about—your claims, you inevitably oversimplify. As we note in Chapter 3, meanings are multiple, which is to say that most things, even the simplest everyday objects and gestures, mean different things at the same time, depending on context.

If you are doing 10 on 1 and using The Method (see Chapters 5 and 2, respectively) in a genuinely exploratory fashion, rest assured that you will find things for which your thesis does not account. Often these emerge when you look for what we have called difference within similarity. The examples in the strands you detect won't be *exactly* alike, and the very act of deciding that your "1" is a representative case will have made you aware of subtle differences among the examples from which you have chosen the typical one. So, too, the organizing contrasts you find will point to conflicts, to issues that are at stake within your subject. These are all sources of complication. Alternatively, the complicating evidence may at first have seemed not to fit within the scope of your thesis, or it may actually lie outside your scope—in either case, it is evidence that will help you to specify more accurately the limits of your thesis.

Faced with evidence that complicates your thesis, the one thing *not* to do is run away. The "problem" you have discovered offers a chance to modify your thesis rather than abandon it. *The complications you encounter are an opportunity to make your thesis evolve.* Formulating a claim, seeking out conflicting evidence, and then using these conflicts to revise the claim are primary movements of mind in analytical writing. The savvy writer will take advantage of opportunities to make complications overt in order to make his or her claim respond more fully to the evidence. This is how a thesis evolves.

A. MAKING THE THESIS EVOLVE

Let's begin with an example of how to make a thesis evolve. Say that you're looking for a trend (strand) in contemporary films you've seen and, as a working thesis, you claim that "women are more sensitive than men." If you were to seek out data that would complicate this overstated claim, you would soon encounter evidence that would press you to make some distinctions that the initial formulation of this claim leaves obscure. You would need, for example, to clarify what you mean by "sensitive" and how you were assessing its presence and absence. Evidence might also lead you to consider whether men, although not demonstrative about certain kinds of tender feelings, nonetheless show them in ways different from the ways women do. And surely you would want to think about how the films represent women's sensitivity. Are women punished for it in the plots? Are they rewarded with being liked (approved of) by the films, even if this trait does cause them problems?

Such considerations as these would require significant reformulation of the working thesis. By the end of the paper, the claim that "women are more sensitive than men" should have evolved into a more carefully defined and qualified statement that reflects the thinking you have done in your analysis of evidence. This, by and large, is what good concluding paragraphs do; they reflect back on and reformulate your paper's initial position in light of the thinking you have done about it (see Figure 6.1).

But, you might ask, isn't this reformulating of the thesis something a writer does before he or she writes the essay? Certainly some of it is accomplished in your prewriting—the exploratory drafting and note taking you do before you begin to compose the first draft of the essay. But your finished paper will necessarily be more than a list of conclusions. To an extent, all good writing recreates the chains of thought that leads writers to their conclusions. Your revision process will have weeded out various false starts and dead ends that you may have wandered into on the way to your finished

FIGURE 6.1

The Evolving Thesis. A strong thesis evolves as it confronts and assimilates evidence; the evolved thesis may expand or restrict the original claim. The process may need to be repeated a number of times.

ideas, but the main routes of your movement from a tentative idea to a refined and substantiated theory should remain visible for readers to follow. (See "Locating the Evolving Thesis in the Final Draft" later in this chapter for a more extensive discussion of how much thesis evolution to include in your final draft.)

❦*Try this:* Using as a model of inquiry the treatment of the example thesis "Women are more sensitive than men," seek out complications in one of the overstated claims in the following list. These complications might include conflicting evidence (which you should specify) and questions about the meaning or appropriateness of key terms (again, which you should exemplify). Illustrate a few of these complications, and then reformulate the claim in language that is more carefully qualified and accurate.

Welfare encourages recipients not to work.

Religious people are more moral than those who are not religious.

School gets in the way of education.

Herbal remedies are better than pharmaceutical ones.

The book is always better than the film. □

The Reciprocal Relationship Between Thesis and Evidence: The Thesis As a Camera Lens

What we have said so far about the thesis does not mean that all repetition is bad or that a writer's concluding paragraph should have no reference to the way the paper began. One function of the thesis is to provide the connective tissue, so to speak, that holds together a paper's three main parts—its beginning, middle, and end. Periodic reminders of your paper's thesis, its unifying idea, are essential for keeping both you and your readers on track.

But, as we also argue, developing an idea requires more than repetition. It is in light of this fact that the analogy of a thesis to connective tissue proves inadequate. A better way of envisioning how a thesis operates is to think of it as a camera lens. This analogy more accurately describes the relationship between the thesis and the subject it seeks to explain: while the lens affects how we see the subject (what evidence we select and what questions we ask about that evidence), the subject we are looking at also affects how we adjust the lens.

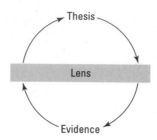

FIGURE 6.2

The Reciprocal Relationship Between Thesis and Evidence. Like a lens, the thesis affects the way a writer sees evidence. Evidence should also require the writer to readjust the lens.

Here is the principle that the camera-lens analogy allows us to see: the relationship between thesis and subject is *reciprocal* (see Figure 6.2). In good analytical writing, especially in the early, investigatory stages of writing and thinking, *the thesis not only directs the writer's way of looking at evidence; the analysis of evidence should also direct and redirect (bring about revision of) the thesis.* Even in a final draft, writers are usually fine-tuning their governing idea in response to their analysis of evidence.

The enemy of good analytical writing is the fuzzy lens—an imprecisely worded thesis statement. Very broad thesis statements, those that are made up of imprecise (fuzzy) terms, make bad camera lenses. They blur everything together and muddy important distinctions. If your lens is insufficiently sharp, you are not likely to see much in your evidence. If you say, for example, that the economic situation today is bad, you will at least have some sense of direction, but the imprecise terms "bad" and "economic situation" don't provide you with a focus clear enough to distinguish significant detail in your evidence. Without significant detail to analyze, you can't develop your thesis, either by showing readers what the thesis is good for (what it allows us to understand and explain) or by clarifying its terms.

A writer's thesis is usually fuzzier in a paper's opening than it is in the conclusion. As we argue in our critique of five-paragraph form, a paper ending with a claim worded almost exactly as it is in the beginning has not made its thesis adequately responsive to evidence. The body of the paper should not only substantiate the thesis by demonstrating its value in selecting and explaining evidence, but also bring the opening version of the thesis into better focus.

Procedure for Making the Thesis Evolve Through Successive Complications

This section of the chapter presents an extended example that illustrates how the initial formulation of a thesis might evolve—through a series of complications—over the course of a draft.

The procedure for evolving a thesis can be described in the following steps:

1. Formulate an idea about your subject.

This *working thesis* should be some claim about the meaning of your evidence that is good enough to get you started.

2. See how far you can make this thesis go in accounting for evidence.

Use the thesis to explain as much of your evidence as it reasonably can. Try it on. This initial application of thesis to evidence will already begin the process of pressing you to develop your thesis—to ponder the accuracy of key terms, and so forth.

3. Locate evidence that is not adequately accounted for by the thesis.

You will need to look actively for such evidence because the initial version of the thesis will incline you to see only what fits and not to notice the evidence that doesn't fit.

4. Ask "So what?" about the apparent mismatch between the thesis and selected evidence.

Explain how and why some pieces of evidence do not fit the thesis.

5. Reshape your claim to accommodate the evidence that hasn't fit.

This will mean rethinking (and rewording) your thesis to resolve or explain apparent contradictions or the way your thesis first led you to see the evidence. Perhaps you will discover that what seemed to be contradictory in the evidence actually isn't. If the contradiction cannot be resolved, it will put pressure on you to evolve your claim.

6. Repeat steps 2, 3, 4, and 5 several times.

Repeat these steps until you are satisfied that the thesis statement accounts for your evidence as fully and accurately as possible. This is to say that the procedure for making a thesis evolve is *recursive:* it requires you to go over the same ground repeatedly, formulating successive versions of the thesis that are increasingly accurate in wording and idea.

As an overarching guideline, acknowledge the questions that each new formulation of the thesis prompts you to ask. Keep asking "So what?" relentlessly of each new formulation. Remember that the thesis develops through successive complications. Allowing your thesis to run up against potentially conflicting evidence ("But what about this?") enables you to build upon your initial idea, extending the range of evidence it can accurately account for by clarifying and qualifying its key terms.

Let's consider the stages you might go through within a more finished draft to evolve a thesis about a film. In *Educating Rita,* a working-class English hairdresser (Rita) wants to change her life by taking courses from a professor (Frank) at the local university, even though this move threatens her relationship with her husband (Denny), who burns her books and puts pressure on her to quit school and get pregnant. Frank, she discovers, has his own problems: he's a divorced alcoholic who is bored with his life, bored with his privileged and complacent students, and bent on self-destruction. The film follows the growth of Frank and Rita's friendship and the changes it brings about in their lives. By the end of the film, each has left a limiting way of life behind and has set off in a seemingly more promising direction. She leaves her constricting marriage, passes her university examinations with honors, and begins to view her life in terms of choices; he stops drinking and sets off, determined but sad, to make a new start as a teacher in Australia.

Formulate an idea about your subject (step 1)

Working thesis: *Educating Rita* celebrates the liberating potential of education.

The film's relatively happy ending and the presence of the word "educating" in the film's title make this thesis a reasonable opening claim.

See how far you can make this thesis go in accounting for evidence (step 2)   The working thesis seems compatible, for example, with Rita's achievement of greater self-awareness and independence. You would go on to locate more data like this that would support the idea that education is potentially liberating. She becomes more articulate, allowing her to free herself from otherwise disabling situations. She starts to think about other kinds of work she might do, rather than assuming that she must continue in the one job she has always done. She travels, first elsewhere in England and then to the Continent. So, the thesis checks out as viable: there is enough of a match with evidence to make it worth pursuing.

Locate evidence that is not adequately accounted for by the thesis and ask "So what?" about the apparent mismatch between the thesis and selected evidence (steps 3 and 4)   Other evidence troubles the adequacy of the working thesis, however: Rita's education causes her to become alienated from her husband, her parents, and her social class; at the end of the film she is alone and unsure about her direction in life. In Frank's case, the thesis runs into even more problems. His boredom, drinking, and alienation seem to have been caused, at least in part, by his education rather than by his lack of it. He sees his book-lined study as a prison. Moreover, his profound knowledge of literature has not helped him to control his life: he comes to class drunk, fails to notice or care that his girlfriend is having an affair with one of his colleagues, and asks his classes whether it is worth gaining all of literature if it means losing one's soul.

Reshape your claim to accommodate the evidence that hasn't fit (step 5)

Question: What are you to do? You cannot convincingly argue that the film celebrates the liberating potential of education, since that thesis ignores such a significant amount of the evidence. Nor can you "switch sides" and argue that the film attacks education as life-denying and disabling, because this thesis is also only partially true.

What not to do. Faced with evidence that complicates your thesis, you should not assume that it is worthless and that you need to start over from scratch. View the "problem" you have discovered as an opportunity to modify your thesis rather than abandon it. After all, the thesis still fits a lot of significant evidence. Rita is arguably better off at the end of the film than at the beginning: we are not left to believe that she should have remained resistant to education, like her husband Denny, whose world doesn't extend much beyond the corner pub.

What to do. Make apparent complications—the film's seemingly contradictory attitudes about education—explicit, and then modify the wording of your thesis in a way that might resolve or explain these contradictions. You might, for example, be able to resolve an apparent contradiction between your initial thesis (the film celebrates the liberating potential of education) and the evidence by proposing that there is more than one version of education depicted in the film. You would, in short, start qualifying and clarifying the meaning of key terms in your thesis.

In this case, you could divide education as represented by the film into two kinds, enabling and stultifying. Then, the next step in the development of your thesis would be to elaborate on how the film seeks to distinguish true and enabling forms of education from false and debilitating ones (as represented by the self-satisfied and status-conscious behavior of the supposedly educated people at Frank's university).

> **Revised thesis:** *Educating Rita* celebrates the liberating potential of enabling—in contrast to stultifying—education.

Repeat steps 2, 3, 4, and 4 (step 6)   Having refined your thesis in this way, you would then repeat the step of seeing what the new wording allows you to account for in your evidence. The revised thesis might, for example, explain Frank's problems as being less a product of his education than of the cynical and pretentious versions of education that surround him in his university life. You could posit further that, with Rita as inspiration, Frank rediscovers at least some of his idealism about education.

What about Frank's emigration to Australia? If we can take Australia to stand for a newer world, one where education would be less likely to become the stale and exclusive property of a self-satisfied elite, then the refined version of the thesis would seem to be working well. In fact, given the possible thematic connection between Rita's working-class identity and Australia (associated, as a former frontier and English penal colony, with lower-class vitality as opposed to the complacency bred of class privilege), the thesis about the film's celebration of the contrast between enabling and stultifying forms of education could be sharpened further. You might propose, for example, that the film presents institutional education as desperately in need of frequent doses of "real life" (as represented by Rita and Australia)—infusions of working-class pragmatism, energy, and optimism—if it is to remain healthy and open, as opposed to becoming the oppressive property of a privileged social class. This is to say that the film arguably exploits stereotypical assumptions about social class.

> **Revised thesis:** *Educating Rita* celebrates the liberating potential of enabling education, defined as that which remains open to healthy doses of working-class, real-world infusions.

Similarly, you can make your supporting ideas (those on which your thesis depends) more accurate and less susceptible to oversimplification, by seeking evidence that might challenge their key terms. *Sharpening the language of your supporting assertions will help you develop your thesis.*

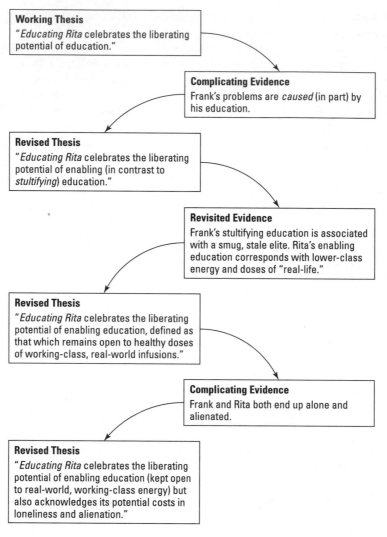

Working Thesis
"*Educating Rita* celebrates the liberating potential of education."

Complicating Evidence
Frank's problems are *caused* (in part) by his education.

Revised Thesis
"*Educating Rita* celebrates the liberating potential of enabling (in contrast to *stultifying*) education."

Revisited Evidence
Frank's stultifying education is associated with a smug, stale elite. Rita's enabling education corresponds with lower-class energy and doses of "real-life."

Revised Thesis
"*Educating Rita* celebrates the liberating potential of enabling education, defined as that which remains open to healthy doses of working-class, real-world infusions."

Complicating Evidence
Frank and Rita both end up alone and alienated.

Revised Thesis
"*Educating Rita* celebrates the liberating potential of enabling education (kept open to real-world, working-class energy) but also acknowledges its potential costs in loneliness and alienation."

FIGURE 6.3
Successive Revisions of a Thesis. An initial thesis about *Educating Rita* evolves through successive complications as it reexamines evidence in the film.

Consider, for example, the wording of the supporting idea that *Educating Rita* has a happy ending. Some qualification of this idea through consideration of possibly conflicting evidence could produce an adjustment in the first part of the working thesis, that the film celebrates education and presents it as liberating. At the end of the film, Frank and Rita walk off in opposite directions down long, empty airport corridors. Though promising to remain friends, the two do not become a couple. This closing emphasis on Frank's and Rita's alienation from their respective cultures, and the film's apparent insistence on the necessity of each going on alone, significantly qualifies the happiness of the "happy ending."

Once you have complicated your interpretation of the ending, you will again need to modify your thesis in accord with your new observations. Does the film simply celebrate education if it also presents it as being, to some degree, incompatible with conventional forms of happiness? By emphasizing the necessity of having Frank and Rita each go on alone, the film may be suggesting that in order to be truly liberating, education—as opposed to its less honest and more comfortable substitutes—inevitably produces and even requires a certain amount of loneliness and alienation. Shown in Figure 6.3 are the successive revisions of the thesis.

> **Final version of thesis:** *Educating Rita* celebrates the liberating potential of enabling education (kept open to real-world, working-class energy) but also acknowledges its potential costs in loneliness and alienation.

❧ *Try this:* Using a highlighter, find and track the evolutions of the thesis in a piece of reading, perhaps one for a course and preferably an essay or article rather than an excerpt from a textbook. This exercise will improve your handling of a thesis in your own writing by training you to become more aware of how the thesis operates in material you read. □

B. LOCATING THE EVOLVING THESIS IN THE FINAL DRAFT

An evolving thesis not only stimulates analytical thinking but provides a form. Having achieved a final version of a thesis, such as the one above, *what next?* How and where do you locate the fully evolved thesis in the final draft? Why, for example, wouldn't a writer just offer this last statement of the thesis in his or her first paragraph and then prove it?

One answer to this last question has to do with the reader. The position articulated in the fully evolved thesis is in most cases too complex and too dependent on the various considerations that preceded it to be stated intelligibly and concisely in the introduction. By the time you get to drafting the final, or close-to-final, version of the essay, you will be writing with a reasonably secure sense of how you will conclude, but even then it is not always possible or desirable to try to encapsulate in a paper's first couple of sentences what it will actually take the whole paper to explain.

Another answer has to do with the writer: writing is a matter not just of communicating with and persuading readers but of communicating with and persuading yourself. The evolution of a thesis involves the discovery of new ways of thinking brought about by successive confrontations with evidence. *The history of your various changes in thinking is what the evolving thesis records (and in some cases, it's the essay itself).*

A full answer to the questions of where to locate the fully evolved thesis in a final draft and how much of its evolution to include involves two separate but related issues: (1) the location of the thesis statement in relation to the conventional shapes of argument—induction and deduction—and (2) the customary location of the thesis according to the protocols (ways of proceeding) of different disciplines.

The Evolving Thesis and Common Thought Patterns: Deduction and Induction

Put simply, in a deductive paper a fairly full-fledged version of the thesis appears at the beginning; in an inductive paper, it appears at the end (see Figure 6.4).

The standard definition of "deduction" is "a process based on inference from accepted principles" or "the process of drawing a conclusion from something known or assumed." A deductive argument draws out the implications—infers the consequences—of a position you already agree to. As a thought process, deduction reasons from the general to the particular.

For example, a deductive paper might state in its first paragraph that attitudes toward and rules governing sexuality in a given culture can be seen, at least in part, to have economic causes. The paper might then apply this principle, already assumed to be true, to the codes governing sexual behavior in several cultures or several kinds of sexual behavior in a single culture. The writer's aim would be to use the general principle as a means of explaining selected features of particular cases. (She or he would, it should be added, thereby articulate what is implicit in the general principle as well.)

A deductive paper will thus state at or near its beginning the general principle governing its examination of evidence. *It is important to note that the general principle stated at the beginning of the paper and the idea stated as the paper's conclusion are usually not the same.* Rather, the conclusion presents the idea that the writer has arrived at through the application of the principle.

An inductively organized paper typically begins not with a principle already assumed to be true but with particular data for which it seeks to generate some explanatory principle. While deduction moves by applying a generalization to particular cases in point, induction moves from the observation of individual cases to the formation of a general principle.

Ideally, the principle arrived at through inductive reasoning is not deemed a workable theory until the writer has examined all possible instances (every left-handed person, for example, if he or she wishes to theorize that left-handed people are better at spatial thinking than right-handers). But since this comprehensiveness is usually impossible, the thesis of an inductive paper (the principle or theory arrived at through the examination of particulars) is generally deemed acceptable if a writer can demonstrate that the theory is based on a reasonably sized sampling of representative instances. This matter of a writer's establishing the representativeness of his or her examples is taken up in detail in the previous chapter. For present purposes, suffice it to say that a child who arrives at the thesis that all orange food tastes bad on the basis of squash and carrots has not based that theory on an adequate sampling of available evidence.

We argue in this chapter that a thesis—the governing idea of an analysis—evolves through successive confrontations with evidence. *This evolution occurs whether the paper is primarily deductive or inductive.* Because the full version of the thesis statement doesn't emerge until the end in our "Procedure for Making the Thesis Evolve," it might appear that the six steps will only work if you are thinking inductively. But in fact, as the *Educating Rita* example illustrates, in most cases induction and deduction operate in tandem.

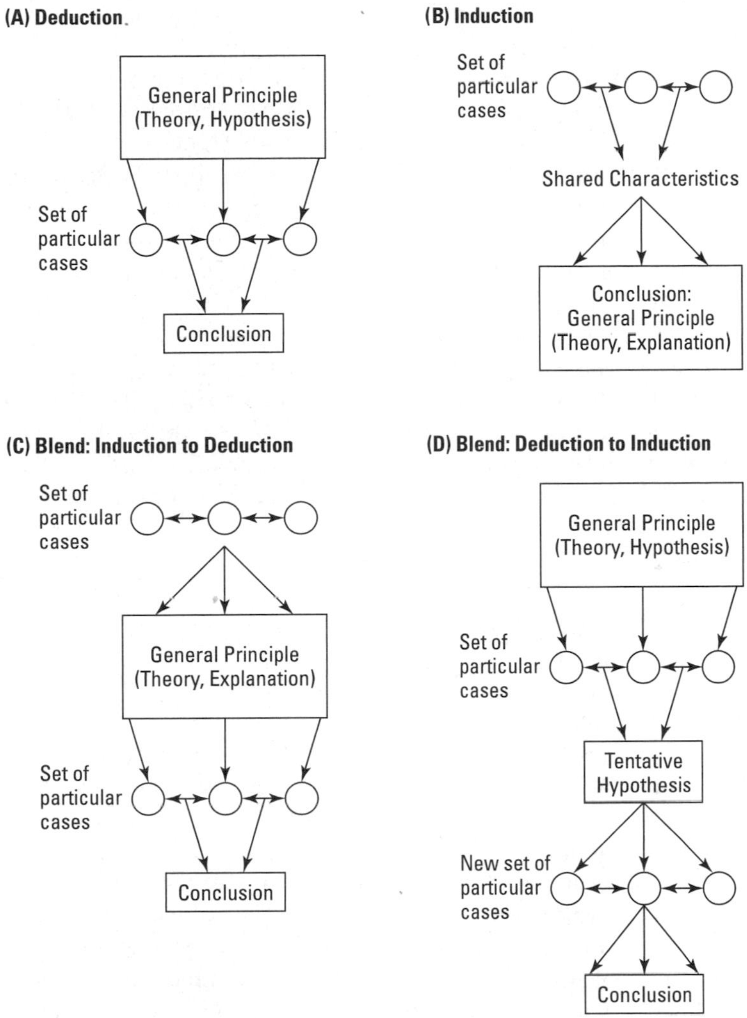

(A) Deduction

(B) Induction

(C) Blend: Induction to Deduction

(D) Blend: Deduction to Induction

FIGURE 6.4
Deduction and Induction. Deduction (A) uses particular cases to exemplify general principles and analyze their implications. Induction (B) constructs general principles from the analysis of particular cases. In practice, analytical thinking and writing blend deduction and induction and start either with particular cases (C) or a general principle (D).

It's true that in some disciplines (philosophy, for example) something close to an entirely deductive pattern of argument prevails. But writers using this thought pattern still, for the most part, repeatedly rearticulate and develop their deductive claims through a series of smaller, essentially inductive moves. In other words, the examination of particular cases that constitute a writer's evidence will be both deductive and inductive—clearly reflective of the general principle but also leading to new formula-tions that will in various ways modify the general principle.

There is some danger, then, in conceiving of deduction and induction as essen-tially separate and alternative ways of proceeding. Whether the overall shape of the argument—its mode of progression—is primarily inductive or deductive, it will still *gain in complexity* from beginning to end. The statement with which you begin is not also the end (see Figure 6.4).

❧*Try this:* Study a group of like things inductively. You might, for example, use greet-ing cards aimed at women versus greeting cards aimed at men, a group of poems by one author, or ads for one kind of product (jeans) or aimed at one target group (teenage girls). Make use of The Method to compile and organize a set of significant details about the data and then leap to a general claim about the group that you think is interesting and accurate. This generalization is your inductive principle. Then use the principle to examine deductively more data of the same kind. That is, you will be using your claim not only to explain the pool of data but also to explore and evolve the claim more fully □.

The Evolving Thesis As Hypothesis and Conclusion in the Natural and Social Sciences

It is important to note that the way a thesis functions in a paper—whether it must be stated in full at the outset, for example, and what happens to it between the beginning of the paper and the end—is not the same for all disciplines. Disciplinary differences appear largest as you move back and forth between courses in the humanities and courses in the natural and certain of the social sciences.

Broadly speaking, papers in the humanities are inclined to proceed inductively, and papers in the natural and social sciences deductively. The natural and social sciences generally use a pair of terms, *hypothesis* and *conclusion,* for the single term *thesis.* Because writing in the sciences is patterned according to the scientific method, writers in disci-plines such as biology and psychology must report how the original thesis (hypothesis) was tested against empirical evidence and then conclude on this basis whether or not the hypothesis was confirmed.

The gap between this way of thinking about the thesis and the concept of an evolving thesis is not as large as it may seem. In fact, one of the chapter's main points—if not *the* main point—is that something must happen to the thesis between the intro-duction and the conclusion so that the conclusion does more than just reassert what had already been asserted in the beginning. To put this concept in the language of the sciences, the paper's hypothesis needs to be carefully tested against evidence, the results of which allow the writer to draw conclusions about the hypothesis's validity. So, in the sciences, while the hypothesis itself does not change, the testing of it and subsequent interpretation of those results produces commentary on and, often, qualifications of the paper's central claim.

The Hypothesis in the Sciences

It should go without saying that if the empirical evidence doesn't confirm your hypothesis, you rethink your hypothesis, but it's a complex issue. Researchers whose hypotheses are not confirmed in fact often question their *method* ("if I had more subjects," or "a better manipulation of the experimental group," or "a better test of intelligence," etc.) as much as their hypothesis. And that's often legitimate. Part of the challenge of psychological research is its reliance on a long array of assumptions. Failure to confirm a hypothesis could mean a problem in any of that long array of assumptions. So failure to confirm your hypothesis is often difficult to interpret.

—Alan Tjeltveit, Professor of Psychology

The thesis in Experimental Psychology papers is the statement of the hypothesis. It is always carefully and explicitly stated in the last few sentences of the introduction. The hypothesis is usually a deductive statement such as: if color does influence mood, then an ambiguous picture printed on different colors of paper should be interpreted differently, depending on the color of the paper. Specifically, based on the results of Jones (1997), the pink paper should cause participants to perceive the picture as a more calm and restful image, and the green paper should cause the picture to be interpreted as a more anxious image.

—Laura Snodgrass, Professor of Psychology

The thesis is usually presented in the abstract and then again at the end of the introduction. Probably the most frequent writing error is not providing a thesis at all. Sometimes this is because the student doesn't *have* a thesis; other times it is because the student wants to maintain a sense of mystery about the paper, as if driving toward a dramatic conclusion. This actually makes it harder to read. The best papers are clear and up front about what their point is, then use evidence and argument to support and evaluate the thesis. I encourage students to have a sentence immediately following their discussion of the background on the subject that can be as explicit as: "In this paper I will argue that while research on toxic effects of methyl bromide provides troubling evidence for severe physiological effects, conclusive proof of a significant environmental hazard is lacking at this time."

I try to avoid the use of the term "hypothesis." I think it gives the false sense that scientists always start with an idea about how something works. Frequently, that is not the case. Some of the best science has actually come from observation. Darwin's work on finches is a classic example. His ideas about adaptation probably derived *from* the observation.

—Bruce Wightman, Professor of Biology

Economists do make pretense to follow scientific methodology. Thus we are careful not to mix hypothesis and conclusion. I think it's important to distinguish between what is conjectured, the working hypothesis, and what ultimately emerges as a result of an examination of the evidence. Conclusions come only after some test has been passed.

—James Marshall, Professor of Economics

So, in the natural and social sciences, successive reformulations of the thesis are less likely to be recorded and may not even be expressly articulated. But, as in all disciplines, the primary analytical activity in the sciences is to repeatedly reconsider the assumptions upon which a conclusion is based.

The Evolving Thesis and Introductory and Concluding Paragraphs

If you are not using the hypothesis/conclusion format, your final drafts could often begin by predicting the evolution of their theses. Thus, the *Educating Rita* paper might open by using a version of the seems-to-be-about-X gambit, claiming that *at first glance* the film seems to celebrate the liberating potential of education. You could then lay out the evidence for this view and proceed to complicate it in the ways we've discussed.

What typically happens is that you lead (usually at the end of the first paragraph or at the beginning of the second) with the best version of your thesis that you can come up with that will be understandable to your readers without a lengthy preamble. If you find yourself writing a page-long introductory paragraph in order to get to your initial statement of thesis, try settling for a simpler articulation of your central idea in its first appearance. As you move through the paper, substantiate, elaborate on, test, and qualify your paper's opening gambit.

The most important thing to do in the introductory paragraph of an analytical paper is to lay out a *genuine issue,* which is to say, something that seems to be *at stake* in whatever it is you are studying. Preferably, you should select a complex issue—one not easily resolved, seeming to have some truth on both sides—and not an overly general one. Otherwise you run the risk of writing a paper that proves the obvious or radically oversimplifies.

Set up this issue as quickly and concretely as you can, avoiding generic (fits anything) comments, throat clearing, and review-style evaluations. As a general rule, you should assume that readers of your essay will need to know on page 1—preferably by the end of your first paragraph—what your paper is attempting to resolve or negotiate.

The first paragraph does not need to—and usually can't—offer your conclusion; it will take the body of your paper to accomplish that. It should, however, provide a quick look at particular details that set up the issue. Use these details to generate a *theory,* a *working hypothesis,* about whatever it is you think is at stake in the material. The rest of the paper will test and develop this theory.

Your concluding paragraph will offer the more carefully qualified and evolved version of your thesis that the body of your paper has allowed you to arrive at. Rather than just summarize and restate what you said in your introduction, the concluding paragraph should leave readers with what you take to be your single best insight, and it should put what you have had to say into some kind of *perspective.* See Chapter 10 for a more extended discussion of introductions and conclusions.

Recognizing Your Thesis

For an analytical or interpretive historical essay, "thesis" is a conventional term and one of much value. The thesis usually is that point of departure from the surfaces of evidence to the underlying significance, or problems, a given set of sources reveal to the reader and writer. In most cases, the thesis is best positioned up front, so that the writer's audience has a sense of what lies ahead and why it is worth reading on. I say "usually" and "in most cases" because the hard and fast rule should not take precedence over the inspirational manner in which a thesis can be presented. But the inspiration is not to be sought after at the price of the thesis itself. It is my experience, in fact, that if inspiration strikes, one only realizes it after the fact.

Recognizing a thesis can be extremely difficult. It can often be a lot easier to talk "about" what one is writing, than to say succinctly what the thrust of one's discussion is. I sometimes ask students to draw a line at the end of a paper after they have finished it off, and then write one, at most two sentences, stating what they most want to tell their readers. My comment on that postscript frequently is: "Great statement of your thesis. Just move it up to your first paragraph."

—Ellen Poteet, Professor of History

C. PUTTING IT ALL TOGETHER

Let's look at one more example, this time using it to bring together all of the strategies that we have suggested so far for writing an analytical paper. The example is a student writer's exploratory draft on a painting called *Las Meninas* (Spanish for "the ladies-in-waiting") by the seventeenth-century painter, Diego Velázquez. We have, by the way, selected a paper on a painting because all of the student's data (the painting) is on one page where you can keep referring back to it, trying to share in the writer's thought process.

Look at the painting on the next page (Figure 6.5), and then read the student's draft. As you read, you will notice that much of the essay is still unfocused and list like description, but as we noted in our chapter on interpretation (Chapter 3), careful description is a necessary stage in moving toward interpretations of evidence, especially in an exploratory draft where the writer is not yet committed to any single position. Notice how the writer's word choice in her descriptions prompts various kinds of interpretive leaps. We have added in blue our observations about how the writer is proceeding.

Velázquez's Intentions in *Las Meninas*

[1] Velázquez has been noted as being one of the best Spanish artists of all time. It seems that as Velázquez got older, his paintings became better. Towards the end of his life, he painted his masterpiece, *Las Meninas*. Out of all of his works, *Las Meninas*

FIGURE 6.5
Las Meninas by Diego Velázquez, 1656. Approximately 10'5" x 9'. Museo del Prado, Madrid.

is the only known self-portrait of Velázquez. There is much to be said about *Las Meninas*. The painting is very complex, but some of the intentions that Velázquez had in painting *Las Meninas* are very clear. [The writer opens with background information and a broad working thesis (underlined).]

[2] First, we must look at the painting as a whole. The question which must be answered is, who is in the painting? The people are all members of the Royal Court of the Spanish monarch, Philip IV. In the center is the daughter of the king who would eventually become Empress of Spain. Around her are her *meninas* or ladies in waiting. These *meninas* are all daughters of influential men. To the right of the *meninas* are dwarfs who are servants, and the family dog who looks fierce but is easily tamed by the foot of the little dwarf. The more unique people in the painting are Velázquez himself who stands to the left in front of a large canvas, the king and queen whose faces

are captured in the obscure mirror, the man in the doorway, and the nun and man behind the *meninas*. To analyze this painting further, the relationship between characters must be understood. [The writer describes the evidence and arrives at an operating assumption—focusing on the relationship between characters.]

[3] Where is this scene occurring? Well, most likely it is in the palace. But, why is there no visible furniture? Is it because Velázquez didn't want the viewers to become distracted from his true intentions? I believe it is to show that this is not just a painting of an actual event. This is an event out of his imagination. [The writer begins pushing observations to tentative conclusions by asking "So what?"]

[4] Now, let us become better acquainted with the characters. The child in the center is the most visible. All the light is shining on her. Maybe Velázquez is suggesting that she is the next light for Spain and that even God has approved her by shining all the available light on her. Back in those days there was a belief in the divine right of kings, so this just might be what Velázquez is saying. [The writer starts ranking evidence for importance and continues to ask "So what?"; she arrives at a possible interpretation of the painter's intention.]

[5] The next people of interest are the ones behind the *meninas*. The woman in the habit might be a nun and the man a priest.

[6] The king and queen are the next group of interesting people. They are in the mirror, which is to suggest they are present, but they are not as visible as they might be. Velázquez suggests that they are not always at the center where everyone would expect them to be. [The writer continues using Notice and Focus plus asking "So what?"; the writer has begun tackling evidence that might conflict with her first interpretation.]

[7] The last person and the most interesting is Velázquez. He dominates the painting along with the little girl. He takes up the whole left side along with his gigantic easel. But what is he painting? As I previously said, he might be painting the king and queen. But I also think he could be pretending to paint us, the viewers. The easel really gives this portrait an air of mystery because Velázquez knows that we, the viewers, want to know what he is painting. [The writer starts doing 10 on 1 with her selection of the most significant detail.]

[8] The appearance of Velázquez is also interesting. His eyes are focused out here. They are not focused on what is going on around him. It is a steady stare. Also interesting is his confident stance. He was confident enough to place himself in the painting of the royal court. I think that Velázquez wants the king to give him the recognition he deserves by including him in the "family." And the symbol on his vest is the symbol given to a painter by the king to show that his status and brilliance have been appreciated by the monarch. It is unknown how it got there. It is unlikely that Velázquez put it there himself. That would be too outright and Velázquez was the type to give his messages subtly. Some say that after Velázquez's death, King Philip IV himself painted it to finally give Velázquez the credit he deserved for being a loyal friend and servant. [The writer continues doing 10 on 1 and asking "So what?"; she arrives at three tentative theses (underlined).]

[9] I believe that Velázquez was very ingenious by putting his thoughts and feelings into a painting. He didn't want to offend the king who had done so much for him. It paid off for Velázquez because he did finally get what he wanted, even if it was after he died. [The writer concludes and is now ready to redraft in order to tighten links between evidence and claims, formulate a better working thesis, and make this thesis evolve.]

There are a number of good things about this draft. If you take the time to study it and our observations about it, you can train yourself to turn a more discerning eye on your own works in progress, especially in that all-important early stage where you are writing in order to discover ideas. As we say at the beginning of this chapter, far and away the biggest problem for student writers when required to produce a thesis-driven paper is that their anxiety about finding a thesis causes them to ignore the evidence and to choose instead to "match" it demonstration-style to the first tenable idea they conjure up. That is, they revert to the pattern we referred to earlier as 1 on 10, wherein one unchanging idea is repeated over and over again about each piece of evidence.

Description to Analysis: The Exploratory Draft

In our chapter on observing (Chapter 2), we argue that most writers do not spend enough time in the data-gathering stage because they try to rush prematurely to conclusions. In that chapter we suggest some key words and procedures for making the observation stage more systematic. We suggest that the words "interesting," "strange," "revealing," and "significant" are useful for guiding the observation process, as is the tactic of shifting in the observation stage from "What do I think?" to "What do I notice?" The move from description to analysis and interpretation begins at the point when you select certain details in your evidence as more important—more telling—than others and explain why you chose as you did. Study the student's draft for this Notice and Focus (selection) process. The writer has, for example, used the "interesting" prompt to press herself to notice and emphasize particular details in her evidence. In her next draft she might want to try one or more of the other prompts. Allowing herself to notice things that seem strange in the painting could be a fruitful move. In a final draft, she will want to craft more substantive, less listlike transitions. For an exploratory draft, however, cataloguing and starting to ask "So what?" about interesting detail is a productive tactic.

As you can see, the writer has not wasted time trying for a polished introductory paragraph. There will be time for that later. She has instead crafted an opening that allows her to get started and to start fast—no rambling prefatory material. This introduction, with its overly broad working thesis, does its job. It provides enough direction to guide the writer in her initial examination of evidence, using the artist's intention as her *interpretive context*. The purpose of the exploratory draft is to use writing as a means of arriving at a working thesis that your next draft can more fully evolve. Most writers find that potential theses emerge near the end of the exploratory draft—which is the case in the student draft (see the three claims that are underlined in paragraph 8). We will say more later on about what might happen to this introduction and working thesis in a subsequent draft.

Interpretive Leaps and Complicating Evidence

Notice that as early as paragraphs 3 and 4, the writer has begun to push herself to tentative conclusions (interpretive leaps) about the meaning of selected features of her evidence. What is especially good about the draft is that it reveals the writer's willingness to push on from her first idea (reading the painting as an endorsement of the divine right of kings, expressed by the light shining on the princess) by seeking out *complicating evidence*. The main point of this chapter is that you need to actively seek out evidence that seems not to fit your ideas and use it to make your thesis evolve. As we say in the section on the thesis as a camera lens, the thesis not only directs a writer's way of looking at evidence; the analysis of evidence should also direct and redirect (bring about revision of) the thesis.

The writer could have settled for the divine-right-of-kings idea, and then simply foregrounded details in the picture that would corroborate this idea, such as the deferential bowing of the *meninas* arranged in a circle with the princess at the center. But this potential thesis would not have accounted for enough of the evidence, and it would have forced the writer to ignore evidence which clearly doesn't fit, such as the small size and decentering of the king and queen and the large size and foregrounding of the painter himself. Rather than ignoring these potentially troublesome (for her initial idea) details, the writer instead zooms in on them, making the painter's representation of himself and of his employers the "1" for doing 10 on 1 (making a number of observations about a single representative piece of evidence and analyzing it in depth). This analytical move produces a burst of interpretive thinking in the form of three related claims (underlined in the student's draft), all of which have thesis potential.

Revising the Exploratory Draft

Now what? The writer is ready to rewrite the paper in order to more carefully formulate and evolve her thesis. What could she do better as she reviews her evidence in preparation for starting this next draft?

First, she could make more use of The Method (see Chapter 2), looking for significant patterns of repetition and contrast (exact repetition, strands, and binaries—organizing contrasts). What kinds of exact or nearly *exact repetitions* are there in the picture? Examples: the pictures in the background, the fact that both the dwarf and the painter, each on his own side of the painting, stare confidently and directly at the viewer. What might you select as *strands* (repetition of a similar kind of detail)? Examples: One strand might be details having to do with family. Another might include servants (dwarf, *meninas,* dog? painter?). There are also a number of details having to do with 'art and the making of art. Where in the painting, and in the student's draft, do you find *organizing contrasts*—binaries? Examples: royalty/commoners; employers/servants; large/small; foreground/background; central (prominent)/marginalized (less prominent).

Along with searching out significant patterns of repetition and opposition in her evidence, the writer also needs to make more aggressive use of the "So what?" question, asking it repeatedly about pieces of evidence and about her own claims, thus pressing herself to arrive at a range of possible answers until she finds the one that seems to best fit the evidence. The key in revision is to ask "So what?" not just of the evidence but also of your own observations. "So what?" is shorthand for questions like the following: Where does this get me? What am I getting at here? What (and what else) might I conclude about this feature of my evidence?

So what that the king and queen are small, but the painter, princess, and dwarf are all large and fairly equal in size and prominence? *So what* that there are size differences in the painting? What might large or small size mean? Here are some possible answers to these "So what?" questions:

- Perhaps the king and queen have been reduced so that Velázquez can showcase their daughter, the princess.
- Perhaps the size and physical prominence of the king and queen are relatively unimportant. In that case, what matters is that they are a presence, always overseeing events (an idea implied but not developed by the writer in paragraph 6).
- Perhaps the relative size and/or prominence of figures in the painting can be read as indicators of their importance or of what the painter wants to say about their importance.
- Perhaps the painter is demonstrating his own ability to make the king and queen any size—any level of importance—he chooses. Although the writer does not overtly say so, the king and queen are among the smallest as well as the least visible figures.

The writer's answers to these "So what?" questions cause her to generate a new set of claims about the painter's intention. The writer has, in other words, made her way through the first five steps of the procedure for making a thesis evolve using complication (see page 101). She is now ready for step 6, which calls first for a return to step 2. Here she will begin again by seeing how well the evolved claims can be made to account for evidence. She will locate evidence that is not yet adequately accounted for and query the significance of the evidence that seems not to fit in order to further evolve the claim (steps 3, 4, and 5).

Testing the Adequacy of the Thesis

As we see, the writer of the *Las Meninas* paper has already begun the process of testing her thesis against evidence that seems not to fit and then using that evidence to reformulate her thesis. The evidence that the writer included in paragraphs 6 and 7 (the decentering of the king and queen and the prominence and confident stare of the painter) caused her to drop her initial thinking—the idea that the painter's intentions were clear and that the primary intention was to endorse the divine-right-of-kings. The direction that her thinking takes next is not, however, an entirely new idea. The shift she is apparently making (but not yet overtly articulating) is from the painting as showcase of royal power to the painting as showcase of the painter's own power.

Given the answers posed above to the "So what?" question about the size and importance of the king and queen relative to the size and importance of the painter—parallel if not greater in prominence to the princess herself—the writer should probably choose the second of the two potential theses arrived at in paragraph 8. That idea—that the painting is a bid for recognition of the painter's status and brilliance—explains more of the evidence than anything else she has come up with so far. It explains, for example, the painter's prominence and the relative insignificance of the monarchs; the painter, in effect, creates their stature (size, power) in the world through his paintings. Framed in a mirror and appearing to hang on the wall, the king and queen are, arguably, suspended among the painter's paintings, mere reflections of themselves—or, rather, the painter's reflection of them.

We are not going to rewrite the student's draft, but here is how the next draft might go. Having chosen the status-and-brilliance idea as a more satisfactory theory, she would use the first part of her next draft to share with her readers the thinking that got her to the three ideas that emerged at the end of her exploratory draft and caused her to pick one of them. The working thesis of this new draft might be worded using the Seems-to-Be-About-X formula: the painting seems to be about the princess and how all are waiting upon her but may actually be more concerned with the painter himself. (Notice that this new working thesis sums up the history of the writer's thinking about the picture in a way that is more specific than her first working thesis but is not so specific that it would leave no room for leading readers through her chain of thought.)

The writer would next utilize steps 2 and 3 of the procedure on page 101, offering first summary and analysis of details in the picture that endorse the centrality of the princess and the power of monarchy, noting potentially conflicting details, and explaining why these details don't fit. Using step 4—asking "So what?" repeatedly of the details that seem not to fit—she would show us how it is possible to arrive at the three claims in the eighth paragraph of her first draft. In this way the paper retraces and shares with readers the evolution of the thesis. This recursive process of trying on, testing, and evolving the thesis continues until you are satisfied that the thesis statement accounts for your evidence as fully and accurately as possible.

Let's see how well the status-and-brilliance idea does in accounting for details in the painting. This thesis seems useful in accounting for the presence of the large dwarf in the right-hand foreground. Positioned in a way that links him with the painter, the dwarf arguably furthers the painting's message and does so, like much else in the painting, in the form of a loaded joke: the small ("dwarfed" by the power of others) are brought forward and made big. What other features of the painting might the thesis account for? How about the various ways that the painting seems to deny viewers' expectations? Both by decentering the monarchs and concealing what is on the easel, the painter again emphasizes his power, in this case, over the viewers (among whom might be the king and queen if their images on the back wall are mirrored reflections of them standing, like us, in front of the painting). He is not bound by anyone's expectations and in fact appears to take a certain pleasure in using viewers' expectations in order to manipulate them: he can make them wish to see something he has the power to withhold.

Does this mean that the status-and-brilliance thesis is adequately evolved? In this case, as the writer locates additional evidence that the thesis explains, it will continue to evolve but perhaps only slightly. For example, if (as the writer has said) the painter is demonstrating that he can make the members of the royal family any size he wants, then the painting is not only a bid for recognition but also a playful, though not so subtle, threat: be aware of my power and treat me well, or suffer the consequences. As artist, the painter decides how the royal family will be seen. The king and queen depend on the painter, as they do in a different way on the princess, with whom Velázquez makes himself equal in prominence, to extend and perpetuate their power.

Before leaving this example we want to emphasize that the version of the thesis that we have just proposed is not necessarily the "right" answer. Looked at in a different context, the painting might have been explained primarily as a demonstration of the painter's mastery of the tools of his trade—light, for example, and perspective. But our proposed revision of the thesis for the *Las Meninas* paper meets two important criteria for evaluating the adequacy of a thesis statement.

1. It unifies the observations the writer has made.
2. It is capable of accounting for a wide range of evidence.

A plausible thesis in an analytical paper makes a claim about the meaning of features of the evidence that would not have been immediately obvious (not obviously true) to readers.

Remember that the thesis develops through successive complications. Allowing your thesis to run up against potentially conflicting evidence ("But what about this?") enables you to build upon your initial idea, extending the range of evidence it can accurately account for by clarifying and qualifying its key terms. Although throwing out the old thesis and starting over may be what is needed, you should first try to use evidence that is not accounted for by your current thesis as a means of evolving the thesis further.

Guidelines for Finding and Developing a Thesis

1. A thesis is an idea that you formulate and reformulate about your subject. It should offer a theory about the meaning of evidence that would not have been immediately obvious to your readers.
2. Look for a thesis by focusing on an area of your subject that is open to opposing viewpoints or multiple interpretations. Rather than attempting to locate a single right answer, search for something that raises questions.
3. Treat your thesis as a hypothesis to be tested rather than an obvious truth.
4. The body of your paper should serve not only to substantiate the thesis by demonstrating its value in selecting and explaining evidence, but also to bring the opening version of the thesis into better focus.
5. Evolve your thesis—move it forward—by seeing the questions that each new formulation of it prompts you to ask.
6. Develop the implications of your evidence and of your observations as fully as you can by repeatedly asking "So what?"

7. When you encounter potentially conflicting evidence (or interpretations of that evidence), don't simply abandon your thesis. Take advantage of the complications to expand, qualify, and refine your thesis until you arrive at the most accurate explanation of the evidence that you can manage.

8. Arrive at the final version of your thesis by returning to your initial formulation—the position you set out to explore—and restating it in the more carefully qualified way you have arrived at through the body of your paper.

9. To check that your thesis has evolved, locate and compare the various versions of it throughout the draft. Have you done more than demonstrate the general validity of an unqualified claim?

ASSIGNMENT

Formulate and evolve a thesis on a film or painting. The chapter has already modeled this process with these forms. Alternatively, you might use an episode of a television show or an advertisement.

First, begin by formulating a variety of possible statements about the film or painting that could serve as a working thesis. These might be in answer to the question "What is the film/painting about?" or "What does it 'say'?" Or you might begin with The Method and formulate a thesis to explain a pattern of repetition or contrast you have observed. In any case, you shouldn't worry that these initial attempts will inevitably be overstated and thus only partially true—you have to start somewhere. At this point you will have completed step 1.

Next, follow the remainder of the procedure for making the thesis evolve, listed again here for convenience:

1. Formulate an idea about your subject.
2. See how far you can make this thesis go in accounting for evidence.
3. Locate evidence that is not adequately accounted for by the thesis.
4. Make explicit the apparent mismatch between the thesis and selected evidence.
5. Reshape your claim to accommodate the evidence that hasn't fit.
6. Repeat steps 2, 3, 4, and 5 several times.

7

Recognizing and Fixing
Weak Thesis Statements

It takes time and effort to make a thesis evolve. The path from your working thesis to the final, fully articulated and qualified version of the central claim is usually circuitous—fraught with false starts, dead-ends, recursive returns to earlier pieces of evidence and evolutions of the thesis. And in any piece of writing, you can only get so far from the start to the finish. Virtually any thesis can be evolved further—taken in another direction and/or fine-tuned—by adding complicating evidence to broaden or narrow its scope.

Obviously, the farther along you *begin* on the path from your working thesis to its final version, the more efficiently you will proceed and the farther you will get. A working thesis that is already partially qualified, in language you have already subjected to reworking, is far more likely to produce a successful paper than an opening claim that is overstated, absent, unsupportable, or otherwise weak.

So it matters a lot what kind of thesis you start with. The point at which inexperienced writers choose a thesis is, as we discuss early in Chapter 5, a chronic problem site. It's at this point in the paper-writing process—as writers turn from preliminary data gathering and analysis to actually composing a draft—that they are most likely to revert to the kinds of weak theses characteristic of five-paragraph form demonstrations.

The aim of this chapter is to discuss ways of *starting* with an improved claim. Towards that end, the chapter will make you conscious of what weak theses look and sound like, in the hope that you will then be less likely to revert to them. Think of the chapter as a version of habits of mind (Chapter 1) that is specifically addressed to thesis construction. This chapter is organized in problem-solution format. Using actual excerpts from student papers, it will exemplify five kinds of weak thesis statements and show how they can be reworded in ways that will stimulate a thesis to evolve.

A. FIVE KINDS OF WEAK THESES AND HOW TO FIX THEM

A *strong thesis* makes a claim that (1) requires analysis to support and evolve it and (2) offers some point about the significance of your evidence that would not have been immediately obvious to your readers. By contrast, a *weak thesis* either makes no claim or makes a claim that does not need proving. As a quick flash-forward, here are the five kinds of weak thesis statements—ones that

1. make no claim ("This paper will examine the pros and cons of . . .")

2. are obviously true or a statement of fact ("Exercise is good for you").

3. restate conventional wisdom ("Love conquers all").

4. offer personal conviction as the basis for the claim ("Shopping malls are wonderful places").

5. make an overly broad claim ("Individualism is good").

Weak Thesis Type 1: The Thesis Makes No Claim

The following statements are not productive theses because they do not advance an idea about the topics the papers will explore.

Problem Examples

I'm going to write about Darwin's concerns with evolution in *The Origin of Species*.

This paper will address the characteristics of a good corporate manager.

The problem examples each name a subject and link it to the intention to write about it, but they don't make any claim about the subject. As a result, they direct neither the writer nor the reader toward some position or plan of attack. The second problem example begins to move toward a point of view through the use of the value judgment "good," but this term is too broad to guide the analysis. The statement-of-intention thesis invites a list: one paragraph for each quality the writer chooses to call good. Even if the thesis were rephrased as "This paper will address why a good corporate manager needs to learn to delegate responsibility," the thesis would not adequately suggest why such a claim would need to be argued or defended. *There is, in short, nothing at stake, no issue to be resolved.* A writer who produces a thesis of this type is probably unduly controlled by banking—that relatively passive, information in/information out approach to learning we discussed in Chapter 1, "Habits of Mind."

Solution

Raise specific issues for the essay to explore.

Solution Examples

Darwin's concern with survival of the fittest in *The Origin of Species* initially leads him to neglect a potentially conflicting aspect of his theory of evolution—survival as a matter of interdependence.

The very trait that makes for an effective corporate manager—the drive to succeed—can also make the leader domineering and therefore ineffective.

Some disciplines expect writers to offer statements of method and/or intention in their papers' openings. Generally, however, these openings also make a claim: for example, "In this paper I will examine how Congressional Republicans undermined the attempts of the Democratic administration to legislate a fiscally responsible health care policy for the elderly," *not* "In this paper I will discuss America's treatment of the elderly." (See Chapter 10, "Introductions and Conclusions" for further discussion of using overt statements of intention.)

Weak Thesis Type 2: The Thesis Is Obviously True or Is a Statement of Fact

The following statements are not productive theses because they do not require proof. A thesis needs to be an assertion with which it would be possible for readers to disagree.

Problem Examples

The jean industry targets its advertisements to appeal to young adults.

The flight from teaching to research and publishing in higher education is a controversial issue in the academic world. I will show different views and aspects concerning this problem.

If few people would disagree with the claim that a thesis makes, there is no point in writing an analytical paper on it. Though one might deliver an inspirational speech on a position that virtually everyone would support (such as the value of tolerance), endorsements and appreciations don't usually lead to analysis; they merely invite people to feel good about their convictions.

In the second problem example, few readers would disagree with the fact that the issue is "controversial." In the second sentence of that example, the writer has begun to identify a point of view—that the flight from teaching is a "problem"—but her next declaration, that she will "show different views and aspects," is a statement of fact, not an idea. The phrasing of the claim is noncommittal and so broad that it prevents the writer from formulating a workable thesis. If you find yourself writing theses of this type, review the discussion of the first three habits of mind presented in Chapter 1, banking, generalizations, and clichés.

Solution

Find some avenue of *inquiry*—a question about the facts or an issue raised by them. Make an assertion with which it would be possible for readers to disagree.

Solution Examples

> By inventing new terms, such as "loose fit" and "relaxed fit," the jean industry has attempted to normalize, even glorify, its product for an older and fatter generation.

> The "flight from teaching" to research and publishing in higher education is a controversial issue in the academic world. As I will attempt to show, the controversy is based to a significant degree on a false assumption, that doing research necessarily leads teachers away from the classroom.

Weak Thesis Type 3: The Thesis Restates Conventional Wisdom

Restatement of one of the many clichés that constitute a culture's conventional wisdom is not a productive thesis unless you have something to say about it that hasn't been said many times before.

Problem Examples

> An important part of one's college education is learning to better understand others' points of view.

> From cartoons in the morning to adventure shows at night, there is too much violence on television.

> "*I* was supposed to bring the coolers; *you* were supposed to bring the chips!" exclaimed ex-Beatle Ringo Starr, who appeared on TV commercials for Sun County Wine Coolers a few years ago. By using rock music to sell a wide range of products, the advertising agencies, in league with corporate giants such as Pepsi, Michelob and Ford, have corrupted the spirit of rock and roll.

All of these examples say nothing worth proving because they are clichés. ("Conventional wisdom" is a polite term for cliché.) Most clichés were fresh ideas once, but over time they have become trite, prefabricated forms of nonthinking. Faced with a phenomenon that requires a response, many inexperienced writers rely on a knee-jerk reaction: they resort to a small set of culturally approved "answers." In this sense, clichés resemble statements of fact. So commonly accepted that most people nod to them without thinking, statements of conventional wisdom make people feel a comfortable sense of agreement with one another. The problem with this kind of packaged solution is that because conventional wisdom is so general and so conventional, it doesn't teach anybody—including the writer—anything. Worse, since the cliché appears to be an idea, it prevents the writer from engaging in a fresh, open-minded exploration of his or her subject.

There is some truth in all of the problem examples above, but none of them *complicates* its position. A thoughtful reader could, for example, respond to the claim that advertising has corrupted the spirit of rock and roll by suggesting that rock and roll was highly commercial long before it colonized the airwaves. The conventional wisdom that rock and roll is somehow pure and honest while advertising is phony and exploitative invites the savvy writer to formulate a thesis that overturns these clichés. As our solution example demonstrates, one could argue that rock actually has improved advertising, not that ads have ruined rock—or, alternatively, that rock has shrewdly marketed idealism to a gullible populace. At the least, a writer deeply committed to the original thesis would do better to examine what it was that Ringo was selling—what he stands for in this particular case—than to discuss rock and advertising in such general terms.

To help you liberate yourself from enslavement to conventional wisdom, take another look at the various discussions in Chapter 1 of how our culture influences us as thinkers and writers. See in particular the preliminary discussion about skepticism and the sections on cliches, judging, debate-style argument, and opinions.

Solution

Seek to complicate—see more than one point of view on—your subject. Avoid conventional wisdom unless you can qualify it or introduce a fresh perspective on it.

Solution Examples

While an important part of one's college education is learning to better understand others' points of view, a persistent danger is that the students will simply be required to substitute the teacher's answers for the ones they grew up uncritically believing.

While some might argue that the presence of rock and roll soundtracks in TV commercials has corrupted rock's spirit, this point of view not only falsifies the history of rock but also blinds us to the ways that the music has improved the quality of television advertising.

❧ *Try this:* You can learn a lot about writing strong thesis statements by analyzing and rewriting weak ones. Rewrite the three weak theses below. As in the case of our solution examples, revising will require you to add information and thinking to the weak theses. Try, in other words, to come up with some interesting claims that most readers would not already have thought of to develop the subject of television violence. (The third thesis you will recognize as a problem example for which we offered no solution.)

1. In this paper I will discuss police procedures in recent domestic violence cases.
2. The way that the media portrayed the events of April 30, 1975, when Saigon fell, greatly influenced the final perspectives of the American people toward the end result of the Vietnam War.
3. From cartoons in the morning to adventure shows at night, there is too much violence on television. □

Weak Thesis Type 4: The Thesis Offers Personal Conviction As the Basis for the Claim

A statement of one's personal convictions or one's likes or dislikes does not alone supply sufficient grounds for a productive thesis.

Problem Examples

> The songs of the punk rock group Minor Threat relate to the feelings of individuals who dare to be different. Their songs are just composed of pure emotion. Pure emotion is very important in music, because it serves as a vehicle to convey the important message of individuality. Minor Threat's songs are meaningful to me because I can identify with them.

> Sir Thomas More's *Utopia* proposes an unworkable set of solutions to society's problems because, like communist Russia, it suppresses individualism.

> Although I agree with Jeane Kirkpatrick's argument that environmentalists and business should work together to ensure the ecological future of the world, and that this cooperation is beneficial for both sides, the indisputable fact is that environmental considerations should always be a part of any decision that is made. Any individual, if he looks deeply enough into his soul, knows what is right and what is wrong. The environment should be protected because it is the right thing to do, not because someone is forcing you to do it.

Like conventional wisdom, personal likes and dislikes can lead inexperienced writers into knee-jerk reactions of approval or disapproval, often expressed in a moralistic tone. The writers of the problem examples above assume that their primary job is to judge their subjects, or testify to their worth, not to evaluate them analytically. As a result, such writers lack critical detachment not only from their topics but, crucially, from their own assumptions and biases. They have *taken personal opinions for self-evident truths.* You can test a thesis for this problem by asking if the writer's response to questions about the thesis would be "because I think so."

The most blatant version of this tendency occurs in the third problem example, which asserts, "Any individual, if he looks deeply enough into his soul, knows what is right and what is wrong. The environment should be protected because it is the right thing to do." Translation (only slightly exaggerated): "Any individual who thinks about the subject will obviously agree with me because my feelings and convictions feel right to me and therefore they must be universally and self-evidently true." The problem is that this writer is not distinguishing between his own likes and dislikes (or private convictions) and what he takes to be right, real, or true for everyone else. Testing an idea against your own feelings and experience is not an adequate means of establishing whether something is accurate or true.

Solution

Try on other points of view honestly and dispassionately; *treat your ideas as hypotheses to be tested rather than obvious truths.* In the following solution examples, we have replaced opinions (in the form of self-evident truths) with ideas—theories about the meaning and significance of the subjects that could be supported and qualified with evidence.

Solution Examples

> Sir Thomas More's *Utopia* treats individualism as a serious but remediable social problem. His radical treatment of what we might now call "socialization" attempts to redefine the meaning and origin of individual identity.

> Although I agree with Jeane Kirkpatrick's argument that environmentalists and business should work together to ensure the ecological future of the world, her argument undervalues the necessity of pressuring businesses to attend to environmental concerns that may not benefit them in the short run.

It is fine, of course, to write about what you believe and to consult your feelings as you formulate an idea. But the risk you run in arguing from your unexamined feelings and convictions is that you will prematurely dismiss from consideration anything that is unfamiliar or does not immediately conform to what you already believe. The less willing you are to test these established and habitual convictions, the less chance you will have to refine or expand the ways in which you think. You will continue to play the same small set of tunes in response to everything you hear. And without the ability to think from multiple perspectives, you will be less able to defend your convictions against the ideas that challenge them because you won't really have examined the logic of your own beliefs—you just believe them.

At the root of this problem lurks an antianalytical bias that predisposes many writers to see any challenge to their habitual ways of thinking as the enemy and to view those who would raise this challenge as cynics who don't believe in anything. Such writers often feel personally attacked, when in fact the conviction they are defending is not really so personal after all. Consider, for example, the first two problem examples above, in which both writers take individualism to be an incontestable value. Where does this conviction come from? Neither of the writers arrived at the thesis independent of the particular culture in which they were raised, permeated as it is by the "rugged individualism" of John Wayne and Sylvester Stallone movies.

In other words, "individualism" as an undefined blanket term verges on *cultural cliché*. That it is always good or positive is a piece of conventional wisdom. But part of becoming educated is to take a look at such global and undefined ideas that one has uncritically assimilated. Clearly, the needs and rights of the individual in contemporary American culture are consistently being weighed and balanced against the rights of other individuals and the necessity of cooperation in groups. Look at the recent nationwide concerns with health maintenance organizations (HMOs), which control health costs but constrain the individual prerogative of the physician, or with the rights of crime victims who are banding together to seek support from a government they believe is protecting the individual rights of the criminal at the expense of the individual rights of the victim.

In light of these considerations, the writers of the first two problem examples would have to question *to what extent* they should attack a book or support a rock band merely on the basis of whether or not each honors individualism. If the author of the second problem example had been willing to explore how Thomas More conceives of and critiques individualism, he or she might have been able to arrive at a revealing analysis of the tension between the individual and the collective rather than merely dismissing the entire book.

This is not to say that the first requirement of analytical writing is that you abandon all conviction or argue for a position that you do not believe. But we are suggesting that the risk of remaining trapped within a limited set of culturally inherited opinions is greater than the risk that you will run by submerging your personal likes or dislikes and instead honestly and dispassionately trying on different points of view. The energy of analytical writing comes not from rehearsing your convictions but from treating them as hypotheses to be tested, as scientists do—from finding the boundaries of your ideas, reshaping parts of them, seeing connections you have not seen before.

When a writing assignment asks for your ideas about a subject, it is usually not asking for your opinion, what you think *of* the subject, but for your reasoning on what and how the subject means. As we discussed in the first chapter, *an idea is not the same thing as an opinion.* The two are closely related, since both, in theory, are based on reasoning. Opinions, however, often take the form of judgments, the reflections of our personal attitudes and beliefs. While having ideas necessarily involves your attitudes and beliefs, it is a more disinterested process than opinion making. The formulation of ideas, which is one of the primary aims of analysis, involves questioning. By contrast, opinions are often habitual responses, mental reflexes that kick in automatically when an answer seems to be called for. (The sections on personalizing, judging, and opinions in Chapter 1 explain more fully how placing too much emphasis on yourself can interfere with your thinking.)

Weak Thesis Type 5: The Thesis Makes an Overly Broad Claim

An overly general claim is not a productive thesis because it oversimplifies and is too broad to direct development. Such statements usually lead either to say-nothing theses or to reductive either/or thinking.

Problem Examples

> Violent revolutions have had both positive and negative results for man.

> There are many similarities and differences between the Carolingian and the Burgundian Renaissances.

> *Othello* is a play about love and jealousy.

> It is important to understand why leaders act in a leadership role. What is the driving force? Is it an internal drive for the business or group to succeed, or is it an internal drive for the leader to dominate over others?

Overly generalized theses avoid complexity. (See the discussion of generalizing in Chapter 1.) At their worst, as in our first three examples, they settle for assertions broad enough to fit almost any subject and thus say nothing in particular about the subject at hand. A writer in the early stages of his or her drafting process might begin working from a general idea, such as what is positive and negative about violent revolutions or how two historical periods are like and unlike, but these formulations are not specific enough to guide the development of a paper. Such broad categories are likely to generate listing, not thinking. We can, for example, predict that the third thesis will prompt the writer to produce a couple of paragraphs demonstrating that *Othello* is about love and then a couple of paragraphs demonstrating that *Othello* is about jealousy, without analyzing what the play says about either.

Our fourth problem example, inquiring into the motivation of leaders in business, demonstrates how the desire to generalize can drive writers into logical errors. Because this thesis overtly offers readers two possible answers to its central question, it appears to avoid the problem of oversimplifying a complex subject. But this appearance of complexity is deceptive because the writer has reduced the possibilities to only two answers—an either/or choice: Is "the driving force" of leadership a desire for group success or a desire to dominate others? Readers can only be frustrated by being asked to choose between two such options when the more logical answer probably lies somewhere in between or somewhere else altogether. (See the discussion of binaries in Chapter 1.)

The best way to avoid the problem evident in the first three examples is to sensitize yourself to the characteristic phrasing of such theses: "both positive and negative," "many similarities and differences," or "both pros and cons." Virtually everything from meatloaf to taxes can be both positive and negative.

Solution

Convert broad categories and generic (fits anything) claims to more specific, more qualified assertions; find ways to bring out the complexity of your subject.

Solution Examples

The differences between the Carolingian and Burgundian Renaissances outweigh the similarities.

Although *Othello* appears to attack jealousy, it also supports the skepticism of the jealous characters over the naïveté of the lovers.

Although violent revolutions begin to redress long-standing social inequities, they often do so at the cost of long-term economic dysfunction and the suffering that attends it.

B. HOW TO REPHRASE THESIS STATEMENTS: SPECIFY AND SUBORDINATE

Clear symptoms of an overly generalized thesis can be found by looking at its grammar. Each of the first three problem examples on page 128, for example, relies mostly on nouns rather than verbs; the nouns announce a broad heading, but the verbs don't do anything with or to the nouns. In grammatical terms, these thesis statements don't *predicate* (affirm or assert something about the subject of a proposition). Instead, they rely on anemic verbs like "is" or "are," which function as equal signs that link general nouns with general adjectives rather than specify more complex relationships.

By replacing the equal sign with a more active verb, you can force yourself to advance some sort of claim, as in one of our solutions; for example, "The differences between the Carolingian and Burgundian Renaissances *outweigh* the similarities." While this reformulation remains quite general, it at least begins to direct the writer along a more particular line of argument. Replacing the "is" or "are" equal signs with stronger verbs will usually impel you to rank ideas in some order of importance and to assert some conceptual relation among them.

In other words, the best way to remedy the problem of overgeneralization is to *move toward specificity in word choice, in sentence structure, and in idea.* If you find yourself writing "The economic situation is bad," consider revising it to "The tax policies of the current administration threaten to reduce the tax burden on the middle class by sacrificing education and health-care programs for everyone."

Here's the problem/solution in schematic form:

Broad Noun The economic situation	+	**Weak Verb** is	+	**Vague, Evaluative Modifier** bad
Specific Noun (The) tax policies (of the current administration)	+	**Active Verb** threaten to reduce (the tax burden on the middle class)	+	**Specific Modifier** by sacrificing education and health-care programs for everyone

By eliminating the weak thesis formula—broad noun plus "is" plus vague evaluative adjective—a writer is compelled to qualify, or define carefully, each of the terms in the original proposition, arriving at a more particular and conceptually rich assertion.

A second way to rephrase overly broad thesis statements, in tandem with adding specificity, is to subordinate one part of the statement to another. The both-positive-and-negative and both-similarity-and-difference formulas are recipes for say-nothing theses, since they encourage pointless comparisons. Given that it is worthwhile to notice both strengths and weaknesses—that your subject is not all one way or all another— what, then, can you do to convert the thesis from a say-nothing to a say-something claim? Generally, there are two strategies for this purpose that operate together. The first we have already discussed.

1. *Specify*—Replace the overly abstract terms—terms like "positive" and "negative" (or "similar" and "different")—with something specific; *name* something that is positive and something that is negative instead.

2. *Subordinate*—Rank one of the two items in the pairing underneath the other. When you subordinate, you put the most important, pressing, or revealing side of the comparison in what is known as the main clause and the less important side in what is known as the subordinate clause, introducing it with a word like "while" or "although." (See Chapter 13 for the definitions and more discussion of main and subordinate clauses.)

Voices from Across the Curriculum

Making the Thesis Specific

Good thesis: "While Graham and Wigman seem different, their ideas on inner expression (specifically subjectivism versus objectivism) and the incorporation of their respective countries' surge of nationalism bring them much closer than they appear."

Not so good thesis/question: "What were Humphrey's and Weidman's reasons behind the setting of *With My Red Fires*, and of what importance were the set and costume design to the piece as a whole?"

What I like about the good thesis is that it moves beyond the standard "they are different, but alike" (which can be said about anything) to actually tell the reader what specific areas the paper will explore. I can also tell that the subject is narrow enough for a fairly thorough examination of one small slice of these two major choreographers' work rather than some overgeneralized treatment of these two historic figures. I would probably encourage the writer of the not so good thesis to search for a better thesis with the question: How does the costume design of *With My Red Fires* support this story of young lovers and their revolt against the family matriarch?

—Karen Dearborn, Professor of Dance

In short, specify to focus the claim, and subordinate to qualify (further focus) the claim still more. This strategy produces the remedies to both the *Othello* and the violent revolution examples in "Weak Thesis Type 5: The Thesis Makes an Overly Broad Claim." As evidence of the refocusing work that fairly simple rephrasing accomplishes, consider the following version of the violent revolution example, in which we merely invert the ranking of the two items in the pair.

> Although violent revolutions often cause long-term economic dysfunction and the suffering that attends it, such revolutions at least begin to redress long-standing social inequities.

Another Note on the Phrasing of Thesis Statements: Questions

The following question is frequently asked about thesis statements: is it okay to phrase a thesis as a question? The answer is both "yes" and "no." Phrasing a thesis as a question makes it more difficult for both the writer and the reader to be sure of the direction the paper will take, because a question doesn't make an overt claim. Questions, however, can clearly imply claims. And many writers, especially in the early, exploratory stages of drafting, will begin with a question. As we note in the discussion in Chapter 1, "What It Means to Have an Idea," an idea answers a question; it explains something that needs to be explained. Also, an idea may result from the discovery of a question where there seemed not to be one. Ideas start with something you want to figure out rather than with something that you and possibly most of your readers already understand.

As a general rule, use thesis questions cautiously, especially in final drafts. While a thesis question often functions well to spark a writer's thinking, it can too often muddy the thinking by leaving the area of consideration too broad. Just make sure that you do not let the thesis-question approach allow you to evade the responsibility of making some kind of claim. Especially in the drafting stage, a question posed overtly by the writer can provide focus, but only if he or she then proceeds to answer it with what would become a first statement of thesis.

❦ *Try this:* Learning to diagnose the strengths and weaknesses of thesis statements is a skill that comes in handy as you read the claims of others and revise your own. A good question for diagnosing a thesis is "*What does the thesis require the writer to do next?*" This question should help you to figure out what the thesis actually wants to claim, which can then direct you to possible rephrasings that would better direct your thinking. Using this question as a prompt, list the strengths and weaknesses of the two thesis statements below, and then rewrite them. In the first statement, just rewrite the last sentence (the other sentences have been included to provide context).

1. Many economists and politicians agree that, along with the Environmental Protection Agency's newest regulations, a global-warming treaty could damage the American economy. Because of the great expense that such environmental standards require, domestic industries would financially suffer. Others argue, however, that severe regulatory steps must be taken to prevent global warming, regardless of cost. Despite both legitimate claims, the issue of protecting the environment while still securing our global competitiveness remains critical.
2. Regarding the promotion of women into executive positions, they are continually losing the race because of a corporate view that women are too compassionate to keep up with the competitiveness of a powerful firm. □

C. COMMON LOGICAL ERRORS IN CONSTRUCTING A THESIS

In further service to our project of giving you ways of avoiding weak thesis statements, this section will move briefly to the field of logic, which has given us terms that are shorthand for certain common thinking errors. We will treat six errors, all of which involve the root problem of oversimplification in the way the thesis explains the meaning of evidence.

1. Simple cause–complex effect

One of the most common problems of thinking, the fallacy of simple cause–complex effect, involves assigning a simple cause to a complex phenomenon that cannot be so easily explained. A widespread version of this fallacy is seen in arguments that blame individual figures for broad historical events, for example, "Eisenhower caused America to be involved in the Vietnam War." This claim ignores the Cold War ethos, the long history of colonialism in Southeast Asia, and a multitude of other factors. When you reduce a complex sequence of events to a simple and single cause—or assign a simple effect to a complex cause—you will virtually always be wrong.

2. False cause

Another common cause/effect thinking error, false cause, is produced by assuming that two events are causally connected when such causal connection does not necessarily exist. One of the most common forms of this fallacy—known as *post hoc, ergo propter hoc* (Latin for "after this, therefore because of this")—assumes that because *A* precedes *B* in time, *A* causes *B*. For example, it was once thought that the sun shining on a pile of garbage caused the garbage to conceive flies.

This error is the stuff that superstition is made of. "I walked under a ladder, and then I got hit by a car" becomes "Because I walked under a ladder, I got hit by a car." Because one action precedes a second one in time, the first action is assumed to be the cause of the second. A more dangerous form of this error goes like this:

> **Evidence:** A new neighbor moved in downstairs on Saturday. My television disappeared on Sunday.
> **Conclusion:** The new neighbor stole my TV.

As the examples illustrate, *typically in false cause some significant alternative has not been considered,* such as the presence of flies' eggs in the garbage. Similarly, it does not follow that if a person watches television and then commits a crime, television watching necessarily causes crime; there are other causes to be considered.

Predictably, instances of simple cause/complex effect and false cause are harder to spot when we encounter them in published settings. Consider how the information offered in the following real-life example might be interpreted in terms of cause and effect. A newspaper article on a study conducted at Stanford University about the connection between adolescents' television viewing habits and drinking reports that high school students who watch a lot of television and music videos are more likely to start drinking than are other students. In the study of fifteen hundred fifty-three ninth-graders, with each increase of one hour per day of watching music videos there was a thirty-one percent greater risk of starting to drink. Each hour increase of watching other kinds of television corresponded with a nine percent greater risk. Each hour spent watching movies in a video cassette recorder (VCR) corresponded to an eleven percent *decreased* risk of starting to drink alcohol. Computer and video games had no effect either way, and among those who already drank, watching television and videos made no difference. Because these data were reported in the newspaper in very abbreviated form, there was little interpretation of the evidence except for the observations that alcohol is the most common beverage shown on television and that drinking on television is done by attractive people, often in association with sexually suggestive content.

❦ *Try this:* Identify possible sites of simple cause/complex effect and false cause in the report (above) on teen drinking. Then, formulate a few alternative explanations one might offer to the theory that television watching is the primary cause of the increased risk of starting drinking. What explanations might there be for the decreased risk of drinking that corresponds with adolescents watching movies on the VCR? □

3. Analogy and false analogy

An analogy is a device for understanding something that is relatively foreign in terms of something that is more familiar. When you argue by analogy, you are saying that what is true for one thing is necessarily true for something else that it in some way resembles. The famous poetic line "my love is like a red, red rose" is actually an argument by analogy. At first glance, this clichéd comparison seems too far-fetched to be reasonable. But is it a false analogy, or a potentially enabling one? Past users of this analogy have thought the thorns, the early fading, the beauty, and so forth, sufficient to argue from the comparison. Similarly, glance back to the first paragraph of the Tiananmen Square essay on page 92 in Chapter 5, in which the writer's deft use of an extended analogy opens up his subject analytically. Analogies, in short, are not bad or illogical in themselves. In fact, they can be incredibly useful, depending on how you handle them.

The danger that arguing analogically can pose is that an *inaccurate* comparison (usually one that oversimplifies) prevents you from looking at the evidence. Flying to the moon is like flying a kite? Well, it's a little bit like that, but this kind of oversimplification is essentially falsifying. In most ways that matter, sending a rocket to the moon does not resemble sending a kite into the air.

Another way that an analogy can become false is when it becomes *overextended:* there is a point of resemblance at one juncture, but the writer then goes on to assume that the two items being compared necessarily resemble each other in most other respects. To what extent is balancing your checkbook really like juggling? On the other hand, an analogy that first appears overextended may not be. How far, for example, could you reasonably go in comparing a presidential election to a sales campaign or an enclosed shopping mall to a village main street?

Let's examine one more false analogy, from a recent ad campaign: "You choose the president; why not choose your cable company?" What's wrong with this comparison? For one thing, each of us is not entitled to our choice of president. If we were, there would be a lot of presidents. And, second, the rules and circumstances covering what is best in the nation's communication network are not necessarily the same as the rules and circumstances guiding the structure of our federal government. So the analogy doesn't work very well. What is true for one side of the comparison is not necessarily true for the other side; the differences are greater than the similarities.

When you find yourself reasoning by analogy, ask yourself two questions: (1) are the basic similarities greater and more significant than the obvious differences? and (2) am I overrelying on surface similarities and ignoring more essential differences?

4. Equivocation

Equivocation is the first of three logical errors that deal with matters of phrasing. As the thesis chapters in Part II show, finding and developing a thesis emphasizes the importance of word choice—of carefully casting and recasting the language with which you categorize and name your ideas.

Equivocation—slipping between two meanings for a single word or phrase—confuses an argument. An example would be: "Only man is capable of religious faith. No woman is a man. Therefore, no woman is capable of religious faith." Here the first use of "man" is generic, intended to be gender neutral, while the second use is decidedly masculine. One specialized form of equivocation results from what are sometimes called *weasel words*. A weasel word is one that has been used so loosely that it ceases to have much of any meaning (the term derives from the weasel's reputed practice of sucking the contents from an egg without destroying the shell). The word "natural," for example, can mean good, pure, and unsullied, but it can also refer to the ways of nature (flora and fauna). Such terms ("love," "reality," and "experience" are others) invite equivocation because they mean so many different things to different people.

5. Begging the question

To beg the question is to argue in a circle by asking readers to accept without argument a point that is actually at stake. This kind of fallacious argument hides its conclusion among its assumptions. For example, "*Huckleberry Finn* should be banned from school libraries as obscene because it uses obscene language" begs the question by presenting as obviously true issues that are actually in question: the definition of obscenity and the assumption that the obscene should be banned because it is obscene.

6. Overgeneralization

An overgeneralization is an inadequately qualified claim. It may be true that some heavy drinkers are alcoholics, but it would not be fair to claim that all heavy drinking is or leads to alcoholism. As a rule, be wary of "totalizing" or making global pronouncements; the bigger the generalization, the more likely it will admit of exceptions. See for examples the process of qualifying a claim we illustrate in the discussion of *Educating Rita* in Chapter 6 and in the solutions in "Weak Thesis Type 5" in this chapter.

One particular form of overgeneralization, the *sweeping generalization,* occurs when a writer overextends the reach of the claim. The claim itself may be adequately qualified, but the problem comes in an overly broad application of that generalization, suggesting that it applies in every case when it applies only in some.

When you move prematurely from too little evidence to a broad conclusion, you have fallen into *hasty generalization.* Much of this book addresses ways of avoiding this problem, also known as an unwarranted inductive leap. See "Demonstrating the Representativeness of Your Example" in Chapter 5.

There are, of course, other common logical errors that can undermine the construction of valid claims. For one more example, see the section called "Strategy 3: Put Your Sources into Conversation with One Another" in Chapter 8 for a discussion of the problem in argument called *straw man,* in which a writer builds his or her case on a misrepresentation of an opponent's argument.

ASSIGNMENT

Because this is a troubleshooting chapter that can be applied to various stages of the writing process, we are not supplying writing assignments.

8

Writing the Researched Paper

A. WHAT TO DO WITH SECONDARY SOURCES

This chapter addresses three characteristic problems that writers often have when incorporating research into their writing:

1. Leaving quotations and paraphrases to speak for themselves
2. Not differentiating themselves from their sources (ventriloquizing)
3. Resorting to overly global agreeing and disagreeing as their only means of response other than summary

The chapter offers a remedy to these problems, building around a concept we call *conversing with sources*. The next chapter then treats such practical matters as finding and evaluating sources in print and electronic media, integrating quotations into one's own prose, and citing sources.

We use the terms *source* and *secondary source* interchangeably to designate ideas and information about your subject that you find in the work of other writers. Secondary sources allow you to gain a richer, more informed, and complex vantage point on your *primary sources*. Here's how primary and secondary sources can be distinguished: if you were writing a paper on the philosopher Nietzsche, his writing would be your primary source, and critical commentaries on his work would be your secondary sources. If, however, you were writing on the poet Yeats, who read and was influenced by Nietzsche, a work of Nietzsche's philosophy would become a secondary source of yours on your primary source, Yeats's poetry.

"Source Anxiety" and What to Do about It

Typically, inexperienced writers either use sources as "answers"—they let the sources do too much of their thinking—or ignore them altogether as a way of avoiding "losing their own ideas." Both of these approaches are understandable but inadequate. We will take up the first of these in some detail in a moment, but for now let's concentrate on the second, using sources as answers.

Confronted with the seasoned views of experts in a discipline, you may well feel that there is nothing left for you to say because it has all been said before or, at least, it has been said by people who greatly outweigh you in reputation and experience. This anxiety explains why so many writers surrender to the role of conduit for the voices of the experts, providing conjunctions between quotations. So why not avoid what other people have said? Won't this avoidance insure that your ideas will be original and that, at the same time, you will be free from the danger of getting brainwashed by some "expert"?

The answer is "no." If you don't consult what others have said, you run at least two risks: you will waste your time reinventing the wheel, and you will undermine your analysis (or at least leave it incomplete) by not considering information or acknowledging positions that are commonly discussed in the field.

By remaining unaware of existing thinking, you choose, in effect, to stand outside of the conversation that others interested in the subject are having. Standing in this sort of intellectual vacuum sometimes appeals to writers who fear that consulting sources will leave them with nothing to say. But it is possible, as this chapter shows, to find *a middle ground* between developing an idea that is entirely independent of what experts have written on a subject and producing a paper that does nothing but repeat other people's ideas. A little research—even if it's only an hour's browse in the reference collection of the library—will virtually always raise the level of what you have to say above what it would have been if you had consulted only the information and opinions that you carry around in your head.

A good rule of thumb for coping with "source anxiety" is to formulate a tentative position on your topic before you consult secondary sources. In other words, give yourself time to do some preliminary thinking. Try writing informally about your topic, analyzing some piece of pertinent information already at your disposal. That way you will have your initial responses written down to weigh in relation to what others have said. Writing of this sort can also help you to select what to look at in the sources you eventually consult.

The Conversation Analogy

Now, let's turn to *the major problem in using sources—a writer leaving the experts he or she cites to speak for themselves.* In this situation, the writer characteristically makes a generalization in his or her own words, juxtaposes it to a quotation or other reference from a secondary source, and assumes that the meaning of the reference will be self-evident. This practice not only leaves the connection between the writer's thinking and his or her source material unstated but also substitutes mere repetition of someone else's viewpoint for a more active interpretation. The source has been allowed to have the final word, with the effect that it stops the discussion and the writer's thinking.

First and foremost, then, you need to do something with the reading. *Clarify the meaning of the material you have quoted, paraphrased, or summarized and explain its significance* in light of your evolving thesis.

It follows that the first step in using sources effectively is to *reject the assumption that sources provide final and complete answers.* If they did, there would be no reason for others to continue writing on the subject. As in conversation, we raise ideas for others to respond to. Accepting that no source has the final word does not mean, however, that you should shift from unquestioning approval to the opposite pole and necessarily assume an antagonistic position toward all sources. Indeed, *a habitually antagonistic response to others' ideas is just as likely to bring your conversation with your sources to a halt* as is the habit of always assuming that the source must have the final word.

Most people would probably agree on the attributes of a really good conversation. There is room for agreement and disagreement, for give and take, among a variety of viewpoints. Generally, people don't deliberately misunderstand each other, but a significant amount of the discussion may go into clarifying one's own as well as others' positions. Such conversations construct a genuinely collaborative *chain* of thinking: Karl builds on what David has said, which induces Jill to respond to Karl's comment, and so forth.

There are, of course, obvious differences between conversing aloud with friends and conversing on paper with sources. As a writer, you need to construct the chain of thinking, orchestrate the exchange of views with and among your sources, and give the conversation direction. A good place to begin in using sources is to recognize that you need not respond to everything another writer says, nor do you need to come up with an entirely original point of view—one that completely revises or refutes the source. You are using sources analytically, for example, when you note that two experiments (or historical accounts, or whatever) are similar but have different priorities or that they ask similar questions in different ways. Building from this kind of observation, you can then analyze what these differences imply.

There are, in any case, many ways of approaching secondary sources, but these ways generally share a common goal: *to use the source as a point of departure.* Here is a partial list of ways to do that.

- Make as many points as you can about a single representative passage from your source, and then branch out from this center to analyze other passages that "speak" to it in some way. (See "Analyzing Evidence in Depth: Doing 10 on 1" in Chapter 5.)
- Use Notice and Focus to identify what you find most strange in the source (see Chapter 2); this will help you cultivate your curiosity about the source and find the critical distance necessary to thinking about it.
- Use The Method to identify the most significant organizing contrast in the source (see Chapter 2); this will help you see what the source itself is wrestling with, what is at stake in it.
- Apply an idea in the source to another subject. (See "Applying a Reading As a Lens" in Chapter 4.)
- Uncover the assumptions in the source, and then build upon the source's point of view, extending its implications. (See "Uncovering the Assumptions in a Reading" in Chapter 4.)

- Agree with most of what the source says, but take issue with one small part that you want to modify.
- Identify a contradiction in the source, and explore its implications, without necessarily arriving at a solution.

The first chapter of this book, "Habits of Mind: Getting Ready to Have Ideas," ends with a brief description of ideas—what they are and especially what they do. We call that section "What It Means to Have an Idea." We say that it's one thing to acquire knowledge, but you also need to learn how to produce knowledge, to think for yourself. In this chapter we offer ways of using secondary sources to help you arrive at ideas. Sources don't relieve you of the responsibility of thinking for yourself; they up the stakes, so to speak, and increase the chances of you arriving at better ideas. Here is a slightly reordered version of the original list in "What It Means to Have an Idea" that stresses goals and methods you'll find in this chapter:

- An idea may be the discovery of a question where there seemed not to be one.
- An idea may make explicit and explore the meaning of something implicit—an unstated assumption upon which an argument rests or a logical consequence of a given position.

Voices from Across the Curriculum

Reporting Versus Analyzing in Scientific Experiments

There is a big difference between simply reporting on what has been done in a scientific venture and analyzing and evaluating the venture. One of the problems with trying to *read* critical analyses of scientific work is that few scientists want to be in print criticizing their colleagues. That is, for political reasons scientists who write reviews are likely to soften their criticism or even avoid it entirely by reporting the findings of others simply and directly. However, by definition such a review is not critical. That author stakes out no particular point of view and thus does not have to defend anything.

What I want from students in molecular biology is a critical analysis of the work they have researched. This can take several forms.

First, *analyze* what was done. What were the assumptions (hypotheses) going into the experiment? What was the logic of the experimental design? What were the results?

Second, *evaluate* the results and conclusions. Here, it's even appropriate to use the first person. *You* are commenting on the field. Foremost, how well do the results support the conclusions? What alternative interpretations are there? What additional experiments could be done to strengthen or refute the argument? This is hard, no doubt, but it is what you should be doing every time you read anything in science or otherwise.

Third, *synthesize* the results and interpretations of a given experiment in the context of the field. How does this study inform other studies? Even though practicing scientists are hesitant to do this in print, everyone does it informally in journal clubs held usually on a weekly basis in every lab all over the world.

—Bruce Wightman, *Professor of Biology*

- An idea usually starts with an observation that is puzzling, with something that you want to figure out rather than with something that you think you already understand.
- An idea may connect elements of a subject and explain the significance of that connection.
- An idea often accounts for some *dissonance*—that is, something that seems not to fit together.
- An idea answers a question; it explains something that needs to be explained.

Most strong analytical ideas launch you in a process of resolving problems and bringing competing positions into some kind of alignment. They locate you where there is something to negotiate, where you are required not just to list answers but also to ask questions, make choices, and engage in reasoning about the significance of your evidence.

If you quote with the aim of conversing with your sources rather than allowing them to do your thinking for you, you will discover that sources can promote rather than stifle your analysis. In short, think of sources not as answers but as voices inviting you into a community of interpretation, discussion, and debate. As the discussion in the "Voices from Across the Curriculum" box demonstrates, this practice is common to different academic disciplines.

B. SIX STRATEGIES FOR ANALYZING SOURCES

Many people never get beyond like/dislike responses with secondary materials. If they agree with what a source says, they say it's "good," and they cut and paste the part they can use as an answer. If the source somehow disagrees with what they already believe, they say it's "bad," and they attack it or—along with readings they find "hard" or "boring"—discard it. As readers they have been conditioned to develop a point of view on a subject without first figuring out the conversation (the various points of view) that their subject attracts. They assume, in other words, that their subject probably has a single meaning—a gist—disclosed by experts, who mostly agree. The six strategies that follow offer ways to avoid this trap.

Strategy 1: Make Your Sources Speak

Quote, paraphrase, or summarize *in order to* analyze—not *in place of* analyzing. Don't assume that either the meaning of the source material or your reason for including it is self-evident. Stop yourself from the habit of just stringing together citations for which you provide little more than conjunctions. Instead, explain to your readers what the quotation or paraphrase or summary of the source means. What elements of it do you find interesting or revealing or strange? Emphasize how those affect your evolving thesis.

In making a source speak, focus on articulating how the source has led to the conclusion you draw from it. Beware of simply putting a generalization and a quotation next to each other (juxtaposing them) without explaining the connection. Instead fill the crucial site between claim and evidence (see Figure 5.2) with your *thinking*. Consider this problem in the following paragraph from a student's paper on political conservatism.

> Edmund Burke's philosophy evolved into contemporary American conservative ideology. There is an important distinction between philosophy and political ideology: philosophy is "the knowledge of general principles that explain facts and existences." Political ideology, on the other hand, is "an overarching conception of society, a stance that is reflected in numerous sectors of social life" (Edwards 22). Therefore, conservatism should be regarded as an ideology rather than a philosophy.

The final sentence offers the writer's conclusion—what the source information has led him to—but how did it get him there? The writer's choice of the word "therefore" indicates to the reader that the idea following it is the result of a process of logical reasoning, but this reasoning has been omitted. Instead, the writer assumes that the reader will be able to connect the quotations with his conclusion. The writer needs to *make the quotation speak* by analyzing its key terms more closely. What is "an overarching conception of society," and how does it differ from "knowledge of general principles"? More important, what is the rationale for categorizing conservatism as either an ideology or a philosophy?

Here, by contrast, is a writer who makes her sources speak. Focus on how she integrates analysis with quotation.

> Stephen Greenblatt uses the phrase "self-fashioning" to refer to an idea he believes developed during the Renaissance—the idea that one's identity is not created or born but rather shaped, both by one's self and by others. The idea of self-fashioning is incorporated into an attitude toward literature that has as its ideal what Greenblatt calls "poetics of culture." A text is examined with three elements in mind: the author's own self, the cultural self-fashioning process that created that self, and the author's reaction to that process. Because our selves, like texts, are "fashioned," an author's life is just as open to interpretation as that of a literary character.
>
> If this is so, then biography does not provide a repository of unshakeable facts from which to interpret an author's work. Greenblatt criticizes the fact that the methods of literary interpretation are applied just to art and not to life. As he observes, "We wall off literary symbolism from the symbolic structures operative elsewhere, as if art alone were a human creation" (Begley 37). If the line between art and life is indeed blurred, then we need a more complex model for understanding the relationship between the life and work of an author.

In this example, the writer shows us how her thinking has been stimulated by the source. At the end of the first paragraph and the beginning of the second, for example, she not only specifies what she takes to be the meaning of the quotation but also draws a conclusion about its implications (that the facts of an author's life, like his or her art, require interpretation). And this manner of proceeding is habitual: the writer repeats the pattern in the second paragraph, *moving beyond what the quotation says to explore what its logic suggests.*

Strategy 2: Use Your Sources to Ask Questions, Not Just to Provide Answers

Use your selections from sources as a means of raising issues and questions. Avoid the temptation to plug in such selections as answers that require no further commentary or elaboration. You will no doubt find viewpoints you believe to be valid, but it is not enough to drop these answers from the source into your own writing at the appropriate spots. You need to *do* something with the reading, even with those sources that seem to have said what you want to say.

As long as you consider only the source in isolation, you may not discover much to say about it. Once you begin considering it in other contexts and with other sources, you may begin to see aspects of your subject that your source does not adequately address. Having recognized that the source does not answer all questions, you should not conclude that the source is "wrong"—only that it is limited in some ways. Discovering such limitations is in fact advantageous, because it can lead you to identify a place from which to launch your own analysis.

It does not necessarily follow that your analysis will culminate in an answer to replace those offered by your sources. Often—in fact, far more often than many writers suspect—it is enough to discover issues or problems and raise them clearly. Phrasing *explicitly* the issues and questions that remain *implicit* in a source is an important part of what analytical writers do, especially with cases in which there is no solution, or at least none that can be presented in a relatively short paper. Here, for example, is how the writer on Stephen Greenblatt's concept of self-fashioning concludes her essay:

> It is not only the author whose role is complicated by New Historicism; the critic also is subject to some of the same qualifications and restrictions. According to Adam Begley, "it is the essence of the new-historicist project to uncover the moments at which works of art absorb and refashion social energy, an endless process of circulation and exchange" (39). In other words, the work is both affected by and affects the culture. But if this is so, how then can we decide which elements of culture (and text) are causes and which are effects? If we add the critic to this picture, the process does indeed appear endless. The New Historicists' relationship with their culture infuses itself into their assessment of the Renaissance, and this assessment may in turn become part of their own self-fashioning process, which will affect their interpretations, and so forth... .

Notice that this writer *incorporates the quotation into her own chain of thinking.* By paraphrasing the quotation ("In other words"), she arrives at a question ("how then") that follows as a logical consequence of accepting its position ("but if this is so"). Note, however, that she does not then label the quotation right or wrong. Instead, she tries to figure out *to what position it might lead* and to what possible problems.

By contrast, the writer of the following excerpt, from a paper comparing two films aimed at teenagers, settles for plugging in sources as answers and consequently does not pursue the questions implicit in her quotations.

> In both films, the adults are one-dimensional caricatures, evil beings whose only goal in life is to make the kids' lives a living hell. In *Risky Business,* director Paul

Brickman's solution to all of Joel's problems is to have him hire a prostitute and then turn his house into a whorehouse. Of course, as one critic observes, "the prostitutes who make themselves available to his pimply faced buddies are all centerfold beauties: elegant, svelte, benign and unquestionably healthy (after all, what does V.D. have to do with prostitutes?)" (Gould 41)—not exactly a realistic or legal solution. Allan Moyle, the director of *Pump Up the Volume,* provides an equally unrealistic solution to Mark's problem. According to David Denby, Moyle "offers self-expression as the cure to adolescent funk. Everyone should start his own radio station and talk about his feelings" (59). Like Brickman, Moyle offers solutions that are neither realistic nor legal.

This writer is having a hard time figuring out what to do with sources that offer well-phrased and seemingly accurate answers (such as "self-expression is the cure to adolescent funk"). Her analysis of both quotations leads her to settle for the bland and undeveloped conclusion that films aimed at teenagers are not "realistic"—an observation that most readers would already recognize as true. But unlike the writer of the previous example, she does not ask herself, "*If this is true, then what follows?*" Had she asked some such version of the "So what?" question, she might have inquired how the illegality of the solutions is related to their unrealistic quality. So what, for example, that the main characters in both films are not marginalized as criminals and made to suffer for their illegal actions, but rather are celebrated as heroes? What different kinds of illegality do the two films apparently condone, and how might these be related to the different decades in which each film was produced? Rather than use her sources to think with, in order to clarify or complicate the issues, the writer has used them only to confirm an obvious generalization.

Strategy 3: Put Your Sources into Conversation with One Another

Rather than limiting yourself to agreeing or disagreeing with your sources, aim for conversation with and among them. Although it is not wrong to agree or disagree with your sources, it is wrong to see these as your only possible moves. You should also understand that although it is sometimes useful and perhaps even necessary to agree or disagree, these judgments should (1) always be *qualified* and (2) occur only *in certain contexts.*

Selective analytical summarizing of a position with which you essentially agree or disagree, especially if located early in a final draft (after you've figured out what to think in your previous drafts), can be extraordinarily helpful in orienting your readers for the discussion to follow. This practice of *framing the discussion* typically locates you either for or against some well-known point of view or frame of reference; it's a way of sharing your assumptions with the reader. You introduce the source, in other words, to succinctly summarize a position that you plan to develop or challenge in a qualified way. This latter strategy—sometimes known as *straw man,* because you construct a "dummy" position specifically in order to knock it down—can stimulate you to formulate a point of view, especially if you are not accustomed to responding critically to sources.

As this boxing analogy suggests, however, setting up a straw man can be a dangerous game. If you do not fairly represent and put into context the straw man's argument, you risk encouraging readers to dismiss your counterargument as a cheap shot and to dismiss you for being *reductive*. On the other hand, if you spend a great deal of time detailing the straw man's position, you risk losing momentum in developing your own point of view. In any case, if you are citing a source in order to frame the discussion, the more reasonable move is both to agree *and* disagree with it. First, identify shared premises; give the source some credit. Then distinguish the part of what you have cited that you intend to develop or complicate or dispute. This method of proceeding is obviously less combative than the typically blunt straw man approach; it verges on conversation.

In the following passage from a student's paper on Darwin's theory of evolution, the student clearly recognizes that he needs to do more than summarize what Darwin says, but he seems not to know any way of conversing with his source other than indicating his agreement and disagreement with it.

> The struggle for existence also includes the dependence of one being on another being to survive. Darwin also believes that all organic beings tend to increase. I do not fully agree with Darwin's belief here. I cannot conceive of the fact of all beings increasing in number. Darwin goes on to explain that food, competition, climate, and the location of a certain species contribute to its survival and existence in nature. I believe that this statement is very valid and that it could be very easily understood through experimentation in nature.

This writer's use of the word "here" in his third sentence is revealing. He is tagging summaries of Darwin with what he seems to feel is an obligatory response—a polite shake or nod of the head: "I can't fully agree with you there, Darwin, but here I think you might have a point." The writer's tentative language lets us see how uncomfortable, even embarrassed, he feels about venturing these judgments on a subject that is too complex for this kind of response. It's as though the writer moves along, talking about Darwin's theory for a while, and then says to himself, "Time for a response," and lets a particular summary sentence trigger a yes/no switch. Having pressed that switch, which he does periodically, the writer resumes his summary, having registered but not analyzed his own interjections. There is no reasoning in a chain from his own observations, just random insertions of unanalyzed agree/disagree responses.

Here, by contrast, is the introduction of an essay that uses summary to frame the conversation that the writer is preparing to have with her source.

> In *Renaissance Thought: The Classic, Scholastic and Humanist Strains,* Paul Kristeller responds to two problems that he perceives in Renaissance scholarship. The first is the haze of cultural meaning surrounding the word "humanism": he seeks to clarify the word and its origins, as well as to explain the apparent lack of religious concern in humanism. Kristeller also reacts to the notion of humanism as an improvement upon medieval Aristotelian scholasticism.

Rather than leading with her own beliefs about the source, the writer emphasizes the issues and problems she believes are central in it. Although the writer's position on her source is apparently neutral, she is not summarizing passively. In addition to making choices about what is especially significant in the source, she has also located it within the conversation that its author, Kristeller, was having with his own sources—the works of other scholars whose view of humanism he wants to revise ("Kristeller responds to two problems").

As an alternative to formulating your opinion of the sources, try constructing the conversation that you think the author of one of your sources might have with the author of another. *How might they recast each other's ideas, as opposed to merely agreeing or disagreeing with those ideas?* Notice how, farther on in the paper, the writer uses this strategy to achieve a clearer picture of Kristeller's point of view:

> Unlike Kristeller, Tillyard [in *The Elizabethan World Picture*] also tries to place the seeds of individualism in the minds of the medievals. "Those who know most about the Middle Ages," he claims, "now assure us that humanism and a belief in the present life were powerful by the 12th century" (30). Kristeller would undoubtedly reply that it was scholasticism, lacking the humanist emphasis on individualism that was powerful in the Middle Ages. True humanism was not evident in the Middle Ages.
>
> In Kristeller's view, Tillyard's attempts to assign humanism to medievals are not only unwarranted, but also counterproductive. Kristeller ends his chapter on "Humanism and Scholasticism" with an exhortation to "develop a kind of historical pluralism. It is easy to praise everything in the past that appears to resemble certain favorable ideas of our own time, or to ridicule and minimize everything that disagrees with them. This method is neither fair nor helpful" (174). Tillyard, in trying to locate humanism within the medieval world, allows the value of humanism to supersede the worth of medieval scholarship. Kristeller argues that there is inherent worth in every intellectual movement, not simply in the ones that we find most agreeable.
>
> Kristeller's work is valuable to us primarily for its forthright definition of humanism. Tillyard has cleverly avoided this undertaking: he provides many textual references, usually with the companion comment that "this is an example of Renaissance humanism," but he never overtly and fully formulates the definition in the way that Kristeller does.

As this excerpt makes evident, the writer has found something to say about her source by putting it into conversation with another source with which she believes her source, Kristeller, would disagree ("Kristeller would undoubtedly reply"). Although it seems obvious that the writer prefers Kristeller to Tillyard, her agreement with him is not the main point of her analysis. She focuses instead on foregrounding the problem that Kristeller is trying to solve and on relating that problem to different attitudes toward history. In so doing, she is deftly orchestrating the conversation between her sources. Her next step would be to distinguish her position from Kristeller's. Having used Kristeller to get perspective on Tillyard, she now needs somehow to get perspective on Kristeller. The next strategy addresses this issue.

Strategy 4: Find Your Own Role in the Conversation

Even in cases in which you find a source's position entirely congenial, it is not enough simply to agree with it. In order to converse with a source, you need to find some way of having a distinct voice in that conversation. This does not mean that you should feel compelled to attack the source but rather that you need to find something of your own to say about it.

In general, you have two options when you find yourself strongly in agreement with a source. You can *apply it in another context to qualify or expand its implications.* Or you can seek out other perspectives on the source in order to break the spell it has cast upon you. "To break the spell" means that you will necessarily become somewhat disillusioned but not that you will then need to dismiss everything you previously believed.

How, in the first option, do you take a source somewhere else? Rather than focusing solely on what you believe your source finds most important, *locate a lesser point, not emphasized by the reading, that you find especially interesting and develop it further.* This strategy will lead you to uncover new implications that depend upon your source but lie outside its own governing preoccupations. In the preceding humanism example, the writer might apply Kristeller's principles to new geographic (rather than theoretical) areas, such as Germany instead of Italy.

The second option, researching new perspectives on the source, can also lead to uncovering new implications. Your aim need not be simply to find a source that disagrees with the one that has convinced you and then switch your allegiance, because this move would perpetuate the problem from which you are trying to escape. Instead, you would use additional perspectives to gain some critical distance from your source. An ideal way of sampling possible critical approaches to a source is to consult book reviews on it found in scholarly journals. Once the original source is taken down from the pedestal through additional reading, there is a greater likelihood that you will see how to distinguish your views from those it offers.

You may think, for example, that another source's critique of your original source is partly valid and that both sources miss things that you could point out; in effect, you *referee* the conversation between them. The writer on Kristeller might play this role by asking herself: "So what that subsequent historians have viewed his objective—a disinterested historical pluralism—as not necessarily desirable and in any case impossible? How might Kristeller respond to this charge, and how has he responded already in ways that his critics have failed to notice?" Using additional research in this way can lead you to *situate* your source more fully and fairly, acknowledging its limits as well as its strengths.

In other words, this writer, in using Kristeller to critique Tillyard, has arrived less at a conclusion than at her next point of departure. A good rule to follow, especially when you find a source entirely persuasive, is that if you can't find a perspective on your source, you haven't done enough research.

Strategy 5: Supply Ongoing Analysis of Sources (Don't Wait Until the End)

Unless disciplinary conventions dictate otherwise, analyze *as* you quote or paraphrase a source, rather than summarizing everything first and leaving your analysis for the end. A good conversation does not consist of long monologues alternating among the speakers. Participants exchange views, query, and modify what other speakers have said. Similarly, when you orchestrate conversations with and among your sources, you need to *integrate your analysis into your presentation* of them.

Voices from Across the Curriculum

Bringing Sources Together

Avoid serial citation summaries; that is, rather than discussing what Author A found, then what Author B found, then what Author C found, and so forth, *integrate* material from all of your sources. For instance, if writing about the cause and treatment of a disorder, discuss what all authors say about cause, then what all authors say about treatment, and so forth, addressing any contradictions or tensions among authors.

—Alan Tjeltveit, *Professor of Psychology*

In supplying ongoing analysis, you are much more likely to explain how the information in the sources fits into your unfolding presentation, and your readers will be more likely to follow your train of thought and grasp the logic of your organization. You will also prevent yourself from using the sources simply as an answer. A good rule of thumb in this regard is to *force yourself to ask and answer "So what?" at the ends of paragraphs*. In laying out your analysis, however, take special care to distinguish your voice from the sources'. (For further discussion of integrating analysis into your presentation of sources, see the commentary on the research paper later in this chapter.)

Strategy 6: Attend Carefully to the Language of Your Sources by Quoting or Paraphrasing Them

Rather than generalizing broadly about ideas in your sources, you should spell out what you think is significant about their key words. In those disciplines in which it is permissible, *quote sources if the actual language that they use is important to your point*. This practice will help you to represent the view of your source fairly and accurately. In situations where quoting is not allowed—such as in the report format in psychology— you still need to attend carefully to the meaning of key words in order to arrive at a paraphrase that is not overly general. As we have suggested repeatedly, paraphrasing provides an ideal way to begin interpreting, since the act of careful rephrasing usually illuminates attitudes and assumptions implicit in a text. It is almost impossible not to have ideas and not to see the questions when you start paraphrasing.

Another reason that quoting and paraphrasing are important is that your analysis of a source will nearly always benefit from attention to the way the source represents its position (not just from dwelling on the position itself). Although focusing on the manner of presentation matters more with some sources than with others—more with a poem or scholarly article in political science than with a paper in the natural sciences— the information is never wholly separable from how it is expressed. If you are going to quote *Newsweek* on Pakistan, for example, you will be encountering not "the truth" about American involvement in this Asian nation but rather one particular representation of the situation—in this case, one crafted to meet or shape the expectations of mainstream popular culture. Similarly, if you quote President Bush on terrorism, what probably matters most is that the president chose particular words to represent—and promote—the government's position. *It is not neutral information.* The person speaking and the kind of source in which his or her words appear usually acquire added significance when you make note of these words rather than just summarizing them.

❦ *Try this:* Select a passage from a secondary source that appears important to your evolving thinking about a subject you are studying, and try doing a passage-based focused freewrite on it. You might choose the passage in answer to the question "What is the one passage in the source that I need to discuss, that poses a question or a problem or that seems, in some way perhaps difficult to pin down, anomalous or even just unclear?" Copy the passage at the top of the page, and go for twenty minutes. As we discuss in the section entitled "Passage-Based Focused Freewriting" in Chapter 4, try to isolate and paraphrase key terms as you relentlessly ask "So what?" about the details. Also, remember to consider how the passage is representative of broader issues in the source; you may wish to refer to a similar passage for this purpose. □

❦ *Try this:* As a variation on the preceding exercise, *apply a brief passage from a secondary source to a brief passage from a primary source.* Choose the secondary source passage first—one that you find particularly interesting, revealing, or problematic. Then locate a corresponding passage from the primary source to which the sentence from the first passage can be connected in some way. Copy both passages at the top of the page, and then write for twenty minutes. You should probably include paraphrases of key phrases in both, but your primary goal is to think about the two together, to allow them to interact. □

C. MAKING THE RESEARCH PAPER MORE ANALYTICAL: A SAMPLE ESSAY

The following is an example of a typical college research paper. We offer a brief analysis of each paragraph with an eye to diagnosing what typically goes wrong in writing a research paper and how applying a version of the six strategies for analyzing sources can be used to remedy the problems.

The Flight from Teaching

[1] The "flight from teaching" (Smith 6) in higher education is a controversial issue of the academic world. The amount of importance placed on research and publishing is the major cause of this flight. I will show different views and aspects concerning the problem plaguing our colleges and universities, through the authors whom I have consulted. [The introductory paragraph needs to be revised to eliminate prejudgment. Calling the issue "controversial" implies that there are different points of view on the subject. The writer, however, offers only one and words it in a way that suggests she has already leaped to a premature and oversimplified conclusion. Instead, she needs to better *frame the issue* and then replace the procedural opening (see Chapter 10) with a more hypothetical working thesis that will enable her to explore the subject.]

[2] Page Smith takes an in-depth look at the "flight from teaching" in *Killing the Spirit*. Smith's views on this subject are interesting, because he is a professor with tenure at UCLA. Throughout the book, Smith stresses the sentiment of the student being the enemy, as expressed by many of his colleagues. Some professors resent the fact that the students take up their precious time—time that could be better used for research. Smith goes on about how much some of his colleagues go out of their way to avoid their students. They go as far as making strange office hours to avoid contact. Smith disagrees with the hands-off approach being taken by the professors: "There is no decent, adequate, respectable education, in the proper sense of that much-abused word, without personal involvement by a teacher with the needs and concerns, academic and personal, of his/her students. All the rest is 'instruction' or 'information transferral,' 'communication technique,' or some other impersonal and antiseptic phrase, but it is not teaching and the student is not truly learning" (7). [The writer summarizes and quotes one of her sources but does not analyze or offer any perspective on it.]

[3] Page Smith devotes a chapter to the ideal of "publish or perish," "since teaching is shunned in the name of research." Smith refutes the idea that "research enhances teaching" and that there is a "direct relationship between research and teaching" (178). In actuality, research inhibits teaching. The research that is being done, in most cases, is too specialized for the student. As with teaching and research, Smith believes there is not necessarily a relationship between research and publication. Unfortunately those professors who are devoted to teaching find themselves without a job and/or tenure unless they conform to the requirements of publishing. Smith asks, "Is not the atmosphere hopelessly polluted when professors are forced to do research in order to validate themselves, in order to make a living, in order to avoid being humiliated (and terminated)?" (197). Not only are the students and the professors suffering, but also as a whole, "Under the publish-or-perish standard, the university is perishing" (180). [The writer continues her summary of her source, using language that implies but does not make explicit her apparent agreement with it. She appears to use the source to speak for her but has not clearly distinguished her voice from that of her source. See, for example, the third sentence and the last sentence of the paragraph. Is the writer only reporting what Smith says or appropriating his view as her own?]

[4] Charles J. Sykes looks at the "flight from teaching" in *Profscam: Professors and the Demise of Higher Education*. Sykes cites statistics to show the results of the reduction of professors' teaching loads enabling them time for more research. The call to research is the cause of many problems. The reduced number of professors actually teaching increases both the size of classes and the likelihood that students will find at registration that their courses are closed. Students will also find they do not have to write papers, and often exams are multiple choice, because of the large classes. Consequently, the effects of the "flight from teaching" have "had dramatic ramifications for the way undergraduates are taught" (40). [The writer summarizes another of her sources without analysis of its reasoning and again blurs the distinction between the source's position and her own.]

[5] E. Peter Volpe, in his chapter "Teaching, Research, and Service: Union or Coexistence?" in the book *Whose Goals for American Higher Education?*, disagrees strongly that there is an overemphasis on research. Volpe believes that only the research scholar can provide the best form of teaching because "Teaching and research are as inseparable as the two faces of the same coin" (80). The whole idea of education is to increase the student's curiosity. When the enthusiasm of the professor, because of his or her research, is brought into the classroom, it intensifies that curiosity and therefore provides "the deepest kind of intellectual enjoyment" (80). Volpe provides suggestions for solving the rift between students and professors, such as "replacing formal discourse by informal seminars and independent study programs" (81). He feels that this will get students to think for themselves and professors to learn to communicate with students again. Another suggestion is that the government provide funding for "research programs that are related to the education function" (82). This would allow students the opportunity to share in the research. In conclusion, Volpe states his thesis to be, "A professor in any discipline stays alive when he carries his enthusiasm for discovery into the classroom. The professor is academically dead when the spark of inquiry is extinguished within him. It is then that he betrays his student. The student becomes merely an acquirer of knowledge rather than an inquirer into knowledge" (80). [Here the writer summarizes a source that offers an opposing point of view. It is good that she has begun to represent multiple perspectives, but as with the preceding summaries, there is not yet enough analysis. If she could put Volpe's argument into active conversation with those of Sykes and Smith, she might be able to articulate more clearly the assumptions her sources share and to distinguish their key differences. How, for example, do the three sources differ in their definitions of research and of teaching?]

[6] The "flight from teaching" is certainly a problem in colleges and universities. When beginning to research this topic, I had some very definite opinions. I believed that research and publication should not play any role in teaching. Through the authors utilized in this paper and other sources, I have determined that there is a need for some "research" but not to the extent that teaching is pushed aside. College and universities exist to provide an education; therefore, their first responsibility is to the student. [Here the writer begins to offer her opinion of the material, which she does, in effect, by choosing sides. She appears to be compromising—"there is a need for some 'research' but not to the extent that teaching is pushed aside"—but as her last sentence shows, she has in fact dismissed the way that Volpe complicates the relationship between teaching and research.]

[7] I agree with Smith that research, such as reading in the professor's field, is beneficial to his or her teaching. But requiring research to the extent of publication in order to secure a tenured position is actually denying education to both the professors and their students. I understand that some of the pressure stems from the fact that it is easier to decide tenure by the "tangible" evidence of research and publication. The emphasis on "publish or perish" should revert to "teach or perish" (Smith 6). If more of an effort is required to base tenure upon teaching, then that effort should be made.

After all, it is the education of the people of our nation that is at risk. [The writer continues to align herself with one side of the issue, which she continues to summarize but not to raise questions about.]

[8] In conclusion, I believe that the problem of the "flight from teaching" can and must be addressed. The continuation of the problem will lead to greater damage in the academic community. The leaders of our colleges and universities will need to take the first steps toward a solution. [The writer concludes with a more strongly worded version of her endorsement of the position of Smith and Sykes on the threat of research to teaching. Notice that the paper has not really evolved from the unanalyzed position it articulated in paragraph 2.]

D. STRATEGIES FOR WRITING AND REVISING RESEARCH PAPERS

Here we offer some general strategies gleaned from and keyed to our analysis of a typical paper, "The Flight from Teaching," that can be applied to any research project.

1. Be sure to make clear who is talking.

When, for example, the writer refers to the professors' concern for their "precious time" in paragraph 2 or when she writes that "In actuality, research inhibits teaching" in paragraph 3, is she simply summarizing Smith or endorsing his position? You can easily clarify who's saying what by inserting attributive tag phrases such as "in Smith's view" or "in response to Smith, one might argue that." Remember that your role is to provide explanation of and perspective on the ideas in your source—not, especially early on, to cheerlead for it or attack it.

2. Analyze as you go along rather than saving analysis for the end (disciplinary conventions permitting).

It is no coincidence that a research paper that summarizes its sources and delays discussing them, as "The Flight from Teaching" does, should have difficulty constructing a logically coherent and analytically revealing point of view. The *organization* of this research paper interferes with the writer's ability to have ideas about her material because the gap is too wide between the presentation and analysis of her sources. As a result, readers are left unsure how to interpret the positions she initially summarizes, and her analysis, by the time she finally gets to it, is too general.

3. Quote *in order to* analyze: make your sources speak.

Even if the language you quote or paraphrase seems clear in what it means to you, the aim of your analysis is to put what you have quoted or paraphrased into some kind of frame or perspective. Quoting is a powerful form of evidence, but recognize that you can quote *very* selectively—a sentence or even a phrase will often suffice. After you quote, you will usually need to paraphrase in order to discover and articulate the implications of the quotation's key terms. *As a general rule, you should not end a discussion with a quotation but rather with some point you want to make about the quotation.*

The following sentence from the second paragraph of "The Flight from Teaching" demonstrates the missed opportunities for analysis that occur when a quotation is allowed to speak for itself.

> Smith disagrees with the hands-off approach being taken by the professors: "There is no decent, adequate, respectable education, in the proper sense of that much-abused word, without personal involvement by a teacher with the needs and concerns, academic and personal, of his/her students" (7).

This sentence is offered as part of a neutral summary of Smith's position, which, the writer informs us "disagrees with the hands-off approach." But notice how Smith's word choices convey additional information about his point of view. The repetition of "personal" and the quarrelsome tone of "much-abused" suggest that Smith is writing a polemic—that he is so preoccupied with the personal that he wishes to restrict the definition of education to it. The writer may agree with Smith's extreme position, but the point is that if she attends to his actual language, she will be able to characterize that position much more accurately.

By contrast, notice how the writer in the following example quotes *in order to* analyze the implications of the source's language:

> If allegations that top levels of U.S. and British governments acted covertly to shape foreign policy are truthful, then this scandal, according to Friedman, poses serious questions concerning American democracy. Friedman explains, "The government's lack of accountability, either to Congress or to the public, was so egregious as to pose a silent threat to the principles of American democracy" (286). The word "principles" is especially important. In Friedman's view, without fundamental ideals such as a democracy based on rule by elected representatives *and* the people, where does the average citizen stand? What will happen to faith in the government, Friedman seems to be asking, if elected representatives such as the president sully that respected office?

By emphasizing Friedman's word choice ("principles"), this writer uses quotation not only to convey information but also to frame it, making a point about the source's point of view.

4. Try converting key assertions in the source into questions.

When you are under the spell of a source, its claims sound more final and unquestionably true than they actually are. So, a useful habit of mind is to experiment with rewording selected assertions as questions. Consider, for example, what the writer of "The Flight from Teaching" might have discovered had she tried converting the following conclusions (in paragraph 4) drawn from one of her sources into questions.

> The call to research is the cause of many problems. The reduced number of professors actually teaching increases both the size of classes and the likelihood that students will find at registration that their courses are closed. Students will also find they do not have to write papers, and often exams are multiple choice, because of the large classes.

Some questions: Is it only professors' desire to be off doing their own research that explains closed courses, large class sizes, and multiple-choice tests? What about other causes for these problems, such as the cost of hiring additional professors or the pressure universities put on professors to publish in order to increase the status of the institution? We are not suggesting that the writer should have detected these particular problems in the passage but rather that she needs, somewhere in the paper, to *raise questions about the reasoning implicit in her sources.*

By *querying how your sources are defining, implicitly and explicitly, their key terms,* you can gain perspective on the sources, uncovering their assumptions. Consider in this context the writer's own fullest statement of her thesis.

> Through the authors utilized in this paper and other sources, I have determined that there is a need for some 'research' but not to the extent that teaching is pushed aside. Colleges and universities exist to provide an education; therefore, their first responsibility is to the student (paragraph 6).

More questions: What do she and her sources mean by "research" and what by "teaching"? To what extent can the writer fairly assume that the primary purpose of universities is and should be "to provide an education"? Can't an education include being mentored in the skills that university teachers practice in their own research? And isn't teaching only one of a variety of contributions that universities make to the cultures they serve?

5. Get your sources to converse with one another, and actively referee the conflicts among them.

By doing so, you will often find the means to reorganize your paper around issues rather than leave readers to locate these issues for themselves as you move from source to source. Both looking for difference within similarity and looking for similarity despite difference are useful for this purpose (see Chapter 4).

The organizing contrast that drives "The Flight from Teaching" is obviously that between teaching and research, but what if the writer actively sought out an unexpected similarity that spanned this binary? For example, Smith asserts that "research inhibits teaching" (paragraph 3), whereas Volpe contends that "only the research scholar can provide the best form of teaching because 'teaching and research are as inseparable as the two faces of the same coin'" (paragraph 5). But both sides *agree* that educating students is the "first responsibility" of colleges and universities, despite differing radically on how this responsibility is best fulfilled. Given this unexpected similarity, the writer could then explore the significance of the difference—that Smith believes professors' research gets in the way of excellent teaching, whereas Volpe believes research is essential to it. If the writer had brought these sources into dialogue, she could have discovered that the assertion she offers as her conclusion is, in fact, inaccurate, even an evasion.

By way of conclusion, we would like to emphasize that these five strategies share a common aim: to get you off the hot seat of judging the experts when you are not an expert. Most of us are more comfortable in situations in which we can converse amicably rather than judge and be judged. Think of that as you embark on research projects, and you will be far more likely to learn and to have a good time doing it.

An Analytical Research Paper: a Good Example

What does an effective analytical research paper look like? Look at the following piece, which demonstrates the analytical skills we discuss in this chapter. We include brief commentary at the ends of selected paragraphs, but for the most part, you should notice how the writer uses her sources to focus questions, analyzing as she goes along. Also, note her habitual use of complicating evidence to evolve the conversation she is having with her sources.

Horizontal & Vertical Mergers Within the Healthcare Industry

[1] The United States healthcare industry is constantly changing, as new ideas and strategies are developed to make healthcare more accessible and affordable for a greater number of people. Mergers within the industry are one of the new influential methods of altering the relationship between buyers and sellers of healthcare. Mergers distort the traditional roles of physicians, hospitals, and patients, but do so with an emphasis on cost-cutting, more efficient management, and better quality of care. Whether these mergers actually succeed in their outward goals is debatable; many studies have shown that these acquisitions seldom fully meet their objectives. Mergers are business deals, occurring in every market. But the healthcare market is unique in that its product, a necessity, often becomes an economic luxury—not everyone can afford the costs of medical coverage or care. [The introduction opens with a clear premise—constant change—and rapidly limits the focus to mergers as one cause of change. The writer raises but does not prematurely resolve the question of mergers' successes and ends the paragraph by distinguishing what is at stake in her topic.]

[2] The first distinct type of acquisition is known as a horizontal merger. It describes the joining of two hospital systems into one. Some simple examples of horizontal mergers include the transaction between Memorial Health System and Adventist Health System, both located in Florida: the four-hospital Memorial purchased the thirty-two-hospital Adventist in late August, 2000. Another example is the purchase of St. Mary Medical Hospital by Trinity Health, in separate parts of Michigan, completed in July 2000. In this case, the new hospital system was renamed St. Mary Mercy Hospital.[1] There are advantages and disadvantages to horizontal mergers, which will be explored, but a hospital system's main objectives in merging include reducing managerial costs, combining marketing efforts, pooling capital, and reducing excess equipment. [Having used a panning shot to establish context in the first paragraph, the writer now tracks one kind of merger and suggests that further debate is to come.]

[3] A vertical merger, however, is one in which a company is bought by another company within the same "supply chain" – that is, a firm might purchase its merchandise supplier.[2] In healthcare economies, this applies to suppliers and buyers of

---

[1] "Mergers & Acquisitions," *Business Watch:* July 2000, p. 63.
[2] Ibid, 1.

healthcare services, such as hospitals and HMO's, or hospitals and physicians. There are several complications to vertical mergers, especially apparent when the level of competition between the two merging entities is explored. Esther Gal-Or's article, "The Profitability of Vertical Mergers Between Hospitals and Physician Practices," will be used to illustrate these complications. [The writer begins to foreground a complication that she will develop into an organizing contrast in the next paragraph, that between private profit and public good.]

[4] The selling point for all horizontal and vertical mergers is the expected increase in efficiency under the new system. But mergers benefit the merging parties immensely; are their public goals of efficiency and, in turn, lowered costs, really being achieved? In their article, "Are Multihospital Systems More Efficient?," economists Dranove, Durkac, and Shanley write that although "the conventional wisdom is that [horizontal mergers] will generate efficiencies in the production of services, surprisingly little systematic evidence exists to support this view."[3] By studying local Californian hospital systems in the 1980's and 1990's, the three researchers found that "the benefits of horizontal integration stem from greater efficiencies in marketing hospital systems ... than from efficiencies in the production of services." [The writer uses sources to frame questions. She then cites sources offering slightly different answers to the question of efficiency.]

[5] Using data from the California Office of Statewide Health Planning and Development, the researchers selected eleven hospital systems that met their requirements for inclusion in the study. After investigating costs per admission, administrative costs, price/cost margins, and limitations, the research "[challenged the idea] that horizontally integrated hospitals generate production efficiencies." More specifically, the study showed that the multihospital systems did not consistently reduce high-tech services, or have lower patient costs. In fact, the study concluded that "integrated hospital systems are more likely than their nonintegrated hospital counterparts to have unusually high administrative costs" and that they had "unusually high price/cost margins and operating profits."[4] These findings raise questions as to why hospitals merge if a merger does not provide a substantial increase in the method of operation's efficiency. If it actually results in higher costs for consumers in certain instances, what benefit does a merger bring? [The writer again uses her sources to focus relevant questions. Notice how she moves beyond what one of her sources says to query what it suggests.]

[6] The instance is similar with vertical mergers. Many times, the joining of a hospital and HMO plan or hospital and physician practice does not result in the expected lowered costs and higher quality care for consumers. In her article "The Profitability of Vertical Mergers Between Hospitals and Physician Practices," Esther Gal-Or outlines her complex and thorough study of vertical mergers. Gal-Or details several different

---

[3] Dranove, Durkac, Shanley. "Are Multihospital Systems More Efficient?" *Health Affairs:* Volume 15, 1996.

[4] Ibid, 102.

facets of the vertical merger: there are possible restrictions that these new systems face, all of which jeopardize their original intent for efficiency. She also notes the importance of the competition between the two, writing

> When the degree of competitiveness [between the hospital and physician prac-
> tice] is comparable, a vertical merger enhances the bargaining position of both
> merging parties vis-à-vis insurers. In contrast, when one provider's market is
> much more competitive than the other a vertical merger may reduce the joint
> profits of the merged entity.[5]

Therefore, the success of a vertical merger depends upon the relationship between the two merging parties. [Here the writer leads with similarity despite difference to get her to her next source, which she briefly summarizes before zooming on a selected piece. Her final sentence draws a conclusion from the quotation, though more analysis of it might have enriched the conversation.]

[7] Two examples noted in Gal-Or's study show the types of vertical mergers that are changing U.S. healthcare today. One of these is Allina Health System, a Minnesota-based system that covers over 25% of the state's residents through its HMO and PPO plans. A 1994 merger between a hospital chain and a health plan, Allina is continuing to acquire more hospitals and physician practices. Blue Cross of Western Pennsylvania, another example in the article, has also been purchasing physician practices.[6] Gal-Or's study eventually finds that when "two providers' markets are characterized by comparable degrees of competitiveness . . . both the merging hospital and the merging physician can negotiate higher rates with insurers . . . Consumers are obviously worse off, as a result, since the higher rates translate to higher premia charged by insurers."[7] This offers a major criticism of vertical mergers because consumers are surely not looking to raise the cost of their premiums. These mergers, especially with the evidence provided in this article, seem to benefit the suppliers of healthcare but only at the financial expense of the patients. [Using representative examples from her source, the writer interprets significant detail to draw a conclusion.]

[8] By contrast, in a study entitled "What Types of Hospital Mergers Save Consumers Money," four researchers studied 3,500 United States hospitals from 1986–1994, including 122 horizontal mergers. Their study found that the mergers saved consumers by approximately 7%, which may show that vertical mergers (which also accounted for a large section of the systems studied) do reduce costs to consumers.[8] [The paper pauses here to introduce complicating evidence, which leads to a brief concession (see Chapter 11). Note how the writer qualifies it with her choice of the word "may."]

---

[5] Gal-Or, Esther. "The Profitability of Vertical Mergers Between Hospitals and Physician Practices. *Journal of Health Economics:* October 1999, p.623.

[6] Ibid, 624.

[7] Ibid, 625.

[8] "Which Types of Hospital Mergers Save Consumers Money?" *Health Affairs:* Volume 16, p. 62-74.

[9] Mergers, especially between hospitals, also provoke an interesting ethical dilemma. Special interest groups like Planned Parenthood and the American Civil Liberties Union (ACLU) have recently argued that these mergers are being treated as business contracts between two "sellers" and that the emphasis on providing better coverage for all has been disregarded. They argue that mergers aim not to help consumers, but to reduce internal costs and therefore raise profits for the hospitals. There are two aspects of hospital mergers that most concern these groups: first, the acquisition between religious and non-religious health facilities, resulting in religiously restrictive hospital systems, and, second, the possibility of a system becoming the only option for patients in rural communities. The ACLU recently released the following:

> Many nonsectarian hospitals have recently been merging with religiously controlled hospitals. As a condition of the merger . . . these hospitals observe religious prohibitions against providing certain health services. The most publicized and significant prohibitions are found in the *Ethical and Religious Directives for Catholic Health Care Services.* . . . The *Directives* bar Catholic health care facilities from providing tubal ligation, vasectomy, abortion, in vitro fertilization, contraception, and emergency contraception in the case of rape.[9]

[Notice the evolving conversation, as the writer shifts from economic issues to the ethics these issues entail. Also note her habitual focus on complication, citing the "aspects that most concern."]

[10] In many instances, even when a Catholic hospital is acquired by a non-religious facility, the terms of the agreement include the system's adherence to these Catholic provisions. A statement from Planned Parenthood notes, "a Catholic hospital, or an HMO contracted with a Catholic hospital, is a community's only provider—leaving women with little or no access to reproductive health services."[10] For some, the decision to choose a hospital is religiously motivated; for others, especially women, they believe it is a personal right to have access to these reproductive health services. The ACLU and Planned Parenthood, however, feel strongly that it is a patient's right to choose whether or not to use these specific services. They also feel that mergers between hospitals jeopardize that right by creating a system in which certain services may not be available, regardless of patient preference. [The conversation continues to evolve as the writer introduces new complicating evidence ("the second ethical issue") and analyzes its implications. Notice as well the diverse range of sources she has brought to bear.]

[11] This argument is closely related to the second ethical issue against horizontal hospital mergers. In more rural communities, where there may be few options from which medical care consumers can choose, mergers create a monopolistic environment. The ACLU states that "low-income women and women in rural areas with few

---

[9] "Hospital Mergers: The Threat to Reproductive Health Services." www.aclu.org.
[10] "Opposing Dangerous Hospital Mergers." www.plannedparenthood.org.

choices in medical care are the most vulnerable ... Women who live in rural communities frequently have little choice . . ."[11] This is detrimental to consumer choice because mergers in rural communities most likely create only one hospital system. A dissatisfied consumer in this situation does not have the power to switch medical suppliers; the power is taken away from the consumer and the seller has the ultimate control over the cost, type, and quality of care. Mergers in rural communities greatly resemble a monopolistic market force, and for this reason, are often the targets of antitrust cases against the new hospital system.

The issue of antitrust violations frequently arises regarding mergers in the healthcare industry. This, too, is a criticism of the acquisitions. The majority of the antitrust cases in the United States involve horizontal mergers because, often, they produce one hospital system that borders closely on the definition of a monopoly. But there have also been antitrust questions raised regarding vertical mergers. The Marshfield Clinic case, from 1996, shows some of the questions. The Marshfield Clinic was a physician-owned clinic in Wisconsin that had vertically integrated with its HMO. But in the merger, the clinic had also excluded Blue Cross/Blue Shield HMO coverage from its services. Eventually, the courts found in favor of the Marshfield Clinic because its HMO obviously did not have the power to eliminate Blue Cross/Blue Shield from the healthcare market. [As has been the case throughout the paper, the writer continues to focus on the important questions raised by her representative examples.]

[12] The most recent development in the antitrust cases of hospital mergers is the influential lobby groups, petitioning state governments on behalf of the hospital systems to exempt mergers within the medical industry from antitrust laws. The state of Maine lately encountered such a request. The 565-bed Maine Medical Center, in an effort to merge with two other hospitals, successfully lobbied the state government in 1996 to pass legislation exempting hospitals from state antitrust laws. Since the enactment of the Maine law, nearly twelve other states have also passed laws to free multihospital systems from antitrust regulations.[12] These laws have significant implications for the future of horizontal hospital mergers. They create a safer environment for mergers to occur: without antitrust laws, hospitals can freely merge and even assume a monopolistic form that jeopardizes the market of healthcare. [As the paper approaches its end, the writer cites the "most recent" developments and opens out the conversation to "significant implications for the future."]

[13] The advantages for horizontal and vertical mergers seem clear – by combining efforts, and creating one system, a multihospital facility should manage its administrative duties more efficiently, provide a higher level of care, and lower costs for its patients. Mergers should make the healthcare industry more successfully directed.

---

[11] "Hospital Mergers: The Threat to Reproductive Health Services." www.aclu.org.
[12] "Smaller Hospitals Quicker to Use Maine Merger Law." *Modern Healthcare:* October 7, 1996.

The ultimate aim of any improvement or change in the industry should be to make better healthcare more accessible to a broader number of Americans. It appears as though horizontal and vertical mergers have the opposite effect on the industry. Their failure to provide a more efficient means of business and the way multihospital systems capitalize on reduced costs by simply earning a larger profit show that these mergers serve the providers, not the consumers. Additionally, multihospital systems jeopardize choices in care for those patients who would want specific services (which might not be available from a large system, religiously controlled). They also create a monopoly for consumers geographically distant from other choices. The horizontal and vertical mergers within the medical care market have not met expectations; instead, they reduce medical choices for consumers, do not guarantee increased efficiency, and create additional profits for the hospitals, physicians, and insurance companies involved. [The paper concludes by coming full circle—back to change—and focusing on an unexpected similarity between horizontal and vertical mergers that leads her to take a stand in the debate that the paper's sources have been staging.]

Guidelines for Writing the Researched Paper

1. Avoid the temptation to plug in sources as answers. Aim for a *conversation* with them. Think of sources as voices inviting you into a community of interpretation, discussion, and debate.

2. Quote, paraphrase, or summarize *in order to* analyze. Explain what you take the source to mean, showing the reasoning that has led to the conclusion you draw from it.

3. Quote sparingly. You are usually better off centering your analysis on a few quotations, analyzing their key terms, and branching out to aspects of your subject that the quotations illuminate.

4. Don't underestimate the value of close paraphrasing. You will almost invariably begin to interpret a source once you start paraphrasing its key language.

5. Locate and highlight what is at stake in your source. Which of its points does the source find most important? What positions does it want to modify or refute, and why?

6. Attribute sources ("According to Einstein, ...") in the text of your paper, not just in parenthetical citations. This practice will distinguish source material from your remarks about it and allow readers to evaluate its credibility up front.

7. Look for ways to develop, modify, or apply what a source has said, rather than simply agreeing or disagreeing with it.

8. If you challenge a position found in a source, be sure to represent it fairly. First, give the source some credit by identifying assumptions you share with it. Then, isolate the part that you intend to complicate or dispute.

9. Look for sources that address your subject from different perspectives. Avoid relying too heavily on any one source.

10. When your sources disagree, consider playing mediator. Instead of immediately agreeing with one or the other, clarify areas of agreement and disagreement among them.

ASSIGNMENTS

At the end of the next chapter, we place a research sequence that makes use of the skills discussed in both chapters.

1. Here are a series of exercises organized in ascending order of complexity that go into writing a researched paper. You can practice these one at a time, and then learn to put them together.
   a. Compose an analytical summary of a single source (try ranking).
   b. Write about a primary source using a single secondary source as a lens.
   c. Compose a comparative analytical summary of two sources (try difference within similarity or similarity despite difference).
   d. Write a synthesis that brings together three or more sources, using them to raise questions and allowing each to help you complicate positions in the others (as the paper on mergers in healthcare does).

2. Here are a set of writing assignments, each using a strategy discussed in the chapter. The skills called for in the following sequence are also discussed in Chapter 4, "Reading: How to Do It and What to Do with It."
   a. Practice making quotations speak by using paraphrase as a means of uncovering assumptions and bringing out implications. Use this method to zoom in on how sources define key terms.
   b. Practice putting two or more sources in conversation with each other: figure out how each source might see and recast the other's ideas. Construct and referee a conversation among your sources.
   c. Practice finding your voice in the conversation: take a source and apply it to another context, or locate a point it makes but does not dwell on and develop it further.
   d. Repeatedly do the two "Try this" exercises on passage-based focused freewriting on page 149. Make these into regular exercises—habits of mind. Also try The Method (see Chapter 2) as a means of developing a more detailed and in-depth knowledge of your source and what is at stake in it.

9

Finding and Citing Sources

With this chapter we shift to more practical and technical matters associated with writing the researched paper. After offering advice on finding and evaluating sources in print and electronic media, we target a chronic problem area for many writers—how to integrate quotations into your own prose—and conclude with a brief discussion of how to cite secondary materials and how to compose abstracts of sources.

A. GETTING STARTED

The problem with doing research in the Information Age is that there is so much information available. How do you know which information is considered respectable in a particular discipline and which isn't? How can you avoid wasting time with source materials that have been effectively refuted and replaced by subsequent thinking? A short answer to these questions is that you should start not in the stacks but in the reference room of your library or with its electronic equivalent.

If you start with specialized dictionaries, abstracts, and bibliographies, you can rapidly gain both a broad perspective on your subject and a summary of what particular sources contain. This is the purpose of the reference room: it offers sources that review and summarize material for you in shorthand forms. In any case, you should take care not to get bogged down in one author's book-length argument until you've achieved a wider view of how other sources treat your subject.

You should be aware that reference sources use agreed-upon keywords for different subjects. Thus, don't be surprised if the subject headings you enter initially yield nothing. Always check first at the reference desk for the *Library of Congress Subject Headings* to see what headings might be appropriate for your subject. It will tell you, for example, that fraternities and sororities are listed not under "fraternities and sororities" but rather under "Greek letter organizations."

Ask your reference librarian to direct you to the printed and on-line *indexes, bibliographies, specialized dictionaries,* and compilations of *abstracts* that are pertinent to your subject or discipline. These tools vary in their scope and in the information they contain.

An index offers a list of titles directing you to scholarly journals; often this list is sufficient to give you a clearer idea of the kinds of topics about which writers in the field are conversing. Here are a few index titles, indicating the range of what's available: *Applied Science and Technology Index, Art Index, Biography Index, Business Periodicals Index, Education Index, General Science Index, Humanities Index, Literary Criticism Index, New York Times Index, Philosopher's Index, Religion Index, Reader's Guide to Periodical Literature,* and *Social Sciences Index.* A number of these index both book reviews and scholarly articles. They are generally compiled annually.

Compilations of abstracts and annotated bibliographies provide more information—anywhere from a few sentences to a few pages that summarize each source. (See the section on abstracts and how to write them at the end of this chapter.) Here are a few commonly used titles: *Abstracts of English Studies, Chemical Abstracts, Communication Abstracts, Dissertation Abstracts, Historical Abstracts, MLA (Modern Language Association) International Bibliography, Psychological Abstracts, Monthly Catalog of United States Government Publications, Sociological Abstracts.*

Specialized dictionaries and encyclopedias are sometimes extraordinarily useful in sketching the general terrain for a subject, and they often include bibliographical leads as well. Here are some titles, ranging from the expected to the eccentric: *Dictionary of the History of Ideas, Dictionary of Literary Biography, Encyclopedia of American History, Encyclopedia of Bioethics, Encyclopedia of Crime and Justice, Encyclopedia of Economics, Encyclopedia of Native American Religions, Encyclopedia of Philosophy, Encyclopedia of Psychology, Encyclopedia of Unbelief, Encyclopedia of World Art, Encyclopedic Dictionary of Mathematics, Macmillan Encyclopedia of Computers, Encyclopedia of Medical History, McGraw Hill Encyclopedia of Science and Technology, New Grove Dictionary of Music and Musicians, Oxford English Dictionary.*

Most of the indexes just listed also include book reviews. The *Reader's Guide to Periodical Literature* will locate reviews as well as articles in popular—general audience—publications such as *Time* and *Newsweek.* For a broader range of titles, you might also consult *Book Review Index, Book Review Digest,* and *Subject Guide to Books in Print.* Indexes organized by discipline are more likely to take you to sources reviewed in academic journals; consult with your reference librarian for the indexes most pertinent to your subject.

Periodicals and journals offer an effective next step in finding sources once you've surveyed your topic in digest form. These are generally more up to date than either reference materials or books. Most library reference rooms have either a booklet that lists all of the periodicals and journals to which the library subscribes or a means of accessing a list of such holdings through the electronic catalogue. There are thousands of specialized journals available. If an index or bibliography refers you to a journal that your library does not hold, the library can usually get it for you (sometimes for a small fee) through a service known as interlibrary loan. Now, many articles and reviews can be downloaded electronically; see the next section entitled "Electronic Research: Locating Scholarly Information."

Tips for Starting Your Research

A useful research technique is to begin with indexes that will take you to specialized periodicals rather than beginning with books. Most scholarly journals have an index in the last issue for each year. Listed alphabetically by author, subject, or title are articles for a given year. Also, you may want to use any number of indexes. Here you look up a key word or phrase (of your choosing), and the index tells you when, what, where, and so forth for the word/phrase. Some of the key indexes are: *Social Science Index, Wall Street Journal Index* (for *WSJ* stories), *New York Times Index* (for *NYT* stories), and the *Public Affairs Information Service.*

A critical part of the bibliographic effort is to find a topic on which there are materials. Most topics can be researched. The key is to choose a flexible keyword/phrase and then try out different versions of it. For example, a bibliography on "women in management" might lead you to look up *women, females, business* (women in), *business* (females in), *gender in the workplace, sexism and the workplace, careers* (of men, of women, in business), *women and CEOs, women in management, affirmative action and women, women in corporations, female accountants,* and so forth. Be imaginative and flexible. A little bit of time with some of the indexes, listed earlier, will provide you with a wealth of sources.

—Frederick Norling, *Professor of Business*

Use quality psychological references. That is, use references that professional psychologists use and regard highly. *Psychology Today* is not a good reference; *Newsweek* and *Reader's Digest* are worse. And don't even think about the *National Enquirer.* APA journals, such as the *Journal of Abnormal Psychology,* on the other hand, are excellent.

In looking for reference material, be sure to search under several headings. For example, look under *depression, affective disorders,* and *mood disorders.*

Books (e.g., *The Handbook of Affective Disorders*) are often very helpful, especially for giving a general overview of a topic. Books addressing a professional audience are generally preferable to those addressing a general, popular audience.

Finally, references should be reasonably current. In general, the newer, the better. For example, with rare exceptions (classic articles), articles from before 1970 are outdated and so should not be used.

—Alan Tjeltveit, *Professor of Psychology*

We might generalize a rule from the psychology professor's final comment: *Start in the present and work backward.* Usually the most current materials will include bibliographical citations that can help you identify the most important sources in the past. We would also note that *Newsweek* can be a useful source if you want evidence about popular understanding of a subject or issue, but in this case, the fact that the material comes from *Newsweek* provides the central reason for citing it. The evidence is always qualified by the frame. This matter of deciding what kind of source is best suited to your topic is the subject of the following section, written by a reference librarian, on using and evaluating sources via the computer.

B. ELECTRONIC RESEARCH: LOCATING SCHOLARLY INFORMATION

By Kelly Cannon, Reference Librarian

The Internet has dramatically altered public access to information. But the quality of information has also changed; it is almost as easy to publish on the Internet as it is to surf it. A general caveat might well be Reader Beware.

Take as an example http://www.martinlutherking.org. This site appears prominently in any Internet search for information about Martin Luther King, Jr. The Web site is visually appealing, claiming to include "essays, speeches, sermons, and more." But who created the site? Why does the site exist? As it turns out, after a little digging (see tips 1 and 2 in "Quick Tips"), the site is sponsored by Stormfront, Inc. (http://iserver.stormfront.org), an organization out of West Palm Beach, Florida, serving "those courageous men and women fighting to preserve their White Western culture, ideals and freedom of speech." This author is concealed behind the work, a ghostwriter of sorts. While the site is at one's fingertips, identifying the author is a challenge, more so than it would be in the world of print publications, where author and publisher are located on the same pages as the title. For those Web sites with no visible author, no publishing house, no recognized journal title, no peer-review process, and no library-selection process (the touchstones of scholarship in the print world), seemingly easy Internet research is now more problematic: the user must discern for him- or herself what is and is not authoritative information.

Understanding Domain Names

But how is the user to begin evaluating a Web document? Fortunately, there are several clues to assist you through the Internet labyrinth. One clue is in the Web address itself. For example, the Internet Movie Database has http://imdb.com as its Web address (also known as URL, or Uniform Resource Locator). One clue lies at the very end of the URL, in what is known as the domain name, in this case the abbreviation ".com." Web sites ending in ".com" are commercial, often with the purpose of marketing a product. Here are some Web sites with different domain names:

National Right to Life Coalition
http://www.nrlc.org/news

Valley of the Shadow
http://jefferson.village.virginia.edu/vshadow2/

Chronicle of Higher Education
http://chronicle.com

Mutual Funds Interactive
http://www.brill.com

Bureau of the Census
http://www.census.gov/

DCA Net Home Page
http://www.dca.net

Note that ".net" stands for network, ".edu" for educational, ".gov" for government, and ".org" for organizations.

Much like sites ending in ".com," sites ending in ".org" may have a veiled agenda, whether marketing or politics. Getting your own commercial site is today big business. Anyone willing to pay can make a ".org" or ".com" site their own. The stories are legion of well-known corporations and individuals who have spent a lot of money to buy up all the possible commercial sites that might represent their names. The organization that oversees the many vendors of ".com" and ".org" domain names is The Internet Corporation for Assigned Names and Numbers, or ICANN (http://www.icann.org/).

On the other hand, ".edu" and ".gov" sites may indicate less bias, as they are ostensibly nonprofit and are often the producers of bonafide research.

In particular, ".gov" sites contain some of the best information that is on the Internet. This is largely because the U.S. government is required by an act of Congress to disseminate to the general public a large portion of its research. The Internet has in recent years been beset by a commercial motive, if only to pay the cost of Web site maintenance. The U.S. government, floated as it is by tax dollars, has largely escaped this consuming interest in moneymaking and provides the high-quality, free Web sites reminiscent of the precommercial Internet era. This means that government sites offer high-quality data, particularly of a statistical nature. Scholars in the areas of business, law, and the social sciences may benefit tremendously, without subscription fees, from a variety of government databases. Prime examples are the legislative site known as Thomas (http://thomas.loc.gov) and data gathered at the Web site of the Census Bureau (http://www.census.gov). The Thomas site, named after—you guessed it— Thomas Jefferson, is maintained by the Library of Congress and is updated daily. Also, of considerable value to researchers is the archive of legislation going back to the ninety-third Congress (1973)—bills, resolutions, the U.S. Code, and so forth—that allows extensive research of the laws governing the United States. Archives, it should be noted, have come to be another hallmark of good Web sites, as the majority of the Internet seems to offer only today's news.

Print Corollaries

But a domain name can be misleading; it is simply one clue in the process of evaluation. Another clue, perhaps more significant, is the correlation between a Web site and the print world. Many Web sites offer print corollaries, and some have print equivalents. For example, Johns Hopkins University Press now publishes all its journals, known and respected for years by scholars, in both print and electronic formats. Many college and university libraries subscribe to these Johns Hopkins journals electronically, collectively known as Project Muse (http://muse.jhu.edu/). In this case, the scholar can assume that the electronic form of the journal undergoes the same editorial rigor as the print publication, because they are identical in content.

Similarly, Stanford University initiated a project some years ago to provide access to reputable academic journals. The purpose, however, is not to provide access to current issues but to electronically archive older journal issues that might still be invaluable to scholars. This project, called JSTOR (http://www.jstor.org), is now subscribed to by research libraries around the world.

For Subscribers Only

An organized and indexed collection of discreet pieces of information is called a *database*. Two examples of databases are a library's card catalogue and on-line catalogue. The World Wide Web is full of databases, though they are often restricted to subscribers. Subscription fees can be prohibitive, but fortunately for the average researcher, most college and university libraries foot the bill. The names of these databases are now well known and arguably contain the most thoroughly reviewed (i.e., scholarly) full text available on the Internet: Academic Search via EbscoHost (http://www.epnet.com), Expanded Academic ASAP via the Gale Group (http://www.galegroup.com/), ProQuest (http://www.umi.com/), and Dialog (http://www.dialog.com). The databases mentioned earlier—Project Muse and JSTOR—are also for use by subscribers only. Inquire at your library to see if you have access to these databases.

Each of these databases contains its own proprietary search engine, allowing refinement of searches to a degree unmatched by search engines on the Internet at large. Why? For one, these databases are exclusive rather than inclusive, as the Internet is. More is not better in an information age. The fact that information is at your fingertips, and sometimes "in your face," can be a problem. Well-organized databases are shaped and limited by human hands and minds and cover only certain media types or subject areas.

Secondly, *databases allow searching by subject heading, in addition to keyword searching.* This means that a human has defined the main subject areas of each entry, consequently allowing the user much greater manipulation of the search. For example, if I enter the words "New York City" in a simple keyword search, I will retrieve everything that simply mentions New York City even once; the relevance will vary tremendously. On the other hand, if subject headings have been assigned, I can do a subject search on New York City and find only records that are devoted to my subject. This may sound trivial, but in the age of information overload, precision searching is a precious commodity.

While there is no foolproof way to a perfect database search, you can save hours of frustration by consulting with the most frequent users of research databases—reference librarians. Ask them (a) which databases they would use for your research topic and (b) how they would construct a search.

Directories Before Search Engines

Have you ever conducted an Internet search only to retrieve several thousand hits, none of which are the ones you thought you asked for? For example, try finding research articles about the Galapagos Islands in Altavista (http://www.altavista.com/). A search on the term "Galapagos Islands" will retrieve over 3 million records, many of which are advertisements for island tours.

This is because searches on well-known search engines like Altavista (http://www.altavista.com/), Hotbot (http://www.hotbot.com), and Google (http://www.google.com) open a Pandora's box of unreviewed, "raw" information posted by anyone from expert to novice, and everything in between. Typically, these sites lack any sort of peer review. One such site, posted in jest, is Clones-R-Us (http://www.d-b.net/dti/). This site offers testimonials of the many customers who have benefited from human cloning; lacking entirely in documentation, it nevertheless appears prominently in Internet searches on human cloning.

Fortunately, there are Internet search *directories* that evaluate Web sites. These directories include the Librarian's Index to the Internet (http://lii.org/), Looksmart (http://www.looksmart.com), Argus Clearinghouse (http://www.clearinghouse.net/), about.com (http://home.about.com) and britannica.com (http://www.britannica.com). The explicitness of the criteria and the rigor of the evaluation vary widely. Perhaps the most rigorous is the Librarian's Index to the Internet, administered by the California State Library. On the subject of genetic disorders, for instance, this directory points the user to GeneClinics (http://www.geneclinics.org/), a collection of "peer-reviewed articles by experts about inherited diseases." While directories like the Librarian's Index are not meant to be the end in Web site evaluation, they are excellent starting points, as they filter out sites judged to be less authoritative or substantive.

Asking the Right Questions

Finally, it is up to the individual user to evaluate each Web site independently. Here are some critical questions to consider:

Question: Who is the author?
Response: Check the Web site's home page, probably near the bottom of the page.

Question: Is the author affiliated with any institution?
Response: Check the URL to see who sponsors the page.

Question: What are the author's credentials?
Response: Check an on-line database like EBSCOhost Academic Search (http://www.epnet.com) or Lexis-Nexis Academic Universe (http://web.lexis-nexis.com), or Dialog (http://www.dialog.com) to see if this person is published in journals or books.

Question: Has the information been reviewed or peer-edited before posting?
Response: Probably not, unless the posting is part of a larger publication; if so, the submission process for publication can be verified at the publication home page.

Question: Is the page part of a larger publication?
Response: Try the various links on the page, to see if there is an access point to the home page of the publication. Or try the "backspacing" technique mentioned as a tip below.

Question: Is the information documented properly?
Response: Check for footnotes or methodology.

Question: Is the information current?
Response: Check the "last update," usually printed at the bottom of the page.

Question: What is the purpose of the page?
Response: Examine content and marginalia.

Question: Does the Web site suit your purposes?
Response: Review what the purpose of your project is. Review your information needs: primary versus secondary and academic versus popular. And always consult with your instructor.

Bibliographic Research

Up until now, we've only addressed electronic information that is full text. There may come a time when most secondary information needed for research is available on-line and as full text, but because of copyright and other restrictions, much scholarly information is still available only in print. This almost always implies a slight delay in retrieving the information: where full-text databases and the Internet promise instant gratification, more traditional modes of research necessitate either document delivery (fax or mail) or a visit to the library or other holding institution where a copy of the item can be retrieved. As individual journals begin to publish on-line (bypassing print altogether), the access to scholarly material may improve, but for now print copies remain the norm.

What has improved tremendously—with few exceptions—is the *indexing* of scholarly journals. Even if the journals themselves are not readily available in an electronic format, the indexing is available electronically. These electronic indexes provide basic bibliographic information and sometimes an abstract (summary) of the article or a book chapter. When professors refer to bibliographic research, they probably mean research done with indexes. These indexes are available in any of three formats—print, CD-ROM, or on-line—depending on the academic institution. Inquire at your library about index availability.

Many academic institutions now subscribe to the following indexes electronically, whether CD-ROM or on-line: MLA (literary criticism), ERIC (education), PsycInfo (psychology), Historical Abstracts (non-U.S. history), America History & Life (U.S. history), Sociological Abstracts (sociology), Biological Abstracts (biology), Chemical Abstracts (chemistry), ABI-Inform (business), Anthropological Literature (anthropology), Philosopher's Index (philosophy), EconLit (economics), ATLA Religion Index (religion), and a host of others. Note that these indexes are specific to particular subject areas. Their coverage is not broad, but it is deep and very scholarly. *These are the indexes to watch for when seeking the most scholarly information in your area of study.* If a professor asks students to support their papers with scholarly secondary research, these indexes provide that kind of information. While the full text is often not included, the indexing will provide information sufficient to track down the complete article, whether it is in the library or available through interlibrary loan or other document delivery service.

These indexes are a great aid in evaluating the scholarly merit of a publication, as they usually eliminate any reference that isn't considered scholarly by the academy. For example, the MLA only indexes literary criticism that appears in peer-reviewed journals and academically affiliated books. So, consider the publications that appear in these indexes to have an academic "Good Housekeeping" seal of approval.

Popular Press

While the indexes listed above are scholarly, there are others that cover the popular press. If information is needed, for example, from an issue of the *Los Angeles Times* in 1990, a book review from *Time* magazine in 1986, or a play review from the *Baltimore Sun* in 1996, popular indexes will cite these materials. *Book Review Digest*, available in print and on-line, indexes book reviews published in the popular press. The *New York Times Index* and the well-known *Reader's Guide*, available in print and on-line, index newspapers, magazines, and reviews. Indeed, because the popular press profits tremendously from electronic access, indexing for popular titles appears all over the place. Lexis-Nexis Academic Universe (http://web.lexis-nexis.com/universe) and EbscoHost Academic Search (http://www.epnet.com), to name two, index hundreds of newspapers, magazines, and reviews.

Many newspapers and popular magazines now index their own publications at individual Web sites. One example is the *Morning Call* (http://www.mcall.com), the leading newspaper in Allentown, Pennsylvania, whose Web site offers indexing back into the early 1990s. This site is free; other sites may charge a fee. To locate the sites of nearly all newspapers with an on-line presence, worldwide, visit News and Newspapers Online (http://library.uncg.edu/news/), maintained by the library of the University of North Carolina at Greensboro. This site is useful in highlighting whether a newspaper offers a free searchable archive.

Tuning in to Your Environment

Every university and college is different, each with its own points of access to information. Below are some exercises to help you familiarize yourself with your own scholarly environment.

Exercise 1: Go to your library's reference desk and get a list of all scholarly journal indexes that are available electronically at your school. Then, get a list of all on-line, full-text databases that are available to you.

Exercise 2: Go to your library's reference desk, and get a list of all the journals that the library subscribes to electronically. Then, get a list of all journals that are available at your library either in print or electronically in your major area of study.

Exercise 3: Ask the reference librarian about Internet access in general for your major area of study. What tips can the library give you about doing electronic research at your academic institution? Are there any special databases, Internet search engines/directories, or indexes that you should consult in your research?

Exercise 4: Try out some or all of the full-text databases available on your campus. Now, try the same searches on a scholarly index (CD-ROM or on-line). What differences do you see in the quality and scope of the information?

Quick Tips

Tip 1: Backspacing

"Backspacing" a URL can be an effective way to evaluate a Web site. It may reveal authorship or institutional affiliation. To do this, place the cursor at the end of the URL, backspace to the last slash, and press Enter. Continue backspacing to each preceding slash, examining each level as you go.

Tip 2: Using WHOIS

WHOIS (http://www.networksolutions.com/cgi-bin/whois/whois) is an Internet service that allows anyone to find out who's behind a Web site.

Tip 3: Beware of the ~ in a Web Address

Many educational institutions allow the creation of personal home pages by students and faculty. While the domain name remains ".edu" in these cases, the fact that they are personal means that pretty much anything can be posted and that academic quality is not assured.

Tip 4: Phrase Searching

Are you finding relevant information? Trying using quotation marks around key phrases in your search string. For example, search in Google for the phrase, enclosed in quotation marks: "whose woods these are I think I know".

Tip 5: Title Searching

Are you still finding irrelevant information? Limit your search to the titles of documents. A title search is an option in several search engines, among them Altavista, in advanced mode (http://www.altavista.com) and HotBot (http://www.hotbot.com).

Tip 6: Full Text

The widest selection of previously published full text (newspaper, magazine, and journal articles, and book chapters) is available in subscription databases via the Internet. Inquire at your library to see if you have access to Lexis-Nexis Academic Universe (http://web.lexis-nexis.com), OCLC FirstSearch, EbscoHost Academic Search (http://www.epnet.com), ProQuest (http://www.proquest.com), Expanded Academic ASAP (http://www.galegroup.com), or other full-text databases.

The leading *free* full-text site is FindArticles.com (http://www.findarticles.com/PI/index.jhtml). This database of "hundreds of thousands of articles from more than 300 magazines and journals, dating back to 1998" can be searched by all magazines, magazines within categories, or specific magazine.

For the full text of books, try the IPL Online Texts Collection (http://www.ipl.org/reading/books/) with over 17,000 book titles that can be browsed by author, title, or Dewey classification.

For more of the best full-text sites on the Internet, search on the term "full-text" in the Librarian's Index to the Internet (http://lii.org).

Tip 7: Archives of Older Published Materials

Full text for newspapers, magazines, and journals published prior to 1990 is difficult to find on the Internet. One subscription site that your library may offer is JSTOR (http://www.jstor.org), an archive of scholarly full-text journal articles dating back, in some cases, into the late 1800s. Lexis–Nexis Academic Universe, also a subscription service, includes the full text of popular periodicals such as the *New York Times* as far back as 1980.

Three free sites offer the full text of eighteenth- and nineteenth-century periodicals from the United States and Great Britain: Internet Library of Early Journals (http://www.bodley.ox.ac.uk/ilej/), Making of America (http://moa.umdl.umich.edu/), and Nineteenth Century in Print (http://memory.loc.gov/ammem/ndlpcoop/moahtml/snchome.html).

Use interlibrary loan or another document delivery service like Ingenta (http://www.ingenta.com) to have a copy of the print version of older titles sent to you. Electronic indexing (no full text) for older materials, back as early as 1900 and sometimes earlier, is readily available. Inquire at your library.

Tip 8: Best sites, free or subscription, for Quantity and Quality of Scholarly Information Across the Disciplines

Below are a few of the sites most relied upon by academic librarians. For the subscription databases, you will need to inquire at your library for local availability.

Subscription Databases: Indexes
ABC PoliSci
ABELL (literature)
America History and Life
Anthropological Literature
Art Index
ArtBibliographies Modern
ATLA Religion Index
Bibliography of the History of Art
Biological Abstracts/BIOSIS
Chemical Abstracts

Communication Abstracts
EconLit
ERIC (education)
GeoBase (geology, geography)
Historical Abstracts
INSPEC (computer science, physics)
MathSciNet
MLA (language, literature, theatre, film)
PAIS (political science, area studies)
Philosopher's Index
PsycInfo
RILM Abstracts of Music Literature
Science Citation Index
Social Science Citation Index
Sociological Abstracts
WorldCat (all disciplines)

Subscription Databases: Full Text
CIAO (political science, area studies)
Dow Jones (business)
EbscoHost Academic Search (all disciplines)
Ethnic NewsWatch
ERIC w/ Documents (education)
Galenet Business and Company ASAP
Galenet Expanded Academic ASAP (all disciplines)
International Index to Music Periodicals
JSTOR (all disciplines)
Lexis-Nexis (business, law, news, reviews)
Project Muse (all disciplines)
ProQuest (all disciplines)
Simmons Study of Media and Markets
Stat-USA (statistics)
TableBase (statistics)
Westlaw
WilsonWeb Omnifile (all disciplines)

Free Sites: Indexes
AGRICOLA (agriculture) http://www.nal.usda.gov/ag98/ag98.html
Getty Research Institute Online Catalogue (art) http://opac.pub.getty.edu/

Handbook of Latin American Studies http://lcweb2.loc.gov/hlas/hlashome.html

Ingenta (all disciplines) http://www.ingenta.com/

PubMed (medicine) http://www4.ncbi.nlm.nih.gov/PubMed/

TOCS-IN (classical studies) http://www.chass.utoronto.ca/amphoras/tocs.html

Free Sites: Full Text

American Memory (history) http://memory.loc.gov/ammem/amhome.html

Artcyclopedia http://www.artcyclopedia.com/

Arts and Letters Daily http://www.aldaily.com

Bartleby Library (literature) http://www.bartleby.com/

Bureau of the Census (statistics) http://www.census.gov/

EDGAR (business) http://www.sec.gov/edgar.shtml

FedStats (statistics) http://www.fedstats.gov/

FindArticles.com http://www.findarticles.com/

FindLaw http://www.findlaw.com/

GPO Access (law, political science) http://www.access.gpo.gov/su_docs/
index.html

Hoovers (business) http://www.hoovers.com/

IDB International Data Base (statistics) http://www.census.gov/ipc/www/
idbnew.html

Internet Library of Early Journals (history) http://www.bodley.ox.ac.uk/ilej/

LANIC (Latin American studies) http://lanic.utexas.edu/

Making of America (history) http://moa.umdl.umich.edu/

National Climatic Data Center http://www5.ncdc.noaa.gov/pubs/
publications.html

News and Newspapers Online http://library.uncg.edu/news/

Online Literary Criticism Collection http://library.uncg.edu/news/

Project Gutenberg (literature) http://sailor.gutenberg.org/

Thomas (law, political science) http://thomas.loc.gov/

Citation Guides on the Web

The two most common styles of documentation are those established by the Modern Language Association (MLA) and the American Psychological Association (APA). These associations each provide examples of basic citation of electronic and print resources at their Web sites; you will find the MLA at http://www.mla.org and APA at http://www.apastyle.org .

As well, many writing centers have made available citation guides at their Web sites. One recommended site is by the writing center of Purdue University (http://owl.english.purdue.edu/handouts/research/index.html).

For citation examples not given at these web sites, it is advisable to consult the associations' printed manuals—*Publication Manual of the American Psychological Association* or the *MLA Handbook*—in their most recent editions.

Seven Steps to Successful Research

1. Consult with your professor to determine what types of resources will be most appropriate for the project at hand.
2. Consider whether you need scholarly or popular sources or a mixture of both.
3. Consider whether you need primary or secondary works or a mixture of both.
4. With the assistance of a reference librarian, consider which search tools will direct you to the most relevant resources.
5. Range widely. Try a new search tool with each new research project.
6. Begin early, in case interlibrary loan is needed to obtain research owned only by other libraries.
7. Remember that one quality source can, in its bibliography, point to many other resources.

C. PLAGIARISM AND THE LOGIC OF CITATION

It is impossible to discuss the rationale for citing sources without reference to plagiarism, even though the primary reason for including citations is not to prove that you haven't cheated. It's essential that you give credit where it's due as a courtesy to your readers. Along with educating readers about who has said what, citations enable them to find out more about a given position and to pursue other discussions on the subject. Nonetheless, plagiarism is an important issue: academic integrity matters. And because the stakes if you are caught plagiarizing are very high, we think it necessary to pause briefly in order to discuss how to avoid it.

In recent years there has been a significant rise in the number of plagiarism cases nationally. Many commentators blame the Internet, with its easily accessible, cut-and-pasted information, for increasing the likelihood of plagiarism. Others cite a lack of clarity about what plagiarism is and why it is a serious problem. So, let's start by clarifying.

Most people have some idea of what plagiarism is. You already know that it's against the rules to buy a paper from an Internet "paper mill" or to download others' words verbatim and hand them in as your own thinking. And you probably know that even if you change a few words and rearrange the sentence structure, you still need to acknowledge the source. By way of formal definition, plagiarism (as one handbook puts it) gives "the impression that you have written or thought something that you have in fact borrowed from someone else" (Gibaldi 30). It is a form of theft and fraud. Borrowing from someone else, by the way, also includes taking and not acknowledging words and ideas from your friends or your parents. Put another way, any assignment with your name on it signifies that you are the author—that the words and ideas are yours—with any exceptions indicated by source citations and, if you're quoting, by quotation marks.

Knowing what plagiarism is, however, doesn't guarantee that you'll know how to avoid it. Is it okay, for example, to cobble together a series of summaries and paraphrases in a paragraph, provided you include the authors in a bibliography at the end of the paper? Or how about if you insert a single footnote at the end of the paragraph? The answer is that both are still plagiarism, because your reader can't tell where your thinking starts and others' thinking stops. As a basic rule of thumb, *"Readers must be able to tell as they are reading your paper exactly what information came from which source and what information is your contribution to the paper"* (Hult 203). More on this later.

Why Does Plagiarism Matter?

A recent survey indicated that fifty-three percent of Who's Who High Schoolers thought that plagiarism was no big deal (Cole 6). So why should institutions of higher learning care about it? Here are two great reasons:

- Plagiarism poisons the environment. Students who don't cheat get alienated by students who do and get away with it, and faculty can become distrustful of students and even disillusioned about teaching when constantly driven to track down students' sources. It's a lot easier, by the way, than most students think for faculty to recognize language and ideas that are not the student's own. And now there are all those search engines provided by firms like Turnitin.Com that have been generated in response to the Internet paper-mill boom. Who wants another Cold War?
- Plagiarism defeats the purpose of going to college, which is learning how to think. You can't learn to think by just copying others' ideas; you need to learn to trust your own intelligence. Students' panic about deadlines and their misunderstandings about assignments sometimes spur plagiarism. It's a good bet that your professors would much rather take requests for help and give extra time on assignments than have to go through the anguish of confronting students about plagiarized work.

So, plagiarism gets in the way of trust, fairness, intellectual development and, ultimately, the attitude toward learning that sets the tone for a college or university community.

Frequently Asked Questions (FAQs) About Plagiarism

Is it still plagiarism if I didn't intentionally copy someone else's work and present it as my own, that is, if I plagiarized it by accident?

Yes, it is still plagiarism. Colleges and universities put the burden of responsibility on students for knowing what plagiarism is and then making the effort necessary to avoid it. Leaving out the quotation marks around someone else's words or omitting the attribution after a summary of someone else's theory may be just a mistake—a matter of inadequate documentation—but faculty can only judge what you turn in to them, not what you intended.

If I include a list of works consulted at the end of my paper, doesn't that cover it?

No. A works-cited list (bibliography) tells your readers what you read but leaves them in the dark about how and where this material has been used in your paper. Putting one or more references at the end of a paragraph containing source material is a version of the same problem. The solution is to cite the source at the point that you quote or paraphrase or summarize it. To be even clearer about what comes from where, also use what are called in-text attributions. See the next FAQ on these.

What is the best way to help my readers distinguish between what my sources are saying and what I'm saying?

Be overt. Tell your readers in the text of your paper, not just in citations, when you are drawing on someone else's words, ideas, or information. Do this with phrases like "According to X . . ." or "As noted in X . . ."—so-called in-text attributions.

Are there some kinds of information that I do not need to document?

Yes. Common knowledge and facts you can find in almost any encyclopedia or basic reference text generally don't need to be documented (that is, John F. Kennedy became president of the United States in 1960). This distinction can get a little tricky because it isn't always obvious what is and is not common knowledge. Often, you need to spend some time in a discipline before you discover what others take to be known to all. When in doubt, cite the source.

If I put the information from my sources into my own words, do I still need to include citations?

Yes. Sorry, but rewording someone else's idea doesn't make it your idea. Paraphrasing is a useful activity because it helps you to better understand what you are reading, but paraphrases and summaries have to be documented and carefully distinguished from ideas and information you are representing as your own.

If I don't actually know anything about the subject, is it okay to hand in a paper that is taken entirely from various sources?

It's okay if (1) you document the borrowings and (2) the assignment called for summary. Properly documented summarizing is better than plagiarizing, but most assignments call for something more. Often comparing and contrasting your sources will begin to give you ideas, so that you can have something to contribute. If you're really stumped, go see the professor.

You will also reduce the risk of plagiarism if you consult sources after—not before—you have done some preliminary thinking on the subject. If you have become somewhat invested in your own thoughts on the matter, you will be able to use the sources in a more active way, in effect, making them part of a dialogue.

Is it plagiarism if I include things in my paper that I thought of with another student or a member of my family?

Most academic behavior codes, under the category called "collusion," allow for students' cooperative efforts only with the explicit consent of the instructor. The same general rule goes for plagiarizing yourself—that is, for submitting the same paper in more than one class. If you have questions about what constitutes collusion in a particular class, be sure to ask your professor.

What about looking at secondary sources when my professor hasn't asked me to? Is this a form of cheating?

It can be a form of cheating if the intent of the assignment was to get you to develop a particular kind of thinking skill. In this case, looking at others' ideas may actually retard your learning process and leave you feeling that you couldn't possibly learn to arrive at ideas on your own.

Professors usually look favorably on students who are willing to take the time to do extra reading on a subject, but it is essential that, even in class discussion, you make it clear that you have consulted outside sources. To conceal that fact is to present others' ideas as your own. Even in class discussion, if you bring up an idea you picked up on the Internet, be sure to say so explicitly.

How to Cite Sources

In general, you will be expected to follow a formalized style of documentation. The two most common are the MLA (Modern Language Association) style, which uses the author-work format, and the APA (American Psychological Association) style, which uses the author-date format. Most writing handbooks (compilations of the rules of grammar and punctuation, available at most bookstores) contain detailed accounts of documentation styles. In addition, you can access various Web sites that will provide most (though not all) of this information.

The various styles differ in the specific ways that they organize the bibliographical information, but all of them share the following characteristics:

1. They place an extended citation for each source, including the author, the title, the date, and the place of publication, at the end of the paper. These end-of-text citations are organized in a list, usually alphabetically.
2. They insert an abbreviated citation within the text, located within parentheses directly following every use of the source. Usually this in-text citation consists of the author's name and either the page (in MLA) or date (in APA). In-text citations indicate in shorthand form in the body of your paper the source you are using and direct your readers to the complete citation located in a list of references at the end of the paper or report.
3. They distinguish among different kinds of sources—providing slightly differing formulas for citing books, articles, encyclopedias, government documents, interviews, and so forth.
4. They have particular formats for citing electronic sources of various kinds, such as CD-ROMs, the Internet, and on-line journals and databases. These citations replace the publication information typically provided for text references to printed material with what is called an *availability statement*, which provides the method of accessing the source. This statement should provide the information

sufficient to retrieve the source. See the section earlier in this chapter entitled "Electronic Research: Locating Scholarly Information" for ways of accessing pertinent URLs for documenting Web sites.

You have probably already discovered that some professors are more concerned than others that students obey the particulars of a given documentation style. Virtually all faculty across the curriculum agree, however, that *the most important rule for writers to follow in documenting sources is formal consistency.* That is, all of your in-text citations should follow the same abbreviated format, and all of your end-of-text citations should follow the same extended format.

Once you begin doing most of your writing in a particular discipline, you may want to purchase or access on the Internet the more detailed style guide adhered to by that discipline. Because documentation styles differ not only from discipline to discipline but also even from journal to journal within a discipline, you should consult your professor about which documentation format he or she wishes you to use in a given course.

Here are a few basic examples of in-text and end-of-text citations in both MLA and APA form, followed by brief discussion of the rules that apply.

1. Single author, MLA style

In-text citation: The influence of Seamus Heaney on younger poets in Northern Ireland has been widely acknowledged, but Patrick Kavanagh's "plain-speaking, pastoral" influence on him is "less recognized" (Smith 74).

"(Smith 74)" indicates the author's last name and the page number on which the cited passage appears. If the author's name had been mentioned in the sentence—had the sentence begun "According to Smith"—you would include only the page number in the citation. Note that there is no abbreviation for "page," that there is no intervening punctuation between name and page, and that the parentheses precede the period or other punctuation. If the sentence ends with a direct quotation, the parentheses come after the quotation marks but still before the closing period. Also note that no punctuation occurs between the last word of the quotation ("recognized") and the closing quotation mark.

End-of-text book citation: Douglas, Ann. *Terrible Honesty: Mongrel Manhattan in the 1920s.* New York: Farrar, Straus, and Giroux, 1995.

End-of-text article citation: Cressy, David. "Foucault, Stone, Shakespeare and Social History." *English Literary Renaissance* 21 (1991): 121–33.

MLA style stipulates an alphabetical list of references (by author's last name, which keys the reference to the in-text citation). This list is located at the end of the paper on a separate page and entitled "Works Cited."

Each entry in the "Works Cited" list is divided into three parts: author, title, and publication data. Each of these parts is separated by a period from the others. Titles of book-length works are italicized, unless your instructor prefers underlining. (Underlining is a means of indicating italics.) Journal citations differ slightly: article names go inside quotations, no punctuation follows the titles of journals, and a colon precedes the page numbers.

2. Single author, APA style:

In-text citation: Studies of students' changing attitudes towards the small colleges that they attend suggest that their loyalty to the institution declines steadily over a four-year period, whereas their loyalty to individual professors or departments increases "markedly, by as much as twenty-five percent over the last two years" (Brown, 1994, p. 41).

For both books and articles, include the author's last name, followed by a comma, and then the date of publication. If you are quoting or referring to a specific passage, include the page number as well, separated from the date by a comma and the abbreviation "p." (or "pp.") followed by a space. If the author's name has been mentioned in the sentence, include only the date in the parentheses immediately following the author's name.

In-text citation: Brown (1992) documents the decline in students' institutional loyalty.

End-of-text book citation: Tannen, D. (1991). *You just don't understand: Women and men in conversation.* New York: Ballantine Books.

End-of-text article citation: Baumeister, R. (1987). How the self became a problem: A psychological review of historical research. *Journal of Personality and Psychology, 52,* 163–176.

APA style requires an alphabetical list of references (by author's last name, which keys the reference to the in-text citation). This list is located at the end of the paper on a separate page and entitled "References." Regarding manuscript form, the first line of each reference is not indented, but all subsequent lines are indented three spaces.

In alphabetizing the references list, place entries for a single author before entries that he or she has co-authored, and arrange multiple entries by a single author by beginning with the earliest work. If there are two or more works by the same author in the same year, designate the second with an "a," the third a "b," and so forth, directly after the year. For all subsequent entries by an author after the first, substitute three hyphens followed by a period [---.] for his or her name. For articles by two or more authors, use commas to connect the authors, and precede the last one with a comma and an ampersand [&].

The APA style divides individual entries into the following parts: author (using initials only for first and middle names), year of publication (in parentheses), title, and publication data. Each part is separated by a period from the others. Note that only the first letter of the title and subtitle of books is capitalized (although proper nouns would be capitalized as necessary).

Journal citations differ from those for books in a number of small ways. The title of a journal article is neither italicized (or underlined) nor enclosed in quotation marks, and only the first word in the title and subtitle is capitalized. The name of the journal is italicized (or underlined), however, and the first word and all significant words are capitalized. Also, notice that the volume number (which is separated by a comma from the title of the journal) is italicized (or underlined) to distinguish it from the page reference. Page numbers for the entire article are included, with no "p." or "pp.," and are separated by a comma from the preceding volume number. If the journal does not use volume numbers, then "p." or "pp." is included.

How to Integrate Quotations into Your Paper

An enormous number of writers lose authority and readability because they have never learned how to correctly integrate quotations into their own writing. The following guidelines should help.

1. Acknowledge sources in your text, not just in citations.

When you incorporate material from a source, attribute it to the source explicitly in your text—not just in a citation. In other words, when you introduce the material, *frame* it with a phrase such as "according to Marsh" or "as Cartelli argues."

Although it is not required, you are usually much better off making the attribution overtly, even if you have also cited the source within parentheses or with a footnote at the end of the last sentence quoted, paraphrased, or summarized. If a passage does not contain an attribution, your readers will not know that it comes from a source until they reach the citation at the end. Attributing up-front clearly distinguishes what one source says from what another says and, perhaps more important, what your sources say from what you say. Useful verbs for introducing attributions include the following: notes, observes, argues, comments, writes, says, reports, suggests, and claims. Generally speaking, by the way, you should cite the author by last name only—as "Cartelli," not as "Thomas Cartelli" or "Mr. Cartelli."

2. Splice quotations onto your own words.

Always attach quotations to some of your own language; don't let them sit in your text as independent sentences with quotation marks around them. You can normally satisfy this rule with an attributive phrase—commonly known as a tag phrase—that introduces the quotation.

According to Paul McCartney, "All you need is love."

Note that the tag phrase takes a comma before the quote.

Alternatively you can splice quotations into your text with a setup, a statement followed by a colon.

Patrick Henry's famous phrase is one of the first that American schoolchildren memorize: "Give me liberty, or give me death."

The colon, you should notice, usually comes at the end of an independent clause (that is, a subject plus verb that can stand alone), at the spot where a period normally goes. It would be incorrect to write "Patrick Henry is known for: 'Give me liberty, or give me death.'"

The rationale for this guideline is essentially the same as that for the previous one: if you are going to move to quotation, you first need to identify its author so that your readers will be able to put it in context quickly.

Spliced quotations frequently create problems in grammar or punctuation for writers. Whether you include an entire sentence (or passage) of quotation or just a few phrases, you need to take care to integrate them into the grammar of your own sentence.

One of the most common mistaken assumptions is that a comma should always precede a quotation, as in "A spokesperson for the public defender's office demanded, 'an immediate response from the mayor.'" The sentence structure does not call for any punctuation after "demanded."

3. Cite sources after quotations.

Locate citations in parentheses after the quotation and before the final period. The information about the source appears at the end of the sentence, with the final period following the closing parenthesis.

> A recent article on the best selling albums in America claimed that "Ever since Elvis, it has been pop music's job to challenge the mores of the older generation" (Hornby 168).

Note that there is normally *no punctuation* at the end of the quotation itself, either before or after the closing quotation mark. A quotation that ends either in a question mark or an exclamation mark is an exception to this rule, because the sign is an integral part of the quotation's meaning.

> As Hamlet says to Rosencrantz and Guildenstern, "And yet to me what is this quintessence of dust?" (2.2.304-05).

See the section entitled "How to Cite Sources" earlier in this chapter for the appropriate formats for in-text citations.

4. Use ellipses to shorten quotations.

Add ellipsis points to indicate that you have omitted some of the language from within the quotation. Form ellipses by entering three dots (periods) with spaces in between them, or use four dots to indicate that the deletion continues to the end of the sentence (the last dot becomes the period). Suppose you wanted to shorten the following quotation from a recent article about Radiohead by Alex Ross:

> The album "OK Computer," with titles like "Paranoid Android," "Karma Police," and "Climbing Up the Walls," pictured the onslaught of the information age and a young person's panicky embrace of it (Ross 85).

Using ellipses, you could emphasize the source's claim by omitting the song titles from the middle of the sentence:

> The album "OK Computer" . . . pictured the onslaught of the information age and a young person's panicky embrace of it (Ross 85).

In most cases, the gap between quoted passages should be short, and in any case, you should be careful to preserve the sense of the original. The standard joke about ellipses is apposite here: A reviewer writes that a film "will delight no one and appeal to the intelligence of invertebrates only, but not average viewers." An unethical advertiser cobbles together pieces of the review to say that the film "will delight . . . and appeal to the intelligence of . . . average viewers."

5. Use square brackets to alter or add information within a quotation.

Sometimes it is necessary to change the wording slightly inside a quotation in order to maintain fluency. Square brackets indicate that you are altering the original quotation. Brackets are also used when you insert explanatory information, such as a definition or example, within a quotation. Here are a few examples that alter the original quotations cited above.

> According to one music critic, the cultural relevance of Radiohead is evident in "the album 'OK Computer' . . . [which] pictured the onslaught of the information age and a young person's panicky embrace of it" (Ross 85).

> Popular music has always "[challenged] the mores of the older generation," according to Nick Hornby (168).

Note that both examples respect the original sense of the quotation; they have changed the wording only to integrate the quotations gracefully within the writer's own sentence structure.

D. HOW TO PREPARE AN ABSTRACT

There is one more skill essential to research-based writing that we need to discuss: how to prepare an abstract. The aim of the nonevaluative summary of a source known as an abstract is to represent a source's arguments as fairly and accurately as possible, not to critique them. Learning how to compose an abstract according to the conventions of a given discipline is a necessary skill for academic researched writing. Because abstracts differ in format and length among disciplines, you should sample some in the reference section of your library or via the Internet to provide you with models to imitate. Some abstracts, such as those in *Dissertation Abstracts,* are very brief—less than two hundred fifty words. Others may run as long as two pages.

Despite disciplinary differences, abstracts by and large follow a generalizable format. The abstract should begin with a clear and specific explanation of the work's governing thesis (or argument). In this opening paragraph, you should also define the work's purpose, and possibly include established positions that it tries to refine, qualify, or argue against. What kind of critical approach does it adopt? What are its aims? On what assumptions does it rest? Why did the author feel it necessary to write the work— that is, what does he or she believe the work offers that other sources don't? What shortcomings or misrepresentations in other criticism does the work seek to correct?

You won't be able to produce detailed answers to all of these questions in your opening paragraph, but in trying to answer some of them in your note taking and drafting, you should find it easier to arrive at the kind of concise, substantive, and focused overview that the first paragraph of your abstract should provide. Also, be careful not to settle for bland, all-purpose generalities in this opening paragraph. And if you quote there, keep the selections short, and remember that quotations don't speak for themselves.

In sum, your aim in the first paragraph is to define the source's particular angle of vision and articulate its main point or points, including the definition of key terms used in its title or elsewhere in its argument.

Once you've set up this overview of the source's central position(s), you should devote a paragraph or so to the source's *organization* (how it divides its subject into parts) and its *method* (how it goes about substantiating its argument). What kind of secondary material does the source use? That is, how do its own bibliographic citations cue you to its school of thought, its point of view, its research traditions?

Your concluding paragraph should briefly recount some of the source's conclusions (as related to, but not necessarily the same as, its thesis). In what way does it go about culminating its argument? What kind of significance does it claim for its position? What final qualifications does it raise?

Here, as a model, is a good example of an abstract:

Abstract of "William Carlos Williams," an essay
by Christopher MacGowan
in *The Columbia History of American Poetry*,
pp. 395–418, Columbia University Press, 1993.

MacGowan's is a chronologically organized account of Williams' poetic career and of his relation to both modernism as an international movement and modernism as it affected the development of poetry in America. MacGowan is at some pains both to differentiate Williams from some features of modernism (such as the tendency of American writers to write as well as live away from their own cultural roots) and to link Williams to modernism. MacGowan argues, for example, that an essential feature of Williams's commitment as a poet was to "the local—to the clear presentation of what was under his nose and in front of his eyes" (385). But he also takes care to remind us that Williams was in no way narrowly provincial, having studied in Europe as a young man (at Leipzig), having had a Spanish mother and an English father, having become friendly with the poets Ezra Pound and H. D. while getting his medical degree at the University of Pennsylvania, and having continued to meet important figures in the literary and art worlds by making frequent visits to New York and by traveling on more than one occasion to Europe (where Pound introduced him to W. B. Yeats, among others). Williams corresponded with Marianne Moore, he continued to write to Pound and to show Pound some of his work, and he wrote critical essays on the works of other modernists. MacGowan reminds us that Williams also translated Spanish works (ballads) and so was not out of contact with European influences.

Williams had a long publishing career—beginning in 1909 with a self-published volume called *Poems* and ending more than fifty years later with *Pictures from Brueghel* in 1962. What MacGowan emphasizes about this career is not only the consistently high quality of work, but also its great influence on other artists (he names those who actually corresponded with Williams and visited with him, including Charles Olson, Robert Creeley, Robert Lowell, Allen Ginsberg, and Denise Levertov). MacGowan observes that Williams defined himself "against" T. S. Eliot—the more rewarded and internationally recognized of the two poets, especially during their lifetimes—searching for "alternatives to the prevailing mode of a complex, highly allusive poetics," which Williams saw as Eliot's legacy (395). MacGowan depicts Williams as setting himself "against the international school of Eliot and Pound—Americans he felt wrote about rootlessness and searched an alien past because of their failure to write about and live within their own culture" (397).

ASSIGNMENT: A RESEARCH SEQUENCE

The traditional sequence of steps for building a research paper—or for any writing that relies on secondary materials—is summary, comparative analysis, and synthesis. The following sequence of four exercises addresses the first two steps as discrete activities. (You might, of course, choose to do only some of these exercises.)

1. *Compose a relatively informal prospectus,* in which you formulate your initial thinking on a subject before you do more research. Include what you already know about the topic, especially what you find interesting, particularly significant, or strange. This exercise will help to deter you from being overwhelmed by and absorbed into the sources you will later encounter.

2. *Conduct a "what's going on in the field" search, and create a preliminary list of sources.* This exercise is ideal for helping you to find a topic or, if you already have one, to narrow it. The kinds of bibliographic materials you consult for this portion of the research project will depend on the discipline within which you are writing. Whatever the discipline, start in the reference room of your library with specialized indexes (such as the *Social Sciences Index* or the *New York Times Index*), book-review indexes, specialized encyclopedias and dictionaries, and bibliographies (print version or CD-ROM) that will give you an overview of your subject or topic. If you have access to databases through your school or library, you should also search them (see the section in this chapter entitled "Electronic Research: Locating Scholarly Information").

   The "what's going on in the field" search has two aims:

   - To survey materials in order to identify trends—the kinds of issues and questions that others in the field are talking about (and, thus, find important)
   - To compile a bibliography that includes a range of titles that interest you, that could be relevant to your prospective topic, and that seem to you representative of research trends associated with your subject (or topic)

   You will not be committed at this point to pursuing all of these sources but rather to reporting what is being talked about. You might also compose a list of keywords (such as Library of Congress headings) that you have used in conducting your search. If you try this exercise, you will be surprised how much value there is in exploring indexes *just for titles,* to see the kinds of topics people are currently conversing about. And you will almost surely discover how *narrowly* focused most research is (which will get you away from global questions).

Append to your list of sources (a very preliminary bibliography) a few paragraphs of informal discussion of how the information you have encountered (the titles, summaries, abstracts, etc.) has affected your thinking and plans for your paper. These paragraphs might respond to the following questions:

a. In what ways has your "what's going on in the field" search led you to narrow or shift direction in or focus your thinking about your subject?
b. How might you use one or more of these sources in your paper?
c. What has this phase of your research suggested you might need to look for next?

3. *Write an abstract of an article (or book chapter)* from your "what's going on" exercise that you think you might use in your final paper. Use the procedure offered in the preceding section, "How to Prepare an Abstract." Aim for two pages in length. If other members of your class are working on the same or similar subjects, it is often extremely useful for everyone to share copies of their abstracts. Remember that your primary concern should lie with representing the argument and point of view of the source as fairly and accurately as possible.

Append to the end of the abstract a paragraph or two that addresses the question "How has this exercise affected your thinking about your topic?" Objectifying your own research process in this way will help to move you away from the cut-and-paste–provide-only-the-transitions mode of writing research papers.

4. *Write a comparative summary of two reviews of a single source.* Most writers, before they invest the significant time and energy required to study a book-length source, take the much smaller amount of time and energy required to find out more about the book. Although you should always include in your final paper your own analytical summary of books you consult on your topic, it's extremely useful also to find out what experts in the field have to say about the source.

Select from your "what's going on" list one book-length source that you've discovered is vital to your subject or topic. As a general rule, if a number of your indexes, bibliographies, and so forth, refer you to the same book, it's a good bet that this source merits consulting.

Locate two book reviews on the book, and write a summary that compares the two reviews. Ideally, you should locate two reviews that diverge in their points of view or in what they choose to emphasize. Depending on the length and complexity of the reviews, your comparative summary should require two or three pages.

In most cases, you will find that reviews are less neutral in their points of view than are abstracts, but they always do more than simply judge. A good review, like a good abstract, should communicate the essential ideas contained in the source. It is the reviewer's aim also to locate the source in some larger context, by, for example, comparing it to other works on the same subject and to the research tradition the book seeks to extend, modify, and so forth. Thus, your summary should try to encompass how the book contributes to the ongoing conversation on a given topic in the field.

Append to your comparative summary a paragraph or two answering the question "How has this exercise affected your thinking about your topic?"

Obviously, you could choose to do a comparative summary of two articles, two book chapters, and so forth, rather than of two book reviews. But in any event, if you use books in your research, you should always find a means of determining how these books are received in the relevant critical community.

The next step, if you were writing a research paper, would involve the task known as *synthesis,* in which you essentially write a comparative discussion that includes more than two sources. Many research papers start with an opening paragraph that synthesizes prevailing, perhaps competing, interpretations of the topic being addressed. Few good research papers consist only of such synthesis, however. Instead, writers use synthesis to frame their ideas and to provide perspective on their own arguments; the synthesis provides a platform or foundation for their own subsequent analysis.

It is probably worth adding that bad research papers fail to use synthesis as a point of departure. Instead, they line up their sources and agree or disagree with them. To inoculate you against this unfortunate reflex, review the sections entitled "Six Strategies for Analyzing Sources" (especially "Strategy 4: Find Your Own Role in the Conversation") and "Strategies for Writing and Revising Research Papers" in Chapter 8.

PART III

Matters
of Form

CHAPTER

10

Introductions and Conclusions

You have probably noticed that it is difficult to read attentively and do something else at the same time. Imagine, for instance, trying to read a book while playing a guitar. Depending on the difficulty of the reading matter and your powers of concentration, you might not be able even to listen to a guitar and read at the same time. When you read, you enter a world created of written language—a textual world—and to varying degrees, you leave the world "out there." Even if other people are around, we all read in relative isolation; our attention is diverted from the social and physical world upon which the full range of our senses normally operates.

In this context, now place yourself in the position of the writer, rather than a reader, and consider the functions that the introduction and conclusion provide for a piece of writing. Your introduction takes the reader from a sensory world and submerges him or her into a textual one. And your conclusion returns the reader to his or her nonwritten reality. Introductions and conclusions *mediate*—they carry the reader from one way of being to another. They function as the most *social* parts of any written communication, the passageways in which you need to be most keenly aware of your reader.

At both sites, there is a lot at stake. The introduction gives the reader his or her first impression, and we all know how indelible that can be. The conclusion leaves the reader with a last—and potentially lasting—impression of the written world you have constructed.

Most of the difficulties in composing introductions and conclusions will arise in deciding how you should deal with theses. How much of a thesis should you put into the introduction? Should your conclusion summarize the thesis or extend it? The model of organization we recommend—of evolving a thesis through successive encounters with evidence—requires a different kind of introduction and conclusion than those you may have been taught to write. It assumes, for example, that the introduction should not and cannot preview a paper's entire interpretation or argument.

As was discussed in Chapter 6, a fully evolved thesis is usually too complex and too dependent on the various reshapings that have preceded it to be stated succinctly but still coherently at the outset. But readers do need to know early on what your paper is attempting to resolve or negotiate. (See two sections of Chapter 6, "Locating the Evolving Thesis in the Final Draft" and "The Evolving Thesis and Introductory and Concluding Paragraphs.")

To an extent, as the next chapter's discussion of disciplinary formats suggests, the conventions of a particular academic discipline may arbitrate such questions. In regard to introductions, for example, a philosophy paper usually locates the thesis in the paper's first sentence and explains in the rest of the opening paragraph how the claim will be proved. Yet, even this model of beginning, strictly deductive and conclusion-oriented, normally devotes more space to showing readers the issues that the rest of the paper will address than to dwelling on the answers.

As with other aspects of writing analytically, there are no absolute rules for writing introductions and conclusions, but there does seem to be a consensus across the disciplines that *introductions should raise issues rather than settle them and conclusions should go beyond merely restating what has already been said.* Put another way, insofar as disciplinary conventions permit, *in introductions, play an ace but not your whole hand; and in conclusions, don't just summarize—culminate.*

A. THE FUNCTION OF INTRODUCTIONS

As the Latin roots of the word suggest—*intro,* meaning "within," and *ducere,* meaning "to lead or bring"—an introduction brings the reader into a subject. Its length varies, depending on the scope of the writing project. An introduction may take a paragraph, a few paragraphs, a few pages, a chapter, or even a book. In most academic writing that you will do, one or two paragraphs is a standard length. In that space you should try to accomplish some or all of the following objectives:

- Define your topic—the issue, question, or problem—and say why it matters.
- Indicate your method of approach to the topic.
- Provide necessary background or context.
- Offer the working thesis (hypothesis) that your paper will develop.

An objective missing from this list that you might expect to find there is the admonition to engage the reader. Clearly, all introductions need to engage the reader, but this admonition is too often misinterpreted as a directive to be entertaining or cute. In academic writing, you don't need a gimmick to engage your readers; you can assume they care about the subject. You will engage them if you can articulate why your topic matters, doing so in terms of existing thinking in the field.

Especially in a first draft, the objectives just listed are not so easily achieved, which is why many writers defer writing the polished version of the introduction until they have completed at least one draft of the paper. At that point, you will usually have a clearer notion of why your subject matters and which aspect of your thesis to place first. Often the conclusion of a first draft becomes the introduction to the second draft. Other writers find that they can't proceed on a draft until they have arrived at an introduction that clearly defines the question or problem they plan to write about and its significance. For these writers, crafting an approach to the topic in the introduction is a key part of the planning phase, even though they also expect to revise the introduction based on what happens in the initial draft.

In any case, the standard shape of an introduction is a *funnel*. It starts wide, providing background and generalization, and then narrows the subject to a particular issue or topic. Here is a typical example from a student paper.

> People have a way of making the most important obligations perfunctory, even trivial, by the steps they take to observe them. For many people traditions and rituals become actuality; the form overshadows the substance. They lose sight of the underlying truths and what these should mean in their lives, and they tend to believe that observing the formalities fulfills their obligation. This is true of professional ethics as they relate to the practice of examining and reporting on financial data—the primary role of the auditor.

The paragraph begins with a generalization in the first sentence (about making even important obligations perfunctory) and funnels down in the last sentence to a working thesis (about the ethics of an auditor's report on financial data).

Putting an Issue or Question in Context

In the accompanying "Voices from Across the Curriculum" boxes, notice that implicit in all of the professors' accounts is some concept of the funnel. Rather than leaping immediately to the paper's issue, question, or problem, most effective introductions provide some broader context to indicate why the issue matters.

Voices from Across the Curriculum

Providing an Introductory Context

Although some expression of the main idea should find its way into the opening paragraph, that paragraph is also an opportunity to draw the reader in, to convince the reader to read on. What's the point of your paper? Why is the issue important? Is it a theoretical issue? A policy issue? What's the historical context? Is this a question that represents a part of a larger question?

—James Marshall, Professor of Economics

I think it is important to understand that an introduction is not simply the statement of a thesis but also the place where the student needs to set a context, a framework that makes such a thesis statement interesting, timely, or in some other way important. It is common to see papers in political science begin by pointing out a discrepancy between conventional wisdom (what the pundits say) and recent political developments, between popular opinion and empirical evidence, or between theoretical frameworks and particular test cases. Papers, in other words, often begin by presenting *anomalies*.

(continued)

I encourage students to write opening paragraphs that attempt to elucidate such anomalies by:

1. Stating the specific point of departure: are they taking issue with a bit of conventional wisdom? Popular opinions? A theoretical perspective? This provides the context in which a student is able to "frame" a particular problem, issue, and so forth. Students then need to indicate:

2. Why the wisdom/opinion/theory has become problematic or controversial by focusing on a particular issue, event, test case, or empirical evidence. (Here the students' choice of topic becomes important, because topics must be both relevant to the specific point of departure as well as to some degree controversial.) I would also expect in the opening paragraph(s):

3. A brief statement of the tentative thesis/position to be pursued in the paper. This can take several forms, including the revising of conventional wisdom/theory/opinion, discarding it in favor of alternative conceptions, or calling for redefinition of an issue and question. In papers directed toward current political practices (for instance, an analysis of a particular environmental policy or of a proposal to reform political parties), the thesis statement may be stated by indicating (a) hidden or flawed assumptions in current practices or (b) alternative reforms and/or policy proposals.

—Jack Gambino, *Professor of Political Science*

Although the various models we offer here differ in small ways from discipline to discipline, the essential characteristics that they share suggest that most professors across the curriculum want the same things in an introduction: *the locating of a problem or question within a context that provides background and rationale, culminating in a working thesis.*

Using Procedural Openings

In the interests of clear organization, some professors require students to include in the introduction an explanation of how the paper will proceed. Such a general statement of method and/or intention is known as *procedural openings.* Among the disciplines in which you are most likely to find this format are philosophy, political science, and sociology.

As the professor of political science observes, the procedural opening is particularly useful in longer papers, where it can provide a condensed version of what's to come as a guide for readers. Also note that he advises placing it early in the essay but not in the first paragraph, which he reserves for "presenting anomalies." In other words, he seems to value the introduction primarily as a site for the writer's idea, for "stating the specific point of departure," and, that taken care of, only secondarily as a place for forecasting the plan of the paper. These priorities bear mentioning because they imply *a potential danger in relying too heavily on procedural openings—that the writer will avoid making a claim at all.*

The statement of a paper's plan is not the same thing as its thesis. As Chapter 7 discussed, one kind of weak thesis offers a general plan *in place of* supplying an idea about the topic that the paper will explore and defend. Consider the deficiencies of the following procedural opening.

In this paper I will first discuss the strong points and weak points in America's treatment of the elderly. Then I will compare this treatment with that in other industrial nations in the West. Finally, I will evaluate the various proposals for reform that have been advanced here and abroad.

This paragraph does not fare well in fulfilling the four functional objectives of an introduction listed at the beginning of this chapter. It identifies the subject, but it neither addresses why the subject matters nor suggests the writer's approach. Nor does it provide background to the topic or suggest a hypothesis that the paper will pursue. Even though a procedural opening is built into the conventions of report writing, these conventions also stipulate that the writer include some clear statement of the hypothesis, which counteracts the danger that the writer won't make any claim at all.

Voices from Across the Curriculum

Procedural Openings

I encourage students to provide a "road map" paragraph early in the paper, perhaps the second or third paragraph. (This is a common practice in the professional journals.) The "road map" tells the reader the basic outline of the argument. Something like the following: "In the first part of my paper I will present a brief history of the issue. . . . This will be followed by an account of the current controversy. . . . Part III will spell out my alternative account and evidence. . . . I then conclude. . . . " I think such a paragraph becomes more necessary with longer papers.

—Jack Gambino, *Professor of Political Science*

I address the issue of an opening paragraph by having the students conceive of an opening section (or introduction) that tells the uninformed reader what's about to happen. I'll say, "Assume I know next to nothing about what lies ahead; so let me, the reader, know. 'My paper's about boom. In it, I'll do boom, boom. I chose this topic for the following reasons: boom, boom, boom.' Then get on with it."

—Frederick Norling, *Professor of Business*

B. HOW MUCH TO INTRODUCE UP FRONT

Introductions need to do a lot in a limited space. To specify a thesis and locate it within a larger context, to suggest the plan or outline of the entire paper, and to negotiate first relations with a reader—that's plenty to pack into a paragraph or two. In deciding how much to introduce up front, you must make a series of difficult choices. We list some of these choices next, phrased as questions you can ask yourself:

* How much can I assume my readers know about my subject?
* Which parts of the research and/or the background are sufficiently pertinent to warrant inclusion?

- How much of my thesis do I include, and which particular part or parts should I begin with?
- What is the proper balance between background and foreground?
- Which are the essential parts of my plan or road map to include?

Typical Problems That Are Symptoms of Doing Too Much

If you ponder the preceding questions, you can avoid writing introductions that try to turn an introduction into a miniature essay. Consider the three problems discussed next as symptoms of *overcompression,* telltale signs that you need to reconceive, and probably reduce, your introduction.

Digression   *Digression* results when you try to include too much background. If, for example, you plan to write about a recent innovation in video technology, you'll need to monitor the amount and kind of technical information you include in your opening paragraphs. You'll also want to avoid starting at a point that is too far away from your immediate concerns, as in "From the beginning of time humans have needed to communicate."

The standardized formats that govern procedural openings in some disciplines can help you to avoid digressing endlessly. There is a given sequence of steps to follow for a psychology report of an empirical study, for instance. Nonetheless, these disciplinary conventions leave plenty of room for you to lose your focus. You still need to be selective about which contexts are sufficiently relevant to be included up front.

In disciplines that do not stipulate a specific format for contextualizing, the number of choices is greater, and so is the danger that you will get sidetracked into paragraphs of background that bury your thesis and frustrate your readers. One reason that many writers fall into this kind of digression in introductions is that they misjudge how much their audience needs to know. As a general rule in academic writing, *don't assume that your readers know little or nothing about the subject.* Instead, use the social potential of the introduction to negotiate your audience, setting up your relationship with your readers and making clear what you are assuming they do and do not know.

Incoherence   *Incoherence* results when you try to preview too much of your paper's conclusion. Incoherent introductions move in too many directions at once, usually because the writer is trying to conclude before going through the discussion that will make the conclusion comprehensible. The language you are compelled to use in such cases tends to be too dense, and the connections between the sentences tend to get left out, because there isn't enough room to include them. After having read the entire paper, your readers may be able to make sense of the introduction, but in that case, the introduction has not done its job.

The following introductory paragraph is incoherent, primarily because it tries to include too much. It neither adequately connects its ideas nor defines its terms.

> Twinship is a symbol in many religious traditions. The significance of twinship will be discussed and explored in the Native American, Japanese Shinto, and Christian religions. Twinship can be either in opposing or common forces in the form of deities or mortals. There are several forms of twinship that show duality of order versus

chaos, good versus evil, and creation versus destruction. The significance of twinship is to set moral codes for society and to explain the inexplicable.

Prejudgment   *Prejudgment* results when you appear to have already settled the question to be pursued in the rest of the paper. The problem here is logical. In the effort to preview your paper's conclusion at the outset, you risk appearing to assume something as true that your paper will in fact need to test. In most papers in the humanities and social sciences, where the thesis evolves in specificity and complexity between the introduction and conclusion, writers and readers can find such assumptions prejudicial. Opening in this way, at any event, can make the rest of the paper seem redundant. Even in the sciences, where a concise statement of objectives, plan of attack, and hypothesis are usually required up front, a separate "Results" section is reserved for the conclusion.

The following introductory paragraph *prejudges*: it offers a series of conclusions already assumed to be true without introducing the necessary background issues and questions that would allow the writer to adequately explore these conclusions.

> Field hockey is a sport that can be played by either men or women. All sports should be made available for members of both sexes. As long as women are allowed to participate on male teams in sports such as football and wrestling, men should be allowed to participate on female teams in sports such as field hockey and lacrosse. If women press for and receive equal opportunity in all sports, then it is only fair that men be given the same opportunity. If women object to this type of equal opportunity, then they are promoting reverse discrimination.

This paragraph also exemplifies the type of weak thesis that can result when its assumptions are left unstated. Prejudgment is in fact a case of assuming too much up front. Read what an economics professor says on the same subject.

Voices from Across the Curriculum

Avoiding Strong Claims in the Introduction

I might be careful about how tentative conclusions should play in the opening paragraph, because this can easily slide into a prejudging of the question at hand. I would be more comfortable with a clear statement of the prevailing views held by others. For example, a student could write on the question, "Was Franklin Delano Roosevelt a Keynesian?" What purpose would it serve in an opening paragraph to reveal without any supporting discussion that FDR was or was not a Keynesian? What might be better would be to say that in the public mind FDR is regarded as the original big spender, that some people commonly associate New Deal policies with general conceptions of Keynesianism, but that there may be some surprises in store as that common notion is examined.

In sum, I would discourage students from making strong claims at or near the beginning of a paper. Let's see the evidence first. We should all have respect for the evidence. Strong assertions, bordering on conclusions, too early on are inappropriate.

—James Marshall, *Professor of Economics*

Try this: Compare and contrast introductory paragraphs from a popular magazine with those from an academic journal aimed at a more specialized audience. Select one of each and analyze them to determine what each author assumes the audience knows. Where in each paragraph are these assumptions most evident? If you write out your analysis, it should probably take about a page, but this exercise can also be done productively with others in a small group. □

C. OPENING GAMBITS: FIVE GOOD WAYS TO BEGIN

The primary challenge in writing introductions, it should now be evident, lies in occupying the middle ground between overassertive prejudgment and avoidance of taking a position. There are a number of fairly common opening gambits that can help you to stake out an effective middle ground. An opening gambit in games such as chess is the initial move—not an announcement of the entire game plan.

Gambit 1: Challenge a Commonly Held View.

One of the best opening gambits is to challenge a commonly held view. This is what the economics professor advises when he suggests that rather than announcing up front the answer to the question at which the paper arrives, you convey that "there may be some surprises in store as that common notion is examined." This move has several advantages. Most important, it provides you with a framework *against* which to reply; it allows you to begin by reacting. Moreover, because you are responding to a known position, you have a ready way of integrating context into your paper. As the economics professor notes of the FDR example, until we understand why it matters whether or not FDR was a Keynesian, it is pointless to answer the question.

Gambit 2: Begin with a Definition.

In the case of the FDR example, a writer would probably include another common introductory gambit, *defining* "Keynesianism." Beginning with a definition is a reliable way to introduce a topic, so long as that definition has some significance for the discussion to follow. If the definition doesn't do any conceptual work in the introduction, the definition gambit becomes a pointless cliché.

You are most likely to avoid a cliché if you cite a source other than a standard dictionary for your definition. The reference collection of any academic library contains a range of discipline-specific lexicons that provide more precise and authoritative definitions than Webster ever could. A useful alternative is to quote a particular author's definition of a key term (such as Keynesianism) because you want to make a point about his or her particular definition: for example, "Although the *Dictionary of Economics* defines Keynesianism as *XYZ,* Smith treats only *X* and *Y* (or substitutes *A* for *Z,* and so forth)."

Gambit 3: Offer a Working Hypothesis.

But, you may be wondering, where is the thesis in the FDR example? As the economics professor proposes, you are often better off introducing a working hypothesis—an opening claim that stimulates the analytical process—instead of offering some full declaration of the conclusion. The introduction he envisions, for example, would first suggest that the question of FDR's Keynesianism is not as simple as is commonly thought and then imply further that the common association of "New Deal policies with general conceptions of Keynesianism" is, to some extent, false.

Gambit 4: Lead with Your Second-Best Example.

Another versatile opening gambit, where disciplinary conventions allow, is to use your *second-best example* to set up the issue or question that you later develop in depth with your best example. This gambit is especially useful in papers that proceed inductively on the strength of representative examples. As you are assembling evidence in the outlining and prewriting stage, in many cases you will accumulate a number of examples that illustrate the same basic point. For example, several battles might illustrate a particular general's military strategy; several primaries might exemplify how a particular candidate tailors his or her speeches to appeal to the religious right; several scenes might show how a particular playwright romanticizes the working class; and so on.

Save the best example to receive the most analytical attention in your paper. If you were to present this example in the introduction, you would risk making the rest of the essay vaguely repetitive. A quick close-up of another example will strengthen your argument or interpretation. By using a different example to raise the issues, you suggest that the phenomenon exemplified is not an isolated case and that the major example you will eventually concentrate upon is indeed representative.

What kind of example should you choose? By calling it second best, we mean to suggest only that it should be another resonant instance of whatever issue or question you have chosen to focus upon. Given its location up front and its function to introduce the larger issues to which it points, you should handle it more simply than subsequent examples. That way your readers can get their bearings before you take them into a more in-depth analysis of your best example in the body of your paper.

Gambit 5: Exemplify the Topic with a Narrative.

A common gambit in the humanities and social sciences, the narrative opening introduces a short, pertinent, and vivid story or anecdote that exemplifies a key aspect of a topic. Although generally not permissible in the formal reports assigned in the natural and social sciences, narrative openings turn up in virtually all other kinds of writing across the curriculum. Here is an example from a student paper in psychology.

> In the past fifteen years, issues surrounding AIDS have incited many people to examine their thoughts and feelings about homosexuality. As a result, instances of prejudice and discrimination toward gays, lesbians, and bisexuals have risen recently (Herek 1989). Although some instances are sufficiently damaging to warrant criminal charges, other less serious instances of prejudice occur every day. Nonetheless, they demonstrate a problem with our society that needs to be addressed. I witnessed one of these subtle demonstrations of prejudice in a social psychology class. The topic of the class was love and relationships, how they develop, endure, and deteriorate. Although the professor had not specifically stated it previously, the information being presented was relevant to homosexual relationships as well as heterosexual ones. At one point

during her lecture, the professor was presenting an example using a hypothetical sorority member. The professor, in passing, referred to the sorority member's love relationship partner as a "she." This reference to a homosexual relationship did not seem intentional on the professor's part. However, many in the class noticed and reacted with silence at first, then glances at neighbors, which led finally to nervous laughter. After this disruption ended, a student explained to the professor what had been said that caused the disruption. And in response the professor promptly explained that the theories for love and relationships also apply to homosexual relationships.

In that moment of nervous laughter, many in the class displayed prejudice against homosexual relationships. In particular, they were displaying a commonly held belief that homosexual relationships are not founded on the same emotions, thoughts, and feelings that heterosexual relationships are. The main causes of prejudice displayed in class against homosexuality include social categorization and social learning.

As this introduction funnels to its thesis, the readers receive a graphic sense of the issue that the writer will now develop nonnarratively. Such nonnarrative treatment is usually necessary because by itself anecdotal evidence can be seen as merely personal. Storytelling is suggestive but usually does not constitute sufficient proof; it needs to be corroborated. In the preceding paragraph the writer has strengthened his credibility by focusing not on his personal responses but rather on the lesson to be drawn from his experience—a lesson that other people might also draw from it.

Like challenging a commonly held view or using a second-best example, a narrative opening will also help to safeguard you from trying to do too much up front. All three of these gambits enable you to play an ace, establishing your authority with your readers, without having to play your whole hand. They offer a starting position rather than a miniaturized version of the entire paper. As a general rule (disciplinary conventions permitting), use your introduction to pose one problem and offer one enigmatic example—seeking in some way to engage readers in the thought process that you are beginning to unfold. Raise the issue; don't settle it.

Try this: Gather some sample introductory paragraphs and, working on your own or in a small group, figure out how each one works, what it accomplishes. Here are some particular questions you might pose:

* Why does the writer start in this way—what is accomplished?
* What kind of relationship does this opening establish with the audience and to what ends?
* How does the writer let readers know why the writing they are about to read is called for, useful, and necessary?
* Where and by what logic does the introduction funnel? □

D. THE FUNCTION OF CONCLUSIONS

Like the introduction, the conclusion has a key social function: it escorts the readers out of the paper, just as the introduction has escorted them in. What do readers want as they leave the textual world you have taken them through? Although the form and length of the conclusion depend on the purpose and disciplinary conventions of the particular paper, it is possible to generalize a set of shared expectations for the conclusion across the curriculum. In some combination most readers want three things: a judgment, a culmination, and a send-off.

Judgment—The conclusion is the site for final judgment on whatever question or issue or problem the paper has focused upon. In most cases, this judgment occurs in overt connection with the introduction, often repeating some of its key terms. The conclusion normally reconsiders the question raised by the opening hypothesis and, however tentatively, rules yea or nay. It also explicitly revisits the introductory claim for why the topic matters.

Culmination—More than simply summarizing what has preceded or reasserting your main point, the conclusion needs to culminate. The word "culminate" is derived from the Latin *"columen,"* meaning "top or summit." To culminate is to reach the highest point, and it implies a mountain (in this case, of information and analysis) that you have scaled. When you culminate a paper in a conclusion, you bring things together and ascend to one final statement of your thinking.

Send-Off—The climactic effects of judgment and culmination provide the basis for the send-off. The send-off is both social and conceptual, a final opening outward of the topic that leads the reader out of the paper with something further to think about. As is suggested by most of the professors in the accompanying "Voices from Across the Curriculum" boxes, the conclusion needs to move beyond the close analysis of data that has occupied the body of the paper into a kind of speculation that the writer has earned the right to formulate.

Here is an example of a conclusion that contains a final judgment, a culmination, and a send-off. The paper, a student's account of what she learned about science from doing research in biology, opens by claiming that, to the apprentice, "science assumes an impressive air of complete reliability, especially to its distant human acquaintances." Having been attracted to science by the popular view that it proceeds infallibly, she arrives at quite a different final assessment:

> All I truly know from my research is that the infinite number of factors that can cause an experiment to go wrong make tinkering a lab skill just as necessary as reading a buret. A scientist can eventually figure out a way to collect the data she wants if she has the patience to repeatedly recombine her materials and tools in slightly different ways. A researcher's success, then, often depends largely on her being lucky enough to locate, among all the possibilities, the one procedure that works.
>
> Aided more by persistence and fortune than by formal training, I evolved a method that produced credible results. But, like the tests from which it derived, the success of that method is probably also highly specific to a certain experimental environment and so is valid only for research involving borosilicate melts treated with hydrofluoric and boric acids. I've discovered a principle, but it's hardly a universal one: reality is too complex to allow much scientific generalization. Science may appear to sit firmly on

all-encompassing truths, but the bulk of its weight actually rests on countless little rules tailored for particular situations.

This writer deftly interweaves the original claim from her introduction—that "science assumes an impressive air of complete reliability"—into a final *judgment* of her topic, delivered in the last sentence. This judgment is also a *culmination,* as it moves from her account of doing borosilicate melts to the small but acute generalization that "little rules tailored for particular situations" rather than "all-encompassing truths" provide the mainstay of scientific research. Notice that *a culmination does not need to make a grand claim in order to be effective.* In fact, the relative smallness of the final claim, especially in contrast to the sweeping introductory position about scientific infallibility, ultimately provides a *send-off* made effective by its unexpected understatement.

Ways of Concluding

The three professors quoted next all advise some version of the judgment/culmination/send-off combination. The first professor stresses the send-off.

Voices from Across the Curriculum

Expanding Possibilities in the Conclusion

I tell my students that too many papers "just end," as if the last page or so were missing. I tell them the importance of ending a work. One could summarize main points, but I tell them this is not heavy lifting. They could raise issues not addressed (but hinted at) in the main body: "given this, one could consider that." I tell them that a good place for reflection might be a concluding section in which they take the ball and run: react, critique, agree, disagree, recommend, suggest, or predict.

I help them by asking, "Where does the paper seem to go *after* it ends on paper?" That is, I want the paper to live on even though the five pages are filled. I don't want to suddenly stop thinking or reacting just because I've read the last word on the bottom of page 5. I want an experience, as if the paper is still with me.

I believe the ending should be an expansion on or explosion of possibilities, sort of like an introduction to some much larger "mental" paper out there. I sometimes encourage students to see the concluding section as an option to introduce ideas that can't be dealt with now. Sort of a "Having done this, I would want to explore boom, boom, boom if I were to continue further." Here the students can critique and recommend ("Having seen 'this,' one wonders 'that'").

—Frederick Norling, *Professor of Business*

There must be a summation. What part did the stock market crash of 1929 play in the onset of the Great Depression? Let's hear that conclusion one more time. Again, but now in an abbreviated form, what's the evidence? What are the main ambiguities that remain? Has your paper raised any new questions for future research? Are there any other broader ramifications following in the wake of your paper?

—James Marshall, *Professor of Economics*

Limiting Claims in the Conclusion

In the professional journals, conclusions typically appear as a refined version of a paper's thesis—that is, as a more qualified statement of the main claim. An author might take pains to point out how this claim is limited or problematic, given the adequacy of available evidence (particularly in the case of papers dependent on current empirical research, opinion polls, etc.). The conclusion also may indicate the implications of current or new evidence on conventional wisdom/theory—how the theory needs to be revised, discarded, and so forth. Conclusions of papers that deal with contemporary issues or trends usually consider the practical consequences or the expectations for the future.

The conclusion does not appear simply as a restatement of a thesis, but rather as an attempt to draw out its implications and significance (the "So what?"). This is what I usually try to impress upon students. For instance, if a student is writing on a particular proposal for party reform, I would expect the concluding paragraph to consider both the significance of the reform and its practicality.

I should note that professional papers often indicate the tentativeness of their conclusions by stressing the need for future research and indicating what these research needs might be. Although I haven't tried this, maybe it would be useful to have students conclude papers with a section entitled "For Further Consideration" in which they would indicate those things that they would have liked to have known but couldn't, given their time constraints, the availability of information, and lack of methodological sophistication. This would serve as a reminder of the tentativeness of conclusions and the need to revisit and revise arguments in the future (which, after all, is a good scholarly habit).

—Jack Gambino, *Professor of Political Science*

Although it is true that the conclusion is the place for "broader ramifications," this phrase should not be understood as a call for a global generalization. As the professor in the above "Voices from Across the Curriculum" box suggests, often the culmination represents a final limiting of a paper's original claim.

Three Strategies for Writing Effective Conclusions

There is striking overlap in the advice offered in the cross-disciplinary "voices." All caution that the conclusion should provide more than a restatement of what you've already said. All suggest that the conclusion should, in effect, serve as the introduction to some "larger 'mental' paper out there" (as one professor puts it) beyond the confines of your own paper. By consensus, the professors make three recommendations for conclusions:

1. *Pursue implications.* Reason inductively from your particular study to consider broader issues, such as the study's practical consequences or applications, or future-oriented issues, such as avenues for further research. To unfold implications

in this way is to broaden the view from the here and now of your paper by looking outward to the wider world and forward to the future.

2. *Come full circle.* Unify your paper by interpreting the results of your analysis in
   light of the context you established in your introduction.
3. *Identify limitations.* Acknowledge restrictions of method or focus in your analysis,
   and qualify your conclusion (and its implications) accordingly.

Consider the following example, which supplies the concluding paragraphs to the
paper whose introduction we analyzed earlier as an example of a narrative opening on
page 199. That opening anecdote, you may recall, introduced the problems of social categorization and social learning as causes of homophobia in the academic environment.
Where do you see the writer beginning to accomplish each of the three strategies for
concluding effectively—unfolding implications, coming full circle, and limiting claims?

> There are many other instances of prejudice, stereotyping, and discrimination
> against homosexuals. These range from beliefs that homosexual partners cannot be
> adequate parents, to exclusion from the military, to bias (hate) crimes resulting in mur-
> der. But in recent decades, attempts have been made to help end these discrimina-
> tions. One of the first occurred in 1973 when the American Psychological Association
> changed its policy so that homosexuals were no longer regarded as mentally ill
> (Melton, 1989). Thus the stigma that homosexuals are not able to fully contribute to
> society was partially lifted.
>
> Other ways that have been suggested to reduce prejudice regarding homosexuals
> include increasing intergroup contact. In this way, each group may come to recognize
> similarities and encounter counterstereotypical information. Herek (1989) also sug-
> gests that education in elementary through high schools about diversity and tolerance
> of it—for students as well as teachers—may help prevent stereotypes, prejudice, and
> hate crimes. And if people are made aware of their schemas and stereotypes, they
> may consider information they would have ignored based on their schemas. We may
> never be able to eliminate the process of social categorization, but perhaps we may
> be able to teach that all out-groups are not necessarily "bad."

❦*Try this:* First look back at the writer's introduction in gambit 5 on page 199. Then
determine how his conclusion has implemented the three strategies, jotting down
answers to the following questions: What does he repeat of the claims made in the
introduction? How does he change the context in which these claims are now to be
viewed? What words does he use to qualify both the final summary of evidence and his
concluding claim? ☐

E. SOLVING TYPICAL PROBLEMS IN CONCLUSIONS

The primary challenge in writing conclusions, it should now be evident, lies in finding
a way to culminate your analysis without claiming either too little or too much. There
are a number of fairly common problems to guard against if you are to avoid either of
these two extremes.

Redundancy

In Chapter 5 we lampooned an exaggerated example of the five-paragraph form for constructing its conclusion by stating "Thus, we see" and then repeating the introduction verbatim. The result is *redundancy*. As you've seen, it's a good idea to refer back to the opening, but it's a bad idea just to reinsert it mechanically. Instead, reevaluate what you said there in light of where you've ended up, repeating only key words or phrases from the introduction. This kind of *selective repetition* is a desirable way of achieving unity and will keep you from making one of two opposite mistakes—either repeating too much or bringing up a totally new point in the conclusion.

Raising a Totally New Point

Raising a totally new point can distract or bewilder a reader. This problem often arises out of a writer's praiseworthy desire to avoid repetition. As a rule, you can guard against the problem by making sure that you have clearly expressed the conceptual link between your central conclusion and any implications you may draw. *An implication is not a totally new point but rather one that follows from the position you have been analyzing.*

Similarly, although a capping judgment or send-off may appear for the first time in your concluding paragraph, it should have been *anticipated* by the body of your paper. Conclusions often indicate where you think you (or an interested reader) may need to go next, but you don't actually go there. In a paper on the economist Milton Friedman, for example, if you think that another economist offers a useful way of critiquing him, you probably should not introduce this person for the first time in your conclusion.

Overstatement

Many writers are confused over how much they should claim in the conclusion. Out of the understandable (but mistaken) desire for a grand (rather than a modest and qualified) culmination, writers sometimes *overstate* the case. That is, they assert more than their evidence has proven or even suggested. Must a conclusion arrive at some comprehensive and final answer to the question that your paper has analyzed? Depending on the question and the disciplinary conventions, you may need to come down exclusively on one side or another. In a great many cases, however, the answers with which you conclude can be more moderate. Especially in the humanities, good analytical writing seeks to unfold successive layers of implication, so it's not even reasonable for you to expect neat closure. In such cases, you are usually better off qualifying your final judgments, drawing the line at points of relative stability.

Anticlimax

It makes a difference precisely where in the final paragraph(s) you qualify your concluding claim. The end of the conclusion is a "charged" site, because it gives the reader a last impression of your paper. As the next chapter on formats will discuss in more detail, if you end with a concession—an acknowledgement of a rival position at odds with your thesis—you risk leaving the reader unsettled and possibly confused. The term for this kind of letdown from the significant to the inconsequential is "anticli-max." In most cases, you will flub the send-off if you depart the paper on an anticlimax.

There are many forms of anticlimax besides ending with a concession. If your con-clusion peters out in a random list or an apparent afterthought or a last-minute qualifica-tion of your claims, the effect is anticlimactic. And for many readers, *if your final answer comes from quoting an authority in place of establishing your own, that, too, is an anticlimax.*

At the beginning of this section we suggested that a useful rule for the introduc-tion is to play an ace but not your whole hand. In the context of this card-game anal-ogy, it is similarly effective to *save an ace for the conclusion.* In most cases, this high card will provide an answer to some culminating "So what?" question—a last view of the implications or consequences of your analysis.

F. SCIENTIFIC FORMAT: INTRODUCTIONS AND CONCLUSIONS

Formats control fairly strictly the form of standard writing projects in the natural sci-ences and psychology.

Introductions of Reports in the Sciences

The professors quoted in the "Voices from Across the Curriculum" boxes in the remainder of this chapter emphasize the importance of isolating a specific question or issue and locating it within a wider context. Notice, as you read these voices, how *little* the model for an introduction changes in moving from a social science (psychology) to the natural sciences of biology and physics.

In the sciences, the introduction is an especially important and also somewhat challenging section of the report to compose because it requires a writer *not merely to assemble but also to assimilate* the background of information and ideas that frame his or her hypothesis.

Voices from Across the Curriculum

Introductions in the Sciences

A paper usually starts by making some general observation or a description of known phenomena and by providing the reader with some background information. The first paragraphs should illustrate an understanding of the issues at hand and should present an argument for why the research should be done. In other words, a context or framework is established for the entire paper. This background informa-tion must lead to a clear statement of the objectives of the paper and the hypothesis that will be experimentally tested. This movement from broad ideas and observa-tions to a specific question or test starts the deductive scientific process.

—Richard Niesenbaum, *Professor of Biology*

Assimilating Prior Research

The introduction is one of the hardest sections to write. In the introduction, students must summarize, analyze, and integrate the work of numerous other authors and use that to build their own argument.

Students frequently have trouble writing the introduction. They tend to just list the conclusions of previous authors. So-and-So said this, and So-and-So said this, and on and on in a list format. Usually, they *quote* the concluding statements from an article. But the task is really to read the article and *summarize* it in your own words. The key is to analyze rather than just repeat material from the articles so as to make clear the connections among them. (It is important to note that experimental psychologists almost never use direct quotes in their writing. Many of my students have been trained to use direct quotation for their other classes, and so I have to spend time explaining how to summarize without directly quoting or plagiarizing the work that they have read.)

Finally, in the introduction the students must show explicitly how the articles they have summarized lead to the hypothesis they have devised. Many times the students see the connection as implicitly obvious, but I require that they explicitly state the relationships between what they read and what they plan to do.

—Laura Snodgrass, *Professor of Psychology*

One distinctive feature of scientific papers is that a separate prefatory section called the *abstract* precedes the introduction. Authors also produce abstracts for papers in many other disciplines, but these are usually published separately—for example, in a bibliography, in a journal's table of contents, and so forth. (See the end of Chapter 9 for further discussion of abstracts.)

Writing Abstracts

The publishable paper in physics begins with an abstract, which briefly describes the experiment, gives the conclusion, and the significance of the work, all in three or four sentences. In the opening paragraph of the main body of the paper, the writer tries to put the work to be described into some larger context. This context usually includes reference to the following:

- similar experiments, which may, or may not, have shown similar results; and
- theoretical work suggesting the importance of the experiment, the scientific or technological significance of the work.

—Robert Milligan, *Professor of Physics*

Discussion Sections of Reports in the Sciences

As is the case with introductions, the conclusions of reports written in the natural sciences and psychology are regulated by formalized disciplinary formats. Conclusions, for example, occur in a section entitled "Discussion." As the voices in the accompanying "Voices from Across the Curriculum" box demonstrate, the organization and contents of discussion sections vary little from discipline to discipline. For that matter, the imperatives that guide discussion sections share essential traits with conclusions across the curriculum. Look for these similarities in the three comments in the box.

Voices from Across the Curriculum

Writing Conclusions in the Sciences

The conclusion occurs in a section labeled "Discussion" and, as quoted from the *Publication Manual of the American Psychological Association* (4th ed., Washington, DC, 1994), is guided by the following questions:

- What have I contributed here?
- How has my study helped to resolve the original problem?
- What conclusions and theoretical implications can I draw from my study? (p. 19)

In a broad sense, one particular research report should be seen as but one moment in a broader research tradition that *preceded* the particular study being written about and that will *continue after* this study is published. And so the conclusion should tie this particular study into both previous research considering implications for the theory guiding this study and (when applicable) practical implications of this study. One of the great challenges of writing a research report is thus to place this particular study within that broader research tradition. That's an analytical task.

—Alan Tjeltveit, *Professor of Psychology*

Papers are concluded with a "Discussion" section in which conclusions are analyzed and qualified and in which ultimately their implications for the "bigger picture" are presented. The conclusion of the paper often represents the move from the deductive to the inductive aspect of science. The specific results first are interpreted (but not restated), and their implications and limitations are then discussed. The original question should be rephrased and discussed in light of the results presented. Conclusions should be qualified, and alternative explanations should be considered. Finally, conservative generalizations and new questions are posed.

—Richard Niesenbaum, *Professor of Biology*

In the "Discussion" section, students must critically evaluate the extent to which the empirical evidence they have collected supports the hypothesis they put forth in the introduction. If the data does not support their hypothesis, they need to explain why. The reasons typically are either that there was something wrong with the hypothesis or something wrong with the experiment. Interestingly, students usually find it easier to write the "Discussion" section if their hypothesis was not supported than if it was—to guess what went wrong—because it is difficult to integrate new results into existing theory.

—Laura Snodgrass, *Professor of Psychology*

ASSIGNMENT

Select an introductory and a concluding paragraph from your own work, and rewrite them. Your revisions should be guided by the chapter's overarching points: *Introductions should raise issues rather than settle them, and conclusions should culminate, going beyond restating what has already been said.* As you plan your revisions, consciously apply the concrete suggestions contained in the chapter's lists of gambits and discussion of strategies. How might the introduction be rewritten to use one of the opening gambits? Which of the opening gambits would be most appropriate? Experiment with at least two. Then rewrite your conclusion in explicit conversation with your introduction, qualifying your opening claims and pushing to answer one culminating but qualified "So what?" at which the original ending never arrived.

CHAPTER
11

Forms and Formats

This is a chapter about form, about the way writers structure their ideas. The first half of the chapter will, like the previous chapter, consider matters of organization and presentation in some detail, with particular attention to so-called *disciplinary formats*—the rules governing the forms of finished papers in the various disciplines. The second half of the chapter will broaden the focus to *rhetoric*: how a writer's awareness of an audience's attitudes and needs affects the shape of her or his writing.

As you will see, academic disciplines differ in the extent to which they adhere to prescribed organizational schemes to which the members of the discipline must conform. In biology and psychology, for example, formal papers and reports generally follow an explicitly prescribed pattern of presentation. Some other disciplines are less uniform and less explicit about their reliance on formats, but writers in these fields— economics, for example, or political science—usually operate within fairly established forms as well. Thus, we also use the term "format" for organizational schemes that, although not rigidly discipline-specific, are often treated as formats in writing assignments, laying out the form of prospective papers in a series of steps.

Predictably, given the disciplinary emphasis in this chapter, there are a substantial number of "Voices from Across the Curriculum" boxes that provide advice from faculty members in the natural and social sciences. But these voices will also serve to reveal the significant underlying similarities among the various disciplinary formats, for, ultimately, this chapter is less concerned with teaching you particular formats than with teaching you ways of thinking about and putting to the best use whatever formats you are asked to write in.

A. THE TWO FUNCTIONS OF FORMATS: PRODUCT AND PROCESS

The first step in learning to use formats productively is to recognize that they have two related but separate functions: product and process.

- *As sets of rules for organizing a final product,* formats make communication among members of a discipline easier and more efficient. By standardizing the means of displaying thinking in a discipline, the format enables readers to compare more readily one writer's work to that of others in the field, because readers will know where to look for particular kinds of information—the writer's methodology, for example, or his or her hypothesis or conclusions.

- *As guides and stimulants to the writing process,* formats offer writers a means of finding and exploring ideas. The procedures that formats contain seek to guide the writer's thinking process in a disciplined manner, prompting systematic and efficient examination of a subject. The notion of formats functioning as aids to invention—idea generation—goes back at least as far as Aristotle, whose *Rhetoric* defined twenty-eight general "topics" (such as considering causes and effects or dividing a subject into parts) that speakers might pursue in order to invent arguments.

Most of the writing (and thinking) we do is generated by some kind of format, even if we are not aware of it. Writers virtually never write in the absence of instructions. Accordingly, you should not regard most of the formats that you encounter simply as *prescriptive* (that is, strictly required) sets of artificial rules. Rather, think of them as descriptive accounts of the various *heuristics*—sets of questions and categories—that humans typically use to guide and stimulate their thinking.

Perhaps *the biggest problem that formats can create for writers is a premature emphasis on product*—on the form of the finished paper at the expense of process. In effect, the format can rush the writer through the successive steps, inhibiting his or her ways of generating the thinking that the finished product will present. In other words, the concept of formats as lines of inquiry (what Aristotle and other classical rhetoricians called the *topics of invention*) has become partially lost in the concept of formats as methods of arranging a finished piece of writing—imposing shape on a final product.

The primary goal in the first half of this chapter is to suggest the heuristic potential of formats. The conventional format of the scientific paper, for example, stimulates rather than merely contains thought. By stipulating the inclusion of a review of prior research, for instance, this format induces the writer to arrive at thoughtful connections between his or her work and earlier experiments. Nor is the process aspect of formats limited to the sciences. Poets, for example, have continued to write sonnets, one of the most highly structured poetic formats, for hundreds of years because the form has heuristic value. It guides the writer down certain pathways that provoke thought. The sonnet form itself—typically, fourteen lines of rhymed iambic pentameter, moving in one logical and/or emotional direction for eight lines and then shifting direction in the final six—lends itself to the production of certain kinds of thinking, such as putting ideas into dialogue with each other, establishing complex logical relationships.

Clearly, formats can both stimulate the writing process and organize the final product, but not when writers think of formats primarily as packaging and thus concern themselves with rigid adherence to form at the expense of more thoughtful exploration of content. At its worst, this "slot-filler approach" to formats can mislead writers into being more concerned with merely filling the slots than with analyzing the material they are filling them with. This is the primary problem we diagnose in our critique of five-paragraph form at the beginning of Chapter 5. (Typically, this format has a three-part thesis, an example supporting each part, and a concluding paragraph that repeats the thesis from the introduction verbatim.)

Unlike five-paragraph form, most of the formats encountered in college are roomier. They are not as rigidly overspecified, and they usually leave the writer space for more complex development of ideas. Generally speaking, formats provide a logic for dividing a subject into manageable parts and a logical order for dealing with each of these parts. To develop ideas in depth, writers need some means of deciding what to talk about and when. Unlike more mechanical organizational schemes, good formats help you to order your thinking sequentially, according to relatively distinct phases.

Using Formats Heuristically: An Example

As we observe in our discussion of formats as process and product, it is possible to lose sight of the heuristic value of formats and instead become concerned with formats primarily as disciplinary etiquette. The solution to this problem probably sounds easier than it is: you need to *find the space in a format that will allow it to work as a heuristic.* Consider how you might go about using even a highly specified organizational scheme like the following.

1. State the problem.
2. Develop criteria of adequacy for a solution.
3. Explore at least two inadequate solutions.
4. Explicate the proposed solution.
5. Evaluate the proposed solution.
6. Reply to anticipated criticisms.

The comforting feature of this format is that it appears to tell you exactly what to do. Thinking, however, especially in the early stages of the writing process, is rarely as linear as the six numbered steps in this example imply. Only by testing the adequacy of various solutions (step 3) is one likely to arrive at a clear statement of the problem (step 1), for example. And what if the problem has no solution or has several possible solutions, depending on the details of the problem? And couldn't the exploration of inadequate solutions (step 3) be the best means of discovering criteria of adequacy (standards for determining the acceptability of a solution in step 2)?

Our questions about the format, however, also reveal your best means of using one like it:

- In the early stages of drafting, allow yourself to move freely among the steps in the order that best sparks your thinking. There will be time later to reassemble your results in the required order.

- Recognize that few formats insist on the writer's devoting exactly the same amount of space and attention to each of its steps or phases. If, for example, the relative inadequacy of any solution seems to you the most pressing thing you have to say, you should be able to place your emphasis accordingly.

This advice doesn't mean that you can select from the format the steps you wish to attend to and ignore the others. You can, however, lean more heavily on one of the steps and build your paper around it.

The best reason not to ignore any of the six steps in this problem/solution format we've been looking at is that *the format does have a logic,* although it leaves that logic unstated. The purpose of including at least two inadequate solutions (step 3), for example, is to protect the writer against moving to a conclusion too quickly on the basis of too little evidence. The requirements that the writer evaluate the solution and reply to criticisms (steps 5 and 6) are there to press the writer toward complexity, to prevent a one-sided and uncritical answer. In short, heuristic value in the format is there for a writer to use if he or she doesn't allow a premature concern with matters of form to take precedence over thinking.

Formats in the Natural and Social Sciences

In some disciplines, especially in the natural sciences and psychology, the pattern of presentation for formal papers and reports is explicitly prescribed and usually mandatory. As noted in Chapter 9, for example, the American Psychological Association (APA) issues a disciplinary style guide (now in its fifth edition) to which all writers seeking to publish in the field must adhere. In other disciplines, particularly in the humanities and other of the social sciences, the accepted patterns of organization are less rigidly defined. Nonetheless, writers in these fields also operate to a significant extent within established forms, such as those set forth by the Modern Language Association (MLA) handbook.

Because formats offer a means not only of displaying thinking in a discipline but also of shaping (in the sense of creating) it, the format that a discipline tacitly or overtly requires conditions its members to think in particular ways. Learning to use the format that scientists use predisposes you to think like a scientist. Learning the differences among the various disciplines' formats can help you recognize differences in *epistemology* (ways of knowing). As we stress elsewhere in this book, how you say something is always a part of what you say; the two can't be easily separated. Although knowing the required steps of a discipline's writing format won't write your papers for you, not knowing how writers in that discipline characteristically proceed can keep you from being read.

But by concentrating on apparent differences in the surface features of writing in the disciplines, it is possible to overemphasize differences and to underestimate the amount of common ground that writing in the disciplines shares. The various formats across the disciplines, the skeletons that both shape and display thinking in those disciplines, are actually quite similar. They usually contain most of the same elements, although these elements may be called by different names and arranged in slightly different orders. A science paper and a history paper, for example, both advance a hypothesis, provide context for it, specify methodology, and support their claims by carefully weighing the evidence.

You should note that the observations in the accompanying "Voices from Across the Curriculum" boxes apply to much, but certainly not all, of the writing that goes on in the sciences. In one contribution, a professor of biology concentrates on the logic of the scientific format, but he also stresses its relative *flexibility.* That is, the distinctions among the various parts are not always as clear-cut as some students may think they are.

Using the Scientific Format

There are firm rules in organizing scientific writing. Papers are usually divided into four major sections:

1. Introduction: provides context and states the question asked and the hypothesis tested in the study
2. Methodology: accurately describes experimental procedure
3. Results: states the results obtained
4. Discussion: analyzes and interprets results with respect to the original hypothesis; discusses implications of the results

As this organizational model should make clear, scientific papers are largely deductive with a shift to inductive reasoning in the discussion when the writer usually attempts to generalize or extend conclusions to broader circumstances.

Scientific papers also include an abstract, which is placed on the page following the title page. The abstract summarizes the question being investigated in the paper, the methods used in the experiment, the results, and the conclusions drawn. The reader should be able to determine the major topics in the paper without reading the entire paper. Compose the abstract after the paper is completed.

—Richard Niesenbaum, *Professor of Biology*

In writing in the social sciences, there is a standard plot with three alternative endings. The "Introduction" (a standard section of APA style) sets forth the problem, which the "Methods" section promises to address. The "Results" section "factually" reports the outcome of the study, with the "Discussion" section interpreting the results. "The data" are given the starring role in determining which ending is discussed in the "Discussion" section: hypothesis confirmed, hypothesis rejected, or hard to say. (I would say "which ending the author chooses" versus "which ending is discussed," but the data are supposed to be determinative, and the role of the author/investigator neutral.) Analytical thinking comes in setting up the problem and making sense of the results in conjunction with existing literature on the subject.

—Alan Tjeltveit, *Professor of Psychology*

Experimental Psychology uses a very rigid format. I explain to the students the functions of the different sections for the reader. Once students start to read journal articles themselves, the functions of the sections become clear. Readers do not always want to read or reread the whole article. If I want to replicate someone's research, I may read just the "Methods" section to get the technical details I need. I may read just the "Results" section to get a sense of the numerical results I might expect. On the other hand, I may not care about the details of how the experiment was run. I might just want to know if it worked, in which case I would read the first few sentences of the "Discussion" section. The format lets me know exactly where to find whatever I might be looking for, without having to read through the whole article.

—Laura Snodgrass, *Professor of Psychology*

Treating the Format Flexibly

Scientific format appears highly formulaic at first glance. Papers are generally broken into four sections: "Introduction" (What is this all about, what do we already know, why do we care?), "Experimental Procedures" (What did you actually do?), "Results" (What happened in your experiments?), and "Discussion" (What do you think it means, what are the remaining questions?). This breakdown is useful because it emphasizes the process of argument (introduction and results), providing evidence (results), and analysis (discussion). However, although this may seem different from writing in other disciplines, I think of it as a codification of basic analytical writing that is common in most disciplines.

A common mistake made by beginning and intermediate students is taking this breakdown too literally. In order to be comprehensible, the rules must be broken periodically. For example, results frequently must be referred to in the "Experimental Procedures" section in order to understand *why* the next procedure was performed. Similarly, the "Results" section frequently must include some discussion, so that the reader understands the immediate significance of the results, if not the broader implications. For example, the following sentences might appear in a "Results" section: "These data suggest that the p53 protein may function in repressing cell division in potential cancer cells. In order to test this possibility, we overexpressed p53 protein in a transformed cell line." The first sentence provides an interpretation to the results that is necessary to understand why the next experiment was performed.

—Bruce Wightman, *Professor of Biology*

B. THE PSYCHOLOGY OF FORM

Thus far in this book we have talked about form primarily in relation to the search for meaning. We've demonstrated that some forms of arranging ideas (five-paragraph form, for example) have the effect of interfering with a writer's ability to have ideas in the first place. Whatever form one uses, we've argued, has to be flexible enough to allow ideas to evolve. The point is that there are various factors influencing a writer's decisions about forms and formats. These include both the demands of the subject itself and those of the discourse community within which the writing seeks to communicate.

We now wish to expand upon the role that a writer's sense of his or her *audience* plays in determining the formal presentation of ideas. We have entitled this section "The Psychology of Form" to emphasize the effects that a chosen form has on an audience—on its receptiveness to a writer's ideas, for example.

Since classical times, there have been numerous studies of this subject, known as *rhetoric*. The study of rhetoric is primarily concerned with the various means at a writer's (or speaker's) disposal for influencing the views of an audience. In early rhetorics, Greek and Roman writers divided these means into three large categories: *ethos, logos,* and *pathos.* We'll use these categories for organizing what we wish to say about the relationship between formal structures and audience.

1. *Ethos.* The category of ethos has to do with the character of the speaker or writer. The basic idea of ethos is that if an audience perceives a speaker to be ethical and rational, it will be inclined to perceive her or his argument as ethical and rational too. Thus, writers attend to the kind of *persona* they become on the page, the personality conveyed by the words and the tone of the words. In classical orations—the grandparent of virtually all speech and essay formats—the first section was always allotted to particular means of establishing an appealing persona, one that an audience would want to listen to and believe.

Although there are many ways of talking about ethos, throughout this book we implicitly recommend essentially the same kind of writer's persona—one that is primarily interested in understanding a subject and conveying that understanding. Such a persona assumes a relationship of mutual interest with his or her audience and avoids a defensive posture toward the material or the audience.

2. *Logos.* This category has to do with the character of the thinking itself, which has been our emphasis throughout this book—the rational component, evident in the presence and development of the ideas.

3. *Pathos.* This category includes appeals to the audience's emotions—which writing does all of the time, whether a writer wants it to or not. It is possible to think of the form of a paper in terms of how it might negotiate, for example, the likes and dislikes, the hopes and fears, of its assumed audience. If, for instance, you were to present an argument in favor of a position with which you knew in advance that your audience was predisposed to disagree, you would probably choose to delay making a case for this position until you had found various ways of earning that audience's trust. By contrast, when presenting an argument to an audience of like-minded people, you would be much more likely to start out with the position you planned to advance.

In any piece of writing, there are always issues of authority. And so, as a writer you need to concern yourself with using language in a way that will incline readers to credit what you say. We have been advancing as the best source of authority your ability to show others why and how you take the evidence to mean what you say it does. A premise of this book is that rather than spend a lot of time cultivating a set of rhetorical strategies for defeating opponents, writers should find ways to make their thinking about evidence clear and convincing in its clarity.

How to Locate Concessions and Refutations

In the language of argument you *concede* whenever you acknowledge that a position at odds with your own does indeed have merit, even though you continue to believe that your position is the more reasonable one. A central idea of Chapter 6, "The Evolving Thesis," in fact, is that one option for dealing with views that conflict with your own is to use these to evolve your own position, thereby assimilating them. Another option is to argue against these views so as to *refute* their reasonableness.

There are several guidelines for locating concessions and refutations in an argument. It is a rule of thumb, for example, not to make your readers wait too long before you either concede or refute a view that you can assume will already have occurred to them. If you delay too long, you may inadvertently suggest either that you are unaware of the competing view or that you are afraid to bring it up.

In the case of short and easily managed concessions and refutations, writers often house these within the first several paragraphs and, in this way, clear a space for the position they wish to promote. In the case of more complicated and potentially more threatening alternative arguments, writers take care to get their own positions clearly and convincingly expressed first, before addressing the alternatives. But to avoid the rhetorical problem of appearing to ignore substantive opposing arguments, writers will often give these a nod in brief, telling readers that they will return to a full discussion of these once they have laid out their own positions in some detail.

Here are some more specific guidelines:

- Don't end on a concession. If you do include a concession in your concluding paragraph, be sure to return to your own position in the final sentences.
- If you state an opposing argument in your introduction, you should be sure that it can be accurately presented in the brief form that introductory paragraphs require. You need to be careful about turning the opposing view into a straw man—an easily knocked-down version of the opposing view (see Chapter 8 for a full discussion).
- One means of making sure you don't treat an opposing argument unfairly but also don't inadvertently convince your readers that this argument is better than your own is to concede the merits of this opposing view but then argue that, in the particular context you are addressing, your argument is more important, more appropriate, and so forth.
- The placement of arguments has much to do with their relative complexity. Reasonably straightforward and easily explained concessions and refutations can often all be grouped in one place, perhaps as early as the second or third paragraph of a paper. The approach to concession and refutation in more complex arguments does not allow for such grouping. For each part of your argument, you will probably need to concede and refute as necessary, before moving to the next part of your argument and repeating the procedure.

To qualify as a concession, a writer's acknowledgment of a competing point of view should not be completely wiped out by a subsequent refutation. The language, in other words, needs to represent the position that the writer is conceding as creditable—rather than only seemingly creditable until he or she lays out a means of opposing it.

Refutations typically operate not just by revealing poor thinking or inadequate evidence in a competing point of view but also by proposing the greater value of adopting another position. Refutations often concede an opposing argument's merits but refute their importance in favor of a position that seems to hold more promise under a given set of circumstances.

In this context, consider the following passage from a student essay on the relation between gender inequality and language, which exemplifies a skillfully constructed concession and refutation. It is excerpted from the second part of an introductory paragraph, after the writer has set up the issue: whether or not the elimination of sexism in language (the use of male pronouns and words like "mankind," for example, in circumstances applying to both men and women) through the use of generic pronouns (those that do not indicate gender, such as "they" rather than "he") can help to eliminate gender exclusion in the culture. The paragraph names the two sides of the issue and moves from there to a tentative thesis.

Gender Inequality and Linguistic Bias

The more conservative side on this issue questions whether the elimination of generic pronouns can, in fact, change attitudes and whether intentionally changing language is even possible. The reformist side believes that the elimination of generic pronouns is necessary for women's liberation from oppression and that reshaping the use of male pronouns as generic is both possible and effective. Although the answer to the debate over the direct link between a change in language and a change in society is not certain, it is certain that the attitudes and behaviors of societies are inseparable from language. Language conditions what we feel and think. The act of using *they* to refer to all people rather than the generic *he* will not automatically change collective attitudes toward women. These generic pronouns should be changed, however, because (1) the struggle itself increases awareness and discussion of the sexual inequalities in society, and, subsequently, this awareness will transform attitudes and language and because (2) the power of linguistic usage has been mainly controlled by and reserved for men. Solely by participating in linguistic reform, women have begun to appropriate some of the power for themselves.

❦ *Try this:* Locate the parts of the preceding paragraph that function as concession and those that function as refutation. What part of the competing argument does the refutation still appear willing to concede? How is the refutation that the writer offers different from the position to which he concedes? □

Organizing Comparisons and Contrasts

Chapter 4 discussed working comparatively as a reading strategy for getting ideas. We now want to address this subject from the perspective of organizing a paper. The first decision a writer has to make when arranging comparisons and contrasts is whether to address the two items being compared and contrasted *sequentially* in blocks or *point by point*. So, for example, if you are comparing subject A with subject B, you might first make all the points you wish to make about A and then make points about B by explicitly referring back to A as you go. The advantage of this format is that it is easier to use in early drafts when you're not yet sure what your major points will be. Writing about first one subject and then the other will allow you to use comparing and contrasting to figure out what you wish to say.

The disadvantage of this subject-A–then-subject-B format is that it can easily lose focus. If you don't manage to keep the points you raise about each side of your comparison parallel, you may end up with a paper comprised of two loosely connected halves. The solution is to make your comparisons and contrasts in the second half of the paper connect explicitly with what you said in the first half. What you say about subject A, in other words, should set the subtopics and terms for discussion of subject B.

The alternative pattern of organization for comparisons and contrasts is to organize by topic—not A and then B but A_1 and B_1, A_2 and B_2, A_3 and B_3, and so forth. That is, you talk about both A and B under a series of subtopics. If, for example, you were comparing two films, you might organize your work under such headings as directing, script, acting, special effects, and so forth.

The advantage of this format is that it better focuses the comparisons, pressing you to use them to think with. The disadvantage is that organizing in this way is sometimes difficult to manage until you've already done quite a bit of thinking about the two items you're comparing. The solution, particularly in longer papers, is sometimes to use both formats. You begin by looking at each of your subjects separately to make the big links and distinctions apparent and then focus what you've said by further pursuing selected comparisons one topic at a time.

Regardless of which format you adopt, the comparisons and contrasts will not really begin to take shape until you have done enough preliminary drafting to discover what the most significant similarities and differences are and, beyond that, whether the similarities or the differences are most important—whether, that is, your primary goal is to compare or to contrast. At this point, you can begin to operate according to the principle we discuss next: climactic order.

Climactic Order

Climactic order has to do with arranging the elements in a list from least important to most important. The idea is to *build to your best points*, rather than leading with them and thereby allowing the paper to trail off from your more minor and less interesting observations.

But what are your best points? A frequent mistake that writers commit in arranging their points climactically—and one that has much to do with the psychology of form—is to assume that the best point is the most obvious, the one with the most data attached to it and the one least likely to produce disagreement with readers. Such writers end up giving more space than they should to ideas that really don't need much development because they are already evident to most readers.

A better strategy is to define as your best points those that Notice and Focus locates as the *most revealing, most thought-provoking, and often, at first glance, least obvious.* In this case, if you followed the principle of climactic order, you would begin with the most obvious and predictable points—and ones that, psychologically speaking, would get readers assenting—and then build to the more revealing and less obvious ones. So, for example, if the comparisons between film A and film B are fairly mundane but the contrasts are really provocative, you'd get the comparisons out of the way first and build to the contrasts, exploiting difference within similarity (see Chapter 4).

Note that the principle of climactic order works with all kinds of organizational schemes, not just with comparison and contrast. If, for example, there are three important reasons for banning snowmobiling in your town, you might choose to place the most compelling one last. If you were to put it first, you might draw your readers in quickly (a principle used by news stories) but then lose them as your argument seemed to trail off into less interesting rationales. Similarly, if you have four examples for a point you wish to make, you might use a pan to cover the first three to pave the way for a zoom on the one you take to be the best and most revealing.

One of the reasons that thesis statements, as we will discuss shortly, often contain subordinate clauses ("although there are many reasons to believe X, the most compelling reason is . . .") is that this sentence structure allows the reader to predict the paper's use of climactic order.

How Thesis Shapes Predict the Shape of the Paper

Many thesis statements begin with a grammatically subordinate idea that they go on to replace or outweigh with a more pressing claim: "Although X appears to account for Z, Y accounts for it better." (You will probably recognize this sentence structure as a version of one of the prompts to interpretation offered in Chapter 3: saying something "seems to be about X, but is really or could also be about Y.") This formula can also organize a paper, which proceeds by following the pattern predicted by the order of clauses in the thesis statement. The first part of the paper deals with the claims for X and then moves to a fuller embrace of Y (usually in overt relation to X). (See Chapter 13 for a discussion of grammatical subordination.)

The advantage of this *subordinate construction* (and the reason that so many theses are set up this way) is that the subordinate idea helps you to define your own position by giving you something to define it against. As should at this point be evident, both the thesis shape containing subordination and the paper that follows from it are versions of climactic order.

In practice, using this shape will often lead you to arrive at some compromise position between the claims of both X and Y. What appeared to be a *binary opposition*—"not X but Y"—emerges as a complex combination of the two. (See Chapter 2 on refocusing binaries.)

Sometimes this combination is already evident in a thesis shape related to the subordination model: *"not only X but also Y."* Here the emphasis predicts that you will make *additional* claims, probably less obvious ones (Y), after you have discussed X.

As is evident in the previous chapter's discussion of introductory paragraphs, one of the most important things to accomplish in an introduction is to locate an issue, question, or problem—something that is at stake—and then place it in an explanatory context. The subordinate clause of a thesis helps you to demonstrate that there is in fact an issue involved—that is, more than one possible explanation for the evidence you are considering—and thus a reason to be writing the paper in the first place.

Another thesis shape that can predict the shape of a paper is the *list*. This shape, in which a writer might offer three points and then devote a section to each, often leads to sloppier thinking than one having a thesis statement containing both subordinate and independent clauses, because the list often does not sufficiently specify the connections among its various components. As a result, it fails to assert a relationship among ideas. The list is in fact the shape used by five-paragraph form—a form that (in Chapter 5) we concede achieves considerable clarity of organization but at the (very high) cost of oversimplifying and derailing analysis.

Try this: It is a useful skill, both in reading and writing, to predict paper shapes from thesis shapes. Unlike the multiple parts of the thesis that merely lists, productive thesis statements arrange the parts in some sort of overt relation to each other. For each of the two theses below, what shape is predicted? That is, what will probably be discussed first, what second, and why? Which words in the thesis are especially predictive of the shape the paper will take?

1. The reforms in education, created to alleviate the problems of previous reforms, have served only to magnify the very problems they were meant to solve.
2. Joinville paints, though indirectly, a picture of military, social, and political gain having very little to do with religion and more to do with race hatred and the acquisition of material wealth. □

The Shaping Force of Transitions

The preceding critique of the list as an overly loose organizational format also applies to the connective tissue among the parts of an essay. Although transitional wording such as "another example of" or "also" at the beginning of paragraphs does tell readers that a related point or example will follow, it does not specify that relationship beyond piling on another "and." The organizational model at work in this sort of additive scheme is again the list—the most diffuse and potentially illogical form of organization. (For a full analysis of the shortcomings of listing, see the section entitled "Strategies for Making Summary More Analytical" in Chapter 4.)

If you find yourself relying on "another" and "also" at points of transition, force yourself to substitute other transitional wording that indicates *more precisely* the nature of the relationship with what has gone before in the paper. Language such as "similarly" and "by contrast" can sometimes serve this purpose. In many cases, however, some restatement of what has been said and its relation to what will come next is called for. Relatively inexperienced writers tend to underestimate the amount of productive restating that goes on in papers, often because they fail to see that the restatement is not just repetition. It is a "saying again" in different language for the purpose of advancing the writer's thinking further. *A good transition reaches backward, telling where you've been, as the grounds for making a subsequent move forward.*

The linkage between where you've been and where you're going is usually a point in your writing at which thinking is taking place. Often this kind of transitional thinking will require you to concentrate on articulating *how* what has preceded connects to what will follow—the logical links. This is especially the case in the evolving model, rather than static model of thesis development, wherein the writer needs to keep updating the thesis as it moves through evidence. And so it follows that *thinking tends to occur at points of transition.* If it doesn't, you're far more likely to run into problems in organization.

The first step towards improving your use of transitions (and thereby, the organization of your writing) is to become *conscious* of them. To see how the transitions work as a skeleton for something you are reading, actively search out words that function as directional indicators, especially at the beginnings of but also within paragraphs. "And," for example, is a plus sign. It indicates that the writer will add something, essentially continuing in the same direction. The words "but," "yet," "nevertheless," and "however" are among the many transitional words that alert readers to changes in the direction of the writer's thinking. They might indicate, for example, the introduction of a qualification, a potentially contradictory piece of evidence, an alternative point of view, and so forth. Note as well that some additive transitions do more work than "also" or "another." The word "moreover" is an additive transition, but it adds emphasis to the added point. The transitional sequence "not only . . . but also" restates and then adds information in a way that clarifies what has gone before.

❧*Try this:* You can learn much about the shape of a writer's thinking and his or her method of connecting and advancing ideas by tracking the transitions. Take a few pages of something you are reading—preferably a complete piece, such as a short article— and circle or underline all of the directional indicators. Then, survey your markings. What do you notice now about the shape of the piece? This exercise is also a good way to expand your repertoire of transitional words to use in your own writing. □

ASSIGNMENT: INFERRING THE FORMAT OF A PUBLISHED ARTICLE

Often the format governing the organization of a published piece is not immediately evident. That is, it is not subdivided according to conventional disciplinary categories that are obeyed by all members of a given discourse community. Especially if you are studying a discipline in which the writing does not follow an explicitly prescribed format, such as history, literature, or economics, you may find it illuminating to examine representative articles or essays in that discipline, looking for an implicit format. In other words, you can usually discern some underlying pattern of organization: the formal conventions, the rules that are being followed even when these are not highlighted.

The following assignment works well whether you tackle it individually or in a group. It can lead to a paper, an oral report, or both. First, you need to assemble several articles from the same or a similar kind of journal or magazine. "Journal" is the name given to publications aimed at specialized, usually scholarly, audiences, as opposed to general or popular audiences. *Time, Newsweek,* and the *New Yorker* are called "magazines" rather than "journals" because they are aimed at a broader general audience. *Shakespeare Quarterly* is a journal; *Psychology Today* is a magazine.

Having found at least three journal or magazine articles, study them in order to focus on the following question: *Insofar as there appears to be a format that articles in this journal adhere to, what are its parts?*

How, for example, does an article in this journal or magazine typically begin and end? Does there seem to be a relatively uniform place in which these articles include opposing arguments? You will, in other words, be analyzing the articles inductively (reasoning from particular details to general principles). Begin with the product and reason backward to the skeleton beneath the skin.

Note that if your professor directs you to work with magazines rather than journals, you should probably further narrow the focus—to a *Time* cover story, to the *New Yorker's* "Letter from [the name of a city]," or another such recurring feature. Even gossip columns and letters of advice to the lovelorn in teen magazines adhere to certain visible though not explicitly marked formats.

Write up your results. Cite particular language from at least two articles in support of your claims about the implicit format. In presenting your evidence, keep the focus on the underlying form, showing how the different articles proceed in the same or similar ways. Don't let yourself get too distracted by the articles' content, even though there may be similarities here as well. Instead, work toward formulating a rationale for the format—what you take to be its psychology of form. You will need (for example) both to lay out the typical form of the introduction and to account for its taking that typical form. Devote several paragraphs to this rationale, either at the end of your report or integrated within it.

CHAPTER

12

Style: Choosing Words

A. NOT JUST ICING ON THE CAKE

Most people simply don't pay attention to words; that is, they use words as if their sounds and shapes were invisible and their meanings were unitary and self-evident. One goal of this chapter is to interest you in words themselves—as *things* with particularized qualities, complex histories, and varied shades of meaning. Such interest is enormously beneficial in improving your ability to write. There are various ways of nourishing this interest, all of which share the characteristic of focusing on the words as words.

This is the first of two chapters on style. It addresses word choice—also known as *diction*—and its impact on style. The next chapter addresses the effect of sentence shapes, also known as *syntax*.

It is commonly assumed that "getting the style right" is a task that begins at the *editing stage* of producing a paper, as part of polishing the final draft. This assumption is only partly true. You probably should delay a *full-fledged* stylistic revision until a late stage of drafting, but that doesn't mean that you should totally ignore stylistic questions as you draft, because the decisions you make about how to phrase your meaning inevitably exert a powerful influence on the meaning you make.

And what is style? Well, it's not just icing on the cake—cosmetic, a matter of polishing the surface. Broadly defined, *style refers to all of a writer's decisions in selecting, arranging, and expressing what he or she has to say.* Many factors affect your style: your aim and sense of audience, the ways you approach and develop a topic, the kinds of evidence you choose, and, particularly, the kinds of syntax and diction you characteristically select.

Getting the style right is not as simple as proofreading for errors in grammar or punctuation. Proofreading occurs in the relatively comfortable linguistic world of simple right and wrong. Stylistic considerations, by contrast, take place in the more exploratory terrain of *making choices* among more and less effective ways of formulating and communicating your meaning.

In this sense, style is personal. The foundations of your style emerge in the dialogue you have with yourself about your topic. When you revise for style, you consciously reorient yourself toward communicating the results of that dialogue to your audience. Stylistic decisions, then, are a mix of the unconscious and conscious, of chance and choice. You don't simply impose style onto your prose; it's not a mask you don or your way of icing the cake. Revising for style is more like sculpting. As a sculptor uses a chisel to "bring out" a shape from a block of walnut or marble, a writer uses style to "bring out" the shape of the conceptual connections in a draft of an essay. As the two style chapters will suggest in various ways, this "bringing out" demands a certain *detachment from your own language*. It requires that you *become aware of your words as words and of your sentences as sentences.*

If stylistic considerations are not merely cosmetic, then it follows that rethinking the way you have said something can lead you to rethink the substance of what you have said. This point is sufficiently important—and unrecognized by a majority of writers—to illustrate here at the beginning for both syntax and diction, before this chapter narrows its focus to diction alone.

How does the difference in sentence structure affect the meaning of the following two sentences?

Draft: The history of Indochina is marked by colonial exploitation as well as international cooperation.

Revision: The history of Indochina, *although* marked by colonial exploitation, testifies to the possibility of international cooperation.

In the draft, the claim that Indochina has experienced colonial exploitation is equal in weight to the claim that it has also experienced international cooperation. But the revision ranks the two claims. The "although" clause makes the claim of exploitation secondary to the claim of cooperation. The first version of the sentence would probably lead you to a broad survey of foreign intervention in Indochina. The result would likely be a static list in which you judged some interventions to be "beneficial" and others "not beneficial." The revised sentence redirects your thinking, tightens your paper's focus to prioritize evidence of cooperation, and presses you to make decisions, such as whether the positive consequences of cooperation outweigh the negative consequences of colonialism. In short, the revision leads you to examine the dynamic relations between your two initial claims.

Rethinking what you mean is just as likely to occur when you attend to word choice. Notice how the change of a single word in the following sentences could change the entire paper.

Draft: The president's attitude toward military spending is ambiguous.

Revision: The president's attitude toward military spending is ambivalent.

In the draft, the use of the word "ambiguous" (meaning "open to many interpretations") would likely lead to a paper on ways that the president's decisions are unclear. The choice of "ambiguous" might also signal that the writer and not the president is unclear on what the president's actions could be taken to mean. If the president's policies aren't unclear—hard to interpret—but are divided, conflicted over competing ways of thinking, then the writer would want the word "ambivalent." This recognition would lead not only to reorganizing the final draft but also to refocusing the argument, building to the significance of this ambivalence (that the president is torn between adopting one of two stances) rather than to the previous conclusion (that presidential policy is simply incoherent).

B. TONE

Tone is the *implied attitude* of a piece of language toward its subject and audience. Whenever you revise for style, your choices in syntax and diction will affect the tone. There are no hard and fast rules to govern matters of tone, and your control of it will depend upon your sensitivity to the particular context—your understanding of your own intentions and your readers' expectations.

Let's consider, for example, the tonal implications of the warning signs in the subways of London and New York.

London: Leaning out of the window may cause harm.

New York: Do not lean out of the window.

Initially, you may find the English injunction laughably indirect and verbose in comparison with the shoot-from-the-hip clarity of the American sign. But that is to ignore the very thing we are calling *style*. The American version appeals to authority, commanding readers what not to do without telling them why. The English version, by contrast, appeals to logic; it is more collegial toward its readers and assumes they are rational beings rather than children prone to misbehave.

In revising for tone, you need to ask yourself if the attitude suggested by your language is appropriate to the aim of your message and to your audience. Your goal is to keep the tone *consistent* with your rhetorical intentions. The following paragraph, from a college catalogue, offers a classic mismatch between the overtly stated aim and the tonal implications:

> The student affairs staff believes that the college years provide a growth and development process for students. Students need to learn about themselves and others and to learn how to relate to individuals and groups of individuals with vastly different backgrounds, interests, attitudes and values. Not only is the tolerance of differences expected, but also an appreciation and a celebration of these differences must be an outcome of the student's experience. In addition, the student must progress toward self-reliance and independence tempered by a concern for the social order.

The explicit content of this passage—*what* it says—concerns tolerance. The professed point of view is student-friendly, asserting that the college exists to allow students "to learn about themselves and others" and to support the individual in accord with the "appreciation ... of ... differences."

But note that the implicit tone—*how* the passage goes about saying *what* it says—is condescending and intolerant. Look at the verbs. An imperious authority lectures students about what they "*need* to learn," that tolerance is "*expected,*" that "celebration . . . *must* be an outcome," and that "the student *must* progress" along these lines. Presumably, the paragraph does not intend to adopt this high-handed manner, but its deafness to tone subverts its desired meaning.

❦*Try this:* Using the example from the college catalogue as a model, locate and bring to class examples of tonal inconsistency or inappropriateness that you encounter in your daily life. If you have difficulty finding examples, try memos from those in authority at your school or workplace, which often contain excruciating examples of officialese. Type one of your passages, and underneath it compose a paragraph of analysis in which you single out particular words and phrases and explain how the tone is inappropriate. Then rewrite the passage to remedy the problem. □

Levels of Style: Who's Writing to Whom, and Why Does It Matter?

How you say something is always a significant part of *what* you say. To look at words as words is to focus on the *how* as well as the *what*. Imagine that you call your friend on the phone, and a voice you don't recognize answers. You ask to speak with your friend, and the voice responds, "With whom have I the pleasure of speaking?" By contrast, what if the voice instead responds, "Who's this?" What information do these two versions of the question convey, beyond the obvious request for your name?

The first response—"With whom have I the pleasure of speaking?"—tells you that the speaker is formal and polite. He is also probably fastidiously well educated: he not only knows the difference between "who" and "whom" but also obeys the etiquette that outlaws ending a sentence with a preposition ("Whom have I the pleasure of speaking *with?*"). The very formality of the utterance, however, might lead you to label the speaker pretentious. His assumption that conversing with you is a "pleasure" suggests empty flattery. On the other hand, the second version—"Who's this?"—while also grammatically correct, is less formal. It is more direct but also terse to a fault; the speaker does not seem particularly interested in treating you politely.

The two hypothetical responses represent two different levels of style. Formal English obeys the basic conventions of standard written prose, and most academic writing is fairly formal. An informal style—one that is conversational and full of slang—can have severe limitations in an academic setting. The syntax and vocabulary of written prose aren't the same as those of speech, and attempts to import the language of speech into academic writing can result in your communicating less meaning with less precision.

Let's take one brief example:

> Internecine quarrels within the corporation destroyed morale and sent the value of the stock plummeting.

The phrase "internecine quarrels" may strike some readers as a pretentious display of formal language, but consider how difficult it is to communicate this concept economically. "Fights that go on between people related to each other" is awkward; "brother against brother" is sexist and a cliché; and "mutually destructive disputes" is acceptable but long-winded.

It is arguably a part of our national culture to value the simple and the direct as more genuine and democratic than the sophisticated, which is supposedly more aristocratic and pretentious. This "plain-speaking" style, however, can hinder your ability to develop and communicate your ideas. In the case of "internecine," the more formal diction choice actually communicates more, and more effectively, than the less formal equivalents.

When in doubt about how your readers will respond to the formality or informality of your style, you are usually better off opting for some version of "With whom have I the pleasure of speaking?" rather than "Who's this?" The best solution will usually lie somewhere in between: "May I ask who's calling?" would protect you against the imputation of either priggishness or piggishness.

What generalizations about style do these examples suggest?

- There are many ways of conveying a message.
- The way you phrase a message constitutes a significant part of its meaning.
- Your phrasing gives your reader cues that suggest your attitude and your ways of thinking.
- All stylistic decisions depend on your sensitivity to context—who's talking to whom about what subject and with what aims.

The last of these generalizations concerns what is called the *rhetorical situation*. *Rhetoric* is the subject that deals with how writers and speakers behave in given situations and, more specifically, how they can generate language that produces the effects they desire on a particular audience. Obviously, as you make stylistic choices, you need to be aware of the possible consequences of making certain statements to a certain audience in a certain fashion.

C. THE PERSON QUESTION

"The person question" concerns which of the three basic forms of the pronoun you should use when you write. Here are the three forms, with brief examples.

First person: I believe Heraclitus is an underrated philosopher.

Second person: You should believe that Heraclitus is an underrated philosopher.

Third person: He or she believes that Heraclitus is an underrated philosopher.

Which person to use is a stylistic concern, since it involves a writer's *choices* as regards to level of formality, the varying expectations of different audiences, and overall tone.

As a general rule, in academic writing you should discuss your subject matter in the third person and avoid the first and second person. There is logic to this rule: most academic analysis focuses on the subject matter rather than on you as you respond to it. If you use the third person, you will keep the attention where it belongs.

The First-Person Pronoun "I": Pro and Con

Using the first-person "I" can throw the emphasis on the wrong place. Repeated assertions of "in my opinion" actually distract your readers from what you have to say. Omit them except in the most informal cases. You might, however, consider using the first person in the drafting stage if you are having trouble bringing your own point of view to the forefront. In this situation, the "I" becomes a strategy for loosening up and saying what you really think about a subject rather than adopting conventional and faceless positions. In the final analysis, though, most analytical prose will be more precise and straightforward in the third person. When you cut "I am convinced that" from the beginning of any claim, what you lose in personal conviction, you gain in concision and directness by keeping the focus on the main idea in a main clause.

Are there cases when you should use "I"? Contrary to the general rule, some professors actually prefer the first-person pronoun in particular contexts, as noted in the accompanying "Voices from Across the Curriculum" box.

Note that these are not blanket endorsements; they specify a limited context within which "I" is preferred. The biology professor's cautioning against using an overly personal and colloquial tone is also probably the consensus view.

Although a majority of professors may prefer the first-person "I think" to the more awkward "the writer (or 'one') thinks," we would point out that, in the service of reducing wordiness, you can often avoid both options. For example, in certain contexts and disciplines, the first-person-plural "we" is acceptable usage: "The president's speech

---

Voices from Across the Curriculum

Using the First-Person *I* in Academic Writing

Avoid phrases like "*The author* believes (or will discuss) . . ." Except in the paper's abstract, "*I* believe (or will discuss)" is okay, and often best.

—Alan Tjeltveit, Professor of Psychology

I prefer that personal opinion or voice (for example, "I this," or "I that") appear throughout. I like the first person. No "the author feels" or "this author found that," please! Who is the author? Hey, it's you!

—Frederick Norling, Professor of Business

The biggest stylistic problem is that students tend to be too personal or colloquial in their writing, using phrases such as the following: "*Scientists all agree . . .*"; "*I find it amazing that . . .*"; "*The thing that I find most interesting . . .*" Students are urged to present data and existing information in their own words, but in an objective way. My preference in writing is to use the active voice in the past tense. I feel this is the most direct and least wordy approach: *I asked this . . . ; I found out that . . . ; These data show. . . .*

—Richard Niesenbaum, Professor of Biology

---

assumes that *we* are all dutiful but disgruntled taxpayers." The one case in which the first person is particularly appropriate occurs when you are citing an example from your own experience. Otherwise, if you are in doubt about using "I" or "we," avoid these first-person pronouns.

The Second-Person Pronoun "You"
and the Imperative Mood

As for the second person, proceed with caution. Using "you" is a fairly assertive gesture. Many readers will be annoyed, for example, by a paper about advertising that states, "When you read about a sale at the mall, you know it's hard to resist." Most readers resent having a writer airily making assumptions about them or telling them what to do. Some rhetorical situations, however, call for the use of "you." Textbooks, for example, use "you" frequently because it creates a more direct relationship between authors and readers. Yet, even in appropriate situations, directly addressing readers as "you" may alienate them by ascribing to them attitudes and needs they may not have.

The readiest alternative to "you," the imperative mood, requires careful handling for similar reasons. The *imperative mood* of a verb expresses a direct request or command, leaving "you" understood, as in the following instance: "Don't [you] dismiss the European perspective too quickly." Such a sentence, though, runs the same kind of risk as the previous example: readers might resent your assumption that they would dismiss the European perspective or, at any rate, dislike being told so forcefully how to think about it. On the other hand, in certain writing situations the imperative mood is both appropriate and useful: when you are giving a set of step-by-step instructions ("*Take* a right on 12th Street and then turn left at the light onto Vine") or politely soliciting your readers' attention ("*Consider* the plight of Afghan refugees"). In both cases, the imperative engages readers more unobtrusively than would inserting an awkward "you should" or "one should" before the verbs.

The conventional argument for using the first and second person is that "I" and "you" are personal and engage readers. It is not necessarily the case, however, that the third person is therefore impersonal. Just as film directors put their stamps on films by the way they organize the images, move among camera viewpoints, and orchestrate the soundtracks, so writers, even when writing in the third person, have a wide variety of resources at their disposal for making the writing more personal and accessible for their audiences. See, for example, the discussion of the passive voice in the next chapter.

D. SHADES OF MEANING:
CHOOSING THE BEST WORD

The nineteenth-century English statesman Benjamin Disraeli once differentiated between "misfortune" and "calamity" by commenting on his political rival William Gladstone: "If Mr. Gladstone fell into the Thames, it would be a misfortune; but if someone dragged him out, it would be a calamity." "Misfortune" and "calamity" might to some people mean the same thing, but in fact the two words allow a careful writer to discriminate fine shades of meaning.

One of the best ways to get yourself to pay attention to words as words is to practice making subtle distinctions among related words. The "right" word contributes
accuracy and precision to your meaning. The "wrong" word, it follows, is inaccurate or
imprecise. The most reliable guide to choosing the right word and avoiding the wrong
word is a dictionary that includes not only concise definitions but also the origin of
words (known as their *etymology*). A dicey alternative is a thesaurus (a dictionary of synonyms, now included in most word processing software): it can offer you a host of
choices, but you run a fairly high risk of choosing an inappropriate word. If you go the
thesaurus route, check the word you select in the dictionary. The best dictionary for
the job, by the way, is the *Oxford English Dictionary*, which commonly goes by its initials, *OED*. Available in every library reference collection and usually on-line at colleges and universities as well, it provides historical examples of how every word has
been used over time.

Frankly, many of the most common diction errors are caused by ignorance. The
writer has not learned the difference between similar terms that actually have different
meanings. If you confuse "then" and "than," or "infer" and "imply," you will not convey
the meaning that you intend, and you will probably confuse your readers and invite
them to question your control of language. Getting the wrong word is, of course, not
limited to pairs of words that are spelled similarly. A *notorious* figure is widely but unfa-
vorably known, whereas a *famous* person is usually recognized for accomplishments
that are praiseworthy. Referring to a famous person as notorious—a rather comic
error—could be an embarrassing mistake. Take the time to learn the differences among
seemingly similar words.

A slightly less severe version of getting the wrong word occurs when a writer uses
a word with a shade of meaning that is inappropriate or inaccurate in a particular context. Take, for example, the words "assertive" and "aggressive." Often used interchangeably, they don't really mean the same thing—and the difference matters. Loosely
defined, both terms mean "forceful." But "assertive" suggests being "bold and self-con-
fident," whereas "aggressive" suggests being "eager to attack." In most cases, you compliment the person you call assertive but raise doubts about the person you call aggressive (whether you are giving a compliment depends on the situation: "aggressive" is a
term of praise on the football field but less so if used to describe an acquaintance's
behavior during conversation at the dinner table).

One particularly charged context in which shades of meaning matter to many
readers involves the potentially sexist implications of using one term for women and
another for men. If, for example, in describing a woman and a man up for the same
job, we referred to the woman as *aggressive* but the man as *assertive,* our diction would
deservedly be considered sexist. It would reveal that what is perceived as poised and a
sign of leadership potential in a man is being construed as unseemly belligerence in a
woman. The sexism enters when word choice suggests that what is assertive in a man is
aggressive in a woman.

In choosing the right shade of meaning, you will get a sharper sense for the word by
knowing its etymological history—the word or words from which it evolved. In the
preceding example, "aggressive" derives from the Latin "*aggressus,*" meaning "to go to or

approach"; and "*aggressus*" is itself a combination of "*ad,*" a prefix expressing motion, and "*gradus,*" meaning "a step." An aggressive person, then, is "coming at you." "Assertive," on the other hand, comes from the Latin "*asserere,*" combining "*ad*" and "*serere,*" meaning "to join or bind together." An assertive person is "coming to build or put things together"—certainly not to threaten.

❧ *Try this:* One of the best ways to get yourself to pay attention to words as words is to practice making fine distinctions among related words, as we did with "aggressive" and "assertive." The following exercise will not only increase your vocabulary but also acquaint you with that indispensable reference work for etymology, the *Oxford English Dictionary (OED).* Look up one of the following pairs of words in the *OED.* Write down the etymology of each word in the pair, and then, in a paragraph for each, summarize its linguistic histories—how their meanings have evolved across time. (The *OED*'s dated examples of how the word has been used will be helpful here.)

ordinal/ordinary	explicate/implicate
tenacious/stubborn	induce/conducive
enthusiasm/ecstasy	adhere/inhere
monarchy/oligarchy	overt/covert

Alternatively, select a pair of similar words or, for that matter, any key words from your reading for a course, and submit them to this exercise. There's no better way to learn about—and remember—a word. □

What's Bad about "Good" and "Bad" (and Other Broad, Judgmental Terms)

Vague evaluative terms such as "good" and "bad" can seduce you into stopping your thinking while it is still too general and ill-defined—a matter discussed at length in Chapter 1 in the section entitled "Judging." If you train yourself to select more precise words whenever you encounter these words in your drafts, not only will your prose become clearer but also the search for new words will probably start you thinking again, sharpening your ideas. If, for example, you find yourself writing a sentence such as "The subcommittee made a *bad* decision," ask yourself *why* you called it a bad decision. A revision to "The subcommittee made a shortsighted decision" indicates what in fact is bad about the decision and sets you up to discuss why the decision was myopic, further developing the idea.

Be aware that often these evaluative terms are disguised as neutrally descriptive ones—"natural," for instance, and "realistic." Realistic according to whom and defined by what criteria? Something is natural according to a given idea about nature—an assumption—and the same goes for "moral." These are not terms that mean separately from a particular context or ideology (that is, an assumed hierarchy of value). Similarly, in a sentence such as "Society disapproves of interracial marriage," the broad and apparently neutral term "society" can blind you to a host of important distinctions about social class, about a particular culture, and so on.

Concrete and Abstract Diction

At its best, effective analytical prose uses both concrete and abstract words. Simply defined, *concrete diction* evokes: it brings things to life by offering your readers words that they can use their senses upon. "Telephone," "eggshell," "crystalline," "azure," "striped," "kneel," "flare," and "burp" are examples of concrete diction. In academic writing, there is no substitute for concrete language whenever you are describing what happens or what something looks like—in a laboratory experiment, in a military action, in a painting or film sequence. In short, the language of evidence and of detail usually consists of concrete diction.

By contrast, *abstract diction* refers to words that designate concepts and categories. "Virility," "ideology," "love," "definitive," "desultory," "conscientious," "classify," and "ameliorate" are examples of abstract diction. So are "democracy," "fascism," "benevolence," and "sentimentality." In academic writing, by and large, this is the language of ideas. We cannot do without abstract terms, and yet writing made up only of such words loses contact with experience, with the world that we can apprehend through our senses.

The line between abstract and concrete is not always as clear as these examples may suggest. You may recall the concept of the ladder of abstraction that we discuss in the section entitled "Generalizing" in the first chapter. There we propose that abstract and concrete are not hard-and-fast categories so much as a continuum, a sliding scale. Word A (for example, "machine") may be more abstract than word B ("computer") but more concrete than word C ("technology").

Just as evidence needs to be organized by a thesis and a thesis needs to be developed by evidence, so *concrete and abstract diction need each other.* Use concrete diction to illustrate and anchor the generalizations that abstract diction expresses. Note the concrete language used to define the abstraction "provinciality" in this example.

> There is no cure for *provinciality* like traveling abroad. In America the waiter who fails to bring the check promptly at the end of the meal we rightly convict for not being watchful. But in England, after waiting interminably for the check and becoming increasingly irate, we learn that only an ill-mannered waiter would bring it without being asked. We have been rude, not he.

In the following example, the abstract terms "causality," "fiction," and "conjunction" are integrated with concrete diction in the second sentence.

> According to the philosopher David Hume, *causality* is a kind of *fiction* that we ascribe to what he called "the constant *conjunction* of observed events." If a person gets hit in the eye and a black semicircle develops underneath it, that does not necessarily mean the blow caused the black eye.

A style that omits concrete language can leave readers lost in a fog of abstraction that only tangible details can illuminate. The concrete language helps readers see what you mean, much in the way that examples help them understand your ideas. Without the shaping power of abstract diction, however, concrete evocation can leave you with a list of graphic but ultimately pointless facts. The best academic writing integrates concrete and abstract diction.

❦ Try this: Compose a paragraph using only concrete diction and then one using only abstract diction. Compare results with another person who has done the same task, as this can lead to an interesting discussion of kinds of words, where they reside on the ladder of abstraction, and why. ☐

❦ Try this: Rewrite the sentences listed below, substituting more concrete language and/or more precise abstractions. Support any abstractions you retain with appropriate detail. Just for the challenge, try to rewrite so that your sentences include no abstract claims; that is, use only concrete details to convey the points.

> It was a great party; everybody had fun.
> It was a lousy party; everybody disliked it.
> The book was really boring.
> The film was very interesting.
> Marxism is stupid.
> Asking that question to subjects is a waste of time.
> He became extraordinarily angry. ☐

Latinate Diction

One of the best ways to sensitize yourself to the difference between abstract and concrete diction is to understand that many abstract words are examples of what is known as Latinate diction. This term describes words in English that derive from Latin roots, words with such endings as "–tion," "–ive," "–ity," "–ate," and "–ent." (Such words will be designated by an *L* in the etymological section of dictionary definitions.) Taken to an extreme, Latinate diction can leave your meaning vague and your readers confused. Note how impenetrable the Latinate terms make the following example:

> The examination of different perspectives on the representations of sociopolitical anarchy in media coverage of revolutions can be revelatory of the invisible biases that afflict television news.

This sentence actually makes sense, but the demands it makes upon readers will surely drive off most of them before they have gotten through it. Reducing the amount of Latinate diction can make it more readable.

> Because we tend to believe what we see, the political biases that afflict television news coverage of revolutions are largely invisible. We can begin to see these biases when we focus on how the medium reports events, studying the kinds of footage used, for example, or finding facts from other sources that the news has left out.

Although the preceding revision retains a lot of Latinate words, it provides a ballast of concrete, sensory details that allows readers to follow the idea. Although many textbooks on writing argue against using Latinate terms where shorter, concrete terms (usually of Anglo-Saxon origin) might be used instead, such an argument seems needlessly limiting in comparison with the advantages offered by a thorough mixture of the two levels of diction. It's fine to use Latinate diction; just don't make it the sole staple of your verbal diet.

Try this: Select a paragraph or two from one of your papers and identify the Latin and Anglo-Saxon diction. Actually mark the draft—with an *L* or an *A,* with a circle around one kind of word and a square around the other. Then find as many Anglo-Saxon substitutes for Latinate terms and as many Latinate substitutes for Anglo-Saxon terms as you can (with the help of a dictionary and perhaps a thesaurus). Ideally, you might then do a final revision in which you synthesize the best from both paragraphs to arrive at a consummate revision of your original paragraph. □

Using and Avoiding Jargon

Many people assume that all jargon—the specialized vocabulary of a particular group—is bad: pretentious language designed to make most readers feel inferior. Many writing textbooks attack jargon in similar terms, calling it either polysyllabic balderdash or a specialized, gatekeeping language designed by an in-group to keep others out.

Yet, in many academic contexts, jargon is downright essential. It is a conceptual shorthand, a technical vocabulary that allows the members of a group (or a discipline) to converse with one another more clearly and efficiently. Certain words that may seem odd to outsiders in fact function as connective tissue for a way of thought shared by insiders. The following sentence, for example, although full of botanical jargon, is also admirably cogent:

> In angiosperm reproduction, if the number of pollen grains deposited on the stigma exceeds the number of ovules in the ovary, then pollen tubes may compete for access to ovules, which results in fertilization by the fastest growing pollen tubes.

We would label this use of jargon acceptable, because it is written, clearly, by insiders *for* fellow insiders. It might not be acceptable language for an article intended for readers who are not botanists, or at least not scientists.

The problem with jargon comes when this insiders' language is ostensibly directed at outsiders as well. The language of contracts offers a prime example of such jargon at work.

> The Author hereby indemnifies and agrees to hold the Publisher, its licensees, and any seller of the Work harmless from any liability, damage, cost, and expense, including reasonable attorney's fees and costs of settlement, for or in connection

with any claim, action, or proceeding inconsistent with the Author's warranties or representations herein, or based upon or arising out of any contribution of the Author to the Work.

Run for the lawyer! What does it mean to "hold the Publisher . . . harmless"? To what do "the Author's warranties or representations" refer? What exactly is the author being asked to do here—release the publisher from all possible lawsuits that the author might bring? We might label this use of jargon *obfuscating;* although it may aim at precision, it leaves most readers bewildered. Although average readers are asked to sign them, such documents are really written by lawyers for other lawyers.

As the botanical and legal examples suggest, the line between *acceptable* and *obfuscating* jargon has far more to do with the audience to whom the words are addressed than with the actual content of the language. Because most academic writing is addressed to insiders, students studying a particular area need to learn its jargon. Using the technical language of the discipline is a necessary skill for conversing with others in that discipline. Moreover, by demonstrating that you can "talk the talk," you will validate your authority to pronounce an opinion on matters in the discipline.

Here are two guidelines that can help you in your use of jargon: (1) when addressing *insiders,* use jargon accurately ("talk the talk"), and (2) when addressing *outsiders—* the general public or members of another discipline—either define the jargon carefully or replace it with a more generally known term, preferably one operating at the same level of formality (which is to say that you would not substitute "gut" for "abdominal cavity").

As the anecdote in the accompanying "Voices from Across the Curriculum" box illustrates, questions of jargon—which are also questions of tone—are best resolved by considering the particular contexts for given writing tasks.

Voices from Across the Curriculum

When to Use and Not Use Jargon

I worked for the Feds for many years before seeking the doctorate. My job required immense amounts of writing: reports, directives, correspondence, and so forth. But, on a day-to-day basis for almost seven years I had to write short "write-ups" assessing the qualifications of young people for the Peace Corps and VISTA programs. I'd generate "list-like," "bullet-like" assessments: "Looks good with farm machinery, has wonderful volunteer experience, would be best in a rural setting, speaks French." But I had to conclude each of these assessments with a one-page narrative. Here I tended to reject officious governmentese for a more personal style. I'd write as I spoke. Rather than "Has an inclination for a direction in the facilitation of regulation," I'd write "Would be very good directing people on projects." I'd drop the "-tion" stuff and write in "speak form," not incomplete sentences, but in what I call "candid, personal" style. I carry this with me today.

—Frederick Norling, Professor of Business

The Politics of Language

We cannot leave the domain of style without reflecting on its place in what we label in Chapter 1 the culture of inattention and cliché that surrounds us. To make this move is to acknowledge that style has political and ethical implications. A little over a half-century ago, in his famous essay "Politics and the English Language," George Orwell warns of the "invasion of one's mind by ready-made phrases . . . [which] can only be prevented if one is constantly on guard against them." The worst modern writing, he declares, "consists in gumming together long strips of words which have already been set in order by someone else, making the results presentable by sheer humbug."

Insofar as style is an expression of the writer's self, Orwell implies, (1) we are under attack from broad cultural clichés and sentimental nostrums that do our thinking for us, and (2) it is thus a matter of personal integrity and civic responsibility to ask ourselves a series of questions about the sentences that we write.

> What am I trying to say? What words will express it? What image or idiom will make it clearer? Is this image fresh enough to have an effect? [. . .] Could I put it more shortly? Have I said anything that is avoidably ugly?"

Words matter. They matter in how we name things, in how we phrase meanings—but also in how we are shaped by the words we read and hear in the media. Words don't simply reflect a neutral world that is out there in some objectively hard way that offers self-evident meanings we can universally agree upon. Words don't reflect—they constitute; they call the world into being. They call us into being when we write them.

Earlier in this chapter we noted, for example, that the decision to call a woman "aggressive" as opposed to "assertive" matters. There are examples all around you of language creating rather than merely reflecting reality. Start looking for these on the front page of your newspaper, in political speeches, in advertising, even in everyday conversation. Does it matter, for instance, that there are no equivalents to the words "spinster" or "whore" for men? Does it change things to refer to a bombing mission as a "containment effort" or, by way of contrast, to call an enthusiastic person "a fanatic"?

A recent article in *Foreign Affairs* by Peter van Ham (October 2001) offers one last dispatch from the frontier of the culture of inattention and cliché. The article is about the rise of the so-called brand state—about how nations market themselves not only to consumers but to other nations. A brand, defined as "a customer's idea about a product," is a powerful tool to replace what a thing is with what other people, for reasons of their own, would have you think it is. This is the world we inhabit, and style can be its adversary or its accomplice. In the last analysis, that's what's at stake in choosing to care about style.

ASSIGNMENT: STYLE ANALYSIS

Write a paper that analyzes the style of a particular group or profession (for example, sports, advertising, bureaucracy, show business, or music reviewing). Or as an alternative, adopt the voice of a member of this group, and write a parody that critiques or analyzes the language practices of the group. If you choose (or are assigned) the latter, be aware that there is always a risk in parody of belittling in an unduly negative way a style that is not your own.

Obviously, you will first need to assemble and make observations about a number of samples of the style that you are analyzing or parodying. Use The Method to help you uncover the kinds of words that get repeated, the most common strands, and so forth. Look at the level of formality, the tone, the use of concrete and abstract diction, and the predilection for Latinate as opposed to Anglo-Saxon words. Who's writing to whom about what, and so what that the writing adopts this style?

Also, see the assignments at the end of Chapter 13.

13

Style: Shaping Sentences
(and Cutting the Fat)

When you write, you build. Writing, after all, is also known as composition—from the Latin *compositio,* meaning "made up of parts." We speak of *constructing* sentences and paragraphs and essays. The fundamental unit of composition is the sentence. *Every sentence has a shape, and learning to see that shape is essential to editing for style.* Once you can recognize the shape of a sentence, you can recast it to make it more graceful or logical or emphatic.

When you revise your sentences for style, your goal is not to prettify your language but rather to reveal the organization of your thought, clarifying your meaning and delivering it more accessibly to your readers. Because meanings are rarely simple themselves, clarifying often does not involve simplifying. Meanings usually involve complex relationships, placing two or more items in balance or elevating one over the others. These relationships can be built into the structure of your sentences. A series of short sentences that breaks up items that belong together will make your prose less readable than a long sentence that overtly makes the connections for your readers. Note the choppiness of the following passage:

> Interactive computer games teach children skills. The games introduce kids to computers. The games enact power fantasies of destroying enemies. These power fantasies are potentially disturbing.

Compare that to the following revision:

> Although interactive computer games teach children certain skills, they also encourage certain potentially disturbing power fantasies.

Because this version connects the items with tighter logic, it generates more forward momentum and is easier to comprehend than the first version, even though the sentence structure is more complex.

If you can approach stylistic editing in this technical, syntactic way, determining how to revise your sentences will become less vague and undirected. If something sounds awkward, but you don't know why, or if you want to make a passage more forceful, but you don't know how, there are fairly standard ways of assessing and altering the shapes of your sentences to make them communicate more effectively.

A. HOW TO RECOGNIZE THE FOUR BASIC SENTENCE SHAPES

Style, defined in Chapter 12, has to do with choices—the choices a writer makes about how to express something. But these decisions can be realized only if you can recognize and use the basic building blocks of composition. Although many of these building blocks are named in the rest of the chapter, you may encounter some terms you're not sure about. If that happens, consult the Glossary of Grammatical Terms located at the end of the next chapter. (In particular, see entries for the following terms: clause, conjunction, conjunctive adverb, coordination, direct object, phrase, preposition, subject, subordination, and verbals.)

Every sentence is built upon the skeleton of its independent clause(s), the subject and verb combination that can stand alone. Consider the following four sentences:

Consumers shop.

Consumers shop; producers manufacture.

Consumers shop in predictable ways, so producers manufacture with different target groups in mind.

Consumers shop in ways that can be predicted by such determinants as income level, gender, and age; consequently, producers use market research to identify different target groups for their products.

Certainly these four sentences become progressively longer, and the information they contain becomes increasingly detailed, but they also differ in their structure—specifically, in the number of independent and dependent clauses they contain. Given that the sentence is the fundamental unit of composition, you will benefit immensely, both in composing and in revising your sentences, if you can identify and construct the four basic sentence types.

The Simple Sentence

The *simple sentence* consists of a single independent clause. At its simplest, it contains a single subject and verb.

Consumers shop.

Other words and phrases can be added to this sentence, but it will remain simple so long as "Consumers shop" is the only clause.

Most consumers shop unwisely.

Even if the sentence contains more than one grammatical subject or more than one verb, it remains simple in structure.

> Most consumers *shop* unwisely and *spend* more than they can afford. [two verbs]

> Both female consumers and their husbands shop unwisely. [two subjects]

The sentence structure in the example that uses two verbs ("shop" and "spend") is known as a *compound predicate*. The sentence structure in the example that uses two subjects ("consumers" and "husbands") is known as a *compound subject*. If, however, you were to add both another subject and another verb to the original simple sentence, then you would have the next sentence type, a compound sentence.

The Compound Sentence

The *compound sentence* consists of at least two independent clauses and no subordinate clauses. The information conveyed in these clauses should be of roughly equal importance.

> Producers manufacture, and consumers shop.

> Producers manufacture, marketers sell, and consumers shop.

As with the simple sentence, you can also add qualifying phrases to the compound sentence, and it will remain compound, as long as no dependent clauses are added.

> Consumers shop in predictable ways, so producers manufacture with different target groups in mind.

> Consumers shop recklessly during holidays; marketers are keenly aware of this fact.

Note that a compound sentence can connect its independent clauses with either a coordinate conjunction or a semicolon. (The primary use of the semicolon is as a substitute for a coordinate conjunction, separating two independent clauses.) If you were to substitute a subordinating conjunction for either of these connectors, however, you would then have a sentence with one independent clause and one dependent clause. For example:

> *Because* consumers shop in predictable ways, producers manufacture with different target groups in mind.

This revision changes the compound sentence into the next sentence type, the complex sentence.

The Complex Sentence

The *complex sentence* consists of a single independent clause and one or more dependent clauses. The information conveyed in the dependent clause is subordinated to the more important independent clause (a matter we take up in more detail momentarily under subordination). In the following example, the subject and verb of the main clause are underlined, and the subordinating conjunctions are italicized:

> *Although* mail-order merchandising—*which* generally saves shoppers money—has increased, most <u>consumers</u> still <u>shop</u> unwisely, buying on impulse rather than deliberation.

This sentence contains one independent clause ("consumers shop"). Hanging upon it are two introductory dependent clauses ("although merchandising has increased" and "which saves") and a participial phrase ("buying on impulse"). If you converted either of these dependent clauses into an independent clause, you would have a sentence with two independent clauses (a compound sentence) and a dependent clause. In the following example, the subjects and verbs of the two main clauses are underlined, and the conjunctions are italicized:

> Mail-order <u>merchandising</u>—*which* generally saves shoppers money—<u>has increased</u>, *but* <u>consumers</u> still <u>shop</u> unwisely, buying on impulse rather than deliberation.

This revision changes the complex sentence into the next sentence type, the compound-complex sentence.

The Compound–Complex Sentence

The *compound–complex sentence* consists of two or more independent clauses and one or more dependent clauses.

> Consumers shop in ways that can be predicted by such determinants as income level, gender, and age; consequently, producers use market research that aims to identify different target groups for their products.

This sentence contains two independent clauses ("consumers shop" and "producers use") and two dependent ones ("that can be predicted" and "that aims").

❦*Try this:* As we have done with the consumers-shop example, compose a simple sentence and then a variety of expansions: a compound subject, a compound predicate, a compound sentence, a complex sentence, and a compound–complex sentence. To prevent this exercise from becoming merely mechanical, keep in mind how different sentence shapes accomplish different ends. In other words, make sure that your compound sentence balances two items of information, that your complex sentence emphasizes one thing (in the main clause) over another (in the subordinate clause), and that your compound–complex sentence is required to handle and organize complexity. ☐

B. COORDINATION, SUBORDINATION, AND EMPHASIS

A *clause* is a group of words containing a subject and a predicate. The syntax of a sentence can give your readers cues about whether the idea in one clause is equal to (coordinate) or subordinate to the idea in another clause. In this context, grammar operates as a form of implicit logic, defining relationships among the clauses in a sentence according to the choices that you make about coordination, subordination, and the order of clauses. In revising your sentences, think of coordination and subordination as tools of logic and emphasis, helping to rank your meanings.

Coordination

Coordination uses grammatically equivalent constructions to link ideas. These ideas should carry roughly equal weight as well. Sentences that use coordination connect clauses with coordinating conjunctions (such as "and," "but," and "or"). Here are two examples.

> Historians organize the past, *and* they can never do so with absolute neutrality.

> Homegrown corn is incredibly sweet, *and* it is very difficult to grow.

If you ponder these sentences, you may begin to detect the danger of the word "and." It does not specify a precise logical relationship between the things it connects but instead simply adds them.

Notice that the sentences get more precise if we substitute "but" for "and."

> Historians organize the past, *but* they can never do so with absolute neutrality.

> Homegrown corn is incredibly sweet, *but* it is very difficult to grow.

These sentences are still coordinate in structure; they are still the sentence type known as compound. But they achieve more emphasis than the "and" versions. In both cases, the "but" clause carries more weight, because "but" always introduces information that qualifies or contradicts what precedes it.

Reversing the Order of Coordinate Clauses

In both the "and" and "but" examples, the second clause tends to be stressed. The reason is simple: *the end is usually a position of emphasis.*

You can see the effect of *clause order* more starkly if we reverse the clauses in our examples.

> Historians are never absolutely neutral, but they organize the past.

> Homegrown corn is very difficult to grow, but it is incredibly sweet.

Note how the meanings have changed in these versions by our emphasizing what now comes last. Rather than simply having their objectivity undermined ("Historians are never absolutely neutral"), historians are now credited with at least providing organization ("they organize the past"). Similarly, whereas the previous version of the sentence about corn was likely to dissuade a gardener from trying to grow it ("it is very difficult to grow"), the new sentence is more likely to lure him or her to nurture corn ("it is incredibly sweet").

Nonetheless, all of these sentences are examples of coordination because the clauses are grammatically equal. As you revise, notice when you use coordinate syntax, and think about whether you really intend to give the ideas equal weight. Consider as well whether reversing the order of clauses will more accurately convey your desired emphasis to your readers.

Try this: Rearrange the parts of the following coordinate sentence, which is composed of four sections, separated by commas. Construct at least three versions, and jot down how the meaning changes in each version.

> I asked her to marry me, two years ago, in a shop on Tremont Street, late in the fall.

Then subject two sentences from one of your own papers to the same treatment. □

Subordination

In sentences that contain *subordination,* there are two "levels" of grammar—the main clause and the subordinate clause—that create two levels of meaning. When you put something in a main clause, you emphasize its significance. When you put something in a subordinate clause, you make it less important than what is in the main clause.

As noted in the discussion of complex sentences, a subordinate clause is linked to a main clause by words known as *subordinating conjunctions.* Here is a list of the most common ones: after, although, as, as if, as long as, because, before, if, rather than, since, than, that, though, unless, until, when, where, whether, and while. All of these words define something *in relation to* something else:

> *If* you study hard, you will continue to do well.

> You will continue to do well, *if* you study hard.

In both of these examples, *if* subordinates "you study hard" to "you will continue to do well," regardless of whether the *if* clause comes first or last in the sentence.

Reversing Main and Subordinate Clauses

Unlike the situation with coordinate clauses, the emphasis in sentences that use subordination virtually always rests on the main clause, regardless of the clause order. Nevertheless, the principle of end-position emphasis still applies, though to a lesser extent than among coordinate clauses. Let's compare two versions of the same sentence.

> Although the art of the people was crude, it was original.

> The art of the people was original, although it was crude.

Both sentences emphasize the idea in the main clause ("original"). Because the second version locates the "although" clause at the end, however, the subordinated idea ("crude") has more emphasis than it does in the first version.

You can experiment with the meaning and style of virtually any sentence you write by reversing the clauses. Here, taken almost at random, is an earlier sentence from this chapter, followed by two such transformations.

When you put something in a subordinate clause, you make it less important than what is in the main clause.

Put information in a subordinate clause if you want to make it less important than what is in the main clause.

If you want to make information less important than what is in the main clause, put it in a subordinate clause.

❦*Try this:* Do two rewrites of the following sentence, changing the order of clauses and subordinating or coordinating as you wish. We recommend that you make one of them end with the word "friendly."

Faculty members came to speak at the forum, and they were friendly, but they were met with hostility, and this hostility was almost paranoid.

How does each of your revisions change the meaning and emphasis? ☐

Parallel Structure

One of the most important and useful devices for shaping sentences is *parallel structure* or, as it is also known, *parallelism.* Parallelism is a form of symmetry: it involves placing sentence elements that correspond in some way into the same (that is, parallel) grammatical form. Consider the following examples, in which the parallel items are underlined or italicized:

The three kinds of partners in a law firm who receive money from a case are popularly known as <u>finders</u>, <u>binders</u>, and <u>grinders</u>.

The Beatles acknowledged their musical debts <u>to</u> American rhythm and blues, <u>to</u> English music hall ballads and ditties, and later <u>to</u> classical Indian ragas.

There was <u>no way that</u> the president <u>could gain</u> the support of party regulars *without alienating* the Congress, and <u>no way that</u> he <u>could appeal</u> to the electorate at large *without alienating* both of these groups.

In the entertainment industry, the money that <u>goes out</u> to hire *film stars* or *sports stars* <u>comes back</u> in increased ticket sales and video or television rights.

As all of these examples illustrate, at the core of parallelism lies repetition—of a word, a phrase, or a grammatical structure. *Parallelism uses repetition to organize and emphasize certain elements in a sentence, so that readers can perceive more clearly the shape of your thought.* In the Beatles example, each of the prepositional phrases beginning with "to" contains a musical debt; in the president example, the repetition of the phrase "no way that" emphasizes his entrapment.

Parallelism has the added advantage of *economy*: each of the musical debts or presidential problems might have had its own sentence, but in that case the prose would have been wordier and the relationships among the parallel items more obscure. Along with this economy come *balance* and *emphasis.* The trio of rhyming words ("finders," "binders," and "grinders") that concludes the law-firm example gives each item equal weight; in the entertainment-industry example, "comes back" answers "goes out" in a way that accentuates their symmetry.

❦*Try this:* List all of the parallelisms in the following famous passage from the beginning of the Declaration of Independence:

> We hold these truths to be self-evident: that all men are created equal; that they are endowed by their Creator with certain inalienable rights; that, among these, are life, liberty, and the pursuit of happiness.

What do you notice about the way that the parallel structures accumulate? ☐

One particularly useful form of balance that parallel structure accommodates is known as *antithesis* (from the Greek word for *opposition*), a conjoining of contrasting ideas. Here the pattern sets one thing against another thing, as in the following example:

> Where <u>bravura failed</u> to settle the negotiations, <u>tact and patience succeeded</u>.

"Failed" is balanced antithetically against "succeeded," as "bravura" against "tact and patience." Antithesis commonly takes the form of "if not X, at least Y" or "not X, but Y."

When you employ parallelism in revising for style, there is one grammatical rule you should obey. It is important to avoid what is known as *faulty parallelism,* which occurs when the items that are parallel in content are not placed in the same grammatical form.

> **Faulty:** *To study* hard for four years and then *getting* ignored once they enter the job market is a hard thing for many recent college graduates to accept.

> **Revised:** *To study* hard for four years and then *to get* ignored once they enter the job market is a hard thing for many recent college graduates to accept.

As you revise your draft for style, search for opportunities to place sentence elements in parallel structure. Try this consciously: include and underline three uses of it in a draft of your next writing assignment. Remember that parallelism can occur with *clauses, phrases,* and *prepositional phrases.* Often the parallels will be hidden in the sentences of your draft, but they can be brought out with a minimum of labor. After you've acquired the habit of casting your thinking in parallel structures, they will rapidly become a staple of your stylistic repertoire, making your prose more graceful, clear, and logically connected.

❦*Try this:* Rewrite the following examples of faulty parallelism using correct parallel structure. In the last of these sentences you will need to contemplate the thinking behind it as well as its form.

1. Our personalities are shaped by both heredity and what type of environment we have been exposed to.
2. Venus likes to play tennis and also watching baseball games.

3. In the 1960s the use of drugs and being a hippie was a way for some people to let society know their political views and that they were alienated from the mainstream. □

C. ADDING SHAPES TO THE MAIN CLAUSE: PERIODIC AND CUMULATIVE SENTENCES

The shape of a sentence governs the way it delivers information. The order of clauses, especially the placement of the main clause, affects what and how the sentence means. There are two common sentence shapes defined by the location of their main clauses; these are known as *periodic* and *cumulative* sentences.

The Periodic Sentence: Snapping Shut

The main clause in a periodic sentence builds to a climax that is not completed until the end. Often, a piece of the main clause (such as the subject) is located early in the sentence, as in the following example.

> The *way* that beverage companies market health—"No Preservatives," "No Artificial Color," "All Natural," "Real Brewed"—*is* often, because the product also contains a high percentage of sugar or fructose, *misleading.*

We have italicized the main clause to clarify how various modifiers interrupt it. The effect is suspenseful: not until the final word does the sentence consummate its fundamental idea. Pieces of the main clause are spread out across the sentence. (The term *periodic* originates in classical rhetoric to refer to the length of such units within a sentence.)

Another version of the periodic sentence locates the entire main clause at the end, after introductory modifiers.

> Using labels that market health—such as "No Preservatives," "No Artificial Color," "All Natural," and "Real Brewed"—while producing drinks that contain a high percentage of sugar or fructose, *beverage companies are misleading.*

As was previously discussed, the end of a sentence normally receives emphasis. When you use a periodic construction, the pressure on the end intensifies because the sentence needs the end to complete its grammatical sense. In both of the preceding examples, the sentences "snap shut." They string readers along, delaying *grammatical closure*—the point at which the sentences can stand alone independently—until they arrive at climactic ends. (Periodic sentences are also known as *climactic sentences.*)

You should be aware of one risk that accompanies periodic constructions. If the delay lasts too long because there are too many "interrupters" before the main clause gets completed, your readers may forget the subject that is being predicated. To illustrate, let's add more subordinated material to one of the preceding examples.

> The way that beverage companies market health—"No Preservatives," "No Artificial Color," "All Natural," "Real Brewed"—is often, because the product also contains a high percentage of sugar or fructose, not just what New Agers would probably term

"immoral" and "misleading" but what a government agency such as the Food and Drug Administration should find illegal.

Arguably, the additions (the "not just" and "but" clauses after "fructose") push the sentence into incoherence. The main clause has been stretched past the breaking point. If readers don't get lost in such a sentence, they are at least likely to get irritated and wish the writer would finally get to the point.

Nonetheless, with a little care, periodic sentences can be extraordinarily useful in giving emphasis. *If you are revising and want to underscore some point, try letting the sentence snap shut upon it.* Often the periodic *potential* will already be present in the draft, and stylistic editing can bring it out more forcefully. Note how minor the revisions are in the following example:

Draft: The novelist Virginia Woolf suffered from acute anxieties for most of her life. She had several breakdowns and finally committed suicide on the eve of World War II.

Revision: Suffering from acute anxieties for most of her life, the novelist Virginia *Woolf* not only *had* several *breakdowns but,* finally, on the eve of World War II, *committed suicide.*

This revision has made two primary changes. It has combined two short sentences into a longer sentence, and it has made the sentence periodic by stringing out the main clause (italicized). What is the effect of this revision? Stylistically speaking, the revision radiates a greater sense of its writer's authority. The information has been arranged for us. Following the opening dependent clause ("Suffering . . ."), the subject of the main clause ("Woolf") is introduced, and the predicate is protracted in a *not only/but* parallelism. The interrupters that follow "had several breakdowns" ("finally, on the eve of World War II") increase the suspense, before the sentence snaps shut with "committed suicide." In general, when you construct a periodic sentence with care, you can give readers the sense that you are in control of your material. You do not seem to be writing off the top of your head but rather, from a position of greater detachment, rationally composing your meaning.

The Cumulative Sentence: Starting Fast

The cumulative sentence is in many respects the opposite of the periodic. Rather than delaying the main clause or its final piece, the cumulative sentence begins by presenting the independent clause as a foundation and then *accumulates* a number of modifications and qualifications. As the following examples illustrate, the independent clause provides quick grammatical closure, freeing the rest of the sentence to amplify and develop the main idea.

Robert F. Kennedy was assassinated by Sirhan B. Sirhan, a twenty-four-year-old Palestinian immigrant, prone to occultism and unsophisticated left-wing politics and sociopathically devoted to leaving his mark in history, even if as a notorious figure.

There are two piano concerti composed solely for the left hand, one by Serge Prokofiev and one by Maurice Ravel, and both commissioned by Paul Wittgenstein, a concert pianist (and the brother of the famous philosopher Ludwig Wittgenstein) who had lost his right hand in combat during World War I.

Anchored by the main clause, a cumulative sentence moves serially through one thing and another thing and the next thing, close to the associative manner in which people think. To an extent, then, cumulative sentences can convey more immediacy and a more conversational tone than can other sentence shapes. Look at the following example:

> The film version of *Lady Chatterley's Lover* changed D. H. Lawrence's famous novel a lot, omitting the heroine's adolescent experience in Germany, making her husband much older than she, leaving out her father and sister, including a lot more love-making, and virtually eliminating all of the philosophizing about sex and marriage.

Here we get the impression of a mind in the act of thinking. Using the generalization of changes in the film as a base, the sentence then appends a series of parallel participial phrases ("omitting," "making," "leaving," "including," "eliminating") that moves forward associatively, gathering a range of information and laying out possibilities. Cumulative sentences perform this outlining and prospecting function very effectively. On the other hand, if we were to add four or five more changes to the sentence, readers would likely find it tedious, or worse, directionless. As with periodic sentences, overloading the shape can short-circuit its desired effect.

If you consciously practice using periodic and cumulative constructions, you will quickly learn to produce their respective effects (where appropriate) in your own writing. As you go over your drafts, look for opportunities to bring out these shapes, for you can assume that they are already present in some unrefined way in the sentence shapes you normally compose. Try including at least one of each in the next paper you write. Here is an example using the simple sentence "James Joyce was a gifted singer."

> **Periodic:** Although known primarily as one of the greatest novelists of the twentieth century, James Joyce, the son of a local political functionary who loved to tip a few too many at the pub, was also a gifted—and prize-winning—singer.

> **Cumulative:** James Joyce was a gifted singer, having listened at his father's knee to the ballads sung in the pubs, having won an all-Ireland prize in his early teens, and having possessed a miraculous ear for the inflections of common speech that was to serve him throughout the career for which he is justly famous, that of a novelist.

❧ *Try this:* Compose a simple sentence on any subject, preferably one with a direct object. Then construct two variations expanding it, one periodic and one cumulative. □

D. CUTTING THE FAT

If you can reduce verbiage, your prose will communicate more directly and effectively. In cutting the fat, you need to consider both the diction and the syntax. As regards diction, the way to eliminate superfluous words is deceptively simple: ask yourself if you need all of the words you've included in order to say what you want to say. Such revision requires an aggressive attitude. *Expect* to find unnecessary restatements or intensifiers such as "quite" and "very" that add words but not significance.

As regards syntax, there are a few technical operations that you can perform—particularly on the *verbs* in your sentences—to reduce the number of words. The remainder of the chapter discusses these matters in more depth, but here's a preview.

- Convert sentences from the passive into the active voice. Writing "He read the book" reduces by a third "The book was read by him," and eliminating the prepositional phrase ("by him") clarifies the relationships within the sentence.
- Replace anemic forms of the verb "to be" with vigorous verbs and direct subject-verb-object syntax. Often you will find such verbs lurking in the original sentence, and once you've recognized them, conversion is easy: "The Watergate *scandal* was an event whose effects were felt across the nation" becomes "Watergate *scandalized* people across the nation."
- Avoid unnecessary subordination. It is illogical to write, "*It is true that* more government services mean higher taxes." If "it is true," then just write, "More government services mean higher taxes"—don't muffle your meaning in a subordinate "that" clause.

Beyond these technical operations, perhaps the most useful way to cut the fat is to have confidence in your position on a subject and state it clearly in your paper. A lot of fat in essays consists of "throat clearings," attempts to avoid stating a position. Move quickly to an example that raises the question or issue you wish to analyze.

Expletive Constructions

The syntactic pattern for "It is true *that* more government services mean higher taxes" is known as an *expletive* construction. The term "expletive" comes from a Latin word that means "serving to fill out." The most common expletives are "it" and "there." Consider how the expletives function in the following examples.

> *There* are several prototypes for the artificial heart.

> *It* is obvious that the American West exerted a profound influence on the photography of Ansel Adams.

Compare these with versions that simply eliminate the expletives.

> The artificial heart has several prototypes.

> The American West obviously exerted a profound influence on the photography of Ansel Adams.

As the revisions demonstrate, most of the time you can streamline your prose by getting rid of expletive constructions. The "It is obvious" opening, for example, causes the grammar of the sentence to subordinate its real emphasis. In some cases, however, an expletive can provide a useful way of emphasizing, as in the following example:

"There are three primary reasons that you should avoid litigation." Although this sentence subordinates its real content (avoiding litigation), the expletive provides a useful frame for what is to follow.

Static (Intransitive) Versus Active (Transitive) Verbs: "To Be" or "Not to Be"

Verbs energize a sentence. They do the work, connecting the parts of the sentence with each other. In a sentence of the subject–verb–direct object pattern, the verb—known as a *transitive verb*—functions as a kind of engine, driving the subject into the predicate, as in the following examples.

> John F. Kennedy effectively *manipulated* his image in the media.

> Thomas Jefferson *embraced* the idea of America as a country of yeoman farmers.

By contrast, "is" and other forms of the verb "to be" provide an equal sign between the subject and the predicate but otherwise tell us nothing about the relationship between them. "To be" is an *intransitive* verb; it cannot take a direct object. Compare the two preceding transitive examples with the following versions of the same sentences using forms of the verb "to be."

> John F. Kennedy *was* effective at the manipulation of his image in the media.

> Thomas Jefferson's idea *was* for America to be a country of yeoman farmers.

Rather than making things happen through an active transitive verb, these sentences let everything just hang around in a state of being. In the first version, Kennedy did something—*manipulated* his image—but in the second he just *is* (or *was*), and the energy of the original verb has been siphoned into an abstract noun, "manipulation." The revised Jefferson example suffers from a similar lack of momentum compared with the original version: the syntax doesn't help the sentence get anywhere. Yet, because the forms of "to be" are so easy to use, writers tend to place them everywhere, habitually, producing relatively static and wordy sentences.

Certain situations, however, dictate the use of forms of "to be." For definitions in particular, in which a term does in fact equal some meaning, "is" works well. For instance, "Organic gardening *is* a method of growing crops without using synthetic fertilizers or pesticides." As with choosing between active and passive voices, the decision to use "to be" or not should be just that—a conscious decision on your part.

If you can train yourself to eliminate every unnecessary use of "to be" in a draft, you will make your prose more vital and direct. In most cases, you will find the verb that you need to substitute for "is" lurking somewhere in the sentence in some other grammatical form. In the preceding sentence about Kennedy, "manipulate" is implicit in "manipulation." In Table 13.1, each of the examples in the left-hand column uses a form of "to be" for its verb (italicized) and contains a potentially strong active verb lurking in the sentence in some other form (underlined). These "lurkers" have been converted into active verbs (italicized) in the revisions in the right-hand column.

TABLE 13.1
Static and Active Verbs

Action Hidden in Nouns and "to Be" Verbs	Action Emphasized in Verbs
The cost of the book *is* ten dollars.	The book *costs* ten dollars.
The acknowledgment of the fact *is* increasingly widespread that television *is* a replacement for reading in American culture.	People increasingly *acknowledge* that television *has replaced* reading in American culture.
A computer *is* ostensibly a labor-saving device —until the hard disk *is* the victim of a crash.	A computer ostensibly *saves labor*—until the hard disk *crashes.*
In the laying of a flagstone patio, the important preliminary steps to remember *are* the excavating and the leveling of the area and then the filling of it with a fine grade of gravel.	To *lay* a flagstone patio, first *excavate* and *level* the area and then *fill* it with a fine grade of gravel.

Clearly, the examples in the left-hand column have problems other than their reliance on forms of "to be"—notably wordiness. "To be" syntax tends to encourage this circumlocution and verbosity.

❧*Try this:* Take a paper you've written, and circle the sentences that rely on forms of "to be." Then, examine the other words in these sentences, looking for "lurkers." Rewrite the sentences, converting the lurkers into vigorous verbs. You will probably discover many lurkers, and your revisions will acquire more energy and directness. □

Active and Passive Voices: Doing and Being Done To

In the *active voice,* the grammatical subject acts; in the *passive voice,* the subject is acted upon. Here are two examples.

Active: Adam Smith wrote *The Wealth of Nations* in 1776.

Passive: *The Wealth of Nations* was written by Adam Smith in 1776.

The two sentences convey identical information, but the emphasis differs—the first focuses on the author, the second on the book. As the examples illustrate, using the passive normally results in a longer sentence than using the active. If we consider how to convert the passive into the active, you can see why. In the passive, the verb requires a form of "to be" plus a past participle (for more on participles, see the "Glossary of Grammatical Terms" in Chapter 14). In this case, the active "wrote" becomes the passive "was written," the subject ("Smith") becomes the object of the preposition "by," and the direct object ("*The Wealth of Nations*") becomes the grammatical subject.

Consider the activity being described in the two versions of the preceding example about Adam Smith: a man wrote a book. That was what happened in life. The grammar of the active version captures that action most clearly: the grammatical subject ("Smith") performs the action, and the direct object ("*The Wealth of Nations*") receives it, just as in life. By contrast, the passive version alters the close link between the syntax and the event: the object of the action in life ("*The Wealth of Nations*") has become the grammatical subject, whereas the doer in life ("Smith") has become the grammatical object of a prepositional phrase.

Note, too, that the passive would allow us to omit "Smith" altogether: "*The Wealth of Nations* was written in 1776." A reader who desired to know more and was not aware of the author would not appreciate this sentence. More troubling, the passive can also be used to avoid naming the doer of an action—not "I made a mistake" (active) but rather "A mistake has been made" (passive).

In sum, there are three reasons for avoiding the passive voice when you can: (1) it's longer, (2) its grammatical relationships often reverse what happened in life, and (3) it can omit the performer responsible for the action.

On the other hand, sometimes there are good reasons for using the passive. If you want to emphasize the object or recipient of the action rather than the performer, the passive will do that for you: "*The Wealth of Nations* was written in 1776 by Adam Smith" places the stress on the book. The passive is also preferable when the doer remains unknown: "The president has been shot!" is probably a better sentence than "Some unknown assailant has shot the president!"

Try this: Circle and identify every verb in a passage (use the abbreviations *VA* = active voice, *VP* = passive voice, *VB* = verb of being). The passage might come from a book you are reading or from one of your own drafts. This exercise will give necessary training in identifying the forms of verbs. □

Especially in the natural sciences, the use of the passive voice is a standard practice. There are sound reasons for this disciplinary convention: *science tends to focus on what happens to something in a given experiment, rather than on the actions of that something.* Compare the following sentences.

Passive: Separation of the protein was achieved by using an electrophoretic gel.

Active: The researcher used an electrophoretic gel to separate the protein.

If you opted for the active version, the emphasis would then rest, *illogically,* on the agent of the action (the researcher) rather than on what happened and how (electrophoretic separation of the protein).

More generally, the passive voice can provide a way to avoid using the pronoun "I," whether for reasons of convention, as indicated earlier, or for other reasons. For example, the following passive sentence begins a business memo from a supervisor to the staff in her office.

The Inventory and Reprint departments have recently been restructured and merged.

Like many passive sentences, this one names no actor; we do not know for sure who did the restructuring and merging, though we might imagine that the author of the memo is the responsible party. The supervisor might, then, have written the sentence in the active voice.

I have recently restructured and merged the Inventory and Reprint departments.

But the active version is less satisfactory than the passive one for two reasons: one of practical emphasis and one of sensitivity to the audience (tone). First, the fact of the changes is more important for the memo's readers than is the announcement of who made the changes. The passive sentence appropriately emphasizes the changes; the active sentence inappropriately emphasizes the person who made the changes. Second, the emphasis of the active sentence on "I" (the supervisor) risks alienating the readers by taking an autocratic tone and by seeming to exclude all others from possible credit for the presumably worthwhile reorganization.

On balance, "consider" is the operative term when you choose between passive and active as you revise the syntax of your drafts. What matters is that you recognize there is a choice—in emphasis, in relative directness, and in economy. All things being equal and disciplinary conventions permitting, the active is usually the better choice.

❦ *Try this:* Identify all of the sentences that use the passive voice in one of your papers. Then, rewrite these sentences, converting passive into active wherever appropriate. Then, count the total number of words, the total number of prepositions, and the average sentence length (words per sentence) in each version. What do you discover? □

❦ *Try this:* Compose a paragraph of at least half a page in which you use only the passive voice and verbs of being, followed by a paragraph in which you use only the active voice. Then, rewrite the first paragraph using only active voice, if possible; and rewrite the second paragraph using only passive voice and verbs of being, as much as possible. How do the paragraphs differ in shape and coherence? □

Experiment!

A key idea of this chapter is that there are not necessarily right and wrong choices when it comes to sentence style but instead better and best choices for particular situations. The from-the-hip plain style of a memo or a set of operating instructions for your lawn mower is very likely not the best style choice for a good-bye letter to a best friend, a diplomatic talk on a sensitive political situation, or an analysis of guitar styles in contemporary jazz. Is style a function of character and personality? Is it, in short, personal—and thus something to be preserved in the face of would-be meddlers carrying style manuals and grammar guides? Well, as you might guess at this point in the book, the answer is "yes" and "no." We all need to find ways of using words that do not succumb to the mind-numbing environment of verbal cliché in which we dwell. But effective style is not inborn and is not hurt by experimentation. Staying locked into one way of writing because that is "your style" is as limiting as remaining locked into only one way of thinking.

This chapter has presented some terms and techniques for experimenting with sentence styles. Equipped with these, what you need to do is read and listen for style. Find models. When a style appeals to you, figure out what makes it work. Copy sentences you like. Try imitating them, knowing, by the way, that imitation will not erase your own style: it will allow you to experiment with new moves, new shapes into which to cast your words.

Voices from Across the Curriculum

Reading Attentively to Improve One's Style

Aside from the usual basic writing errors, the stylistic problems I most frequently encounter in students' papers are odd word selection and awkward sentence structure. I think both problems find their genesis in the same broader problem. You learn how to make telling use of the vocabulary you've been forced to memorize only by reading. You fashion an appealing sentence based on what you've read others doing.

—James Marshall. Professor of Economics

ASSIGNMENTS: STYLISTIC ANALYSIS

1. Analyze the style—the syntax but also the diction—of two writers doing a similar kind of writing, for example, two sportswriters, two rock music reviewers, or two presidents. Study first the similarities. What style characteristics does this type of writing seem to invite? Then study the differences. How is one writer (Bush, Clinton, or Reagan, for example) recognizable through his or her style?

2. Analyze your own style, past and present. Assemble some pieces you have written, preferably of a similar type, and study them for style. Do you have some favorite stylistic moves? What sentence shapes (simple, compound, complex, compound–complex, highly parallel, periodic, or cumulative) dominate in your writing? What verbs? Do you use forms of "to be" a lot, and so forth?

3. For many people, Lincoln's Gettysburg Address is one of the best available examples of the careful matching of style to situation. Delivered after a long talk by a previous speaker at the dedication of a Civil War battlefield on a rainy day, the speech composed by Abraham Lincoln (some say on the back of an envelope) is a masterpiece of style. Analyze its sentence structure, for example, its use of parallelism, antithesis, and other kinds of repetition. Which features of Lincoln's style seem to you to be most important in creating the overall effect of the piece? (Or do this with any popular journalist whom you read regularly and who you think has an especially effective style. Or look for another inspirational speech and see if such occasional writing has anything in common.)

4. Do a full-fledged stylistic revision of a paper. The best choice might well be an essay you already have revised, resubmitted, and had returned, because in that case, you will be less likely to get distracted by conceptual revision and so can concentrate on stylistic issues. As you revise, try to accomplish each of the following:
   a. Sharpen the diction.
   b. Blend concrete and abstract diction.
   c. Experiment with the order of and relation among subordinate and coordinate clauses.

d. Choose more knowingly between active and passive voice.
e. Cut the fat, especially by eliminating unnecessary "to be" constructions.
f. Vary sentence length and shape.
g. Use parallelism.
h. Experiment with periodic and cumulative sentences.
i. Fine-tune the tone.

CHAPTER

14

Nine Basic Writing Errors and How to Fix Them

A. WHY CORRECTNESS MATTERS

This chapter addresses the issue of grammatical correctness and offers ways of recognizing and fixing (or avoiding) the most important errors. The first guideline in editing for correctness is to *wait* to do it until you have arrived at a reasonably complete conceptual draft. We have delayed until the end of the book our consideration of technical revisions precisely because if you get too focused on producing polished copy right up front, you may never explore the subject enough to learn how to have ideas about it. In other words, it doesn't make sense for you to let your worries about proper form or persuasive phrasing prematurely distract you from the more important matter of having something substantial to polish in the first place. Writers need a stage in which they are allowed to make mistakes and use writing to help them discover what they want to say. But at the appropriate time—the later stages of the writing process—editing for correctness becomes very important.

When a paper obeys the rules of grammar, punctuation, and spelling, it has achieved *correctness.* Unlike editing for style, which involves you in making choices between more and less effective ways of phrasing, editing for correctness locates you in the domain of right or wrong. As you will see, there are usually a number of ways to correct an error, so you are still concerned with making choices, but leaving the error uncorrected is not really a viable option.

Correctness matters deeply because your prose may be unreadable without it. If your prose is ungrammatical, not only will you risk incoherence (in which case your readers will not be able to follow what you are saying) but also you will inadvertently invite readers to dismiss you. Is it fair of readers to reject your ideas because of the way you've phrased them? Perhaps not, but the fact is they often will. A great many readers regard technical errors as an inattention to detail that also signals sloppiness at more important levels of thinking. If you produce writing that contains such errors, you risk not only distracting readers from your message but also *undermining your authority* to deliver the message in the first place.

B.   THE CONCEPT OF BASIC WRITING ERRORS (BWEs)

You get a paper back, and it's a sea of red ink. But if you look more closely, you'll often find that you haven't made a million mistakes—you've made only a few, but over and over in various forms. This phenomenon is what the rhetorician Mina Shaughnessy addressed in creating the category of "basic writing errors," or BWEs. Shaughnessy argues that in order to improve your writing for style and correctness, you need to do two things:

- Look for a *pattern of error,* which will require you to understand your own logic in the mistakes you typically make.
- Recognize that not all errors are created equal, which means that you need to *address errors in some order of importance*—beginning with those most likely to interfere with your readers' understanding.

The following BWE guide, "Nine Basic Writing Errors and How to Fix Them," that we have composed reflects Shaughnessy's view. First, it aims to teach you how to recognize and correct the basic kinds of errors that are potentially the most damaging to the clarity of your writing and to your credibility with readers. Second, the discussions in the guide seek to help you become aware of the patterns of error in your writing and discover the logic that has misled you into making them. If you can learn to see the pattern and then look for it in your editing and proofreading—expecting to find it—you will get in the habit of avoiding the error. In short, you will learn that your problem is not that you can't write correctly but simply that you have to remember, for example, to check for possessive apostrophes.

Our BWE guide does not, as we've mentioned, cover *all* of the rules of grammar, punctuation, diction, and usage, such as where to place the comma or period when you close a quotation or whether or not to write out numerals. For comprehensive coverage of the conventions of standard written English, you can consult one of the many handbooks available for this purpose. Our purpose is to provide a short guide to grammar—one that identifies the most common errors, provides remedies, and offers the logic that underlies them. This chapter's coverage of nine basic writing errors and how to fix them will help you eliminate most of the problems that routinely occur. We have arranged the error types in a hierarchy, moving in descending order of severity (from most to least problematic).

What Punctuation Marks Say: A "Quick-Hit" Guide

These little signs really aren't that hard to use correctly, folks. A few of them will be treated in more specific contexts in the upcoming discussion of BWEs, but here are the basic rules of punctuation for the five basic signs.

The **period** [.] marks the end of a sentence. Make sure that what precedes it is an independent clause, that is, a subject plus verb that can stand alone.

The period says to a reader, "This is the end of this particular statement. I'm a mark of closure."

Example: Lennon rules.

The **comma** [,] separates the main (independent) clause from dependent elements that modify the main clause. It also separates two main clauses joined by a conjunction—known as a compound sentence. Information that is not central to the main clause is set off in a comma sandwich. The comma does not signify a pause.

The comma says to the reader, "Here is where the main clause begins (or ends)," or "Here is a break in the main clause." In the case of compound sentences (containing two or more independent clauses), the comma says, "Here is where one main clause ends, and after the conjunction that follows me, another main clause begins."

Examples: Lennon rules, and McCartney is cute.

Lennon rules, although McCartney is arguably more tuneful.

The **semicolon** [;] separates two independent clauses that are not joined by a conjunction. Secondarily, the semicolon can separate two independent clauses that are joined by a conjunction if either of the clauses already contains commas. In either case, the semicolon both shows a close relationship between the two independent clauses that it connects and distinguishes where one ends and the other begins. It is also the easiest way to fix comma splices (see "BWE 2" on page 265).

The semicolon says to the reader, "What precedes and what follows me are conceptually close but grammatically independent and thus equal statements."

Example: Lennon's lyrics show deep sympathy for the legions of "Nowhere Men" who inhabit the "Strawberry Fields" of their imaginations; McCartney's lyrics, on the other hand, are more upbeat, forever bidding "Good Day, Sunshine" to the world at large and "Michelle" in particular.

The **colon** [:] marks the end of a setup for something coming next. It provides a frame, pointing beyond itself, like a spotlight. The colon is quite dramatic, and unlike the semicolon, it links what precedes and follows it formally and tightly rather than loosely and associatively. It usually operates with dramatic force. It can frame a list to follow, separate cause and effect, or divide a brief claim from a more expanded version of the claim. The language on at least one side of the colon must be an independent clause, though both sides can be.

The colon says to the reader, "Concentrate on what follows me for a more detailed explanation of what preceded me" or "What follows me is logically bound with what preceded me."

Examples: *Rubber Soul* marked a change in The Beatles' song-writing: the sentimentality of earlier efforts gave way to a new complexity, both in the range of their subjects and the sophistication of their poetic devices.

Nowhere is this change more evident than in a sequence of songs near the album's end: "I'm Looking Through You," "In My Life," "Wait," and "If I Needed Someone."

The **dash** [—] provides an informal alternative to the colon for adding information to a sentence. Its effect is sudden, of the moment—what springs up impulsively to disrupt and extend in some new way the ongoing train of thought. A **pair of dashes** provides an invaluable resource to writers for inserting information within a sentence. In this usage, the rule is that the sentence must read coherently if the inserted information is left out. (Note that to type a dash, type two hyphens with no space between, before, or after. This distinguishes the dash from a hyphen [-], which is the mark used for connecting two words into one.)

The dash says to the reader, "This too!" or, in the case of a pair of them, "Remember the thought in the beginning of this sentence because we're jumping to something else before we come back to finish that thought."

> **Examples:** For all their loveliness, the songs on *Rubber Soul* are not without menace—"I'd rather see you dead little girl than to see you with another man."
>
> In addition to the usual lead, rhythm, and bass guitar ensemble, *Rubber Soul* introduced new instruments—notably, the harpsichord interlude in "In My Life," the sitar spiraling though "Norwegian Wood"—that had not previously been heard in rock'n'roll.

Nine Basic Writing Errors and How to Fix Them

If you're unsure about some of the terms you encounter in the discussions of BWEs, see the "Glossary of Grammatical Terms" at the end of this chapter. You'll also find brief "Test Yourself's" interspersed throughout this section. Do them: it's easy to conclude that you understand a problem when you are shown the correction, but understanding is not the same thing as actively practicing. There's an appendix to this chapter that contains answers to these sections, along with explanations.

BWE 1: Sentence Fragments   The most basic of writing errors, a *sentence fragment,* is a group of words punctuated like a complete sentence but lacking the necessary structure: it is only part of a sentence. Typically, a sentence fragment occurs when the group of words in question (1) lacks a subject, (2) lacks a predicate, or (3) is a subordinate (or dependent) clause.

To fix a sentence fragment, either turn it into an independent clause by providing whatever is missing—a subject or a predicate—or attach it to an independent clause upon which it can depend.

Noun Clause (No Predicate) As a Fragment
A world where imagination takes over and sorrow is left behind.

This fragment is not a sentence but rather a noun clause—a sentence subject with no predicate. The fragment lacks a verb that would assert something about the subject. (The verbs "takes over" and "is left" are in a dependent clause created by the subordinating conjunction "where.")

Corrections

A world *arose* where imagination takes over and sorrow is left behind. [new verb matched to "a world"]

She entered a world where imagination takes over and sorrow is left behind. [new subject and verb added]

The first correction adds a new verb ("arose"). The second introduces a new subject and verb, converting the fragment into the direct object of "she entered."

Verbal As a Fragment

Falling into debt for the fourth consecutive year.

"Falling" in the preceding fragment is not a verb. Depending on the correction, "falling" is either a verbal or part of a verb phrase.

Corrections

The company was falling into debt for the fourth consecutive year. [subject and helping verb added]

Falling into debt for the fourth consecutive year *led the company to consider relocating.* [new predicate added]

Falling into debt for the fourth consecutive year, *the company considered relocating.* [new subject and verb added]

In the first correction, the addition of a subject and the helping verb "was" converts the fragment into a sentence. The second correction turns the fragment into a gerund phrase functioning as the subject of a new sentence. The third correction converts the fragment into a participial phrase attached to a new independent clause. (See the section entitled "Glossary of Grammatical Terms" under "verbal" for definitions of "gerund" and "participle.")

Subordinate Clause As a Fragment

I had an appointment for 11:00 and was still waiting at 11:30. Although I did get to see the dean before lunch.

"Although" is a subordinating conjunction that calls for some kind of completion. Like "if," "when," "because," "whereas," and other subordinating conjunctions (see the "Glossary of Grammatical Terms"), "although" *always* makes the clause that it introduces dependent.

Corrections

I had an appointment for 11:00 and was still waiting at *11:30, although* I did get to see the dean before lunch. [fragment attached to preceding sentence]

As the correction demonstrates, the remedy lies in attaching the fragment to an independent clause on which it can depend (or, alternatively, making the fragment into a sentence by dropping the conjunction).

Sometimes writers use sentence fragments deliberately, usually for rhythm and emphasis or to create a conversational tone. In less formal contexts, they are generally permissible, but you run the risk that the fragment will not be perceived as intentional. In formal writing assignments, it is safer to avoid intentional fragments.

Test Yourself: Fragments

There are fragments in each of the following three examples, probably the result of their proximity to legitimate sentences. What's the problem in each case, and how would you fix it?

1. Like many other anthropologists, Margaret Mead studied non–Western cultures in such works as *Coming of Age in Samoa.* And influenced theories of childhood development in America.
2. The catastrophe resulted from an engineering flaw. Because the bridge lacked sufficient support.
3. In the 1840s the potato famine decimated Ireland. It being a country with poor soil and antiquated methods of agriculture.

A Note on Dashes and Colons

One way to correct a fragment is to replace the period with a dash: "The campaign required commitment. Not just money." becomes "The campaign required commitment—not just money." The dash offers you one way of attaching a phrase or dependent clause to a sentence without having to construct another independent clause. In short, it's succinct. (Compare the correction that uses the dash with another possible correction: "The campaign required commitment. It also required money.") Moreover, with the air of sudden interruption that the dash conveys, it can capture the informality and immediacy that the intentional fragment offers a writer.

You should be wary of overusing the dash in this way, as the slightly more presentable cousin of the intentional fragment. The energy it carries can clash with the decorum of formal writing contexts; for some readers, its staccato effect quickly becomes too much of a good thing.

One alternative to this usage of the dash is the colon. It can substitute because it also can be followed by a phrase, a list, or a clause. As with the dash, it must be preceded by an independent clause. And it, too, carries dramatic force because it abruptly halts the flow of the sentence.

The colon, however, does not convey informality. In place of a slapdash effect, it offers a *spotlight* on what is to follow it. Hence, as in this sentence you are reading, it is especially appropriate for setting up certain kinds of information: explanations, lists, or results. In the case of results, the cause or action precedes the colon; the effect or reaction follows it.

Let us quickly offer the other legitimate use of the dash: to enclose information within a sentence. In this use, dashes precede and follow the information, taking the role usually assigned to commas. Consider the following example:

> Shortly before the election—timing its disclosures for maximal destructive effect—the candidate's campaign staff levied a series of charges against the incumbent.

Note that if the information within the dashes is omitted, the sentence must still read grammatically. That is the rule for using dashes to sandwich information in this way.

BWE 2: Comma Splices and Fused (or Run-On) Sentences A comma splice consists of two independent clauses connected ("spliced") with a comma; a fused (or run-on) sentence combines two such clauses with no conjunction or punctuation. The solutions for both comma splices and fused sentences are the same.

1. Place a conjunction (such as "and" or "because") between the clauses.
2. Place a semicolon between the clauses.
3. Make the clauses into separate sentences.

All of these solutions solve the same logical problem: they clarify the boundaries of the independent clauses for your readers.

Comma Splice

He disliked discipline, he avoided anything demanding.

Correction

Because he disliked discipline, he avoided anything demanding. [subordinating conjunction added]

Comma Splice

Today most TV programs are violent, almost every program is about cops and detectives.

Correction

Today most TV programs are violent; almost every program is about cops and detectives. [semicolon replaces comma]

Because the two independent clauses in the first example contain ideas that are closely connected logically, the most effective of the three comma-splice solutions is to add a subordinating conjunction ("because") to the first of the two clauses, making it depend on the second. For the same reason—close conceptual connection—the best solution for the next comma splice is to substitute a semicolon for the comma. The semicolon signals that the two independent clauses are closely linked in meaning. In general, you can use a semicolon where you could also use a period.

The best cures for the perpetual comma splicer are to learn to recognize the difference between independent and dependent clauses and to get rid of the "pause theory" of punctuation. All of the clauses in our two examples are independent. As written, each of these should be punctuated not with a comma but rather with a period or a semicolon. Instead, the perpetual comma splicer, as usual, acts on the "pause theory": because the ideas in the independent clauses are closely connected, the writer hesitates to separate them with a period. And so the writer inserts what he or she takes to be a shorter pause—the comma. But a comma is not a "breath" mark; it provides readers with specific grammatical information, in each of these cases (erroneously) that there is only one independent clause separated by the comma from modifying information. In the corrections, by contrast, the semicolon sends the appropriate signal to the reader: the message that it is joining two associated but independent statements. (Adding a coordinating conjunction such as "and" would also be grammatically correct, though possibly awkward.)

Fused Sentence

The Indo-European language family includes many groups most languages in Europe belong to it.

Correction

The Indo-European language family includes many groups. Most languages in Europe belong to it. [period inserted after first independent clause]

You could also fix this fused sentence with a comma plus the coordinating conjunction "and." Alternatively, you might condense the whole into a single independent clause.

Most languages in Europe belong to the Indo-European language family.

Comma Splices with Conjunctive Adverbs

Quantitative methods of data collection show broad trends, however, they ignore specific cases.

Sociobiology poses a threat to traditional ethics, for example, it asserts that human behavior is genetically motivated by the "selfish gene" to perpetuate itself.

Corrections

Quantitative methods of data collection show broad trends; however, they ignore specific cases. [semicolon replaces comma before "however"]

Sociobiology poses a threat to traditional ethics; for example, it asserts that human behavior is genetically motivated by the "selfish gene" to perpetuate itself. [semicolon replaces comma before "for example"]

Both of these examples contain one of the most common forms of comma splices. Both of them are compound sentences—that is, they contain two independent clauses. (See the section entitled "The Compound Sentence" in Chapter 13.) Normally, connecting the clauses with a comma and a conjunction would be correct; for example, "Most hawks hunt alone, but osprey hunt in pairs." In the preceding two comma splices, however, the independent clauses are joined by transitional expressions known as conjunctive adverbs (see the "Glossary of Grammatical Terms"). When a conjunctive adverb is used to link two independent clauses, it *always* requires a semicolon. By contrast, when a coordinating conjunction links the two clauses of a compound sentence, it is *always* preceded by a comma.

In most cases, depending on the sense of the sentence, the semicolon precedes the conjunctive adverb and has the effect of clarifying the division between the two clauses. There are exceptions to this general rule, though, as in the following sentence:

The lazy boy did finally read a *book, however;* it was the least he could do.

Here "however" is a part of the first independent clause and qualifies its claim. The sentence thus suggests that the boy was not totally lazy, because he did get around to reading a book. Note how the meaning changes when "however" becomes the introductory word for the second independent clause.

The lazy boy did finally read a *book; however,* it was the least he could do.

Here the restricting force of "however" suggests that reading the book was not much of an accomplishment.

Test Yourself: Comma Splices

What makes each of the following sentences a comma splice? Determine the best way to fix each one and why, and then make the correction.

1. "Virtual reality" is a new buzzword, so is "hyperspace."
2. Many popular cures for cancer have been discredited, nevertheless, many people continue to buy them.
3. Elvis Presley's home, Graceland, attracts many musicians as a kind of shrine, even Paul Simon has been there.
4. She didn't play well with others, she sat on the bench and watched.

BWE 3: Errors in Subject–Verb Agreement   The subject and the verb must agree in number, a singular subject taking a singular verb and a plural subject taking a plural verb. Errors in subject–verb agreement usually occur when a writer misidentifies the subject or verb of a clause.

Agreement Problem

Various kinds of vandalism has been rapidly increasing.

Correction

Various kinds of vandalism *have* been rapidly increasing. [verb made plural to match "kinds"]

When you isolate the grammatical subject ("kinds") and the verb ("has") of the original sentence, you can tell that they do not agree. Although "vandalism" might seem to be the subject because it is closest to the verb, it is actually the object of the preposition "of." The majority of agreement problems arise from mistaking the object of a preposition for the actual subject of a sentence. If you habitually make this mistake, you can begin to remedy it by familiarizing yourself with the most common prepositions. (See the "Glossary of Grammatical Terms," which contains a list of these.)

Agreement Problem

Another aspect of territoriality that differentiates humans from animals are their possession of ideas and objects.

Correction

Another aspect of territoriality that differentiates humans from animals *is* their possession of ideas and objects. [verb made singular to match subject "aspect"]

The subject of the sentence is "aspect." The two plural nouns ("humans" and "animals") probably encourage the mistake of using a plural verb ("are"), but "humans" is part of the "that" clause modifying "aspect," and "animals" is the object of the preposition "from."

Agreement Problem

The Republican and the Democrat both believe in doing what's best for America, but each believe that the other doesn't understand what's best.

Correction

The Republican and the Democrat both believe in doing what's best for America, but each *believes* that the other doesn't understand what's best. [verb made singular to agree with subject "each"]

The word "each" is *always* singular, so the verb ("believes") must be singular as well. The presence of a plural subject and verb in the sentence's first independent clause ("the Republican and the Democrat both believe") has probably encouraged the error.

Test Yourself: Subject–Verb Agreement

Diagnose and correct the error in the following example.

> The controversies surrounding the placement of Arthur Ashe's statue in
> Richmond was difficult for the various factions to resolve.

A Note on Nonstandard English

The term "standard written English" refers to language that conforms to the rules and conventions adhered to by the majority of English-speaking writers. The fact is, however, that not all speakers of English grow up hearing, reading, and writing standard written English. Some linguistic cultures in America follow, for example, a different set of conventions for subject–verb agreement. Their speakers do not differentiate singular from plural verb forms with a terminal "–s," as in standard English.

She walks home after work.

They walk home after work.

Some speakers of English do not observe this distinction, so that the first sentence becomes

She walk home after work.

These two ways of handling subject–verb agreement are recognized by linguists not in terms of right versus wrong but rather in terms of dialect difference. A *dialect* is a variety of a language that is characteristic of a region or culture and is sometimes unintelligible to outsiders. The problem for speakers of a dialect that differs from the norm is that they can't always rely on the ear—on what sounds right—when they are editing according to the rules of standard written English. Such speakers need, in effect, to learn to speak more than one dialect so that they can edit according to the rules of standard written English in situations where this would be expected. This often requires adding a separate proofreading stage for particular errors, like subject–verb agreement, rather than relying on what sounds right.

BWE 4: Shifts in Sentence Structure (Faulty Predication)   This error involves an illogical mismatch between subject and predicate. If you continually run afoul of faulty predication, you might use the exercises in a handbook to drill you on isolating the grammatical subjects and verbs of sentences, because that is the first move you need to make in fixing the problem.

Shift

In 1987, the release of more information became available.

Correction

In 1987, more *information* became available *for release.* [new subject]

It was the "information," not the "release," that "became available." The correction relocates "information" from its position as object of the preposition "of" to the subject position in the sentence; it also moves "release" into a prepositional phrase.

Shift

The busing controversy was intended to rectify the inequality of educational opportunities.

Correction

Busing was intended to rectify the inequality of educational opportunities. [new subject formulated to match verb]

The *controversy* wasn't *intended to rectify,* but *busing* was.

Test Yourself: Faulty Predication

Identify and correct the faulty predication in this example:

The subject of learning disabilities is difficult to identify accurately.

BWE 5: Errors in Pronoun Reference   There are at least three forms of this problem. All of them involve a lack of clarity about whom or what a pronoun (a word that substitutes for a noun) refers to. The surest way to avoid difficulties is to make certain that the pronoun relates back unambiguously to a specific word, known as the antecedent. In the sentence "Nowadays appliances don't last as long as they once did," the noun "appliances" is the antecedent of the pronoun "they."

Pronoun–Antecedent Agreement

A pronoun must agree in number (and gender) with the noun or noun phrase that it refers to.

Pronoun Error

It can be dangerous if a child, after watching TV, decides to practice what they saw.

Corrections

It can be dangerous if *children,* after watching TV, *decide* to practice what *they* saw. [antecedent (and verb) made plural to agree with pronouns]

It can be dangerous if a child, after watching TV, decides to practice what *he or she* saw. [singular pronouns substituted to match singular antecedent "child"]

The error occurs because "child" is singular, but its antecedent pronoun, "they," is plural. The first correction makes both singular; the second makes both plural. You might also observe in the first word of the example—the impersonal "it"—an exception to the rule that pronouns must have antecedents.

Test Yourself: Pronoun–Antecedent Agreement

What is wrong with the following sentence, and how would you fix it?

Every dog has its day, but all too often when that day happens, they can be found barking up the wrong tree.

Ambiguous Reference

A pronoun should have only one possible antecedent. The possibility of two or more confuses relationships within the sentence.

Pronoun Error

Children like comedians because they have a sense of humor.

Corrections

Because children have a sense of humor, *they* like comedians. [subordinate "because" clause placed first, and relationship between noun "children" and pronoun "they" tightened]

Children like comedians because *comedians* have a sense of humor. [pronoun eliminated and replaced by repetition of noun]

Does "they" in the original example refer to "children" or "comedians"? The rule in such cases of ambiguity is that the pronoun refers to the nearest possible antecedent, so here "comedians" possess the sense of humor, regardless of what the writer may intend. As the corrections demonstrate, either reordering the sentence or repeating the noun can remove the ambiguity.

Test Yourself: Ambiguous Reference

As you proofread, it's a good idea to target your pronouns to make sure that they cannot conceivably refer to more than one noun. What's wrong with the following sentences?

1. Alexander the Great's father, Philip of Macedon, died when he was twenty-six.
2. The committee could not look into the problem because it was too involved.

Broad Reference

Broad reference occurs when a pronoun refers loosely to a number of ideas expressed in preceding clauses or sentences. It causes confusion because the reader cannot be sure which of the ideas the pronoun refers to.

Pronoun Error

As a number of scholars have noted, Sigmund Freud and Karl Marx offered competing but also at times complementary critiques of the dehumanizing tendencies of Western capitalist society. We see this in Christopher Lasch's analysis of conspicuous consumption in *The Culture of Narcissism*.

Correction

As a number of scholars have noted, Sigmund Freud and Karl Marx offered competing but also at times complementary critiques of the dehumanizing tendencies of Western capitalist society. We see *this complementary view* in Christopher Lasch's analysis of conspicuous consumption in *The Culture of Narcissism*. [broad "this" clarified by addition of noun phrase]

The word "this" in the second sentence of the uncorrected example could refer to the fact that "a number of scholars have noted" the relationship between Freud and Marx, to the competition between Freud's and Marx's critiques of capitalism, or to the complementary nature of the two men's critiques.

Beware "this" as a pronoun: it's the most common source of broad reference. The remedy is generally to avoid using the word as a pronoun. Instead, convert "this" into an adjective, and let it modify some noun that more clearly specifies the referent: "this complementary view," as in the correction or, alternatively, "this competition" or "this scholarly perspective."

Test Yourself: Broad Reference

Locate the errors in the following examples, and provide a remedy for each.

1. Regardless of whether the film is foreign or domestic, they can be found in your neighborhood video store.
2. Many experts now claim that dogs and other higher mammals dream; for those who don't own such pets, this is often difficult to believe.

A Note on Sexism and Pronoun Usage

Errors in pronoun reference sometimes occur because of a writer's praiseworthy desire to avoid sexism. In most circles, the following correction of the preceding example would be considered sexist.

It can be dangerous if a child, after watching TV, decides to practice what *he* saw.

Though the writer of such a sentence may intend "he" to function as a gender-neutral impersonal pronoun, it in fact excludes girls on the basis of gender. Implicitly, it also conveys sexual stereotypes (for example, that only boys are violent, or perhaps stupid, enough to confuse TV with reality).

The easiest way to avoid the problem of sexism in pronoun usage usually lies in putting things into the plural form, because plural pronouns ("we," "you," "they") have no gender. (See the use of "children" in the first correction of the pronoun–antecedent agreement example.) Alternatively, you can use the phrase "he or she." Many readers, however, find this phrase and its variant, "s/he," to be awkward constructions. Another remedy lies in rewriting the sentence to avoid pronouns altogether, as in the following revision.

> It can be dangerous if a child, after watching TV, decides to practice *some violent activity portrayed on the screen.*

BWE 6: *Misplaced Modifiers and Dangling Participles* Modifiers are words or groups of words used to qualify, limit, intensify, or explain some other element in a sentence. A misplaced modifier is a word or phrase that appears to modify the wrong word or words.

> Misplaced Modifier
>
> At the age of three he caught a fish with a broken arm.

> Correction
>
> At the age of three *the boy with a broken arm* caught a fish. [noun replaces pronoun; prepositional phrase revised and relocated]

The original sentence mistakenly implies that the fish had a broken arm. Modification errors often occur in sentences with one or more prepositional phrases, as in this case.

> Misplaced Modifier
>
> According to legend, General George Washington crossed the Delaware and celebrated Christmas in a small boat.

> Correction
>
> According to legend, General George Washington crossed the Delaware *in a small boat* and *then* celebrated Christmas *on shore.* [prepositional phrase relocated; modifiers added to second verb]

As a general rule, you can avoid misplacing a modifier by keeping it as close as possible to what it modifies. Thus, the second correction removes the implication that Washington celebrated Christmas in a small boat. When you cannot relocate the modifier, separate it from the rest of the sentence with a comma to prevent readers from connecting it to the nearest noun.

A dangling participle creates a particular kind of problem in modification: the noun or pronoun that the writer intends the participial phrase to modify is not actually present in the sentence. Thus, we have the name dangling participle: the participle has been left dangling because the word or phrase it is meant to modify is not there.

> Dangling Participle
>
> After debating the issue of tax credits for the elderly, the bill passed in a close vote.

Correction

After debating the issue of tax credits for the elderly, *the Senate passed the bill* in a close vote. [appropriate noun added for participle to modify]

The bill did not debate the issue, as the original example implies. As the correction demonstrates, fixing a dangling participle involves tightening the link between the activity implied by the participle ("debating") and the entity performing that activity ("the Senate").

Test Yourself: Modification Errors

Find the modification errors in the following examples and correct them.
1. After eating their sandwiches, the steamboat left the dock.
2. The social workers saw an elderly woman on a bus with a cane standing up.
3. Crossing the street, a car hit the pedestrian.

BWE 7: *Errors in Using Possessive Apostrophes*   Adding " 's" to most singular nouns will make them show possession, for example, the plant's roots, the accountant's ledger. You can add the apostrophe alone, without the "s," for example, to make plural nouns that already end with "s" show possession: the flowers' fragrances, the ships' berths (although you may also add an additional "s").

Apostrophe Error

The loyal opposition scorned the committees decisions.

Corrections

The loyal opposition scorned the *committee's* decisions.

The loyal opposition scorned the *committees'* decisions. [possessive apostrophe added]

The first correction assumes there was one committee; the second assumes there were two or more.

Apostrophe Error

The advisory board swiftly transacted it's business.

Correction

The advisory board swiftly transacted *its* business. [apostrophe dropped]

Unlike possessive nouns, possessive pronouns ("my," "your," "yours," "her," "hers," "his," "its," "our," "ours," "their," "theirs") *never* take an apostrophe.

Test Yourself: Possessive Apostrophes

Find and correct any errors in the following sentence.

The womens movement has been misunderstood by many of its detractors.

BWE 8: Comma Errors   As with other rules of punctuation and grammar, the many that pertain to comma usage share an underlying aim: to clarify the relationships among the parts of a sentence. Commas separate the parts of a sentence grammatically. One of their primary uses, then, is to help your readers distinguish the main clause from dependent elements, such as subordinate clauses and long prepositional phrases. They do not signify a pause, as was discussed under "BWE 2."

Comma Error

After eating the couple went home.

Correction

After *eating,* the couple went home. [comma added before independent clause]

The comma after "eating" is needed to keep the main clause "visible" or separate; it marks the point at which the prepositional phrase ends and the independent clause begins. Without this separation, readers would be invited to contemplate cannibalism as they move across the sentence.

Comma Error

In the absence of rhetoric study teachers and students lack a vocabulary for talking about their prose.

Correction

In the absence of rhetoric *study,* teachers and students lack a vocabulary for talking about their prose. [comma added to separate prepositional phrase from main clause]

Without the comma readers would have to read the sentence twice to find out where the prepositional phrase ends—with "study"—in order to figure out where the main clause begins.

Comma Error

Dog owners, despite their many objections will have to obey the new law.

Correction

Dog owners, despite their many *objections,* will have to obey the new law. [single comma converted to a pair of commas]

A comma is needed after "objections" in order to isolate the phrase in the middle of the sentence ("despite their many objections") from the main clause. The phrase needs to be set off with commas because it contains additional information that is not essential to the meaning of what it modifies. (Dog owners must obey the law whether they object or not.) Phrases and clauses that function in this way are called *nonrestrictive.*

The test of nonrestrictive phrases and clauses is to see if they can be omitted without substantially changing the message that a sentence conveys ("Dog owners will have to obey the new law," for example). Nonrestrictive elements always take two commas—a comma "sandwich"—to set them off. Using only one comma illogically separates the sentence's subject ("dog owners") from its predicate ("will have to obey").

This problem is easier to see in a shorter sentence. You wouldn't, for example, write "I, fell down." As a rule, commas virtually never separate the subject from the verb of a sentence. (Here's an exception: "Ms. Taloora, a high fashion model, watches her diet scrupulously.")

Comma Error

Most people regardless of age like to spend money.

Correction

Most *people,* regardless of age, like to spend money. [comma sandwich added]

Here commas enclose the nonrestrictive elements; you could omit this information without significantly affecting the sense. Such is not the case in the following two examples.

Comma Error

People, who live in glass houses, should not throw stones.

Correction

People *who live in glass houses* should not throw stones. [commas omitted]

Comma Error

Please return the library book, that I left on the table.

Correction

Please return the library *book that* I left on the table. [comma omitted]

It is incorrect to place commas around "who live in glass houses" or a comma before "that I left on the table." Each of these is a *restrictive clause*—that is, it contains information that is an essential part of what it modifies. In the first sentence, for example, if "who live in glass houses" is left out, the fundamental meaning of the sentence is lost: "People should not throw stones." The word "who" is defined by restricting it to "people" in the category of glass-house dwellers. Similarly, in the second example the "that" clause contributes an essential meaning to "book"; the sentence is referring to not just any book but to a particular one, the one "on the table."

So remember the general rule: if the information in a phrase or clause can be omitted—if it is nonessential and therefore nonrestrictive—it needs to be separated by commas from the rest of the sentence. Moreover, note that nonrestrictive clauses are generally introduced by the word "which," so a "which" clause interpolated into a sentence takes a comma sandwich. By contrast, a restrictive clause is introduced by the word "that" and takes no commas.

Test Yourself: Comma Errors

Consider the following examples as a pair. Punctuate them as necessary, and then briefly articulate how the meanings of the two sentences differ.

1. The book which I had read a few years ago contained a lot of outdated data.
2. The book that I had read a few years ago contained a lot of outdated data.

BWE 9: Spelling/Diction Errors That Interfere with Meaning   Misspellings are always a problem in a final draft, insofar as they undermine your authority by inviting readers to perceive you as careless (at best). If you make a habit of using the spellchecker of a word processor, you will take care of most misspellings. But the problems that a spellchecker won't catch are the ones that can often hurt you most. These are actually diction errors—incorrect word choices in which you have confused one word with another that it closely resembles. In such cases, you have spelled the word correctly, but it's the wrong word. Because it means something other than what you've intended, you end up misleading your readers. (See "Shades of Meaning" in Chapter 12.)

The best way to avoid this problem is to memorize the differences between pairs of words that are commonly confused with each other but that have distinct meanings. The following examples illustrate a few of the most common and serious of these errors. Most handbooks contain a glossary of usage that *cites* more of these *sites* of confusion.

Spelling/Diction Error: "It's" Versus "Its"

Although you can't tell a book by its' cover, its fairly easy to get the general idea from the introduction.

Correction

Although you can't tell a book by *its* cover, *it's* fairly easy to get the general idea from the introduction. [apostrophe dropped from possessive and added to contraction]

"It's" is a contraction for "it is." "Its" is a possessive pronoun meaning "belonging to it." If you confuse the two, *it's* likely that your sentence will mislead *its* readers.

Spelling/Diction Error: "Their" Versus "There" Versus "They're"

Their are ways of learning about the cuisine of northern India besides going their to watch the master chefs and learn there secrets—assuming their willing to share them.

Correction

There are ways of learning about the cuisine of northern India besides going *there* to watch the master chefs and learn *their* secrets—assuming *they're* willing to share them. [expletive "there," adverb "there," possessive pronoun "their," and contraction "they're" inserted appropriately]

"There" as an adverb normally refers to a place; "there" can also be used as an expletive to introduce a clause, as in the first usage of the correction. (See the discussion of expletives under "Cutting the Fat" in Chapter 13.) "Their" is a possessive pronoun meaning "belonging to them." "They're" is a contraction for "they are."

Spelling/Diction Error: "Then" Versus "Than"

If a person would rather break a law then obey it, than he or she must be willing to face the consequences.

Correction

If a person would rather break a law *than* obey it, *then* he or she must be willing to face the consequences. [comparative "than" distinguished from temporal "then"]

"Than" is a conjunction used with a comparison, for example, "rather X than Y." "Then" is an adverb used to indicate what comes next in relation to time, for example, "first X, then Y."

Spelling/Diction Error: "Effect" Versus "Affect"

It is simply the case that BWEs adversely effect the way that readers judge what a writer has to say. It follows that writers who include lots of BWEs in their prose may not have calculated the disastrous affects of these mistakes.

Correction

It is simply the case that BWEs adversely *affect* the way that readers judge what a writer has to say. It follows that writers who include lots of BWEs in their prose may not have calculated the disastrous *effects* of these mistakes. [verb "affect" and noun "effects" inserted appropriately]

In their most common usages, "affect" is a verb meaning "to influence," and "effect" is a noun meaning "the result of an action or cause." The confusion of "affect" and "effect" is enlarged by the fact that both of these words have secondary meanings: the verb "to effect" means "to cause or bring about"; the noun "affect" is used in psychology to mean "emotion or feeling." Thus, if you confuse these two words, you will inadvertently make a meaning radically different from the one you intend.

Test Yourself: Spelling/Diction Errors

Make corrections as necessary in the following paragraph.

Its not sufficiently acknowledged that the behavior of public officials is not just an ethical issue but one that effects the sale of newspapers and commercial bytes in television news. When public officials don't do what their supposed to do, than their sure to face the affects of public opinion—if they get caught—because there are dollars to be made. Its that simple: money more then morality is calling the tune in the way that the press treats it's superstars.

C. GLOSSARY OF GRAMMATICAL TERMS

adjective   An adjective is a part of speech that usually modifies a noun or pronoun, for example, "blue," "boring," "boisterous."

adverb   An adverb is a part of speech that modifies an adjective, adverb, or verb, for example, "heavily," "habitually," "very." The adverbial form generally differs from the adjectival form via the addition of the ending "–ly"; for example, "happy" is an adjective, and "happily" is an adverb.

clause (independent and dependent)   A clause is any group of words that contains both a **subject** and a **predicate**. An **independent clause** (also known as a **main clause**) can stand alone as a sentence. For example,

The most famous revolutionaries of this century have all, in one way or another, offered a vision of a classless society.

The subject of this independent clause is "revolutionaries," the verb is "have offered," and the direct object is "vision." By contrast, a **dependent** (or **subordinate**) **clause** is any group of words containing a subject and verb that cannot stand alone as a separate sentence because it depends on an independent clause to complete its meaning. The following sentence adds two dependent clauses to our previous example:

> The most famous revolutionaries of this century have all, in one way or another, offered a vision of a classless society, *although* most historians would agree *that* this ideal has never been achieved.

The origin of the word "depend" is "to hang": a dependent clause literally hangs on the independent clause. In the preceding example, neither "although most historians would agree" nor "that this ideal has never been achieved" can stand independently. The "that" clause relies on the "although" clause, which in turn relies on the main clause. "That" and "although" function as **subordinating conjunctions;** by eliminating them, we could rewrite the sentence to contain three independent clauses:

> The most famous revolutionaries of this century have all, in one way or another, offered a vision of a classless society. Most historians would agree on one judgment about this vision: it has never been achieved.

comma splice   A comma splice consists of two independent clauses incorrectly connected (spliced) with a comma. See "BWE 2."

conjunction (coordinating and subordinating)   A conjunction is a part of speech that connects words, phrases, or clauses, for example, "and," "but," "although." The conjunction in some way defines that connection: for example, "and" links; "but" separates. All conjunctions define connections in one of two basic ways. Coordinating conjunctions connect words or groups of words that have equal grammatical importance. The coordinating conjunctions are "and," "but," "or," "nor," "for," "so," and "yet." Subordinating conjunctions introduce a dependent clause and connect it to a main clause. Here is a partial list of the most common subordinating conjunctions: "after," "although," "as," "as if," "as long as," "because," "before," "if," "rather than," "since," "than," "that," "though," "unless," "until," "when," "where," "whether," and "while."

conjunctive adverb   A conjunctive adverb is a word that links two independent clauses (as a conjunction) but that also modifies the clause it introduces (as an adverb). Some of the most common conjunctive adverbs are "consequently," "furthermore," "however," "moreover," "nevertheless," "similarly," "therefore," and "thus." Phrases can also serve this function, such as "for example" and "on the other hand." When conjunctive adverbs are used to link two independent clauses, they always require a semicolon:

> Many pharmaceutical chains now offer their own generic versions of common drugs; however, many consumers continue to spend more for name brands that contain the same active ingredients as the generics.

When conjunctive adverbs occur within an independent clause, however, they are enclosed in a pair of commas, as is the case with the use of "however" earlier in this sentence.

coordination   Coordination refers to grammatically equal words, phrases, or clauses. Coordinate constructions are used to give elements in a sentence equal weight or importance. In the sentence "The tall, thin lawyer badgered the witness, but the judge interceded," the clauses "The tall, thin lawyer badgered the witness" and "but the judge interceded" are coordinate clauses; "tall" and "thin" are coordinate adjectives.

dependent clause (see *clause*)

direct object   The direct object is a noun or pronoun that receives the action carried by the verb and performed by the subject. In the sentence, "Certain mushrooms can kill you," "you" is the direct object.

gerund (see *verbals*)

fused (or run-on) sentence   A fused sentence incorrectly combines two independent clauses with no conjunction or punctuation. See "BWE 2."

independent clause (see *clause*)

infinitive (see *verbals*)

main clause (see *clause*)

noun   A noun is a part of speech that names a person ("woman"), place ("town"), thing ("book"), idea ("justice"), quality ("irony"), or action ("betrayal").

object of the preposition (see *preposition*)

participle and participial phrase (see *verbals*)

phrase   A phrase is a group of words occurring in a meaningful sequence that lacks either a subject or a predicate. This absence distinguishes it from a clause, which contains both a subject and a predicate. Phrases function in sentences as adjectives, adverbs, nouns, or verbs. They are customarily classified according to the part of speech of their key word: "over the mountain" is a **prepositional phrase**; "running for office" is a **participial phrase**; "had been disciplined" is a **verb phrase**; "desktop graphics" is a **noun phrase**; and so forth.

predicate   The predicate contains the verb of a sentence or clause, making some kind of statement about the subject. The predicate of the preceding sentence is "contains the verb, making some kind of statement about the subject." The simple predicate—the verb to which the other words in the sentence are attached—is "contains."

preposition, prepositional phrase   A preposition is a part of speech that links a noun or pronoun to some other word in the sentence. Prepositions usually express a relationship of time (after) or space (above) or direction (toward). The noun to which the preposition is attached is known as the object of the preposition. A preposition, its object, and any modifiers comprise a prepositional phrase. "*With* love *from* me *to* you" strings together three prepositional phrases. Here is a partial list of the most common prepositions: about, above, across, after, among, at, before, behind, between, by, during, for, from, in, into, like, of, on, out, over, since, through, to, toward, under, until, up, upon, with, within, and without.

pronoun   A pronoun is a part of speech that substitutes for a noun, such as I, you, he, she, it, we, and they.

run–on (or fused) sentence   A run–on sentence incorrectly combines two independent clauses with no conjunction or punctuation. See "BWE 2."

sentence   A sentence is a unit of expression that can stand independently. It contains two parts, a **subject** and a **predicate**. The shortest sentence in the Bible, for example, is "Jesus wept." "Jesus" is the subject; "wept" is the predicate.

sentence fragment   A sentence fragment is a group of words incorrectly punctuated like a complete sentence but lacking the necessary structure; it is only a part of a sentence. "Walking down the road" and "the origin of the problem" are both fragments because neither contains a **predicate**. See "BWE 1."

subject   The subject, in most cases a noun or pronoun, names the doer of the action in a sentence or identifies what the predicate is about. The subject of the previous sentence, for example, is "the subject, in most cases a noun or pronoun." The simple subject of that sentence—the noun to which the other words in the sentence are attached—is "subject."

subordination, subordinating conjunctions   "Subordination" refers to the placement of certain grammatical units, particularly phrases and clauses, at a lower, less important structural level than other elements. As with coordination, the grammatical ranking carries conceptual significance as well: whatever is grammatically subordinated appears less important than the information carried in the main clause. In the following example, the 486–based personal computer is subordinated both grammatically and conceptually to the Pentium–based PC:

> Although 486-based personal computers continue to improve in speed, the new Pentium-based PC systems have thoroughly outclassed them.

Here "although" is a **subordinating conjunction** that introduces a subordinate clause, also known as a **dependent clause**.

verb   A verb is a part of speech that describes an action ("goes"), states how something was affected by an action ("became angered"), or expresses a state of being ("is").

verbals (participles, gerunds, and infinitives)   Verbals are words derived from verbs. They are verb forms that look like verbs but, as determined by the structure of the sentence they appear in, they function as nouns, adjectives, or adverbs. There are three forms of verbals.

An **infinitive**—composed of the root form of a verb plus "to" ("to be," "to vote")—becomes a verbal when it is used as a noun ("*To eat* is essential"), an adjective ("These are the books *to read*"), or an adverb ("He was too sick *to walk*").

Similarly, a **participle**—usually composed of the root form of a verb plus "–ing" (present participle) or "–ed" (past participle)—becomes a verbal when used as an adjective. It can occur as a single word, modifying a noun, as in "faltering negotiations" or "finished business." But it also can occur in a participial phrase, consisting of the participle, its object, and any modifiers. Here are two examples:

> *Having been tried and convicted,* the criminal was sentenced to life imprisonment.

> *Following the path of most resistance,* the masochist took deep pleasure in his frustration.

"Having been tried and convicted" is a participial phrase that modifies "criminal"; "Following the path of most resistance" is a participial phrase that modifies "masochist." In each case, the participial phrase functions as an adjective.

The third form of verbal, the **gerund**, resembles the participle. Like the participle, it is formed by adding "–ing" to the root form of the verb, but unlike the participle, it is used as a noun. In the sentence "Swimming is extraordinarily aerobic," the gerund "swimming" functions as the subject. Again like participles, gerunds can occur in phrases. The gerund phrases are italicized in the following example: "*Watching a film adaptation* takes less effort than *reading the book* from which it was made."

When using a verbal, remember that although it resembles a verb, it cannot function alone as the verb in a sentence: "Being a military genius" is a fragment, not a sentence.

Guidelines for Revising for Correctness

1. In correcting grammar, seek to discover the patterns of error in your writing, and unlearn the logic that has led you to make certain kinds of errors recurrently.
2. Check the draft for errors that obscure the boundaries of sentences: fragments, comma splices, and run-ons. Begin by isolating the simple subject and predicate in the main clause(s) of every sentence (to make sure they exist); this check will also help you to spot faulty predication and errors in subject–verb agreement. Then, check to see that each independent clause is separated from others by a period, a comma plus coordinating conjunction, or a semicolon.
3. Check your sentences for ambiguity (the potential of being read in more than one way) by deliberately trying to misread them. If your sentence can be read to mean something other than what you intended, the most common causes are misplaced and dangling modifiers and errors in pronoun reference.
4. Fix errors in pronoun reference and misplaced modifiers by making sure that every pronoun has only one clear antecedent and that every modifying word or phrase is placed as close as possible to the part of the sentence it modifies.
5. Avoid dangling modifiers by being sure that the noun or pronoun being modified is actually present in the sentence. Avoid broad reference by adding the appropriate noun or noun phrase after the pronoun "this." (You can greatly improve the clarity of your prose just by avoiding use of the vague "this," especially at the beginnings of sentences.)

6. Check that commas are separating dependent clauses, long prepositional phrases, or other modifying elements from the main clause. A comma is not a pause; its function is to help readers locate your sentence's main (independent) clause(s).
7. Enclose nonrestrictive modifiers placed between the subject and predicate of a sentence in a pair of commas or—for more emphasis—in a pair of dashes. A nonrestrictive modifier is a phrase, often beginning with "which," that can be deleted from the sentence without changing the sentence's meaning.

ASSIGNMENT: GRAMMAR AND STYLE QUIZ

Here is an error-laden paragraph to rewrite and correct by making changes in grammar and punctuation as necessary. You may need to add, drop, or rearrange words, but do not add any periods. That way, you will be able to test yourself on your ability to use commas plus conjunctions, semicolons, colons, and dashes rather than avoid these options by separating each independent clause into a simple sentence. The quiz also contains a few stylistic problems addressed in Chapters 12 and 13. A discussion of the errors and how to fix them can be found in the Appendix to this chapter.

[1] It is a fact that fraternities and sororities are a major part of student life at the
[2] university, students are preoccupied with pledging. This is not approved of by
[3] most members of the faculty, however, they feel helpless about attacking them.
[4] Perceiving that the greek societies are attractive to the students but at the same
[5] time encouraging anti-intellectualism, it is not an issue that can be addressed
[6] easily. The student, who wants to be popular and cool feels that he should not
[7] talk in class, because interest in academics or having ideas outside class is
[8] uncool. Its more important to pledge the right house then being smart. If the
[9] administration would create alternatives to Greek life such as a honors program
[10] students lives would be more enriched. Although for now raising the cumulative
[11] grade point necessary to pledge and remain active would be a good start.
[12] Contrary to the University's stance against gender discrimination Greek life
[13] perpetuates gender stereotypes; for example, the dances at each house for
[14] freshman women but not men. Some of the best students agree with this but
[15] mistakenly believes that most faculty endorse the system.

Chapter 14 Appendix
Answer Key (with Discussion)

TEST YOURSELF SECTIONS

Test Yourself: Fragments

Original example: Like many other anthropologists, Margaret Mead studied non-Western cultures in such works as *Coming of Age in Samoa*. And influenced theories of childhood development in America.

Problem: The second sentence is actually a fragment, a predicate in need of a subject.

Possible correction: Like many other anthropologists, Margaret Mead studied non-Western cultures (in such works as *Coming of Age in Samoa*) in ways that influenced theories of childhood development in America.

Comment: There are many ways to fix this example, but its original form leaves ambiguous whether the fragment refers only to "Mead" or to "many other anthropologists" as well. The correction offered includes the other anthropologists in the referent and diminishes the emphasis on Mead's book by placing it within parentheses. Although the correction uses a subordinating "that" to incorporate the fragment into the first sentence, it keeps this information in an emphatic position at the end of the sentence.

Original example: The catastrophe resulted from an engineering flaw. Because the bridge lacked sufficient support.

Problem: The second sentence is actually a dependent clause; "because" always subordinates.

Possible correction: The catastrophe resulted from an engineering flaw: the bridge lacked sufficient support.

Comment: Because the colon has causal force, this is an ideal spot to use one, identifying the "flaw."

Original example: In the 1840s the potato famine decimated Ireland. It being a country with poor soil and antiquated methods of agriculture.

Problem: The second sentence is actually a fragment, a subject plus a long participial phrase.

Possible correction: In the 1840s the potato famine decimated Ireland, a country with poor and antiquated methods of agriculture.

Comment: The cause of this kind of fragment is usually that the writer mistakenly believes that "being" is a verb rather than a participle that introduces a long phrase (modifying "Ireland" in this case). It would also be correct simply to change the period to a comma in the original sentence.

Test Yourself: Comma Splices

Original example: "Virtual reality" is a new buzzword, so is "hyperspace."

Problem: This is a comma splice—both clauses are independent, yet they are joined with a comma.

Possible correction: "Virtual reality" is a new buzzword; so is "hyperspace."

Comment: Because the clauses are linked by association—both naming buzz-words—a semicolon would show that association. A writer could also condense the clauses into a simple sentence with a compound subject, for example, "Both 'virtual reality' and 'hyperspace' are new buzzwords."

Original example: Many popular cures for cancer have been discredited, neverthe-less, many people continue to buy them.

Problem: A comma splice results from the incorrectly punctuated conjunctive adverb "nevertheless."

Possible correction: Many popular cures for cancer have been discredited; neverthe-less, many people continue to buy them.

Comment: Without the semicolon to separate the independent clauses, the conjunc-tive adverb could conceivably modify either the preceding or the following clause. This problem is usually worse with "however."

Original example: Elvis Presley's home, Graceland, attracts many musicians as a kind of shrine, even Paul Simon has been there.

Problem: This is a comma splice—the two independent clauses are linked by a comma without a conjunction. The problem is exacerbated by the number of commas in the sentence; the reader cannot easily tell which one is used to separate the clauses.

Possible correction: Elvis Presley's home, Graceland, attracts many musicians as a kind of shrine—even Paul Simon has been there.

Comment: Although one could justly use a semicolon here, the dash conveys the impromptu effect of an afterthought.

Original example: She didn't play well with others, she sat on the bench and watched.

Problem: Because the second clause develops the first one, a writer might think that it is dependent on the first; conceptually, yes, but grammatically, no.

Possible correction: She didn't play well with others; she sat on the bench and watched.

Comment: If the writer wanted to link the two clauses more tightly, a colon would be appropriate instead of the semicolon.

Test Yourself: Subject–Verb Agreement

Original example: The controversies surrounding the placement of Arthur Ashe's statue in Richmond was difficult for the various factions to resolve.

Problem: The grammatical subject of the main clause ("controversies") is plural; the verb ("was") is singular.

Possible corrections: The controversies surrounding the placement of Arthur Ashe's statue in Richmond were difficult for the various factions to resolve (or, The controversy . . . was).

Comment: An error of this kind is encouraged by two factors: the distance of the verb from the subject and the presence of intervening prepositional phrases that use singular objects, either of which a writer might mistake for the grammatical subject of the main clause.

Test Yourself: Faulty Predication

Original example: The subject of learning disabilities is difficult to identify accurately.

Problem: The predicate matches the object of the preposition ("learning disabilities") rather than the subject of the main clause ("subject").

Possible correction: Learning disabilities are difficult to identify accurately.

Comment: Omitting the abstract opening ("The subject of") enables the predicate ("are") to fit the new grammatical subject ("disabilities").

Test Yourself: Pronoun–Antecedent Agreement

Original example: Every dog has its day, but all too often when that day happens, they can be found barking up the wrong tree.

Problem: The plural pronoun "they" that is the grammatical subject of the second clause does not have a plural antecedent in the sentence.

Possible correction: Every dog has its day, but all too often when that day happens, the dog can be found barking up the wrong tree.

Comment: If a writer vigilantly checks all pronouns, he or she will identify the intended antecedent of the pronoun "they" to be the singular "dog" and revise accordingly. The sentence would still be incorrect if the pronoun "it" were used instead of the repeated "dog," because "it" could refer to the nearest preceding noun, "day."

Test Yourself: Ambiguous Reference

Original example: Alexander the Great's father, Philip of Macedon, died when he was twenty-six.

Problem: A reader can't be sure whether "he" refers to Alexander or to Philip.

Possible correction: Alexander the Great's father, Philip of Macedon, died at the age of twenty-six.

Comment: The correction rewords to remove the ambiguous pronoun. This solution is less awkward than repeating "Philip" in place of "he," though that would also be correct.

Original example: The committee could not look into the problem because it was too involved.

Problem: A reader can't be sure whether "it" refers to "the committee" or to "the problem."

Possible correction: The committee was too involved with other matters to look into the problem.

Comment: As with the previous example, rewording to eliminate the ambiguous pronoun is usually the best solution.

Test Yourself: Broad Reference

Original example: Regardless of whether the film is foreign or domestic, they can be found in your neighborhood video store.

Problem: The plural pronoun "they" does not have a plural antecedent in the sentence.

Possible correction: Regardless of whether the film is foreign or domestic, it can be found in your neighborhood video store.

Comment: Although the sentence offers two options for films, the word "film" is singular and so, as antecedent, requires a singular pronoun ("it"). It is probably worth noting here that "it" would still be correct even if the original sentence began, "Regardless of whether the film is a foreign film or a domestic film." The rule for compound subjects that use an either/or construction is as follows: the number (singular or plural) of the noun or pronoun that follows *or* determines the number of the verb. Compare the following two examples: "Either several of his aides *or* the *candidate is* going to speak" and "Either the candidate *or* several of his *aides are* going to speak."

Original example: Many experts now claim that dogs and other higher mammals dream; for those who don't own such pets, this is often difficult to believe.

Problem: The referent of the pronoun "this" is unclear. Precisely what is "difficult to believe"—that mammals dream or that experts would make such a claim?

Possible correction: Many experts now claim that dogs and other higher mammals dream; for those who don't own such pets, this claim is often difficult to believe.

Comment: Often the best way to fix a problem with broad reference produced by use of "this" as a pronoun is to convert "this" to an adjective—a strategy that will require a writer to provide a specifying noun for "this" to modify. As a rule, when you find an isolated "this" in your draft, ask and answer the question "This what?"

Test Yourself: Modification Errors

Original example: After eating their sandwiches, the steamboat left the dock.

Problem: This is a dangling participle—the grammar of the sentence conveys that the steamboat ate their sandwiches.

Corrections: After the girls ate their sandwiches, the steamboat left the dock. Or, After eating their sandwiches, the girls boarded the steamboat, and it left the dock.

Comment: The two corrections model the two ways of remedying most dangling participles. Both provide an antecedent ("the girls") for the pronoun "their." The first correction eliminates the participial phrase and substitutes a subordinate clause. The second correction adds to the existing main clause ("steamboat left") another one ("girls boarded") for the participial phrase to modify appropriately.

Original example: The social workers saw an elderly woman on a bus with a cane standing up.

Problem: Misplaced modifiers create the problems in this sentence, which implies that the bus possessed a cane that was standing up. The problem exemplified here is produced from the series of prepositional phrases—"*on* a bus *with* a cane"—

followed by the participial phrase "standing up," which is used as an adjective and intended to modify "woman."

Possible correction: The social workers saw an elderly woman on a bus. She was standing up with the help of a cane.

Comment: Writers often try to cram too much into sentences, piling on the prepositions. The best remedy is sometimes to break up the sentence, a move that usually involves eliminating prepositions, which possess a sludgy kind of movement, and adding verbs, which possess more distinct movement.

Original example: Crossing the street, a car hit the pedestrian.

Problem: The dangling participle ("Crossing the street") does not have a word to modify in the sentence. The sentence conveys that the car crossed the street.

Possible corrections: Crossing the street, the pedestrian was hit by a car. Or: As the pedestrian crossed the street, a car hit him.

Comment: The first solution brings the participial phrase closest to the noun it modifies ("pedestrian"). The second converts the participial into the verb ("crossed") of a dependent "as" clause and moves "pedestrian" into the clause as the subject for that verb. As in the "steamboat" example, one correction provides an appropriate noun for the participial phrase to modify, and the other eliminates the participle.

Test Yourself: Possessive Apostrophes

Original example: The womens movement has been misunderstood by many of its detractors.

Problem: The possessive apostrophe for "womens" is missing. The trickiness here in inserting the apostrophe is that this word is already plural.

Possible correction: The women's movement has been misunderstood by many of its detractors.

Comment: Because the word is already plural, it takes a simple "–'s" to indicate a movement belonging to women—not "–s'" (womens').

Test Yourself: Comma Errors

Original paired examples: The book which I had read a few years ago contained a lot of outdated data.

The book that I had read a few years ago contained a lot of outdated data.

Problem: In the first example, the modifying clause "which I had read a few years ago" is nonrestrictive: it could be omitted without changing the essential meaning of the sentence. Therefore, it needs to be enclosed in commas—as the "which" signals.

Possible correction: The book, which I had read a few years ago, contained a lot of outdated data.

Comment: The second example in the pair is correct as it stands. The restrictive clause, "that I had read a few years ago," does not take commas around it because the information it gives readers is an essential part of the meaning of "book." That is, it refers to not just any book read a few years ago, as in the first example in the pair, but rather specifies the one containing outdated data. "The book that I had read a few years ago" thus functions as what is known as a *noun phrase*.

Test Yourself: Spelling/Diction Errors

Original example: Its not sufficiently acknowledged that the behavior of public officials is not just an ethical issue but one that effects the sale of newspapers and commercial bytes in television news. When public officials don't do what their supposed to do, than their sure to face the affects of public opinion—if they get caught—because there are dollars to be made. Its that simple: money more then morality is calling the tune in the way that the press treats it's superstars.

Problems: The paragraph confuses the paired terms discussed under "BWE 9." It mistakes

"its" for "it's" before "not sufficiently."
"effects" for "affects" before "the sale."
"their" for "they're" before "supposed."
"than" for "then" before "their sure."
"they're" for "their" before "sure."
"affects" for "effects" before "of public opinion."
"its" for "it's" before "that simple."
"then" for "than" before "morality."
"it's" for "its" before "superstars."

Possible correction: It's not sufficiently acknowledged that the behavior of public officials is not just an ethical issue but one that affects the sale of newspapers and commercial bytes in television news. When public officials don't do what they're supposed to do, then they're sure to face the effects of public opinion—if they get caught—because there are dollars to be made. It's that simple: money more than morality is calling the tune in the way that the press treats its superstars.

Comment: If you confuse similar words, the only solution is to memorize the differences and consciously check your drafts for any problems until habit takes hold.

GRAMMAR AND STYLE QUIZ

The answers offered here are not exclusive—the only ways to correct the problems. In some cases, we have offered various satisfactory remedies, and as previously noted, a few of the suggested revisions—marked by a bullet—address editing for style (Chapters 12 and 13) rather than editing for correctness.

Line 1

- There are no grammatical errors per se, but "It is a fact that" is a wordy expletive that should be cut.

Line 2

- There is a comma splice between "university" and "students": insert a semicolon as the preferred option.
- "This," beginning the next sentence, is a broad reference and should be converted into an adjective, with a noun or noun phrase added, such as "This preoccupation" or "This dominance by Greek societies."
- In addition, a writer might recast the passive verb into the active: "Most faculty members do not approve of . . ."

Line 3

- There is a comma splice after "faculty": insert a semicolon.
- The antecedent of the pronoun "them" is ambiguous: substitute a noun such as "the Greeks."

Line 4

- "Perceiving" is a dangling participle: either recast to include a subject in a dependent clause (such as "Because most faculty members perceive") or insert "most faculty members" as a referent for the participle before "it" in Line 5.
- Capitalize "Greek."

Line 5

- Fix faulty parallelism: introduce the second item ("encouraging anti-intellectualism") with another "that" ("but at the same time that they encourage").
- The "it is" (an expletive) creates problems with broad reference. If Line 4 has been changed by eliminating the participle (using some version of the "Because most faculty members feel" option), recast the main clause. For example, following "anti-intellectualism," the sentence might read, "this issue cannot be addressed easily." If Line 4 has retained the participial phrase, then the revision would need to read something like "most faculty members believe that this issue cannot be addressed easily."

Line 6

- The "who" clause is restrictive: the comma must be dropped.
- The "he" is sexist: use "he or she," or change the number—to "Students who want ... feel that they."

Line 7

- Fix faulty parallelism: change "interest in" to "be*ing* interested in" so as to match "hav*ing* ideas."

Line 8

- Possessive "Its" should be the contraction "It's."
- Temporal "then" should be the comparative "than."
- Fix faulty parallelism: change "being" to "to be" to match "to pledge."

Line 9

- Change "a honors" to "an honors."
- Insert commas around the nonrestrictive modifying phrase "such as an honors program": these will separate it from both the long introductory dependent "if" clause that precedes it and the main clause that follows.

Line 10

- Make "students" a plural possessive: "students' lives."
- The "more enriched" is arguably wordy: "richer" is leaner.
- "Although" is a subordinating conjunction that creates a sentence fragment. The easiest solution is to cut it, though a writer could also attach the entire "although" clause to the previous sentence, using a comma or dash.

Line 11

- This is part of the fragment that began in Line 10.

Line 12

- Fix the possessive: make it "University's."
- Fix the case of the noun: make it "university's."
- Place a comma after "discrimination" to separate the long introductory modifying phrases from the main clause.

Line 13

- The semicolon is incorrect, because the sentence does not contain two independent clauses. A colon is better than a dash here, though both are technically correct.

Line 14

- Most rhetoricians consider "freshman" sexist: substitute "first-year."
- The use of "this" is another egregious case of broad reference (ask, "Agree with *this what?*). The best solution is probably to rewrite this part of the sentence to clarify the meaning. For example, make it "Some of the best students object to Greek life in these terms and oppose the administration's handling of the Greeks ..."

Line 15

- Fix subject–verb agreement: make it "some ... believe."

Here is how one corrected version of the quiz might look:

> Fraternities and sororities are a major part of student life at the university: students are preoccupied with pledging. Most faculty members do not approve of this domi-

nance by Greek societies; however, they feel helpless about attacking the Greeks. Because faculty members perceive that the Greek societies are attractive to the students but at the same time that they encourage anti-intellectualism, this issue cannot be addressed easily. The student who wants to be popular and cool feels that he or she should not talk in class, because being interested in academics or having ideas outside class is uncool. It's more important to pledge the right house than to be smart. If the administration would create alternatives to Greek life, such as an honors program, the students' lives would be richer. For now, raising the cumulative grade point necessary to pledge and remain active would be a good start to solving the problem of Greek domination. Contrary to the university's stance against gender discrimination, Greek life perpetuates gender stereotypes: for example, the dances at each house for first-year women but not men. Some of the best students object to Greek life in these terms and oppose the administration's handling of the Greeks. But many of these same students mistakenly believe that most faculty members endorse the system.

Works Cited

Cole, Sally, and Elizabeth Kiss. "What Can We Do About Student Cheating?" *About Campus* (May-June 2000): 5–12.

Gibaldi, Joseph. *MLA Handbook for Writers of Research Papers*, Fifth Edition. New York: MLA, 1999.

Hult, Christine A. *Researching and Writing Across the Curriculum*. Boston: Allyn and Bacon, 1996

Lodge, David. *The Art of Fiction*. New York: Penguin, 1992.

Owens, Derek. "Introduction" to *The Essay Theory and Pedagogy for an Active Form*. By Paul Heilker. Urbana, ILL: NCTE, 1996.

Stark, Stephen D. "The Oprah Winfrey Show and the Talk-Show Furor," in *Signs of Life in the U.S.A.*, Third Edtion. Eds. Sonia Maasik and Jack Solomon, Boston: Bedford/St. Martin's, 2000.

Credits

PHOTO

Page 28, *The Dancers* by Sara Kersh. Pen and ink drawing, 6" × 13.75".

Page 39, Figure 3.1. REUNION DES MUSEES NATIONAUX, ART RESOURCE, NY. James Abbott McNeil Whistler. Arrangement in Gray and Black No. 1: Portrait of the Artist's Mother, 1871.

Page 91, Figure 5.4. AP/Wide World Photos

Page 112, Figure 6.5. SCALA/ART RESOURCE, NY. Diego Rodrigues Velazquez. Las Meninas. 1656.

LITERARY

Page 67, Fassin, Eric. "Playing by the antioch rules." Copyright © 1993 by the *New York Times*. Reprinted by permission.

Index

Abstract diction, 234–235
Abstraction ladder, 7–8
Abstractions, 83
Abstracts
  compilations of, 164
  preparing and writing, 184–186, 187
  sample, 185–186
  in scientific papers, 207
Abstract terms, replacing, 130
Academic disciplines, differences in, 211
Academic integrity, 176
Academic journals, access to, 167–168
Academic Search via EbscoHost, 168, 171, 172
Academic writing, 234
Active reading, 6
Active voice, 252, 254–256
Adjectives, 277
  evaluative, 10
Adverbs, 277
  evaluative, 10
Age of Enlightenment, 42
Agreement, subject-verb, 267–269
All-purpose organizational scheme, 80–82
Ambiguous references, 270–271
American Psychological Association (APA) disciplinary style guide, 214
American Psychological Association (APA) documentation style, 175–176, 179. *See also* Single-author APA style citations
Analogy, 134
  thinking by, 47
Analysis, 3–4. *See also* In-depth analysis
  attacks on, 46
  creativity and, 18
  missed opportunities for, 153

moving from description to, 114–115
  reliance on reading, 60
  summarizing and, 56
  versus argument, 11–12
Analytical conclusions, 9
  plausibility of, 41
Analytical habit of mind, 7
Analytical ideas, 17, 141
Analytical papers. *See also* Analytical research papers
  on *Las Meninas*, 111–114
  plausible theses in, 118
Analytical questions, 56
Analytical research papers, sample, 155–160
Analytical stance, suspicion about, 42
Analytical summaries, 144
  strategies for writing, 56–59
Analytical thinking, 12, 33–34
  evolving theses and, 105
  five-paragraph form and, 80
  prerequisites for, 50
Analytical writers, persuasion and, 12
Analytical writing, 3
  defined, 49
  prerequisites for, 33–34
  theses in, 75
Anomalies
  looking for, 28–29
  noticing, 38
Antianalytical bias, 127
Anticlimax, in conclusions, 205–206
Antithesis, parallel structure and, 248
"Anything Goes" School of Interpretation, 48–49
Apostrophes, possessive, 273
Argument
  complexity of, 108
  concessions and refutations in, 217–219
  deductive, 106, 107
  opposing, 218
  reading as, 58
  versus analysis, 11–12

Aristotle, 212
Assertions
  groundless, 84
  rewording of, 153–154
  unsubstantiated, 83
Association, thinking by, 47
Assumptions
  having ideas by uncovering, 67–71
  procedure for uncovering, 65–67, 70–71
  stereotypical, 28
  uncovering in reading, 64–67
Attitude
  analytical, 33
  implied, 227
  tracing to concrete causes, 7
Audience, form and, 216
Audience emotions, appeals to, 217
Author-date citation format, 179
Authorial intention, 44–46
Authority issues, in writing, 217
Author-work citation format, 179
Availability statement, 179

Background, providing, 192
Balance, parallelism and, 248
Banking model of education, 5–6
Basic writing errors (BWEs), 260–277
Begging the question, 135
Bibliographical citations, 165
Bibliographic research, 170–171
Bibliographies, 164, 178
Binary oppositions (binaries), 12–13. *See also* Collapsing the binary
  analyzing the terms of, 32
  details or words that form, 25
  false, 70
  finding, 27, 31, 115